Paddle America
A Guide to Trips and Outfitters in all 50 States

Nick and David Shears

Starfish Press
Washington, D.C.

Paddle America
A Guide to Trips and Outfitters in all 50 States

Published by:
Starfish Press
6525 32nd St., N.W.
PO Box 42467
Washington, D.C. 20015

Copyright © 1996 by Nick and David Shears
Previous editions: copyright © 1992 and 1993 by Nick Shears
Library of Congress Card Catalog Number: 95-072415
ISBN 0-9622806-7-4
Printed in the United States of America

Front cover: A paddle crew on a Whitewater Voyages' trip drifts through a calm stretch between rapids on the renowned Class V Forks of the Kern, Sequoia National Forest, California. Photo by Barry Tessman.

Typesetting by: the LetterEdge, Baltimore MD

Table of Contents

Preface to the Third Edition

Putting this book together was a challenge but not a chore. It was fun to contact paddling professionals in all kinds of remote locations and to encounter their support. We learned of great paddling spots in every state from Maine to Hawaii. We were delighted to receive hundreds of brochures depicting the joys of paddling — a recreation enjoyed by over 24 million Americans by the latest count.

This updated and expanded edition contains 871 listings of canoeing, kayaking, rafting, and sea kayaking outfitters across the country. These outfitters responded to questionnaires asking them to describe their operations and the waters their paddlers enjoy. We did not solicit or accept any payment for these listings.

We know that despite mailing more than 2,000 questionnaires to companies on the best available mailing lists, we failed to reach some outfitters. So once again we ask for help: if your company or a company you know of is not included, please send us its name and address for future editions. This book is already a standard resource; we want to make it as comprehensive as possible.

Also we invite advice on other improvements: including any important paddling streams we may have left out of the introductions to each state, updating the list of resources and the bibliography at the end of the book, and any other corrections. Call us directly at (202) 244-STAR or write to Starfish Press, 6525 32nd Street, NW, Washington, DC 20015.

Finally I want to thank all those in the paddling business who have been so helpful with advice, encouragement, and information. Many outfitters kindly contributed photographs and other materials, and in particular I want to thank Jim Thaxton of the Professional Paddlesports Association for his unstinting support.

David Shears
Washington D.C.
March 1996

Introduction

At 17 I took my first canoe trip. Three friends and I spent two glorious, carefree weeks swimming, fishing, and camping in the wilderness of Maine's Syslodobsis Lakes. At dusk we'd pitch our tents on small, breezy islands. Mornings we'd break camp early and paddle to a new lake or campsite.

I came back from the woods amazed that such great trips could be so poorly publicized. In fact, we would have missed our Maine adventure altogether had I not spotted one of the tiny, intermittent advertisements our outfitter ran in *Field & Stream*.

Sixteen years later, minimal advertising is still the rule among many small canoe liveries. Owners of these businesses often are forced to take other jobs in the off-season to supplement their incomes. Such shoe-string operations predictably have little money left over for promotion.

Yet at the same time, I know there are others like me who glance over country bridges, spot enticing rivers, but haven't a clue where to rent a canoe, raft, or tube. Nevertheless, in bookstores I searched in vain for local or national guides to outfitters.

This book is an attempt to fill that gap. It is intended as a guide to tote along while traveling. Then, as you find yourself with some free time and a nice stretch of water, the book will guide you to a local outfitter for a day- or half-day paddle trip. The book also is designed to help you plan longer, more ambitious outings. Particularly as you leaf through the chapters on Maine, Minnesota, and most Western states, you will find a wide selection of week-long expeditions.

Before deciding where to spend your precious vacation time, you will want to do some careful research to ensure that the destination, equipment, food, guides, and service are exactly what you are looking for. This book, with its outfitter listings and descriptions, can help you quickly find the few outfitters whose trips most appeal to you.

Ultimately, you may want to write or call five or more companies to request brochures and information. Doing so you will find that each outfitter has his or her own distinctive character, level of service, and array of trip offerings.

Choosing a Destination

Whether or not you have some idea of where you would like to take your next trip, I urge you to browse through this book from cover to cover. I have spent months poring over outfitters' catalogs, yet I continue to be surprised at how easily some new trip or location catches my fancy.

You may well have the same response. One moment you may be tempted by an adventurous fly-in trip to the Alaskan wilderness, and the next you want to be sea kayaking off the Florida coast. Or, one minute you're set on hair-raising whitewater and the next you want a relaxing, scenic trip.

Here are some of the questions you might ask yourself. Do you want a guided or unguided trip? If guided, how large a group would you be comfortable traveling in? Do you want a whitewater or scenic trip? Do you want to paddle or are you happy to let a guide pilot the boat? On multi-day trips, do you want to camp or stay in lodges? Do you want to pitch in with camp chores or be pampered? Do you want to bring your kids?

Your answers to these questions will help you narrow the list of options. For instance, if it is important to you to have solitude or be alone with friends and family, you may want to forego some of the most popular trips, where you will likely have other boats in view for most of your run. On the other hand, if it's famous whitewater stretches you're after, you may forgive or even take comfort in seeing others on the river.

How the Book is Organized

To help you with your research, the book has state-by-state listings for the entire country. Each chapter begins with a brief introduction to many of the favorite paddling spots in each state, along with an overview of these areas' terrain, scenery, and wildlife. Some of the places mentioned are not served by commercial outfitters. These places are covered, however, as a service to those wanting to shuttle their own canoes, kayaks, or rafts. Material for the introductions was drawn from hundreds of sources, the most helpful of which are listed in the bibliography.

The introductions to each state are followed by listings of outfitters operating trips there. These listings give additional information on the particular areas each outfitter serves.

For additional information to help in selecting a destination, you may want to refer to the guidebooks listed in the bibliography, and write or call state departments of natural resources, state tourist boards, conservation groups, and any of the helpful paddlesports associations listed in the "Resources" section at the end of the book.

Finally, you are likely to want maps of the areas where you will be paddling, particularly on overnight trips. To get a general sense of the "lay of the land," automobile travel maps are often adequate. With these you can locate large bodies of water and nearby towns and major roads. Unfortunately, auto maps seldom show smaller roads, rivers, and lakes.

Auto maps, because they lack such critical detail, are worthless for use when underway, however. For maps that show secondary roads, small bridges, and detailed topographic features, your best source are the topographic maps published by the U.S. Geological Survey. Often you can buy these maps from your outfitter. Call ahead to check, however.

USGS Maps, in various scales, can also be ordered by phoning USGS at (800) 435-7627 or (303) 202-4700. If you call to order maps, you may also wish to request USGS's terrific 63" x 41" wall map of bodies of water all across the country. This map, "Surface-Water and Related Land-Resources Development in the United States and Puerto Rico," is the only single map I know of that shows all the hundreds of rivers, streams, and lakes mentioned in this book. It costs just $4.

Choosing an Outfitter

The companies in this book range from small, family operations to large, multi-state enterprises. Regardless of size, any outfitter should impress you with his or her concern for your having a safe, fun trip. Even if you are just planning a day trip, it is good to call ahead to make reservations. When you have the outfitter on the phone, ask some basic questions.

Will the outfitter provide you with a canoe or raft that is clean, in good condition, and equipped with properly sized paddles and PFDs (personal flotation devices)? Will you receive instruction on paddling, water conditions, hazards, and safety? Will you need to shuttle the boat on your cartop? If the outfitter provides the shuttle, how much extra, if any, will that cost? What is the outfitter's policy on refunds due to rain or low or unsafe water conditions? Does the outfitter have a trip to match your level of ability? On guided trips, are the guides experienced and mature? Is the outfitter licensed by the state or certified by a trade association?

When asking such questions, it is also a good idea to confirm that the trips offered are exactly as listed here in the outfitter descriptions. The outfitter information in this book was supplied by the outfitters themselves via written questionnaires and should, therefore, be accurate. However, because schedules and offerings change, and because Starfish Press cannot independently confirm each listing's accuracy, it is a good idea to double check trips and services before making a booking.

After making these inquiries, you should be satisfied both with the answers themselves and with the manner of the person on the phone. I might add that, if your experiences are like mine, I expect you will be very pleased

with the service of the outfitters you encounter. The outfitters I've patron-
ized and the hundreds more that I have written and spoken to in preparing
this book have been exceptionally helpful and friendly.

Safety

Many of the country's largest outfitters have had tens of thousands of paddlers run wild whitewater runs without a single drowning or serious injury.
Nevertheless, there is always certain inherent risk in paddling, for which all
participants must have a healthy respect.

The United States Coast Guard, the American Canoe Association (ACA),
and the American Red Cross have developed excellent safety education
books, films, and instructional programs. To learn more about safety, contact your local Coast Guard or Red Cross office, or write to the American
Canoe Association to request a copy of their free safety brochure (see the
"Resources" section for the address and phone number).

The ACA offers another excellent primer on safety, a poster titled *River
Canoeing*, which cites these common causes of avoidable accidents: alcohol
consumption, not wearing life jackets, insufficient skill, inability to "read" river
conditions, paddling alone, poorly maintained equipment, inadequate flotation, no spare paddle, no first aid kit, improper dress, high water, cold water,
dams, downed trees, undercut rocks, paddling a remote river, and changing
river conditions.

To be a safe canoeist, it is essential that you learn to take the proper precautions to avoid unnecessary risk. In particular, you should never attempt
more difficult rapids than you are comfortable with, unless accompanied by
a skilled guide, instructor, or trip leader. If in doubt, take an easier trip.

As you may know, rapids are rated on an international scale of difficulty.
These ratings, cited throughout this book, are as follows:

Class I: Moving water with a few riffles and small waves. Few or no obstacles.

Class II: Easy rapids with waves up to 3 feet and wide, clear channels
that are obvious without scouting. Some maneuvering is required.

Class III: Rapids with high, irregular waves often capable of swamping
an open canoe. Narrow passages that often require complex maneuvering.
May require scouting from shore.

Class IV: Long, difficult rapids and constricted passages that often require
precise maneuvering in very turbulent waters. Scouting from shore is often
necessary, and conditions make rescue difficult. Generally not possible for
open canoes. Boaters in covered canoes and kayaks should have the ability
to Eskimo roll.

Class V: Extremely difficult, long, very violent rapids with highly congested routes, which nearly always must be scouted from shore. Rescue conditions are difficult, and there is significant hazard to life in the event of a mishap. Ability to Eskimo roll is essential for boaters in kayaks and closed canoes.

Class VI: Difficulties of Class V carried to the extreme of navigability. Nearly impossible and very dangerous. For teams of experts only, after close study has been made and all precautions have been taken.

A final note on safety — heavy rain, storms, spring runoff, fallen trees, and other hazards can suddenly make waters treacherous. For that reason, you should always inquire about water and weather conditions before beginning any trip. This book, intended as a general guide, cannot possibly anticipate such hazards. Also, while every effort has been made to be make this book as accurate as possible, there may be typographical errors or errors in the information submitted to us by outfitters. As a result, the authors and Starfish Press assume no liability for any loss or damage caused or alleged to have been caused by information in this book.

Conservation

Paddlers can take an enormous toll on rivers. Recognizing this risk, paddlers and outfitters increasingly adhere to the wilderness ethic of packing out trash, not cutting live trees for firewood, building fires in fire rings or not at all, avoiding glass beverage containers, and practicing catch-and-release fishing. Many outfitters also go a step further by sponsoring river clean-up days in which they supply canoes free to paddlers who agree to pick up trash along the river.

As you read this book and plan your trips, you can contribute to this effort by letting outfitters know that you appreciate their efforts protect the environment.

For our part, at Starfish Press, we donate 10 percent of our net profit from the sales of *Paddle America* to American Rivers, the country's foremost river conservation group.

American Rivers

Here is a brief statement from American Rivers describing the organization and its activities:

> American Rivers, a non-profit founded in 1973, is the nation's leading river conservation organization. Its mission is to "preserve and restore America's river systems and to foster a rivers stewardship ethic."

America has more than 3.5 million miles of rivers, comprising more than 100,000 streams. Healthy river systems, however, are a finite and vanishing resource. The vast majority have been drained, dammed, channelized, over-developed, and/or choked with pollution. Many, if not most, of our rivers are in danger of losing their most basic natural features, capacities and ecological balance. ...

American Rivers protects rivers across the nation from numerous threats: ecologically destructive — and harmful — dams, water diversions, dredging, adverse development (including mining and clear-cutting along river banks), and pollution.

If you are interested in joining American Rivers or obtaining more information about a river in your area, contact American Rivers at (202) 547-6900, 1025 Vermont Ave., NW, Suite 720, Washington, D.C. 20005.

Happy paddling!

Nick Shears
Washington D.C.
March 1996

Alabama

Alabama is well served by rivers offering varied paddling from lazy floating to Class V whitewater. They are well spread out over the state, from the Appalachians to the plateaus, the Piedmont and the Gulf Coast plain. You can take your choice of cold mountain streams and warm pastoral rivers, with scenery to match. But John H. Foshee, author of Alabama Canoe Rides and Float Trips, says there is unfortunately a dark side to the story. He writes that Alabama tends to "dam every piece of water that moves" and allows too much riverside development and pollution.

However, the fishing is good. State tourist brochures claim that Lake Eufaula on the Chattahoochee River is the Big Bass Capital of the world. Similarly, they boast that Weiss Lake on the Coosa River is the Crappie Capital of the world.

Alabama's most popular canoeing river is the Cahaba, which flows from Trussville, near Birmingham, to its confluence with the Alabama River near Selma. Ideal for one-day trips, it is broken up by bridges or fords into segments with easy access. The Cahaba's upper section, through rocky territory, gets very low in the summer except when heavy rains suddenly turn it into a torrent. But below Centerville, where it starts meandering across the plain, it is floatable all year. The river is surprisingly undeveloped and is rich in water lilies and fish. The Little Cahaba is described by Foshee as an "excellent training river." It offers outfitted trips of four, six and ten miles, but paddlers should call ahead (205-926-7382) to check water levels.

The Locust Fork of the Black Warrior River offers more of a challenge to whitewater buffs. Located in Blount County, north of Birmingham, this well-known stream has a seven-mile Class III run down to the covered bridge at Nectar. It takes the paddler through rolling, forested country and is runnable from late winter until June after heavy rain. But there is said to be a long-standing antagonism between river-runners and the local private land-owners.

The Mulberry Fork of the Black Warrior, in the same Nectar-Garden City area, has an eight- to eleven-mile stretch with Class I-II rapids. It is an unspoiled river, with scenic bluffs and rock formations alternating with low hills and wooded banks. Again, this stream is only runnable in late winter and after spring rains. Some stretches can be quite hazardous at high water.

Also close to Birmingham is the Blackburn Fork, which flows down from Inland Lake on a ten-mile course to its confluence with Calvert Prong. Thence it continues as the Blackburn Fork — alternatively dubbed Little Warrior River — to join the Locust Fork described above. The countryside is mostly forested and unspoiled, with more bluffs and rock formations.

For the real adventurer, Little River Canyon in season is about as exciting as anyone could wish. This run has a so-called Suicide Section on its upper reach just below Desoto Falls. Richard Penny, in his Whitewater Sourcebook, calls the name "slightly hysterical." But he rates it as Class V-VI and describes it as "totally aggro." Below the 2.5-mile Suicide Section come a three-mile stretch rated Class IV-V followed by a six-mile Class III-IV run down to Canyon Mouth. The time to tackle the Little River Canyon is November to May.

Paddlers preferring easy floats will enjoy the Escatawpa, which runs almost due south, wandering westward across the Mississippi state line as it heads for the Gulf. It displays a sharp contrast between its black water and its many sugar-white sandbars that offer are fine for picnics and camping. The Escatawpa offers slow flatland canoeing, with adequate water depth all year round. Much the same is true of the Mobile-Tensaw River Delta, one of the largest delta systems in the country. The scenery in this area is a mixture of hardwoods and bottom swamp, alive with white-tailed deer, otters, raccoons, and birds including swallowtail kites. Bass, brim, catfish and many marine species can be caught in the brackish waters upstream from Mobile Bay.

Alabama Small Boats, Inc.
Granger Russell
2370 Hwy 52
Helena, AL 35080
(205) 424-3634
Cahaba River
Max. rapids: None
PPA

A small family business, Alabama Small Boats rents canoes and kayaks on the Cahaba, one of the most ecologically diverse rivers of its size in North America. The scenery is great, constantly changing from wooded to rocky, with a wide variety of wildlife.

Trips are easy and suitable for everyone, with bass, catfish, bream, and gar fishing available during the company's year-round season.

Bear Creek Canoe Run
Randall N. Morgan
242 W. Valley Ave., Ste. 309
Birmingham, AL 35209
(800) 788-7070
Bear Creek
Max. rapids: I-II
PPA

Bear Creek Canoe Run offers two canoeing trips, one for beginners and the other, which has both class I and II rapids, for paddlers with some experience. Guided trips, fishing, and camping are available on Bear Creek, a 26-mile public floatway developed by the T.V.A. The outfitter's season runs from March through September.

Escatawpa Hollow, Inc.
Larry D. Godfrey
15551 Moffett Rd.
Wilmer, AL 36587
(334) 649-4233
Escatawpa River
Max. rapids: None
PPA

Open all year, Escatawpa Hollow provides canoe and kayak outings amid beautiful scenery on the Escatawpa, described as the cleanest blackwater river in the nation. White sandbars at every curve offer ideal spots for picnicking, camping, and swimming. Trips last up to three days and are suitable for all comers. Wildlife is varied and fish include bass, bream, and catfish.

Southern Trails, Inc.
5143 Atlanta Highway
Montgomery, AL 36109
(205) 272-0952
Coosa River, Hatchett Creek
Max. rapids: III-IV
PPA, NORS

Southern Trails rents canoes, kayaks, and rafts for both whitewater and flatwater trips with a good current. The Coosa offers the challenge of rivers like the famous Ocoee but also enables novices and families "to enjoy without being munched!"

The one-day outings are designed for small groups, with special attention to environmental harmony with a river habitat. Giant cypresses, Spanish moss, great blue herons, ospreys, deer, and beavers enliven the scenery. Paddlers can also stop to fish for Kentucky spot and big catfish. The season runs from March to October.

Sunshine Canoes
Bob Andrews
5460 Old Shell Road
Mobile, AL 36608
(205) 344-8664
Escatawpa River, Mobile Tensaw River Delta
Max. rapids: None

Sunshine Canoes offers guided trips by canoe and kayak on the Escatawpa and the Mobile-Tensaw River Delta. It also rents canoes and kayaks. River trips can cover up to fifty miles and last anywhere from three hours to five days. The Escatawpa is unspoiled, with no development of any kind along its banks. Its many sandbars offer innumerable opportunities for swimming, picnicking, and camping. During its season from May through September, Sunshine Canoes also provides lessons.

Alaska

Alaska fulfills the wilderness canoeists's dream. In this vast country are virgin canoe trails of rare beauty amid ten thousand undammed rivers. These streams are wild, not just in the whitewater sense but as part of an untamed world where Man is an intruder. Here the solitary paddler can feel like an explorer and not see another canoeist all day. But he or she must be forewarned: river conditions can change from day to day, even by the hour. A rushing torrent can dry to a trickle that will not float a canoe. The same river, floated at the same season, can vary enormously from year to year. For those who want more predictability and enjoy sharing adventure with others, outfitters offer rafts, canoes, and kayaks for trips on a score of waterways. Most of them recommend that guests bring their own bug repellent to deal with Alaska's legendary mosquitoes.

A choice whitewater trip is on the Talkeetna River, on tours lasting up to six days that take stalwart rafters through the Sluice Box, a continuous Class IV rapid within a deep 14-mile canyon. It ranks as the longest runnable rapid in North America. If this does not provide thrills enough, floaters can view grizzly bears, wolves, moose and caribou. They can also enjoy excellent fishing in this salmon spawning river. Although the Talkeetna lies not far north of Anchorage, floaters fly in aboard a small plane, possibly viewing Mt. McKinley and other Alaska Range peaks on the way.

Most Alaskan rivers are remote, but if you yearn for the ultimate escape from civilization the place to go is the arctic north. For there in the Arctic National Wildlife Refuge bordering the Beaufort Sea and Canada's Northern Territories is an 18-million-acre wilderness that is home to some 180,000 caribou as well as dall sheep, wolves, musk oxen, grizzlies and numerous waterfowl and birds of prey. Some have compared the coastal plain to East Africa's Serengeti, and wildlife biologists call it the last intact arctic ecosystem in America. A 10-day raft trip on the Canning River takes the venturesome paddler past high mountains, foothills, ice fields and down into the tundra where the river flows into the Arctic Ocean.

For whitewater in the same area one outfitter offers ten-day trips on a river with the improbable name of Hulahula which runs through the highest peaks of the Brooks Range. It offers Class I-III rapids as well as excellent wildlife and fishing. At the right time of year the paddler may be rewarded by the spectacle of the annual caribou migration.

Comparatively short floatplane flights eastward from Anchorage take the floater to Tazlina and Klutina Lakes, where two- or three-day trips begin on rivers of the same names. Both offer Class III rapids with good scenery, wildlife and fishing. And the Eagle, Matanuska, Lionshead and Six-Mile Creek rivers provide one-day whitewater paddling within easy driving distance from Anchorage.

Visitors to the Glacier Bay region can enjoy a spectacular 184-mile wilderness float on the Alsek and Tatshenshini Rivers. Paddlers revel in glaciers and jagged mountains as they travel from Dolton Post in Canada's Yukon Territory to the take-out at Dry Bay, Alaska.

South of Anchorage, experienced sea kayakers can explore Prince William Sound and the nearby Kenai Fjords National Park, with their glaciers, seals, sea otters and whales.

The river boating season is short — May through September. Highwater usually reaches its peak in July and in August, normally Alaska's wettest month.

ABEC's Alaska Adventures
Ramona Finnoff
1550 Alpine Vista Court
Fairbanks, AK 99712
(907) 457-8907, FAX (907) 457-6689
Kongakut, Hulahula, Koyukuk, Alatna,
Noatak, Canning Rivers
Max. rapids: III-IV

ABEC's Alaska Adventures runs guided trips of seven to 13 days on the Kongakut, Hulahula, Koyukuk, Alatna, Noatak, and other rivers in the Brooks Range. These trips, through pristine wilderness in remote areas of Alaska, offer spectacular mountain scenery and a chance to observe caribou, bears, moose, wolves, foxes, and other tundra wildlife. Guests can fish for grayling, Dolly Varden, pike, and lake trout. Custom river trips and backpacking expeditions are also available.

For its trips, which run from June to August, ABEC requires that participants have camping experience and be in good health.

Adventure Alaska Tours
Todd Bureau
2904 W. 31st Ave.
Anchorage, AK 99517
(800) 365-7057, (907) 248-0400
Yukon, Fortymile, Noatak Rivers, Prince
William Sound, Kodiak Island
Max. rapids: III-IV
America Outdoors

Adventure Alaska runs guided canoe, kayak, and raft trips for small groups during a June-September season. No prior experience is required, although some itineraries are more adventurous than others. Each tour has unique scenery, from the rugged seacoast to the cliffs of remote upcountry rivers. Bears, moose, wolves, and mountain goats can be spotted, along with eagles and falcons. Camping is available, along with fishing for salmon and arctic char.

Rafting on the Kongakut River. Courtesy of ABEC, Fairbanks, Alaska.

Adventures & Delights
Intec, Inc.
P.O. Box 21-0402PA
Anchorage, AK 99521
(907) 276-8282
Prince William Sound, Kenai Fjords,
Resurrection Bay
Max. rapids: None
TASK

Adventures & Delights offers guided and unguided sea kayak tours in Prince William Sound, Kenai Fjords National Park, and Resurrection Bay. On 4-5 day trips, kayakers can explore fjords where ice drops from 300-foot-high tidal glaciers to form icebergs where harbor seals haul out and sea otters play. Other wildlife includes bears, eagles, moose, wolves, and sea birds.

Trips also feature views of orange and gray granite cliffs and seaside waterfalls, camping on black-sand beaches, and walks on glaciers and islands covered in wildflowers. These tours are suitable for beginning and experienced kayakers and are available between May and September.

Air Adventures
Mike McBride
P.O. Box 22
Kenai, AK 99611
(907) 776-5444, FAX (907) 776-5445
Cook Inlet, Bristol Bay
Max. rapids: III-IV

Air Adventures flies paddlers to remote sites for outfitted and guided river raft trips of one to seven days on tributaries of Cook Inlet and the Bristol Bay region. Trips with Class I to V rapids run through pristine wilderness with views of snow-capped mountains, boreal forest, and abundant wildlife, including moose, bears, caribou, sheep, goats, otters, beavers, eagles, and other birds. These areas also feature good fishing for trout, char, grayling, and various species of salmon.

The season for Air Adventures' trips is May to October.

Alaska Discovery

Ken Leghorn/Susan Warner
5449 Shaune Dr., #4
Juneau, AK 99801
(800) 586-1911, (907) 780-6505
Tatshenshini, Alsek, Konyakut & Sheensek
Rivers, Glacier Bay, Icy Bay, Admiralty Is.,
Pt. Adolphus Whale Grounds
Max. rapids: III-IV
America Outdoors, T.A.S.K.

Alaska Discovery is said to be the
oldest and most experienced guiding
company in Alaska, as well as the only
operator of sea kayaks in Glacier Bay. Its
canoe, kayak and rafting trips explore
some of the cleanest, wildest, and most
remote waters of the state, affording
views of glaciers, mountains, whales,
bears, wolves, mountain goats, and bald
eagles. Five species of salmon may be
caught, as well as trout.

Paddlers should be in good shape
physically, but no experience is needed
for these easy-to-moderate trips. Outings last from 3-12 days and the season
goes from mid-May to mid-September.

Alaska Fish & Trails Unlimited

Jerald D. Stansel
1177 Shypoke Dr.
Fairbanks, AK 99709
(907) 479-7630
Koyukuk, Paw Rivers, Central Brooks Range,
various Arctic lakes.
Max. rapids: III-IV

Alaska Fish & Trails Unlimited flies
clients into wilderness for guided trips
for rafting, backpacking, or both. For
these expedition-type excursions, guests
must be in excellent condition. But
anyone can take the unguided tours, in
which customers are flown to a comfortable camp in the Gates of the Arctic
region, one of the most beautiful and
secluded areas in the Brooks Range.
From there they rent rafts to float to
Bettles on the Koyukuk River.

Guided tours, some of which are limited to two to three people, are led by
guides familiar with the terrain and local
history. Guests can fish for Arctic char,

shee fish, trout, grayling, and salmon,
and often see grizzly bears, wolves, caribou, eagles, and falcons.

Alaska Kayak Paddlesport Outfitters

Roger Pollard
Box 233725
Anchorage, AK 99523
(907) 349-4588
Prince William Sound, Kenai Fjords,
Swanson Lakes, Happy River
Max. rapids: III-IV

Alaska Kayak offers canoe, kayak,
and sea kayak trips amid some of the
world's most pristine scenery. Guided
and unguided trips lasting up to a week
take paddlers into regions where grizzly
and black bear, caribou, and moose may
be viewed. Instructors offer basic sea
kayaking courses for beginners and show
them Kenai Fjords and Prince William
Sound.

The 35-lake complex of Swanson
Lakes in the Kenai peninsula offers a
canoe trail rich in wildlife. Inland, expe-
rienced kayakers may sample the Class
III-IV Happy River in the Southern
Alaska Range. Camping and fishing are
available and the season runs May-
October.

Alaska River Adventures

George Heim
1831 Kuskokwim Street
Suite 9
Anchorage, AK 99508
(907) 276-3418, FAX (907) 258-9220
Lake Greer, Talkeetna River, Copper River
Max. rapids: III-IV
Alaska Wilderness Guides Association

Alaska River Adventures offers
guided raft and kayak trips of 1-10 days
on numerous rivers in the far north,
above the Arctic Circle; in Bristol Bay;
and on the Talkeetna, Copper, and other
rivers in southern Alaska. Most trips are
easy for participants in good health who
enjoy camping. A few trips are more
demanding.

The waters traveled are among the
most beautiful, fish-filled wild rivers in

the world. Fishing for salmon, trout, char, grayling, lake trout, and pike is particularly good. On these trips, paddlers can also enjoy the varied terrain, ranging from arctic desert to spectacular mountains, and the remarkably abundant wildlife, which includes moose, bears, caribou, eagles, and wolves.

Alaska Rivers Co.
Gary Galbraith
P.O. Box 827
Cooper Landing, AK 99572
(907) 595-1226
Upper Kenai River, Skilak Lake
Max. rapids: I-II

Alaska Rivers offers raft and dory guided trips for "soft adventure" amid spectacular mountain scenery. The fishing, notably for rainbows, sockeye salmon, and silver salmon, is described as world class. Alaska Rivers has 15 years' experience, rustic hand-hewn log buildings, and excellent equipment.

The season runs from April to October. Camping is available.

Alaska Travel Adventures, Inc.
Robert Dindinger
9085 Glacier Hwy. #301
Juneau, AK 99801
(907) 789-0052, (800) 791-2673
Mendenhall River, Harriet Hunt Lake (Ketchikan), Ocean Waterways at Juneau, Sitka and Skagway
Max. rapids: III-IV
PPA

Specializing in half-day excursions for cruise-ship passengers, Alaska Travel Adventures offers guided paddling trips on mountain lakes and the Mendenhall Lake below the famous glacier. Also available are sea kayak outings from Auke Bay, near Juneau, and from Sitka. Experienced guides provide clients with lifejackets, raingear, paddling instruction, and expertise on local wildlife which may include bears, seals, and Sitka black-tailed deer.

The more adventurous visitors paddle rafts or rent kayaks on their own. All

told, including shore hikes, the company has catered to over 850,000 people aged 4 to 99 during two decades. Its season runs from May-September.

Alaska Whitewater
Mary Matisinez
P.O. Box 142294
Anchorage, AK 99514
(907) 337-RAFT
Eagle River, Tonsina River, Klutina River, Tazlina River, Copper River, Talkeetna River
Max. rapids: III-IV

Alaska Whitewater runs 1-14 day guided raft trips on six pristine glacier rivers amid snow-capped mountains, glaciers, and tundra with "no dams, no houses, and no bridges." Guests can also view moose, caribou, bears, eagles, wolves, and other wildlife.

Trips run between May and October and range in difficulty from easy flatwater scenic floats to Class III-IV whitewater. Most trips are by paddle rafts, but oar boats are available too.

Alaska Whitewater also offers generous provisions beyond the usual life jackets and paddles, including wet suits, dry bags, booties, rainjackets, extra wool gear, and tents.

Alaska Wilderness Journeys
Steve Weller
Box 220204
Anchorage, AK 99522
(907) 349-2964, (800) 349-0064
Sheenjek, Copper, Tazlina Rivers, Wood Tikchik State Park, Prince William Sound
Max. rapids: III-IV

Alaska Wilderness provides guided canoe, kayak, and raft trips lasting 2-10 days amid glaciated high mountain scenery. The company prides itself on the quality of its staff and its eco-tour values. Alaska Wilderness takes only small groups during its May-September season, paddling through virgin uncut forests and glimpsing bears, moose, wolves, eagles, and dall sheep. Camping is available and fishing is for char, rainbow, grayling, and salmon.

Anadyr Adventures
Hedy Sarney
Box 1821
Valdez, AK 99686
(907) 835-2814, (800) TO-KAYAK
Prince William Sound
Max. rapids: None

Anadyr Adventures runs guided and unguided kayak trips lasting up to 10 days on the wide waters of Prince William Sound, with its magnificent mountain views. Whales, otters, seals, sea lions, and eagles may be viewed, while salmon, halibut, and rockfish rise to the bait. Camping and kayak lessons are available during the company's May-October season.

Canoealaska
Lou & Ron Davis
Box 81750
Fairbanks, AK 99708
(907) 479-5183
Fortymile River, Beaver and Birch Creeks, Chena, Delta and Gulkana Rivers
Max. rapids: I-II
PPA, ACA

Canoealaska offers guided canoe and raft trips of one to eight days for adults up to age 70, amid magnificent Alaskan scenery. Tours are custom designed, offering a choice of rivers, and an Elderhostel option. Paddlers enjoy clean air, great campsites, mountains and hills, wildflowers, and wildlife including moose, caribou, and eagles. Guests may also fish for salmon, grayling, and whitefish.

The season runs from June to August. Lessons are also available.

Colorado River and Trail Expeditions
Vicki and David Mackay
5058 S. 300 West
Salt Lake City, UT 84107
(801) 261-1789
Colorado River, Green River, Glacier Bay
Max. rapids: III-IV

Colorado River & Trail Expeditions runs guided raft trips of 5-12 days on the Colorado River in Utah and Arizona, the Green River in Utah, and Glacier Bay and the Arctic National Wildlife Refuge in Alaska. These trips offer excellent whitewater and magnificent scenery in remote locations. Their difficulty varies with the river and season. Generally, all trips are fine for people in good health and good physical condition.

During its May-September season, Colorado River & Trails also offers educational trips, which study photography, history, natural history or ecology.

Denali Floats
Tom Waite
Box 330
Talkeetna, AK 99676
(907) 733-2384
Susitna River, Chulitna River, Talkeetna River
Max. rapids: III-IV

Denali Floats runs 1-10 day guided raft trips on three Alaskan rivers between June and September. Trips are suitable for all skill levels and offer views of Mt. McKinley, excellent trout and salmon fishing, and a chance to spot moose, bears, beavers, and eagles.

Denali Raft Adventures
James Raisis
Drawer 190
Denali National Park, AK 99755
(907) 683-2234
Nenana River
Max. rapids: III-IV

Denali Raft Adventures offers exciting guided raft trips on the glacier-fed Nenana River in Denali National Park. Trips range in length from two to six hours with a scenic trip good for adults and children ages 5 and older, and whitewater trips for those 12 and older.

The season is from mid-May to mid-September, with good wildlife viewing for moose, caribou, Dall sheep, and grizzly bears.

Denali River Guides
Joe Halladay
Box 165
Talkeetna, AK 99676
(800) 474-2697
Southside Denali National Park, Denali State Park
Max. rapids: II-III

Denali River Guides specializes in remote back-country adventures, taking clients on rafts and hikes in fabled Denali Park. Trips last from three to five days during the June-October season, with emphasis on glacier hiking and wildlife photography. The company runs a tent camp beside Ruth Glacier, near Mt. McKinley.

Fishermen may hook arctic grayling and rainbow trout while naturalists search for ancient fossils and watch bear, moose, beaver, and migratory birds.

Denali West Lodge
Jack and Sherri Hayden
Box 40 PA
Lake Minchumina, AK 99757
Phone & FAX (907) 674-3112
Nowitna River, Kantishna River system
Max. rapids: None
Alaska Wilderness Guides Association

Denali West Lodge runs canoe trips on remote wilderness rivers in Alaska's vast interior. Set on the western edge of Denali National Park and Preserve, the lodge is more than 100 miles from the nearest highway and accessible only by seaplane or boat.

With maximum capacity of 10 people, and two to four guests per guide, clients head down the rivers, up the streams, and through the tundra to explore the wilds in canoes, riverboats, and on foot. Guests at the lodge stay in private log cabins and family-style meals are served in the handcrafted log lodge. Available, too, are "flightseeing" tours of Denali with views of Mt. McKinley.

Eagle River Raft Trips
Donna Robinson
P.O. Box 142294
Anchorage, AK 99514
(907) 337-7238
Eagle River
Max. rapids: III-IV

Eagle River runs 1-2 day guided raft trips between May and October. Offering both flatwater and whitewater trips on the Eagle River, the outfitter can treat paddlers "age 8 to 100" to pano-

Rafting on the Nenana River. Courtesy of Nate Mullins, Denali Raft Adventures, Inc., Denali National Park, Alaska.

ramic mountain scenery and views of moose, eagles, and bears. Fishing is for trout and salmon.

Eagle River Raft Trips supplies wet suits, booties, rain jackets, and extra wool gear if necessary. Located just 15 minutes from Anchorage, the outfitter offers free pickup at the Anchorage airport.

Eruk's Wilderness Float Tours
Eruk Williamson
12720 Lupine Rd.
Anchorage, AK 99516
(907) 345-7678
Western Alaska, Arctic
Max rapids: III-IV
Alaska Wilderness Recreation & Tourism Assn.

From June 1 through August, Eruk's Wilderness Float Tours runs guided raft trips on very remote rivers in the unspoiled Alaskan wilderness. Trips range from four to 14 days and are geared to each party's wishes. They are suitable for adults who like to camp and children over 8 years old. Comfort and safety are priorities. Swimming and paddling lessons are also available.

Tours for groups of two to seven are led by a wildlife biologist and offer instruction in fly fishing. All the little-used rivers have outstanding mountain scenery and excellent fishing for rainbow trout and five species of salmon.

Gary King's Alaskan Experience
Gary King
202 E. Northern Lights Blvd.
Anchorage, AK 99502
(907) 276-5425, (800) 777-7055
Rivers throughout Alaska
Max. rapids: III-V

Gary King's Alaskan Experience is a travel agency that books 1-10 day kayak and raft trips throughout Alaska. Claiming the distinction of being the largest booking agency for outdoor travel in Alaska, Alaskan Experience offers trips with dozens of outfitters for paddler of all skill levels. Trips run on remote,

pristine streams and rivers known for fine salmon fishing and chances to spot moose, caribou, and bears.

Trips booked by Alaskan Experience are available between June and September. The agency writes: "We take the risk out of selecting your Alaskan outfitter as we are in Alaska and know firsthand the outfitters whose trips we sell."

Glacier Bay Sea Kayaks
Bonnie Kaden
P.O. Box 26
Gustavius, AK 99826
(907) 697-2257
Glacier Bay
Max. rapids: None

Glacier Bay Sea Kayaks offers 1-10 day unguided kayak trips for paddlers wanting to explore the tidewater glaciers and pristine wilderness of Glacier Bay in Glacier Bay National Park.

The outfitter recommends its trips for novice and experienced kayakers alike, reporting a perfect safety record in 12 years of operation. The company does recommend, however, that paddlers be experienced campers.

Trips run between May 15 and September 15 and offer chances to spot humpback whales, Orcas, brown and black bears, and many sea birds.

Hugh Glass Backpacking Co.
Chuck Ash
Box 110796
Anchorage, AK 99511
(907) 344-1340
Kenai Fjords Nat. Park, Lakes & Rivers of Katmai Nat. Park, Kongakut, Noatak, Canning and Chilikadrotna Rivers

The outfitter offers true wilderness trips for small groups in excellent locations, with good interpretive guides versed in natural history. Hugh Glass Backpacking supplies canoes, kayaks, and sea kayaks for these guided trips, which last 3-10 days during a late May to early September season.

Camping is available and fishing is for salmon, trout, char, grayling, pike, and

— for sea kayakers — ocean species. Naturelovers may spot mountain goats, wolves, foxes, mink, and myriad birds including eagles, ospreys, harriers, and other raptors.

Interior Canoeing & Outfitting

Rich Kruse
Box 85
Ester, AK
(907) 479-9697, (907) 479-9699
Chena, Chatanika, Tanana Rivers
Max. rapids: I-II

Interior Canoeing does not offer guided trips but rents canoes to people of all experience levels. Some waters are calm and suitable for beginners while others in more remote locations have challenging sweepers and sharp turns. The company offers shuttle service to rivers of clients' choice, with friendly and knowledgeable staff. Camping, fishing, and paddling lessons are available during the May-September season. Typical wildlife includes black bear, moose, beaver, otter, fox, and waterfowl.

Jacques Adventure Company

Jerry Jacques
4316 Kingston Drive
Anchorage, AK 99504
(907) 337-9604
Talkeetna River
Max. rapids: III-IV

Jacques Adventure Company offers a variety of guided oar-boat and paddle-boat trips. These include half-day raft trips in Denali Park near Mt. McKinley; 1-day trips on the wild Six-Mile Creek; 3 and 6-day outings on the Talkeetna River; and 12-day trips on the Copper River starting at the ghost town of McCarthy.

The outfitter also offers custom river trips in Alaska, fishing trips of 1-10 days, and natural history and river trips in the Magadan and Siberia regions of the former Soviet Union. Trips, which run between June and August, range in difficulty and are suitable for guests age 12 and older.

Kayak Kodiak Tours

Tom Watson
P.O. Box 228
Kodiak, AK 99615
(907) 486-2604
Sheltered bays around Kodiak Islands, Gulf of Alaska, Pacific Ocean
Max. rapids: None
Trade Association of Sea Kayaking

Kayak Kodiak Tours runs guided sea kayak day trips along the rugged, fjord inlets along Alaska's coast from April 1 to October 15. These outings require no prior experience but customers should be in good health with average stamina.

The outfitter is eco-tourism oriented, devoting part of its fees to the local Audubon chapter. Its two-person kayaks are safe and dry. The trips, limited to six paddlers, offer good opportunities to spot sea lions, sea otters, puffins, kittiwakes, and whales, and fish for rockfish, salmon, and dolly varden.

Keystone Raft & Kayak Adventures

Mike Buck
P.O. Box 1486
Valdez, AK 99686
(907) 835-2606, (800) 328-8460
Lowe River, Tonsina River, Talkeetna River, Kennecott River, Nizina River, Chitina River, Copper River, Tatshenshini River, Tana River
Max. rapids: V
Alaska Wilderness Guides

Keystone Raft & Kayak Adventures offers guided and unguided kayak and raft trips through pristine Alaskan wilderness. One of the most spectacular and exciting river runs is on the Lowe River through Keystone Canyon. A popular day adventure, with Class III-IV rapids, is a Tonsina River trip. For action-packed whitewater and excellent fishing, Talkeetna River trips are exceptional. And Chitina and Cooper River trips in the Wrangell Mountains offer beautiful mountain and glacier scenery, plus a chance to explore ghost towns.

Finally, Tana River offers breathtaking scenery with sand dunes, whitewater, and abundant wildlife. Trips range from very easy to very demanding. Among the wildlife to see are bears, eagles, goats, sheep, and moose. Fishing for salmon, trout, and grayling is excellent. Trips run from May to September.

The National Outdoor Leadership School
Nancy Siegel
River Manager
Box AA
Lander, WY 82520
(307) 332-6973
Prince William Sound, other Alaskan waters, Green River
Max. rapids: IV
America Outdoors, Colorado River Outfitters Association, Utah Guides and Outfitters Organization

The National Outdoor Leadership School specializes in teaching a wide array of backcountry skills including kayaking, rafting, mountaineering, rock climbing, glacier travel, backpacking, and cross-country skiing. Its rafting trips run through Desolation Canyon on the Green River in Utah and Lodore Canyon on the Green River at the Colorado-Utah border. NOLS also offers sea kayaking in Alaska and Baja, Mexico. These instructional trips range in length from 14-31 days, with some trips geared for teenagers 16 and older and some for paddlers 25 and older. All trips are physically challenging; paddlers must be in good shape and excellent health.

These trips, which run between June and late October, feature beautiful scenery and sufficient challenge to ensure that all participants can test and improve their paddling skills.

Nichols Expeditions
Chuck and Judy Nichols
497 North Main
Moab, UT 84532
(801) 259-3999, (800) 648-8488
Copper River, Green River, Koyakuk River, Main Salmon River, Sea of Cortez, Magdalena Bay
Max. rapids: II-IV
Utah Guides and Outfitters, Idaho Guides and Outfitters

Experience the splendor of Alaska from the comfort of a paddle raft or the intimacy of a sea kayak. Nichols' trips pass through pristine wilderness of glaciers and nameless peaks, offering a chance to spot dall sheep, caribou, moose, eagles, and harbor seals. These 8-15 day trips are fine for beginners in good shape, and allow time for photography and fishing.

Nichols Expeditions also offers raft whitewater trips in Idaho (see Idaho listings), Green River trips in Utah's Labyrinth Canyon (see Utah listings), sea kayaking in Baja, Mexico, mountain biking, and combination trips.

North Star Alaska
Bob Parker
Box 1724
Flagstaff, AZ 86002
(520) 773-9917, (800) 258-8434, FAX (520) 773-9917
Kongakut, Noatak, Talkeetna and Copper Rivers, sea kayaking in Prince William Sound & Kenai Fjords Nat. Park
Max. rapids: III-IV

Arizona-based North Star Alaska runs a wide variety of guided paddling trips in remote inland areas of Alaska as well as offshore sea kayaking outings. For its wilderness river journeys, the company provides canoes, kayaks, and rafts with experienced guides and naturalists. Most of the rivers involved are used by no more than 50 to 200 paddlers a year.

Active vacationers who enjoy the wilderness experience and primitive camping may relish mountain views, glaciers, tundra, and abundant wildlife ranging from grizzlies to musk-oxen. Fishing is excellent. The season runs May 15-Sept. 15.

Nova Riverrunners Inc.
Chuck Spaulding and Jay Doyle
P.O. Box 1129
Chickaloon, AK 99674
(907) 745-5753
Rivers throughout Alaska
Max. rapids: V+

NOVA Riverrunners offers kayak rentals and guided kayak and raft trips on wilderness rivers throughout Alaska. Its easiest trip is a one-day float in an oar boat just a one-and-a-half hour drive from Anchorage in the Chugach and Talkeetna Mountains. At the other extreme is the Class V + Six-Mile Creek paddle-boat run for which paddlers must pass a tough whitewater test to confirm their ability to handle the rigors of the trip.

Other offerings between May and October include a 27-mile trip along the edge of Matanuska Glacier and a 3-day trip to remote Salmon Spring River, which offers great fishing and an abundance of bears. Other wildlife to be seen include moose, caribou, bison, beavers, and eagles.

Osprey Expeditions
Aaron & Robin Underwood
P.O. Box 209
Denali National Park, AK 99755
(907) 683-2734
Talkeetna, Copper, Chitina, Fortymile, Tazlina, S. Fork Kuskokwim Rivers
Max. rapids: III-IV
Alaska Wilderness Guides Association

Almost anyone who likes to camp can enjoy a wilderness rafting trip with Osprey Expeditions. The company offers experienced guides, excellent food, and a wide variety of wilderness excursions on remote, seldom travelled Alaskan rivers.

The scenery includes alpine tundra, high mountains, glaciers, and moose,

caribou, bears, wolves, seals, eagles, and other wildlife. The whitewater is excellent, and there is good fishing for salmon, grayling, trout, and dolly varden. The season runs from June to mid-September.

Ouzel Expeditions, Inc.
Paul and Sharon Allred
Box 935
Girdwood, AK 99587
(800) 825-8196, (907) 783-2216
Upper Cook Inlet, Bristol Bay
Max. rapids: IV

Ouzel Expeditions runs guided raft trips on 26 scenic rivers in Alaska. Trips of 6-8 days are generally by oar boat on Class I and II rivers, offering excellent opportunities to enjoy the wild scenery, fishing, and views of grizzly bears, caribou, and moose.

Especially proud of its fishing expeditions, Ouzel flies guests to Alaska's interior to enjoy wilderness fishing for rainbow trout, Dolly Varden, arctic grayling, northern pike, and king, sockeye, silver, calico, and pink salmon. Ouzel uses only debarbed single hooks and maintains a catch-and-release policy on all rivers. Guests may, however, keep two king salmon or three other salmon during the course of a trip.

Ouzel's season runs from June to September.

Quest Expeditions
Paul Jackson
Box 671895
Chugiak. AK 99567
(907) 688-4848
Canning, Hulahula, Sheenjek, Wind, Kobuk, Nigu-Killik, Noatak Rivers, rivers in W. Alaska.
Max. rapids: III

Quest Expeditions runs adventurous, expedition-style trips of 5-14 days in Alaska's Arctic National Wildlife Refuge (ANWR). The ANWR is the calving ground of a Porcupine caribou herd and home to Dall sheep, wolves, musk oxen, grizzly bears, nesting waterfowl, shore birds, and raptors. Trips in this 18-million-acre wilderness pass through high mountains, foothills, and coastal plains, offering beginning or moderate whitewater, and stunning views of wildflowers, ice fields, and abundant wildlife. Trips are also run in the Gates of the Arctic and Kobuk Valley National Parks, and the Noatak Preserve and W. Alaska.

Most trips are of moderate difficulty, in authentic expedition style, requiring guests to paddle and otherwise pitch in. Easy river trips and cabin rentals on remote lakes are also available.

Sourdough Outfitters
Gary, Hulda, Brandon Benson
P.O. Box 90
Bettles, AK 99726
(907) 692-5252
All Brooks Range rivers
Max. rapids: III-IV
Alaska Wilderness Recreation & Tourism Association

Sourdough Outfitters, located on the south side of the Brooks Range, offers a wide variety of adventures from June 1 to September 7. These range from easy canoeing trips to rugged canoeing-backpacking tours and exciting whitewater rafting on the remote Ivishak River.

These are excursions to true wilderness where there are no roads and few, if any, other people. Caribou, bears, moose, and small mammals inhabit the landscape, which varies from mountains to open tundra. Trout, grayline, arctic char, pike, sheefish, and salmon enliven the streams.

Rust's Flying Service
Hank & Todd Rust
Box 190325
Anchorage, AK 99519
(907) 243-1595, (800) 544-2299
All rivers in S. Central and S.W. Alaska
where planes can land safely
Max. rapids: V+

Rust's Flying Service offers guided trips by canoe, kayak, raft, and dory as well as rental canoes, kayaks and rafts for trips of up to 20 days throughout southcentral and southwest Alaska. The

A 35-lb. king salmon caught on the Deshka River. Courtesy of Ouzel Expeditions, Anchorage, Alaska.

company offers good equipment and an unsurpassed safety record. Flight destinations include remote fishing lodges and cabins. Camping, too, is available.

A wide variety of trips is offered, suitable for experts as well as novices. Scenery, fishing and wildlife vary by location, but as the company says: "Alaska landscape speaks for itself."

Spirit Walker Expeditions
Nathan Borson
Box 240PA
Gustavus, AK 99826
(907) 697-2266, (800) KAYAKER,
FAX (907) 697-2701
Icy Strait, Gulf of Alaska
Max. rapids: None

Spirit Walker Expeditions offers guided sea-kayak trips of one to seven days on Icy Strait, the Gulf of Alaska, and numerous smaller bays and inlets. Paddlers including beginners and families pass along wild, rocky coasts, through narrow inlets among the islands of the inside passage, and over colorful reefs inhabited by starfish, sea anemones, and crabs. Travel by kayak permits silent approaches to view seals, sea lions, river otters, whales, deer, and bears. Trips also feature fresh, gourmet meals; fishing for salmon, trout, and halibut; and comfortable camp sites on wilderness beaches or amid spruce or hemlock forests.

Trips run from May to October and are of little to moderate difficulty, suitable for anyone fit enough to walk a few miles.

Sunlight North Expeditions
Clancy Crawford
Box 112983
Anchorage, AK 99511
(907) 346-2027, FAX (907) 346-2063
Kenai Nat. Wildlife Refuge, Kenai Fjords
Nat. Park, Brooks Range, Noatak River
Max. rapids: I-II

Wilderness trips for the moderately fit are Sunlight North's specialty. The company provides knowledgeable personal service to small groups. Clients may canoe in the Kenai Wildlife Refuge, sea kayak in the Kenai Fjords, or spend 10 days rafting on the remote upper stretch of the Noatak River in the western Brooks Range, a true wilderness experience.

Everywhere the scenery, wildlife, and fishing are superbly Alaskan, and the company's season goes from mid-May to mid-September.

Tippecanoe
Ray & Heather Kelley
Box 1175
Mile 66.6 Parks Hwy
Willow, AK 99688-1175
(907) 495-6688
Little Susitna River, Moose Creek, and the
lake-studded Nancy Lake State Rec. Area
Max. rapids: II
PPA

Tippecanoe runs guided tours on the Nancy Lake Recreation Area canoe trail system as well as renting canoes and kayaks. Paddlers have an excellent opportunity to watch wildlife such as bears, moose, eagles, loons, and beavers in their natural habitat. They can also fish for rainbow and grayling trout, salmon, and northern pike. Camping and cabins are also available. The season runs from May 15 to Oct. 15.

Too-loo-uk River Guides
Juliette Boselli & Jim Hendrick
Box 106
Denali National Park, AK 99755
(907) 683-1542
Chitina, Copper, Fortymile, Talkeetna,
John Rivers
Max. rapids: III-IV

Too-loo-uk offers guided raft trips for small groups in wilderness areas rife with bears, moose, caribou, wolves, bald eagles, salmon, and trout. The company caters to people of all ages, with some raft trips suitable for 8-year-olds and up. Scenery is typically northern: glacial and tundra.

Watching caribou along the Naotak River. Courtesy of ABEC, Fairbanks, Alaska.

Wapiti River Guides
Gary Lane
Box 1125
Riggins, ID 83549
(208) 628-3523, (800) 488-9872
*Rivers throughout Alaska, Grande Ronde
River, Owyhee River, Salmon River
Max. rapids: V+
Oregon Guides and Packers Association,
Idaho Outfitters and Guides Association*

Wapiti River Guides, with trips in
Idaho, Oregon, and Alaska, specializes
in small personalized trips of moderate
difficulty "for ages 3 to 103, families, and
nature lovers." The trips are distinctive,
too, for their guides' emphasis on
natural history and Native American
culture, and for the fine scenery.

Trips, ranging in length from 1-12
days, also allow time for interesting side
hikes and viewing elk, deer, bald eagles,
bobcats, cougars, bears, bighorn sheep,
minks and other wildlife. Fishing is for
steelhead, trout, and bass.

White Magic Unlimited
Jack Morison
P.O. Box 5506
Mill Valley, CA 94942
(800) 869-9874, (415) 381-8889
*Tatshenshini, Alsek (AK), Colorado (AZ)
Max. rapids: III-IV*

California-based White Magic runs
guided raft trips on many rivers throughout the western United States. An
adventure travel company, it also offers
rafting and trekking expeditions in 16
countries.

In Alaska, the company provides
10-day rafting and hiking trips on the
Tatshenshini River and similar 13-day
tours on the Alsek River during the
summer. Both trips afford dramatic
closeup views of calving glaciers amid
the pristine wilderness of Alaska, with
its mountains and abundant wildlife.

Wilderness: Alaska/Mexico
Ron Yarnell
Dept. PA, 1231 Sundance Loop
Fairbanks, AK 99709
Phone/FAX: (907) 479-8203
Noatak, Hulahula, Kongakut, Canning,
Kobuk, Alatna, Koyukuk Rivers.
Max. rapids: III-IV
Alaska Wilderness Recreation & Tourism
Assn.

Wilderness Alaska/Mexico runs guided raft and kayak trips in the Brooks Range of northern Alaska, a true wilderness with its caribou migrations and natural rivers without dams or pollution. These tours last eight to 12 days and require no previous river experience.

During the June-September season, guests can experience 24-hour daylight, explore tundra terrain, and see wolves, grizzlies, muskoxen, dall sheep, and caribou. There is fishing for Arctic char, grayling, Dolly Varden, salmon, pike, and sheefish.

The sea kayaking trips of 8-14 days in Prince William Sound are moderately strenuous. While previous sea kayaking experience is not necessary, guests must be able to paddle 10 to 12 miles a day. The scenery is stunning, with glaciers, fjords, mountains, and views of whales, sea otters, and seals.

World Express Tours, Inc.
200 W. 34th Ave., Ste. 412
Anchorage, AK 99503
(800) 544-2235, FAX (206) 828-4712
Kenai, Susitna, Tatshenshini, Alsek,
Eagle Rivers
Max. rapids: none

World Express Tours is a tour operator that specializes in providing custom Alaska itineraries for discriminating groups or individuals. Working with different companies throughout Alaska, it books rafting, canoeing, and kayaking trips on a wide variety of rivers, with excellence as the watchword.

Arizona

To many people, boaters and landlubbers alike, mention of rafting American rivers immediately conjures up the image of the Grand Canyon. No wonder, for this stupendous chasm rivals Mount Everest among the world's natural wonders, and the ideal way to explore it is by raft or kayak. Words can hardly do the Grand Canyon justice. But Major John Wesley Powell, who made the first documented runs of the canyon in 1869-72, came close when he called its billion-year-old cliffs "the library of the gods" whose colorful strata formed the leaves of "one great book." Paddlers and trail riders can read this open book of geology at close range as they explore the 217-mile-long canyon with its mile-high walls. It is a place to linger, to contemplate the gigantic cross-section of the earth's crust laid bare by the Colorado River, to touch rocks more than 1,500,000,000 years old. Sightseers crowding the canyon rim can admire the spectacle from afar. But they cannot handle these primeval rocks or search the valley for fossils.

Commercial floating through the canyon began in 1938, aboard rudimentary wooden boats very different from today's rafts and kayaks. Now it has become so popular that paddlers who do not join an outfitted trip have to compete for a permit to navigate on their own. At present the waiting list is about ten years long. But more than one-third of those who finally reach the top decide to cancel, so applicants lower down can then get vacant slots. Call the River Permits Office at (520) 638-7843 for applications, information and latest word on available dates.

Grand Canyon rapids can be scary — up to Class V+ — and even the best kayakers sometimes overturn in heavy waves. They find the water extremely cold, sometimes less than fifty degrees at the Lees Ferry put-in close to the Utah state line. It has been aptly stated that the Grand Canyon is one of the few places on earth where one may suffer heat prostration and hypothermia within a single ten-minute period. (Summer air temperatures may exceed 100 degrees.)

All kinds of pontoons are available, from small oar-powered and paddle rafts to huge motorized craft that carry 20 passengers on cushioned seats. On luxury trips, guides cook lavish meals for clients to eat at campsite tables.

Bedrolls or foam rubber sleeping pads are provided for added comfort. Some outfitters helicopter people in and out of the canyon. Lovers of nature resent these intrusions on the peace and quiet of what remains of the wilderness. Many outfitters refuse to join the motorized contingent. One makes a point of stressing in his brochure: "All our trips are oar-powered. Given a choice, we think you would prefer the sounds of the canyon and the river, not the sound of a motor." But the canyon is so huge that its majesty can still overwhelm the visitor — especially at sunset as the motors fall silent, the rocks change color and the campfires crackle.

Since completion of the Glen Canyon Dam in 1964, the natural flow of warm and muddy water through the world's biggest gorge has changed to a cold, crystal-clear river with a steadier flow. The Colorado can be floated as well in April or October as in midsummer. People who want to walk into the many beautiful side canyons and look for wildlife such as bighorn sheep try to pick the cooler months of spring and fall.

Obviously the Grand Canyon with its 200 rapids is Arizona's star attraction, but despite its lack of rainfall the state is not without a supporting cast of minor rivers. Close to Phoenix, raft trips are offered down the Gila, Salt and Verde Rivers with modest Class I-II rapids. These year-round scenic tours introduce rafters to the Sonoran Desert. They also provide memorable views of tall cliffs, cactus, mesquite groves and wildlife including bald eagles and wild horses.

American River Touring Association
24000 Casa Loma Rd.
Groveland, CA 95321
(800) 323-2782, (209) 962-7873
Colorado River, Middle Fork and Main Salmon Rivers, Selway River, Merced River, Tuolumne River, Klamath River, Rogue River, Illinois River, Umpqua River, Green River, Yampa River
Max. rapids: IV
America Outdoors, Oregon Guides and Packers, Idaho Outfitters and Guides, Utah Guides and Outfitters

ARTA offers a total of 16 raft trips in five Western states. The trips, in California, Oregon, Utah, Idaho, and Arizona, are by oar rafts, paddle rafts, oar/paddle combination rafts, and inflatable canoes.

Most trips are of Class III difficulty and appropriate for novices and families, as well as those with more experience.

Other trips of up to V+ difficulty challenge even the most advanced paddler. Depending on the location, the trips feature such added attractions as wildflowers, side streams, swimming holes, Indian ruins, warm water, abundant wildlife, good hiking and fishing, and hot springs.

ARTA, a non-profit company, also offers whitewater schools, professional guide training, and family discounts.

Arizona Raft Adventures
Robert Elliott
4050 E. Huntington Drive
Department P
Flagstaff, AZ 86004
(800) 786-7238
San Jose River
Max. rapids: II-III

Arizona Raft Adventures runs guided raft trips of 6-14 days on the Colorado

River through the Grand Canyon, offering tremendous scenery, fishing, hiking, and whitewater. These expeditions are not difficult unless guests opt for the 6-day canyon trip, which includes a strenuous seven-and-a-half mile hike and requires good physical conditioning. Guests can also control the degree of difficulty by the type of boat they select. Oar boats, motor boats, paddle boats, and paddle/oar combination boats are available.

On all trips, guests can also enjoy side hikes, pristine campsites, and spotting ringtail cats, bighorn sheep, mule deer, birds, and other wildlife. Trips run from April to October.

Arizona Raft Adventures also offers trips operated by other outfitters in Idaho, Utah, and Costa Rica.

Arizona River Runners
Judy Marshall
P.O. Box 47788
Phoenix, AZ 85068
(602) 867-4866, (800) 477-7238
Colorado River
Max. rapids: V+
America Outdoors

Arizona River Runners runs guided oar- and motor-powered trips of 3, 4, 6, 8 and 13 days on the Colorado River, from May to September. All trips include food, equipment, guides and various transportation options. Guests are free to enjoy the beauty of the Grand Canyon's wildlife geology, history and folklore, all described by very experienced guides.

Back Bay Canoe & Kayak
John Motshagen
Box 21684
Bullhead City, AZ 86439
(520) 758-6242
Lake Mohave, Lake Havasu, Topock Gorge, Colorado River
Max. rapids: none
PPA

Back Bay runs both guided and unguided trips by canoe and kayak for easy paddling amid rugged desert scenery. Customers find clear water, good fishing for trout and striped bass, and wildlife including bighorn sheep, beaver, and many birds. Custom trips lasting several days are available, as well as half-day outings, during the company's year-round season. Camping, swimming, and paddling lessons are available.

Canyoneers, Inc.
Gaylord and Joy Staveley
Box 2997
Flagstaff, AZ 86003
(520) 526-0924, (800) 525-0924
(outside AZ)
Colorado River
Max. rapids: V+
America Outdoors, National Forest Recreation Association, Grand Canyon River Guides

Canyoneers runs 2-14 day guided trips in the Grand Canyon in pontoon rowboats and pontoon motorboats. Rowing boats carry four to six passengers and offer an exciting, wet ride, while motorboats are more comfortable, with individual, cushioned seats. Trips by either craft are suitable for guests in general good health.

Trips, which run between April and September, are led by knowledgeable guides and allow ample time for fishing and hiking in side canyons.

Cimarron Adventures and River Company
Denny Carr, Jon Colby, Dave Insley
7714 East Catalina
Scottsdale, AZ 85251
(602) 994-1199
Verde River, Salt River, Gila River
Max. rapids: I-II
America Outdoors

Cimarron Adventure and River Company runs guided raft trips on scenic rivers in the Sonoran desert. Trips range in length from one to three days, offering excellent birdwatching and wildlife observation and views of towering cliffs, saguaro cactus, and mesquite groves in a unique desert landscape. Among the wildlife to be seen are eagles, coyotes, wild horses, and desert bighorn sheep.

Cimarron also offers moonlight rafting, combined jeep/raft trips, executive fishing trips, paddle/saddle trips, and hiking tours in the Camelback and Superstitious Mountains.

Colorado River and Trail Expeditions

Vicki and David Mackay
5058 S. 300 West
Salt Lake City, UT 84107
(801) 261-1789
Colorado River, Green River, Glacier Bay
Max. rapids: III-IV

Colorado River & Trail Expeditions runs guided raft trips of 5-12 days on the Colorado River in Utah and Arizona, the Green River in Utah, and Glacier Bay and the Arctic National Wildlife Refuge in Alaska. These trips offer excellent whitewater and magnificent scenery in remote locations. Their difficulty varies with the river and season. Generally, all trips are fine for people in good health and good physical condition.

During its May-September season, Colorado River & Trails also offers educational trips, which study photography, history, natural history or ecology.

Colorado River Outfitters

Larry Thompson, Joe Hernandez
2649 Hwy. 95, Ste. 49
Bullhead City, AZ 86442
(520) 763-2325
Lake Mohave, Lake Mead, Havasu Wildlife
Refuge on the Lower Colorado River
Max. rapids: I-II
PPA

Casinos are featured as well as canyons on the canoe and kayak trips offered by Colorado River Outfitters. The company runs both guided and unguided trips through desert waterways with lots of wildlife, including mountain sheep and beaver. On the Nevada side of the river paddlers also pass high-rise hotels and casinos. Fishing is for trout, catfish, striped bass, smallmouth bass, and crappie. The water quality is excellent and hot springs may be found in the canyons. Camping and paddling lessons

Grand Canyon. Courtesy of Expeditions, Inc., Flagstaff, Arizona.

are available during the January-January season.

Expeditions, Inc.
Dick and Susie McCallum
625 N. Beaver St.
Flagstaff, AZ 86001
(520) 779-3769, FAX: (520) 774-4001
Colorado River - Grand Canyon
Max. rapids: V+

Expeditions Inc., a family-run business, offers 5-16 day trips on the Colorado River through the Grand Canyon. Guided tours are by canoe and kayak support trips and by raft. They offer ample time each day to hike, explore side canyons, and swim. On guided tours, guests can choose between oar-powered boats and paddle boats.

Expeditions Inc. can supply a support boat for running kayaks through the Grand Canyon. Both "kayak-support" and rafting trips includes complete camping equipment and meals.

Scenery is spectacular, with Class V rapids. All trips start and finish in Flagstaff. Guests can also enjoy fishing for trout and viewing bighorn sheep, coyotes, and foxes.

Grand Canyon Expeditions Company
Michael R. Denoyer
P.O. Box O
Kanab, UT 84741
(801) 644-2691, (800) 544-2691
Colorado River
Max. rapids: V+

Grand Canyon Expeditions runs guided raft and dory trips through the Grand Canyon on the Colorado River. Trips last eight days by motorized raft or 14 by oar boat. These expeditions begin and end in Las Vegas, with bus service to and from the Grand Canyon. The company provides gourmet meals and makes all other arrangements, leaving guests free to enjoy the Canyon's scenic and geological wonders. Guests can spot mule deer, bighorn sheep, and other wildlife; fish for rainbow, brook, and cut-

Grand Canyon. Courtesy of Ron Smith, Grand Canyon Expeditions.

throat trout, and hike in side canyons. In addition, special history, archaeology, astronomy, geology, photography, and ecology trips are available.

Grand Canyon Expeditions' trips, suitable for anyone aged eight or older, run between April and September.

James Henry River Journeys
James Katz
P.O. Box 807
Bolinas, CA 94924
(415) 868-1836, (800) 786-1830
Colorado River, Salmon River, Rogue River, Tatshenshini-Alsek Rivers, Noatak River, Stanislaus River, Carson River, Klamath River
Max. rapids: III-IV
Idaho Outfitters and Guides

James Henry River Journeys runs guided canoe, kayak, and raft trips in California, Arizona, Idaho, Oregon, and Alaska. In California, the outfitter offers trips with Class II-III rapids, of one to three days, on the Stanislaus, East Fork of the Carson, and the Lower Klamath.

In Arizona, the company runs Grand Canyon trips, with Class IV+ rapids, of 6, 8, 9, 13, and 14 days. Trips in Idaho, of 4, 5 or 6 days, run on the Class III-IV Main Salmon. In Oregon, trips of 3, 4, and 5 days run on the Class III Rogue. Finally, in Alaska the company offers a natural history expedition on the Tatshenshini-Alsels Rivers.

All trips run through especially scenic wilderness areas and are carefully planned to move at a leisurely pace, allowing ample time for side hikes, fishing, photography, and general relaxation. As a result, participation is open to anyone active and in good health. The company's season runs from May to September.

Jerkwater Canoe Co., Inc.
Eloise Roche & Ernie Doiron
Box 800
Topock, AZ 86436
(602) 768-7753, (800) 421-7803
Colorado River: Hoover Dam to Yuma
Max. rapids: None
PPA

Jerkwater Canoe rents canoes year-round to families and others for relaxing flatwater trips amid scenic canyon country. Paddlers can linger in back bays and quiet lagoons; fish for striped bass, trout, and catfish; and spot bighorn sheep, beavers, herons, rails, and raccoons. The water is very clear and unbroken by rapids, snags, or outfalls. Trips last from 1-6 days.

Laughing Heart Adventures
Dezh Pagen
Trinity Outdoor Center
P.O. Box 669
Willow Creek, CA 95573
(916) 629-3516, (800) 541-1256
Colorado River
Max. rapids: I
PPA, ACA

The Black Canyon section of the Lower Colorado, located below Hoover Dam and Lake Mead, has outstanding canoeing opportunities and the greatest

assortment of hot springs in any river location. Laughing Heart Adventures conducts trips during Thanksgiving week and prepares a barbecue turkey with all the trimmings. Also during Easter vacation guests can enjoy hot springs nestled between towering canyon walls with unique views of the sun and stars. There are also hot waterfalls and a "sauna cave" to ease any tired muscles after a day of canoeing and birding.

Moki Mac River Expeditions, Inc.
Richard, Clair and Robert Quist
P.O. Box 21242
Salt Lake City, UT 84121
(801) 268-6667, (800) 284-7280
Colorado River, Green River
Max. rapids: V+
Utah Guides and Outfitters, PPA

Moki Mac River Expeditions runs guided canoe, raft and "funyak" trips of 1-14 days on the Colorado and Green Rivers. Runs on the Colorado go through the Westwater, Cataract, and Grand Canyons, and on the Green River through the Desolation, Labyrinth, and Stillwater Canyons. Oar boats are available on all runs; motorized boats are available in Cataract Canyon and the Grand Canyon; and oar-boat/funyak trips run through Desolation Canyon. The Grand Canyon has the largest, most frequent rapids, Desolation Canyon is milder, and Cataract Canyon offers great excitement during the high-water runoff season.

Moki Mac also rents canoes for trips through the Labyrinth and Stillwater Canyons. All trips, set on the Colorado Plateau, offer chances to spot eagles, cranes, Canada geese, bighorn sheep and the occasional bear. Guests can also fish for catfish and trout. Moki Mac's season is from April to October.

O.A.R.S.
George Wendt
P.O. Box 67
Angels Camp, CA 95222
(209) 736-4677, (800) 446-7238 (CA),
(800) 346-6277 (U.S.)
*American, Cal-Salmon, Stanislaus,
Tuolumne, Merced, Rogue, Snake, San Juan,
Colorado, Salmon Rivers and Middle Fork of
the Salmon*
Max. rapids: III-IV
America Outdoors

O.A.R.S. runs guided dory, raft, and kayak trips in six Western states. It offers tours in California on the American, Cal-Salmon, Merced, Stanislaus, and Tuolumne Rivers; in Idaho on the Rogue; in Arizona on the Colorado; in Wyoming on the Snake, and in Utah on the San Juan River. These outings last 1-13 days and, depending on the class of river, are fine for children, novices, families, and intermediate and expert rafters. O.A.R.S. trips provide fishing, swimming, camping, side hikes, wildlife viewing, and other activities. Tours run from April to October.

Outdoors Unlimited
John Vail
6900 Townsend Winona Road
Flagstaff, AZ 86004
(602) 526-4546, (800) 637-RAFT
Colorado River
Max. rapids: V+

Outdoors Unlimited runs guided kayak and raft trips of 5-12 days on the Colorado River through the Grand Canyon. Twelve-day trips traverse the entire length of the Grand Canyon, while 5- and 8-day trips run on either upper or lower sections. These partial trips begin deep in the heart of the canyon, requiring a strenuous nine-mile hike. Trips are either in five-person oar boats or six- or seven-person paddle boats. All trips offer Class V rapids, spectacular scenery, and a chance to view bighorn sheep and other wildlife. Outdoors Unlimited's season is from May to October.

Professional River Outfitters
Bruce & Nancy Helin
P.O. Box 635
Flagstaff, AZ 86002
(602) 779-1512
*Colorado, Salt, San Juan, Green Rivers, plus
Tatshensheni and Alsek Rivers in Alaska*
Max. rapids: V+

Professional River Outfitters serves a very small group of people: those who have private permits to run the Colorado and other rivers. It is not, therefore, a commercial outfitter in the usual sense.

The company has over 50 years' experience in the Grand Canyon and provides its clients with top-quality gear and advice. Most customers run the Colorado through the Grand Canyon. The company's season runs from March/April to November but it also serves winter trips through the Canyon.

Sleight Expeditions
Mark Sleight
P.O. Box 40
St. George, UT 84771
(801) 673-1200
Colorado River
Max. rapids: III-IV

Sleight Expeditions runs guided raft tours through the Grand Canyon from April to October at competitive cost, with experienced guides, and in small groups. No previous whitewater experience is needed, but camping experience is helpful. Trips range from 5-12 days and the Grand Canyon scenery is phenomenal.

Sun Country Rafting, Inc.
Scott Seyler
Box 9429
Phoenix, AZ 85068
(602) 493-9011, (800) 272-3353
Upper Salt River
Max rapids: V
America Outdoors

Sun Country Rafting runs guided tours in the majestic Upper Salt River Canyon from March-June. Trip lengths vary from 1-day to 4- and 5-day adventures. Both paddle and oar trips are available. The Upper Salt River is a world-class whitewater system and it is discovered by new enthusiasts each year.

Grand Canyon. Courtesy of Western River Expeditions, Salt Lake City, Utah.

Waters Edge
Thor Lane
2561 East Ft. Lowell
Tucson, AZ 85716
(520) 325-9935
*Desert lakes & rivers, esp. Lake Powell
& Baja*
Max. rapids: None
PPA

Waters Edge offers inflatable kayak lessons and rents kayaks, canoes, rafts, and catarafts year-round. Its trips run through country where paddlers can fish for bass and spot bighorn sheep, raptors, and riparian birds.

Western River Expeditions
Larry Lake
7258 Racquet Club Drive
Salt Lake City, UT 84121
(801) 942-6669, (800) 453-7450
(outside UT)
*Colorado River, Green River, Main
Salmon River*
Max. rapids: III-IV
America Outdoors

Western River Expeditions runs guided raft trips and rents rafts and inflatable kayaks on the Colorado River in Colorado, Utah, and Arizona; the Green River in Utah; and the Main Salmon in Idaho. Green River trips, by oar or paddle raft, provide thrilling whitewater and views of towering red rock cliffs and arches, deep gorges, frontier cabins, and Indian petroglyphs. Colorado River tours offer spectacular scenery in Cataract Canyon, Westwater Canyon, and the upper and lower Grand Canyon. Rapids are moderate to large, and paddlers can swim, take side hikes, and view historic Indian and Old West sites. Finally, trips on the Main Salmon involve scenic blue-green waters, pine-covered mountains, stops at hot springs and abandoned mining camps, and camping on white-sand beaches.

All trips are suitable for anyone in good health above the minimum age set for each trip. During Western River's March-September season, some trips can be combined with a ranch stay.

White Magic Unlimited
Jack Morison
P.O. Box 5506
Mill Valley, CA 94942
(800) 869-9874, (415) 381-8889
Colorado River
Max. rapids: V

California-based White Magic runs raft trips on most rivers throughout the western United States. An adventure travel company, it also offers rafting and trekking trips in 16 countries.

In Arizona, Grand Canyon trips depart daily between April to November and range in length from 5-14 days. Some cover the complete canyon, others only the upper or lower sections. These shorter trips begin or end at Phantom Ranch, requiring a 5,000-foot climb up or down the strenuous nine-mile Bright Angel Trail. Oar, paddle, and motorized rafts are available.

The scenery is world-renowned, and the side canyons contain fascinating fossils, natural history, and springs gushing from the rock.

Whitewater Voyages
William McGinnis
P.O. Box 20400
El Sobrante, CA 94820-0400
(510) 222-5994, (800) 488-RAFT
Colorado River, Kern River, Merced River, Tuolumne River, Cache Creek, American River, Yuba River, Klamath River, Stanislaus River, Trinity River, Middle Fork Salmon River, Rogue River
Max. rapids: III-IV
America Outdoors, American River Recreation Association

Whitewater Voyages offers an extensive array of trips, with guided oar- and paddle-boat runs in California, Arizona, Oregon, and Idaho. Trips by kayak and raft range in length from 1-5 days and in difficulty from Class II to Class V. With runs on nine Wild and Scenic Rivers and on more California rivers than any other outfitter, Whitewater Voyages has trips for paddlers of all level of experience.

The outfitter also has specialty trips, including whitewater schools, family trips, low-cost river-cleanup trips, "team-building" trips and excursions in the former Soviet Union to paddle with Russians as part of project R.A.F.T.

Arkansas

Many of Arkansas' 9,000 miles of streams are great for floating by canoe, raft or johnboat. The state helps the paddler by putting out a "floater's kit" describing 17 favorite waterways with maps, access points, preferred seasons, fishing and scenery on each river, along with an outfitters directory. It can be obtained from the Arkansas Department of Parks and Tourism, 1 Capitol Mall, Little Rock, AR 72201.

Big Piney Creek is considered by some to be a classic Ozark stream. Only 67 miles long, it rises in the Ozark National Forest and offers both wild and calm water as it heads for its confluence with the Arkansas River at Lake Dardanelle. Along one 10-mile stretch, from Treat to Long Pool, its rapids boast such names as Roller Coaster, Surfing Hole and, somewhat ominously Cascades of Extinction. The canoe season begins in late fall and can run on until mid-June after a rainy spell. Steep wooded hillsides, deer, turkeys and even black bears may be seen. Fishing for smallmouth bass is best in late spring or early summer.

For good family floating, the Caddo River in west central Arkansas is hard to beat. Originating in the Ouachita Mountains, the Caddo provides good pastoral scenery, excellent fishing, peaceful waters in most stretches but occasional Class I-II rapids.

Famous for its trout fishing is the White River, a 720-mile stream which follows a zigzag course like a giant questionmark from northwestern Arkansas to the Mississippi on the state's southeastern border. Its best-known section is just below Bull Shoals Dam, where cold water from deep in the lake is discharged at the right temperature for rainbow, brown and cutthroat trout. Arkansas stocks the stream generously, and the resulting fishing draws thousands of anglers every year. Some brown trout reach world record size of 33 lb. or more. Above Bull Shoals Dam the river can only be floated from October-May. But below the dam it is good for year-round paddling, and when all the turbines are running the flow can be very swift.

Crooked Creek and the Buffalo River, both tributaries of the White River are well worth exploring. Crooked Creek has deep pools, fast chutes and clear water. The Buffalo, with nearly 95,000 acres of public land along its

150 miles, has superb scenery and great fishing. Numerous gravel bars, often beside swimming holes, provide perfect campsites along the 24-mile stretch downstream from Ponca.

For whitewater, the Mulberry River is exciting in early spring, when its Class II-III rapids are at their height. Then it becomes an easy float until mid-June. From then on, as the floater's kit puts it, the best floating is "on an air mattress at one of the local swimming holes." Then the paddler should head for the Spring River in north-central Arkansas, floatable year-round because of its massive inflow of cool water from Mammoth Spring. It offers great trout fishing below Dam No. 3 and its South Fork is known for bass, catfish and walleye.

Call the Corps of Engineers at 501-324-5150 for river levels.

Arrowhead Cabin and Canoe Rentals, Inc.
John Carter and Philip Ward
209 E. Portia Terrace
Hot Springs National Park, AR 71913
(501) 767-5326
Caddo River, Little Missouri River, Cossatot River
Max. rapids: I-II

Arrowhead Cabin & Canoe Rentals, set in the Ouachita National Forest, offers canoe trips with long Class I-II rapids and only short and infrequent pools. Unguided 1-2 day trips run on the crystal-clear Caddo River, which has a rocky bottom and excellent fishing for smallmouth bass, catfish, Kentucky bass, and sunfish. Sharp-eyed paddlers can glimpse a wide variety of wildlife along the Caddo, including bears, turkeys, beavers, whitetail deer, and many kinds of waterfowl.

The company also offers canoe rentals for trips on the Little Missouri and Cossatot Rivers and is applying for guide permits for the Caddo, Little Missouri, and Cossatot.

Arrowhead Cabin and Canoe Rental also features a campground, cabins, and what the *Arkansas Times* named the best swimming hole in Arkansas. Arrowhead's season runs from February to October.

Buffalo Camping & Canoeing
B.F. & Cynthia Fruehauf
Box 504 & 45
Gilbert, AR 72636
(501) 439-2888, (501) 439-2386
Buffalo National River
Max. rapids: I-II
PPA, AO

Depending on the time of year, people of all ages can float the clean Buffalo River aboard the canoes and rafts offered by this company for rental and guided trips. While spring canoeing is challenging, summer paddling may be enjoyed by everyone. Deer, elk, mink, and bobcats may be seen amid the tall limestone bluffs, rolling hills, and waterfalls.

Swimming is good, and the fishing includes largemouth and smallmouth bass, trout, crappie, and catfish. The company's season runs from March to November.

Buffalo Outdoor Center
Mike Mills
P.O. Box 1
Ponca, AR 72670
(800) 221-5514
Buffalo National River
Max. rapids: I-II
PPA

Buffalo Outdoor Center rents canoes and rafts and runs guided trips with

these craft on the scenic Buffalo River
with its 500-foot limestone bluffs. The
river winds through some of the most
spectacular sections of the Arkansas
Ozarks.

Trips of one to seven days are available between March and November.
Paddlers of all ages may fish for smallmouth bass and watch for elk, deer, wild
turkeys, and turtles.

Buffalo Point Canoe Rental
Joe Connior
HCR66, Box 383
Yellville, AR 72687
(501) 449-4521
Buffalo National River
Max. rapids: I-II

This outfitter rents kayaks, rafts, and
tubes as well as canoes for very easy,
family-oriented outings of up to a week.
The beautiful Buffalo National River,
with its Ozark bluffs and mountains,
provides paddlers with good fishing for
smallmouth bass and bream as well as
glimpses of deer, beaver, otter, and
varied birdlife.

Camping and swimming are available.
The company, whose season lasts from
April 1 to October 1, has a record of 25
years of continuous service.

Byrd's Canoe Rental & Wayfarer
Barbara Byrd (501) 667-4066 (Byrd's)
Pam & Tammy Byrd (501) 667-4998
(Wayfarer)
HC 61, Box 131
Ozark, AR 72949
Mulberry River
Max. rapids: I-II

These two associated outfitters operate separate facilities a few miles apart
on the scenic Mulberry River, with its
abundant wildlife and fishing. At normal
water levels, the river can be paddled by
anyone. Only experienced canoeists
should run it after heavy rain, however.

Both Byrd's and the Wayfarer rent
canoes, rafts, and tubes. Byrd's also provides guided raft trips. Trips run 1-3 days
during a February-to-June season.

Paddling trips can be combined with
hiking, rock climbing, and mountain
biking.

Gunga-La Lodge River Outfitters
Kenten Hunnell
Rt. 1, Box 147
Lakeview, AR 72642
(501) 431-5606, (800) 844-5606
Crooked Creek
Max. rapids: III-IV
White/Norfork River Outfitters
Association

Gunga-La Lodge, set in the Ozarks,
offers 1-7 day canoe and rafting trips on
Crooked Creek and the White River.
These trips are suitable for both beginners and advanced paddlers, and feature
fine fishing and scenery, with views of
mountain bluffs, woodlands, and historic
river towns where supplies can be replen-
ished on extended trips.

Wildlife to be seen include minks,
muskrats, beavers, deer, coyotes, herons,
and eagles. Fishing is for rainbow, cutthroat, and brown trout, and smallmouth and black bass.

The Lodge also offers well-equipped
log cabins, guided float trips, and rentals
of canoes, rafts, johnboats, and camping
gear.

Moore Outdoors
Kerry and Debbie Moore
Route 2, Box 303M
Dover, AR 72837
(501) 331-3606
Big Piney Creek
Max. rapids: III-IV

Moore Outdoors offers guided raft
trips and canoe and raft rentals for trips
of 1-3 days on Big Piney Creek and the
Illinois Bayou. Big Piney Creek has challenging Class II-III rapids, requiring previous whitewater canoeing experience.
The creek is clear and clean, offering
excellent fishing for catfish and smallmouth and largemouth bass. The creek
also boasts beautiful wilderness scenery
of high bluffs, waterfalls on side streams,
and banks lined with pines, hardwoods,

ferns, and wildflowers. Paddlers also can spot deer, beavers, minks, squirrels, ducks, and, in winter and early spring, bald eagles.

Moore Outdoors' season runs from January to June.

Ouachita Canoe Rentals
Tim and Sandy Williamson
SR 2, Box 200
Mount Ida, AR 71957
(501) 326-4710, (501) 867-2382
Ouachita River, Caddo River
Max. rapids: I-II

Ouachita Canoe Rentals, open year-round, offers 1-4 day trips on the Ouachita River in the Ouachita National Forest. Trips on the Caddo River are also available by special request. With Class I rapids, all trips are fine for families and paddlers of all ages.

The Ouachita trips feature picturesque slate bluffs, gravel bars, and bluff shelters and excellent fishing for small-mouth and largemouth bass, catfish, bream, and crappie. Wildlife includes deer, beavers, turkeys, minks, otters, blue herons, bald eagles, and bears.

Ouachita Canoe Rentals also offers custom trips, a campground with showers, and cabin rentals. Its proprietors, Tim and Sandy Williamson, also operate "Rocky Shoals Float Camp," located two miles east of Ouachita Canoe Rentals.

Rocky Shoals offers camping, cabins, canoe lessons and rentals on the Ouachita, and combined hiking/canoeing trips, where guests hike the Ouachita Trail one day and float the Ouachita River the next.

Southfork Canoe Resort
Jerry Lawson
Rte. 3, Box 124A
Mammoth Spring, AR 72554
(501) 895-2803
Spring River, Myatt Creek
Max. rapids: I-II

Southfork offers guided canoe trips and rents both canoes and tubes for relaxing 1-3 day trips in mountainous country. Guests paddling on these clear waters can also view deer, wild turkeys, and bears, and fish for bass, trout and catfish.

The outfitter's remote and scenic campground and cabins are open from April through October.

Turner Bend
Brad Wimberly
HC 63, Box 216
Hwy 23 North
Ozark, AR 72949
(501) 667-3641
Mulberry River
Max. rapids: I-II

Turner Bend offers unguided white-water canoe trips on the Mulberry River, which has Class I-II rapids and is one of the most challenging rivers in the Ozarks at high-water levels. Trips range in length from 2 to 26 miles, are offered March 1 to June 15, and require some paddling experience. These stretches of the Mulberry feature high bluffs, tree-lined banks, occasional views of deer, turkeys, and beavers, and fishing for catfish and small and large-mouth bass.

Turner Bend also offers a year-round campground (without hook-ups), store, canoe shuttle service, hot showers, and shuttle service for hikers along the Ozark Highlands Trail.

Wayfarer of the Ozarks
Tammy Byrd & Pam Boulder
HC61, Box 131
Ozark, AR 72949
(501) 667-4066, (501) 667-4998
Mulberry River
Max. rapids: III-IV

This outfitter rents canoes and rafts for 1-3 day trips on the Mulberry River amid beautiful bluffs and landscape. At low water these outings are easy and well-suited for families. At high water they are challenging for experienced paddlers. There is camping and swimming along the river, the Ozark Highlands Trail is nearby, and fish include channel catfish, bass, and perch. The season runs March-May.

Wild Bill's Canoe Rental
Bill & Osa Scruggs
HCR 66, Box 380
Yellville, AR 72687
(501) 449-6235, (800) 554-8657
Buffalo River
Max. rapids: I-II
PPA

Wild Bill's rents canoes, kayaks, rafts, and tubes and runs guided canoe, kayak and raft trips on the Buffalo River. The company also has a motel, rustic cabins, and a deli-store.

During easy trips that last from 1 hour to 10 days, paddlers can fish, camp, swim and enjoy great smallmouth bass fishing. Deer, turkeys, bears, wild hogs, and bald eagles may be spotted on this river, which runs through the heart of the Ozarks. Wild Bill's is open year-round.

Woodsman's Sports Shop & Fishing Service
Morrell Woods
HCR 61, Box 461
Norfork, AR 72658
(501) 499-7454
White River, Buffalo River
Max. rapids: I-II

Woodsman's offers 1-5 day guided and unguided canoe trips on the White and Buffalo Rivers in the Ozarks, with Class I and II rapids and cold, clear waters. These rivers offer easy paddling and excellent fishing for rainbow trout, brown trout, cutthroat, trout and small- and largemouth bass.

The unspoiled setting in northern Arkansas offers high bluffs, wooded hillsides, and abundant wildlife, including deer, squirrels, rabbits, and wild turkeys.

Woodsman's also has a campground with cabins and R.V. hookup, and is open year-round.

Wright Way Canoe Rental
Stephen R. Wright
P.O. Box 180
Highway 8 West and 27 North
Glenwood, AR 71943
(501) 356-2055
Caddo River
Max. rapids: I-II

Wright Way Canoe Rentals runs 1-7 day canoe trips on the Caddo, specializing in outfitting small groups for customized overnight trips for beginners and experts alike. Most stretches of the Caddo offer Class I whitewater. After a good rain, however, experienced canoeists can find Class II and III whitewater above Caddo Gap.

Guided and unguided trips run year-round and offer excellent fishing for bream, catfish, and smallmouth, brown, white, Kentucky, largemouth, and rock bass. The Caddo also offers find swimming holes and abundant sand and gravel bars for camping.

California

With its streams frolicking, churning and charging out of the Sierra Nevada range, California is practically made for river runners. Superb white-water, crystal-clear rivers, lush forests, dramatic canyons, unspoiled wilderness — what more could a paddler ask? On top of everything else, California boasts the Cherry Creek/Upper Tuolumne run, which has been called "the Mount Everest of rafting" because of its phenomenal 105 feet per mile average gradient. This ferocious nine-mile dash in the Stanislaus National Forest has nearly continuous Class IV+ and V rapids. Strictly for the expert, it is claimed to be the most challenging stretch of runnable whitewater in America and the standard by which Class V runs are measured.

Starting in the north, Hell's Corner Canyon on the Upper Klamath River offers twenty miles of tough Class IV+ rafting astride the Oregon state line. The Upper Klamath was designated a National Wild and Scenic River as recently as 1994. Rafters able to take time out from running forty major rapids can spot abandoned settlers' cabins on the banks and visit lava caves once used by Indians. Further downstream, the Lower Klamath winds through forested mountains on a 28-mile stretch below Happy Camp, offering Class III floating with possible glimpses of bear, beaver, otter, osprey, bald eagle and great blue heron. Both of these relatively remote California runs can be enjoyed from mid-May until late summer.

Several stretches of the Trinity River, once a focus of intense — and highly destructive — gold mining, can be canoed and 2 rafted with enjoyment. Halfway down its course the Trinity churns through Burnt Ranch Gorge, a seven-mile long, 2,000-foot deep chasm. A Class V adventure, this run takes the rafter at breakneck speed through giant boulder gardens and narrow passageways where both strength and skill are needed to dodge obstacles. Another tough challenge in this area is the California Salmon River, which like the Trinity has been officially designated Wild and Scenic despite the depredations of gold miners in the mid-19th century. The Cal-Salmon, with its North and South Forks, remains a very beautiful river that runs through true wilderness country in the Salmon Mountains. It has mostly Class III runs with some impassable gorges. At least one outfitter offers two-day and three-day trips on a Class V section of the Cal-Salmon through a twisting gorge in the Klamath National Forest.

East of San Francisco, the Stanislaus River cuts through Mother Lode country in central California. Due to releases from the recently-built New Melones Reservoir, the Main Stanislaus now has excellent water flow all summer long. Once California's most popular river, the Stanislaus is back in business with Class III (formerly Class IV-V) rapids bearing names like Cadillac Charlie, Death Rock and Widow Maker. The North Fork of the Stanislaus has another great run within easy distance of city life. It goes five miles to Calaveras Big Trees State Park and combines Class IV rafting in forests of pines and sequoias with opportunities to visit historic gold rush towns.

Also in mid-California is the Tuolumne (pronounced tu-WAL-o-me) River, yet another gold mining stream which runs from Yosemite National Park to join the San Joaquin River. Fed by releases from Hetch Hetchy Reservoir, the Tuolumne is runnable from March to October. It provides superb Class IV whitewater in an unspoiled canyon not far from the Yosemite park's western entrance. Designated a National Wild and Scenic River, the Tuolumne takes the rafter past places redolent with gold rush and Indian history.

For the real whitewater enthusiast the ultimate challenge is the Cherry Creek/Upper Tuolumne run, mentioned above. This lies immediately upstream from the trip just described (and is generally known as the Cherry Creek even though it covers only one mile of that stream and eight miles of the Upper Tuolumne). Its roaring chutes, holes, ledges and falls go by such names as Miracle Mile, Lewis' Leap and Jawbone. Outfitters require clients to pass stiff physical and Class V skill tests before participating in this daunting voyage.

California's most popular waterway, the South Fork of the American River, flows through Coloma, site of James Marshall's 1848 find which touched off the Gold Rush. This trip east of Sacramento takes paddlers on clear, sparkling waters through Class III-IV rapids. The stream moves from rolling hill country to canyons and culminates in the American River Gorge with its whitewater and wildflowers. The most notorious rapid in this stretch is called Satan's John — or Satan's Cesspool.

The North Fork American contains the Giant Gap run, which ranks among the most pristine of wilderness trips. It is also one of the most closely regulated stretches of river in the country. The Giant Gap is a Class V springtime run featuring a 2,000-foot-deep sheer canyon with waterfalls cascading into the river. On one tour, rafters must descend a switchback trail to the put-in while packhorses carry their gear. Paddlers on the Middle Fork

American, another exciting run, raft through a 30-yard tunnel blasted out by gold miners. The Middle and South Forks American are California's only rivers that can be run consistently all year-round.

Another certified Wild and Scenic whitewater river is the Kern in the Sequoia National Forest. The Lower Kern is only a short drive from the Los Angeles metropolitan area. One of the river's toughest sections is an Upper Kern run covering 17 miles down to the town of Kernville. It is a rigorous Class V test of every paddler's mettle, but only runnable from April through June. To reach the put-in at Forks of the Kern for another nearby trip, paddlers must hike three miles down a rocky trail into a canyon, carrying backpacks. Pack animals carry river equipment and food for the Class V run through a spectacular 1,000-foot-deep chasm. For somewhat less energetic floaters, the Kern offers Class IV rapids elsewhere on its turbulent course, notably on a 20-mile Lower Kern trip starting at Isabella Lake.

Just north of the Bay Area runs the comparatively small Russian River, an easy float for beginners. Handsome redwoods line the stream as it slices through coastal hills to the sea. Although crowded at weekends, it offers canoeists a view of varied bird and marine life.

Sea kayakers paddle in San Francisco Bay, Tomales Bay, Humboldt Lagoons and sheltered river estuaries. Sometimes they can view seals close up as well as marine birdlife.

Adventure Connection, Inc.
Nate Rangel
P.O. Box 475
Coloma, CA 95613
(800) 556-6060, (916) 626-7385
North, Middle and South Forks of the American, Upper Klamath, Stanislaus, Kaweah, Middle Fork of the Salmon, and Sacramento Rivers
Max. rapids: IV
America Outdoors, California Outdoors, Friends of the River, American Rivers

Adventure Connection offers luxury river vacations of 1, 2, and 6 days on the finest rivers in California and Idaho. Trips range from easy canoe excursions to advanced whitewater runs. Special half-price family trips, group discounts, and free trips for group leaders are available. Adventure Connection offers experienced guides, deluxe camping, and gourmet food.

Adventure Sports Unlimited
Dennis Judson, Virginia Wedderburn
303 Potrero Street #15
Santa Cruz, CA 95060
(408) 458-3648
Mokelumne River, American River, Kings River, Big Sur, Carmel Bay, Point Lobos, Point Reyes, Elkhorn Slough
Max. rapids: III-IV

Adventure Sports Unlimited offers guided and unguided canoe and sea-kayak trips of 1-3 days. Sea-kayak trips begin with instruction in a heated pool, followed by a trip to Big Sur, Tomales Bay, Carmel Bay, Pt. Lobos, Elkhorn Slough, or Salt Pt. These trips offer pristine beaches and clear water, ideal for viewing whales, sea lions, sea otters, seals, birds, and other coastal and marine wildlife. Sea-kayak trips vary in difficulty to suit anyone from beginners to kayak surfers.

River trips run on the Mokelomne, American, and Kings Rivers. Adventure Sports, open year-round, emphasizes instruction, togetherness, and gourmet food.

Adventure Whitewater
Gene Allred, M.D.
P.O. Box 321
Yreka, CA 96097
(800) 888-5632
Salmon River, Scott River, Klamath River, Trinity River
Max. rapids: V+
America Outdoors

With its personable and highly-qualified guides, Adventure Whitewater offers guided kayak and raft trips for gentle Class II to expert Class V runs. Trips feature great whitewater and spectacular mountain scenery of snow-capped peaks, deep granite gorges, and heavily forested slopes. Set in the Marble Mountains and Trinity Alps, the trips offer fishing for trout, steelhead, and salmon and chances to view bears, deer, coyotes, otters, eagles, ospreys, and herons.

Ahwahnee Whitewater
Jim Gado and Cris Barsanti
P.O. Box 1161
Columbia, CA 95310
(209) 533-1401, (800) 359-9790,
FAX (209) 533-1409
Tuolumne River, Merced River, Stanislaus River, East Fork of the Carson River, Cherry Creek
Max. rapids: V+
America Outdoors

Ahwahnee Whitewater runs half to three-day guided oar- and paddle-raft trips. The minimum age for paddlers is 6 on the East Fork of the Carson River, 7 on the Stanislaus, 12 on the Merced and Tuolumne Rivers, and 18 on Cherry Creek.

Rapids are Class II-III on the East Fork of the Carson River, III on the Stanislaus, III-IV+ on the Tuolumne and Merced, and V-V+ on Cherry

Creek. All rivers have sparkling, clear water, some with gentle rapids that are safe to swim. Along the way, guests can enjoy excellent trout fishing, wildflowers, remote wilderness canyons, gold rush artifacts, hiking, swimming, and wilderness camping. Guests also have a chance to spot otters, deer, foxes, coyotes, eagles, hawks, ospreys and waterfowl. The season runs from April to September.

American River Recreation
Don Hill
P.O. Box 465
Lotus, CA 95651
(916) 622-6802 (803) 333-RAFT
American River, Merced River, Carson River, Klamath River, Cal-Salmon River
Max. rapids: III-IV
America Outdoors

American River Recreation offers guided raft trips from March to October for paddlers of all skill levels. Highlights include skilled guides, an excellent safety record, a wide range of rivers and trips, and reasonable prices. Trips run from March to October and pass through high desert, canyons, and gorges. Guests can also enjoy lessons, fishing for brown and rainbow trout, and viewing deer, ospreys, herons, eagles, and otters.

American River Touring Association
Steve Welch
24000 Casa Loma Rd.
Groveland, CA 95321
(800) 323-2782, (209) 962-7873
American, Merced, Tuolumne, Cal-Salmon, Klamath, Rogue, Illinois, Umpqua, Green, Yampa, Salmon, and Selway Rivers
Max. rapids: V+
America Outdoors, Oregon Guides and Packers, Idaho Outfitters and Guides, Utah Guides and Outfitters

ARTA offers a total of 16 raft trips in five Western states. The trips, in California, Oregon, Utah, Idaho, and Arizona, are by oar rafts, paddle rafts, oar/paddle rafts, and inflatable canoes.

Most trips are of Class III difficulty and appropriate for novices and families, as well as those with more experience. Other trips of up to V+ difficulty challenge even the most advanced paddler. Depending on the location, the trips feature such added attractions as wildflowers, side hikes, swimming holes, Indian ruins, warm water, abundant wildlife, good hiking and fishing, and hot springs.

ARTA, a non-profit company, also offers whitewater schools, professional guide training, and family discounts.

American Whitewater Expeditions, Inc.
Jon Osgood
Box 4280
Sunland, CA 91041-4280
(818) 352-3205, (800) 825-3205
South, Middle & North Forks American River, Stanislaus, West Walker Rivers
Max. rapids: III-V
America Outdoors

American Whitewater Expeditions specializes in paddle boat raft trips,

rewarding paddlers with exceptionally well-appointed campsites that feature professional cooks, hot showers, and rental tents, tipis and sleeping bags. Trips are for one or two days and run through California's Gold Rush region, offering views of steep canyons and spring wildflowers. Deluxe buses run from Los Angeles and San Francisco weekly. The season is from April-October.

Bigfoot Outdoor Company
Marc & Londa Rowley
P.O. Box 729
Willow Creek, CA 95573
(916) 629-2263
Trinity, Trinity South Fork, Klamath, Smith Rivers
Max. rapids: III-IV
California Outdoors

Bigfoot Outdoor Co. rents rafts and kayaks and offers these craft for reasonably-priced trips for a wide range of customers. The Trinity River offers clear, warm water, good scenery, and wildlife.

A Beyond Limits Adventures' trip on the North Fork of the Yuba River. Courtesy of Rapid Shooters/Dennis Stiff.

Trinity's South Fork is a wilderness trip with many rapids. The Smith River features numerous rapids and many exotic plants. Trips last 1-4 days and provide good fishing, camping, and swimming. The season runs from April to October.

Beyond Limits Adventures, Inc.
Mike Doyle/Dave Hammond
P.O. Box 215
Riverbank, CA 95367
(209) 869-6060, (800) 234-RAFT (CA)
Stanislaus River, American River, Yuba River, Trinity River, Klamath River, Scott River, New River
Max. rapids: V
America Outdoors

Beyond Limits Adventures offers 1-4 day trips ranging from "mild to wild," with guided raft trips and rentals of canoes, kayaks, and rafts. The company's specialty, however, is Class IV-V rafting in self-bailing boats with skilled, friendly guides and excellent food.

Set on the pristine, challenging rivers of the Sierras, Beyond Limits trips features scenery of giant sequoias, sheer granite domes, and deep canyons. Also, lucky paddlers may sight otters, eagles, and bears, and catch trout, salmon, and steelhead.

CAL Adventures
Rob Anderson
University of California - Berkeley
2301 Bancroft Avenue
Berkeley, CA 94720
(510) 642-4000
American River, Klamath River, Trinity River
Max. rapids: III-IV
America Outdoors

Cal Adventures offers an excellent array of raft, kayak, and sea-kayak trips and classes at very reasonable rates. A unique outfitter, Cal Adventures is part of the Department of Recreational Sports at the University of California, Berkeley.

Despite its link to the university, Cal Adventures' programs are available to the public. Among the offerings are a three-part sea-kayak class; 12 sea kayak trips; 1- and 2-day raft trips on the American, Klamath, and Stanislaus Rivers; a three-part whitewater kayaking course; kayak roll clinics and pool sessions; and five 1-day kayak river trips.

Cal Adventures also offers year-round rentals of kayaks, rafts, sea kayaks, and camping gear.

Caldera Kayaks
Stuart Wilkinson
Box 726
Mammoth Lakes, CA 93546
(619) 935-4942 Tel/FAX
Mono Lake, Crowley Lake, other lakes in E. Sierra
Max. rapids: none

Caldera Kayaks provides guided and unguided kayak trips on the ancient inland sea of Mono Lake, with its unique alkaline ecosystem. Brine shrimp and alkali flies provide a rich food source for nesting and migratory birds. Fresh underwater springs combine with the salt water to form strange, delicate calcium carbonate tufa towers. Crowley Lake offers freshwater paddling, trout and perch fishing and spectacular mountain views. Camping and paddling lessons are available during the company's April-November season.

California Canoe & Kayak
Keith Miller
11257 S. Bridge St.
Rancho Cordova, CA 95670
(916) 631-1400, (800) 366-9804
San Francisco Bay, Tomales Bay, Drakes Estero (sea kayaking), American River, Stanislaus River, Klamath River, Trinity River, Mokelumne River, Eel River
Max. rapids: III
America Outdoors

California Canoe and Kayak offers 1-5 day trips year-round, suited for paddlers 15 or older. Between the guided and unguided canoe and sea-kayak trips, the company offers access to a wide range of waters and terrain, including

Chamberlain Falls on the North Fork of the American River. Courtesy of Sierra Shutterbug Photography.

limestone canyons, lush rain forests, and scenic coastal waters.

Among the wildlife to be seen are eagles, herons, otters, beavers, and seals. Fishing is for trout and salmon. California Canoe & Kayak also has outposts in Oakland at Jack London Square (510) 893-7833 and Half Moon Bay (415) 728-1803.

Catch A Canoe & Bicycles, Too
Jeff Stanford
P.O. Box 487
44850 Comptche-Ukiah Rd.
Mendocino, CA 95460
(707) 937-0273, (707) 937-5026
Big River
Max. rapids: None
PPA

Catch A Canoe operates year-round on one of California's largest protected and undeveloped estuaries, where paddlers ride the tides and view historic

logging dams, piers, and trestles. The outfitter rents kayaks, outrigger canoes, and fiber glass canoes. Trips are suitable for paddlers of all skill levels.

Customers may take paddling lessons, camp, swim, and fish for salmon and steelhead. Tours run through a redwood forested canyon containing seals, bears, otters, blue herons, and other wildlife.

Chuck Richards Whitewater, Inc.
Box W.W. Whitewater
Lake Isabella, CA 93240
(619) 379-4685
Kern River
Max. rapids: V
American Rivers, NFRA, America Outdoors

Chuck Richards Whitewater, Inc. offers guided and unguided canoe, kayak, and raft trips on three sections of the Kern River. With Class III, IV, and V rapids, trips feature "slambang action" on warm crystal-clear waters. Paddlers pass through pine and sequoia forests and enjoy views of granite spires and cliffs, deer, beavers, and eagles. Fishing is for brown and rainbow trout.

Trips range in length from 1-3 days and the season runs from May 1 to October 31.

Earthtrek Expeditions
Jerry Ashburn
Box 1010
Lotus, CA 95651
(800) 229-8735, (916) 642-1900
American River
Max. rapids: IV
American Outdoors

Earthtrek Expeditions has a wide assortment of 1-4 day trips for rafters in the gold-rush country of California. Paddlers can choose among trips of varying difficulty and accommodations ranging from historic inns to primitive wilderness campgrounds. Trips run from April to October, offering excellent wilderness scenery and chances to fish and view abundant wildlife.

Earthtrek also offers group rates and charter bus service.

ECHO: The Wilderness Company
Dick Linford and Joe Daly
6529 Telegraph Avenue
Oakland, CA 94609
(510) 652-1600, (800) 652-ECHO (3246)
Tuolumne River, South Fork American River
Max. rapids: III-IV
California Outdoors

ECHO runs guided trips on the Tuolumne and South Fork American in California, the Main and Middle Fork Salmon in Idaho, and the Rogue in Oregon. The company has 1- to 11-day trips available for paddlers at all skill levels and offers a variety of boats, including inflatable kayaks, oar rafts, oar/paddle rafts, and oar/paddle rafts.

ECHO also offers a large number of special trips, White (and Red) Wine and Whitewater; Bluegrass on Whitewater; River Trips for Kids; Whitewater School; Aikido and Nature; the Rogue

String Quartet, and Yoga Workshop. The season runs from April to September.

James Henry River Journeys
James Katz
P.O. Box 807
Bolinas, CA 94924
(415) 868-1836, (800) 786-1830
Tatshenshini-Alsek River, Noatak River, Stanislaus River, Carson River, Klamath River, Rogue River
Max. rapids: III-IV
Idaho Outfitters and Guides

James Henry River Journeys runs guided canoe, kayak, and raft trips in California, Arizona, Idaho, Oregon, and Alaska. In California, the outfitter offers trips with Class II-III rapids, of 1-3 days, on the Stanislaus, East Fork of the Carson, and the Lower Klamath. In Arizona, the company runs Grand Canyon trips, with Class IV + rapids, of 6, 8, 9, 13, and 14 days. Trips in Idaho, of 4, 5 or 6 days, run on the Class III-IV Main Salmon. In Oregon, trips of 3, 4, and 5 days run on the Class III Rogue. Many special-interest trips are also available. These include Salmon River Bluegrass, Country, Folk, and Cajun Music Trips; Whitewater Workshops; Organizational Development and Teambuilding; Wine Tasting and Gourmet Cuisine; Lodge Trips on the Rogue and Salmon; Rogue and Salmon Natural History Trips; Alaska Nature Photography; and Alaska Wilderness Literature.

All trips run through especially scenic wilderness areas and are carefully planned to move at a leisurely pace, allowing ample time for side hikes, fishing, photography, and general relaxation. As a result, participation is open to anyone active and in good health. The company's season runs from May to September.

Kids enjoying the ride on the South Fork of the American River. Courtesy of Sierra Shutterbug Photography.

Kayak Tahoe
Steve & Sue Lannoy
Box 11129
Tahoe Paradise, CA 96155
(916) 544-2011
Lake Tahoe & surrounding Alpine lakes,
Truckee and E. Fork Carson Rivers
Max. rapids: I-II

This company runs guided and unguided kayak trips and rents canoes for outings on Lake Tahoe's 99.7% pure waters. Paddlers can peer 70 feet down and maybe spot trout as large as 30 lbs. Above the lake's blue surface, osprey, bald eagles, and Canada geese circle against the mountain background. Kayak Tahoe offers camping, swimming, and paddling lessons during its season, running from Memorial Day to October 1.

Kings River Expeditions
Justin Butchert
211 N. Van Ness
Fresno, CA 93701
(209) 233-4881
Upper Kings River
Max. rapids: III-IV
America Outdoors, NFRA

Kings River Expeditions runs 1-2 day guided raft trips on the Upper Kings River in the Sequoia and Sierra National Forests. The season begins in April and is followed by a period of high water stretching from the middle of May through the middle of June. The outfitter recommends that only physically fit adults raft during this early part of the season. From mid-June until August, the water warms considerably, making trips suitable for children as young as nine.

Guests enjoy the Kings River's clear, clean water and wilderness setting in a moderately steep tree-filled canyon. Fishing is for trout and bass, and the wildlife seen include hawks, bears, and foxes.

Koolriver Adventure Tours
Don Koolmees
16209 Virginia
Paramount, CA 90723
(310) 630-6929, (800) 931-8999
South, Middle and North Forks of
American River
Max. rapids: III-IV
America Outdoors

Koolriver supplies guided raft trips through beautiful canyons in the mother-lode gold rush country. With a combined total of 60 years' rafting experience, the staff attends to individual needs and ensures that floats are fun.

Trips on the South Fork are for beginners, those on the Middle Fork are for intermediate and outings on the North Fork are for advanced paddlers. Camping tours last up to 3 days, trout fishing is available and the wildlife includes deer and ducks. The company's season runs April through September.

Laughing Heart Adventures
Dezh Pagen
Trinity Outdoor Center
P.O. Box 669
Willow Creek, CA 95573
(916) 629-3516, (800) 541-1256 (outside CA only)
Trinity, Klamath, Eel, Smith, Colorado,
Mattole Rivers
Max. rapids: II-III
PPA

Laughing Heart Adventures conducts canoe, raft and kayak outings on N. California Wild and Scenic Rivers. All trips are conducted in a spirit of adventure, fun and discovery. Expert, personable guides give instruction, interpret geology and the natural and human history of the river environment. LHA supports ecotourism and seeks cross-cultural encounters. It also specializes in custom trips on topics such as yoga, birding, African drumming and sweat lodge ceremonies. Trips run May-September and are also conducted in Baja and Belize during the winter.

Mariah Wilderness Expeditions
Donna Hunter
P.O. Box 248
Point Richmond, CA 94807
(510) 233-2303, (800) 462-7424
South, Middle & North Forks of the
American, Merced, Kings, Tuolumne Rivers
Max. rapids: V+
America Outdoors

Mariah Wilderness Expeditions guided raft trips in the Gold Rush country from April to September, catering to families, groups, and individuals. It offers trips of 1-5 days, from beginning whitewater (Class III) to challenging Class V whitewater runs.

Monterey Bay Kayaks
Cass Schrock
693 Del Monte Ave.
Monterey, CA 93940
(408) 373-5357
Monterey Bay, Elkhorn Slough, Salinas River
Max. rapids: none
TASK

This company offers sea kayaking amid sea otters, sea lions and harbor seals in the Monterey Bay National Marine Sanctuary. Kayaks may be rented or paddlers can join guided natural history tours, with kayaking lessons available for beginners. Monterey Bay Kayaks is a full-service outfitter open year-round.

O.A.R.S.
George Wendt
P.O. Box 67
Angels Camp, CA 95222
(209) 736-4677, (800) 446-7238 (CA),
(800) 346-6277 (U.S.)
American, Cal-Salmon Stanislaus,
Tuolumne, Merced, Rogue, Snake, San Juan,
Colorado, Middle Fork Salmon Rivers
Max. rapids: III-IV
America Outdoors

O.A.R.S. runs guided dory, raft, and kayak trips in five Western states. It offers tours in California on the American, Cal-Salmon, Merced, Stanislaus, and Tuolumne Rivers; in Oregon on the

Rogue; in Arizona on the Colorado; in Wyoming on the Snake, and in Utah on the San Juan River. These outings last 1-13 days and, depending on the class of river, are fine for children, novices, families, and intermediate and expert rafters. O.A.R.S. trips provide fishing, swimming, camping, side hikes, wildlife viewing, and other activities. Tours run from April to October.

Otter Bar Lodge
Pete & Kristy Sturges
Box 210
Forks of Salmon, CA 96031
(916) 462-4772
California Salmon, Klamath Rivers
Max. rapids: V

Otter Bar Lodge is a kayak school that offers comprehensive instruction, comfortable accommodations, and spectacular mountain scenery. Twenty five week-long kayaking courses are available: beginners', basic intermediate, intermediate, and advanced. Guests are

housed in a lodge featuring a sauna and excellent meals.

The season runs April-September, with fly fishing instruction also available on the rivers' crystal-clear water. Bears, foxes, mountain lions, otters, ospreys, and other wildlife may be seen along the canyons.

Outdoor Adventures
Bob Volpert
P.O. Box 1149
Point Reyes, CA 94956
(415) 663-8300
Tuolumne River, Kern River, Salmon River, Rogue River
Max. rapids: V+
America Outdoors, Idaho Outfitters and Guides, Oregon Outfitters Association

Outdoor Adventures specializes in guided raft trips and raft rentals on federally designated wild and scenic rivers in Idaho, Oregon, and California. In Idaho, 6-day trips are available on the Middle Fork of the Salmon and the

Mushroom Falls on the upper Tuolumne River. This Class V trip is widely regarded as one of the most challenging in the country. Courtesy of Sierra Mac River Trips, Sonora, California.

Salmon River. Included are all shuttles from Boise, tents and sleeping bags, delicious on-river meals, quality guides, and Avon rafts.

In Oregon, 3- and 4-day trips are available on the Rogue River, featuring lively rapids, wonderful hiking trails, and abundant wildlife. On these trips, the last night is spent at Half Moon Bar, a rustic lodge by the river where paddlers can enjoy hot showers, comfortable beds, and home-cooked meals.

In California, Outdoor Adventures offers 2-day trips on the Tuolomne River, 3-day trips on the Forks of the Kern, and 1-day trips on the Upper Kern. These California trips offer some of the wildest whitewater in the country during the spring run-off in April and May. During this time, wetsuits and previous rafting experience are required. All other Outdoor Adventures trips are fine for families and beginners. The company's season is from April to September.

Ouzel Outfitters
Kent Wickham
Box 827
Bend, OR 97709
(503) 385-5947, (800) 788-RAFT
Rogue River, Owyhee River, North Umpqua River, Deschutes River, McKenzie River, Salmon River
Max. rapids: III-IV
Oregon Guides and Packers

Ouzel Oufitters specializes in trips of 1-5 days on the "loveliest and liveliest" rivers in the Northwest. These rivers include the Rogue, North Umpqua, McKenzie, Lower and Middle Owyhee, and Deschutes Rivers in Oregon and the Lower Salmon in Idaho. All trips but the Middle Owyhee runs have class III-IV rapids and are fine for families and guests of all levels of experience to paddle in paddle rafts, inflatable kayaks, or guide-accompanied, "row-your-own" oar-rafts. The Middle Owyhee run, with class IV-V rapids, is a challenging, expedition-like trip for adventurous, experienced rafters only. Ouzel Outfitters' trips run between May and September. Depending on the river traveled, guests can view bears, deer, eagles, and otters, and fish for bass, trout, steelhead, and salmon.

River Travel Center
Raven Earlygrow and Annie Nelson
15 Riverside Drive
P.O. Box 6
Point Arena, CA 95468
(800) 882-7238,
All commercially run rivers
Max. rapids: V+
America Outdoors

River Travel Center represents more than 100 outfitters offering canoe, raft, kayak, sea kayak, and dory trips in the West and overseas. With knowledge of thousands of trips, River Travel Center can assist you in selecting the destination, trip, and outfitter that is right for you. The company specializes in arranging trips by telephone, providing quick, reliable, and convenient service.

Trips range in length from 2-18 days and are available year-round.

Sierra Mac River Trips
Marty McDonnell
P.O. Box 366
Sonora, CA 95370
(209) 532-1327, (800) 457-2580
Tuolumne River, North Fork of the American River, Stanislaus River, Cherry Creek/Upper Tuolumme, Giant Gap
Max. rapids: V+
America Outdoors

Sierra Mac runs Class III-IV guided raft trips of 1-3 days. The difficulty of the trips offered varies enormously. For novices, there are oar-boat and moderate paddle-boat trips. At the other extreme are several Class V trips, including the famed Cherry Creek/Upper Tuolumne run, which has a phenomenally steep gradient of 105-feet per mile and is widely considered the most challenging in the entire United States. A training seminar and Class V paddler's test are required for this expert's thrill ride.

Sierra Mac, with more than 26 years' experience, runs trips from March to October. In addition to the paddling adventure, guests can enjoy spectacular wilderness scenery, trout fishing, and a chance to view eagles, great blue herons, deer, and coyotes.

Southwind Kayak Center
Joanne Turner, Doug Schwartz
17855 Sky Park Circle #A
Irvine, CA 92714
(714) 261-0200, (800) SOUTHWIND
California coast, Catalina Island, Channel Islands National Park, Lake Mead, and South Colorado River (AZ), Green River (UT)
Max. Rapids: None
TASK, NAPSA

Operating year-round, Southwind rents canoes and kayaks and runs kayak trips of 1-7 days with highly trained guides. Scenery is spectacular, ranging from sea caves and cliffs to desert mountains and canyons, with abundant wildlife at sea and ashore.

Skilled instruction is provided for four levels of expertise, from novice to advanced. Trips are either catered or rustic. For most outings paddlers must be 16 or older; 10-year-olds are welcome on some calm-water outings.

Sunshine River Adventures
Jim Foust
P.O. Box 1445
Oakdale, CA 95361
(209) 881-3236, (800) 829-7238
Stanislaus River, Mokelumne River, Trinity River
Max. rapids: III-IV
America Outdoors

Sunshine River Adventures has guided and unguided canoe and raft trips offering the full range of difficulty, from Class I float trips to Class IV adventure. Among the highlights of these trips is the guided cave tour in the West's largest limestone gorge along the Stanislaus Canyon.

Sunshine's tours, of 1-3 days, are offered April to October 15 at guaranteed lowest rates. Trips permit viewing of deer, otters, beavers, muskrats, ospreys, eagles, falcons, and hawks.

Tamal Saka
John Granatir/Ken Blum
Box 833
Marshall, CA 94940
(415) 663-1743
Tomales Bay and neighboring esteros
Max. rapids: I-II
PPA

Tamal Saka runs guided trips for canoeists and kayakers on Tomales Bay, rated one of the cleanest marine estuaries in the country. It also rents canoes and kayaks year-round and provides camping and paddling lessons. Fishing is for halibut, salmon, shark, crabs, and shellfish. Tours of up to 6 days' duration are custom-designed and enable clients aged 8 and up to explore Point Reyes National Seashore with its great birding.

Tributary Whitewater Tours
Daniel J. Buckley, L.A. Hall
20480 Woodbury Drive
Grass Valley, CA 95949
(916) 346-6812
Yuba, American, Carson, Klamath, Stanislaus, Kaweah, Trinity, New, Salmon, Scott, Sacramento, Eel, Smith and W. Walker Rivers
Max. rapids: V+
America Outdoors

Tributary Whitewater Tours runs 1-6 day guided raft and inflatable kayak tours on 17 Northern California rivers. Trips range from gentle family floats suitable for the young, old, and disabled, to Class V trips for experts only. Depending on the river, guests can choose paddle, oar, or paddle-oar boats. Also, on Class III rivers, paddlers can opt to use exciting one-person inflatable kayaks. These boats are maneuverable, easy to master, and ideal for running some of California's beautiful rivers during the summer, when the water is too low for larger rafts.

Whatever their size, all of Tributary's boats are self-bailing, which makes them more agile and comfortable in big water than conventional rafts. Special charter trips, group discounts and youth, senior and off-season discounts are also available. Tributary's season runs March-October.

Trowbridge Recreation, Inc.

Phil Trowbridge
20 Healdsburg Ave.
Healdsburg, CA 95448
(707) 433-7247, (800) 640-1386
Spring Lake in Santa Rosa, CA
Max. rapids: I

Trowbridge Recreation rents canoes, kayaks, and tubes to novice paddlers and others for trips of up to 5 days in the Sonoma County vineyard region. Although easy to reach from main roads, Spring Lake is rich in smallmouth bass, waterfowl, raptors, and otters. The company's season runs from April to October and it offers camping and swimming as well as fishing.

Turtle River Rafting Company

Richard Demarest and David Wikander
P.O. Box 313
1308 Old U.S. Highway 99
Mt. Shasta, CA 96067
(916) 926-3223, (800) 726-3223
Klamath River, Trinity River, Sacramento River, Scott River, Eel River, Smith River
Max. rapids: V+
America Outdoors

Turtle River Rafting Company runs guided kayak and raft trips and rents kayaks for trips of 1-10 days on the Klamath, Upper Klamath, Scott, Cal-Salmon, Trinity, Upper Sacramento, Owyhee, Smith, and Eel Rivers. Depending on the river and time of year, these trips range in difficulty from Class II to Class V. Families are encouraged to participate, in accordance with the following minimum age requirements: four for "Kid's Klamath"; six for "Gentle Klamath"; eight for Main Klamath, Trinity, and Owyhee; 12 for upper Sacramento

and Middle Eel; and 15 for Upper Klamath, Scott, and Cal-Salmon.

These trips range in length from 1-10 days and feature wild and scenic canyons, waterfalls, clean beaches, excellent food, and abundant wildlife, including bears, eagles, otters, turtles, herons, and deer. During its April-to-October season, Turtle River also offers custom trips for men, women, musicians, and aspiring whitewater guides.

Wantu Canoe Co.

Bill & Imkelina Davis
P.O. Box 839
Forest Ranch, CA 95942
(916) 891-1424
Sacramento, Trinity, Klamath, Russian, Rivers
Max. rapids: I-II
PPA, ACA

Wantu Canoe provides guided excursions on many of the scenic rivers and lakes of northern California, chiefly on the Trinity and Sacramento Rivers. Scenery ranges from mountain wilderness to gold country, vineyards and coastal estuaries. Trips are primarily on Class I-II waters, suitable for beginners to intermediate paddslers. The company offers motivational/teambuilding trips for buisinesses, river rescue training and customized itineraries.

White Magic Unlimited

Jack Morison
P.O. Box 5506
Mill Valley, CA 94942
(800) 869-9874, (415) 381-8889
Tuolumne, American (all Forks), Stanislaus, Merced, Cal Salmon, Kern, Kings, North Fork Yuba Rivers
Max. rapids: V

White Magic Unlimited runs guided raft trips on many rivers throughout the western United States. In California, White Magic operates raft tours at varying times on different rivers, according to water flow. Some are wild, bucking rides in Class V whitewater. Others are less daunting, but all have at least Class III rapids. These 1-3 day trips also boast

"Satan's Cesspool" rapid on the South Fork of the American River. Courtesy of Sierra Shutterbug Photography.

fine scenery and abundant wildlife.

An adventure travel company, it also offers rafting and trekking expeditions in 16 countries.

Whitewater Voyages
William McGinnis
P.O. Box 20400
El Sobrante, CA 94820-0400
(510) 222-5994, (800) 488-RAFT
Colorado, Kaweah, Kern, Merced,
Tuolumne, Salmon, Cache Creek, American
River, Yuba River, Klamath River, Stanislaus
River, Trinity River, Rogue River
Max. rapids: V+
America Outdoors, American River
Recreation Association

Whitewater Voyages offers an extensive array of trips, with guided oar- and paddle-boat runs in California and Oregon, and Idaho. Trips by kayak and raft range in length from 1-5 days and in difficulty from Class II to Class V. With runs on nine Wild and Scenic Rivers and on more California rivers than any other

outfitter, Whitewater Voyages has trips for paddlers of all levels of experience.

The outfitter also has specialty trips, including whitewater schools, whitewater summer camps for young people, family trips, low-cost river-cleanup trips, "teambuilding" trips, whitewater summer camps for young people and inflatable kayaking courses.

Wild Water Adventures
Al Law, Melinda Allan
P.O. Box 249
Creswell, OR 97426
(503) 895-4465, (800) 289-4534
Klamath River
Max. rapids: III-IV
Oregon Guides and Packers Association

Wild Water Adventures specializes in running guided and unguided inflatable kayak trips on wilderness rivers. Trips in rafts and inflatable kayaks range in length from 1/2 day to 9 days and run on rivers ranging from mountain streams to desert waterways and from scenic floats

Pop-up on the South Fork of the American River. Courtesy of Sierra Shutterbug Photography.

to crashing whitewater. On these trips, in addition to paddling, guests can fish, view Indian pictographs and pioneer ruins, and spot deer, eagles, otters, hawks, minks, beavers, and other wildlife.

During the season, which runs from March to November, and year-round for "wetsuiters," guests can also take inflatable kayak lessons, learning brace strokes, ferrying, river rescue, and how to "read" rivers. Kayaking students can enjoy instruction by Melinda Allan, coauthor of *The Inflatable Kayak Handbook.*

Wilderness Adventures
Dean Munroe
P.O. Box 938
Redding, CA 96099
(800) 323-7238
Sacramento River, Scott River, Wooley Creek
Max. rapids: V

Wilderness Adventures runs a number of remarkable trips on rivers along the California-Oregon border. Among the unusual offerings is a raft trip begun on the Class V Woodley Creek after a horseback ride into the Marble Mountain Wilderness. Another exciting trip, called "Hell and High Water," combines all the Class V sections of the Salmon, Scott and Upper Klamath into a weekend trip.

Trips range in length from 1-4 days, are offered from April to October, and are suited for intermediate to advanced paddlers. Set in wilderness areas, trips offer fishing for trout and views of eagles, ospreys, minks, otters, and beavers.

Wilderness Sports
Charlie Fox
12401 Folsom Blvd.
Rancho Cordova, CA 95742
(916) 985-3555, (510) 596-4490
American, Consumnes, Tuolumne, Klamath Rivers, San Francisco Bay, Area lakes
Max. rapids: III-IV

As its name suggests, Wilderness Sports offers clients a wide range of challenges, suitable for advanced as well as novice paddlers. It also caters to backpackers, skiers, and climbers. Paddling trips by canoe and kayak are available year-round, guided or unguided, through majestic scenery of cliffs and rugged terrain. Trout, salmon, and blue gill lurk in the crystal-clear waters, along with abundant wildlife elsewhere. Certified instructors and guides are available and trips last up to 5 days.

Colorado

As a classic Rocky Mountain state, Colorado offers the whitewater enthusiast innumerable rapids to run amid stunning scenery. Rivers that start as snow-fed mountain torrents plunge through deep canyons to irrigate distant deserts. They include some of the greatest American arteries: the Arkansas, the Colorado, the North Platte and the Rio Grande. Rapids bear names that quicken the pulse of the daring: Pinball, Zoom-Flume, Widow-Maker, Needle Eye, Stovepipe and the notorious Snaggletooth.

This is exciting country. Take, for instance, the furious Pine Creek Rapids that run just below Granite on the Arkansas River. Except in August when the flow abates this gorge is rated Class V. Among macho kayakers, running Pine Creek Rapids ranks as a test of manhood — or womanhood. More popular is the six-mile run a little further downstream on the Arkansas which has been the scene of many national championships and the annual Colorado Cup. This Class IV river segment, which begins at a campground about ten miles upstream from Buena Vista, attracts kayakers from far and wide.

But the most popular of all Arkansas River runs is Brown's Canyon, a Class III rafting and kayaking trip which goes ten miles from Nathrop to a highway bridge six miles above Salida. Many commercial rafts crowd this canyon on a busy summer day, with tourists thrilling to its excellent whitewater. But only the seasoned kayaker attempts to run the 1,500-foot-deep Royal Gorge, a Class IV challenge which lies between Parkdale and Canon City. The black-walled chasm has some spectacular scenery including a suspension bridge said to be the world's highest.

A gentler float may be enjoyed on the Upper Colorado, starting near Kremmling and taking rafters through narrow Little Gore Canyon with its Class II rapids. On the second day of this 28-mile, two-day trip the raft emerges into ranchland surrounded by a mountain backdrop. A perfect outing for families, this tour offers natural hot springs, 100-year-old miners' cabins and a stagecoach road. Below Grand Junction, with its waters swelled by the influx of the Gunnison, the celebrated Colorado moves sedately through Ruby and Horsethief Canyons before crossing the state line and entering turbulent Westwater Canyon (see Utah).

The North Gate Canyon stretch of the North Platte, where this un-dammed river flows northward across the Wyoming state line, is described by one outfitter as "the best-kept secret in Colorado." The canyon contains many Class III-IV rapids, and rafters running the entire 30-mile trip eventually come out of forested Medicine Bow mountain wilderness into the rolling hill country of southern Wyoming. The only time to paddle this trail is from late May through June.

The Dolores River in southwestern Colorado offers a great combination of canyon whitewater and colorful desert panoramas. But like the North Platte, its rafting season is short — from early May to mid-June. The Dolores, a tributary of the Colorado, invites trips through aptly-named Ponderosa Gorge and Slick Rock Canyon. Their toughest rapid is Snaggletooth, an infamous Class IV-V obstacle which most rafters portage. Slick Rock is uniquely colorful with its red, white and orange sandstone, prickly pear cactus and pinon and juniper trees sprouting from the canyon walls.

Then there is the famous Gunnison River. Just downstream from the Black Canyon of the Gunnison National Monument with its many dams is Gunnison Gorge, where the river flows freely again and provides Class II-IV whitewater all summer long. This is rugged wilderness country: a spectacular narrow canyon with black cliffs and a river alternating between smooth pools and surging rapids. The put-in is at the foot of a mile-long narrow trail; rafts and equipment have to be carried down by packhorses.

Small rafts, canoes and kayaks can float Colorado sections of the Rio Grande before it crosses into New Mexico and on to Texas. But a more rewarding river in the southern part of the state is the Animas. Its upstream rapids are hazardous for all but experts, but just north of Durango is an easy ten-mile run, and a pleasant 20-mile trip ensues in the Animas Valley close to the New Mexico state line.

Adventure Bound River Expeditions
Tom Kleinschnitz
2392 H Road
Grand Junction, CO 81505
(970) 245-5428, (800) 423-4668
FAX (970) 241-5633
Colorado, Green and Yampa Rivers
Max. rapids: V+
PPA, America Outdoors, Utah Guides &
Outfitters, CROA
    Adventure Bound runs guided inflat-able kayak and raft trips lasting from 1-6

days in wilderness country. They range from family jaunts on Class II-III water to Class V challenges for skilled paddlers. The outfitter's craft include inflatable kayaks, paddle boats, oar rafts, and large, motorized pontoon boats.
    During the April 22-to-November 1 season, customers can camp, swim, fish for catfish, and observe desert bighorn sheep, deer, and other wildlife.

American Adventure Expeditions
Ray and Penny Kitson
P.O. Box 1549
Buena Vista, CO 81211
(800) 288-0675
Arkansas River, Animas River, Colorado River, Piedra River
Max. rapids: V+
America Outdoors, Arkansas River Outfitters Association

American Adventure offers guided oar- and paddle-boat trips on four Colorado rivers set high in the Rockies amid the largest concentration of 14,000-foot peaks in the lower 48 states. Lessons and 1-7 day trips are available for all skill levels from novice to expert. Along the way, guests can fish for trout and perhaps spot elk, deer, bears, and mountain lions.

Trips run from April to October. With experienced guides and fine equipment, American Adventures offers a satisfaction guarantee.

Arkansas River Tours
Box 1032-PA
Buena Vista, CO 81211
(800) 321-4352, FAX (719) 395-8949,
Arkansas River
Max. rapids: V
America Outdoors, Arkansas River Outfitters Association, Colorado River Outfitters Association

Arkansas River Tours specializes in guided paddle rafting trips on the Arkansas in south central Colorado, with trips to suit paddlers of all skill levels. Trips last 1-3 days, run between May and August, and pass through high-desert terrain that offers scenic mountain views and chances to spot bighorn sheep, ouzels, and hawks.

All trips are in self-bailing rafts. Oar boats are an option for those who choose not to paddle. The owners of Arkansas River Tours also operate Four Corners Rafting. (See separate listing.)

Aspen Kayak School
Kirk Baker
P.O. Box 1520
Aspen, CO 81611
(303) 925-6248
Roaring Fork River, Colorado River, Arkansas River, Crystal River, Green River
Max. rapids: III-IV
American Canoe Association

Aspen Kayak School has more than 20 years' experience and an excellent safety record offering kayak instruction and rentals. Its trips run from 1-12 days and include offerings for paddlers of all skill levels. For novices there are trips with good beginner water, and for intermediate and advanced kayakers, there is an excellent variety of Class III and IV runs.

The scenery varies greatly as well, ranging from the Alpine Rockies to high desert. Wildlife to be seen include deer, foxes, and black bears, and fishing is for rainbow and brown trout.

Bighorn Expeditions
Pitchfork Enterprises, Inc.
P.O. Box 365
Bellvue, CO 80512
(303) 221-8110
Dolores River, Green River, Rio Grande
Max. rapids: III-IV
America Outdoors, Utah Guides and Outfitters

Bighorn Expeditions offers 2-8 day guided oar-boat trips on the Rio Grande River in Texas, the Dolores River in Colorado, and the Green River in Utah. Unlike most outfitters offering oar-boat trips, Bighorn encourages guests to do the rowing. The company provides 11-foot, one-person rafts that are lively and riverworthy but small enough for easy handling. Trips include thorough lessons and begin on calm stretches, so they are fine for those with no rowing experience. Those wishing to row, however, should be in good physical condition. If you are unsure of your conditioning or prefer to concentrate on photography or bird-watching, you can elect to ride on one of the company's larger, guide-operated rafts.

Bighorn's trips run March to November through scenic canyon terrain and offer good instruction in whitewater boating and wilderness ethics.

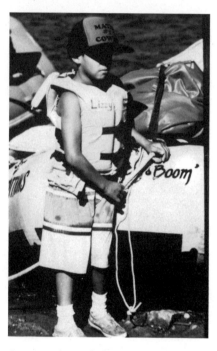

A young rafter ready for action. Courtesy of Dvorak's Kayak and Rafting Expeditions, Inc. Nathrop, Colorado.

Bill Dvorak's Kayak and Rafting Expeditions
Bill and Jaci Dvorak
17921 U.S. Highway 285
Nathrop, CO 81236
(719) 539-6851, (800) 824-3795
Arkansas Colorado, Gunnison, Green, North Platte, Dolores, Middle Fork and Main Salmon, Rio Grande, Salt Rivers
Max. rapids: V+
America Outdoors, Colorado River Outfitters Association, Utah Guides and Outfitters, and New Mexico River Outfitters Association

Dvorak's Kayak and Rafting Expeditions runs a wide array of guided and unguided trips through 29 canyons on a total of 10 rivers in Colorado, Utah, and New Mexico. Scenery ranges from alpine to desert, and whitewater ranges from Class I to Class V. Guests also have a choice of touring by canoe, kayak, or raft. With this selection of locations and trips, Dvorak's has offerings to suit any individual or group.

Trips run for 1-13 days between March and October and allow time for trout fishing and viewing deer, elk, bears, eagles, beavers, and coyotes.

Brown's Royal Gorge Rafting
Mark Brown
45045 U.S. Highway 50
Canyon City, CO 81212
(719) 275-5161, (719) 275-7238
Arkansas River
Max. rapids: V+
America Outdoors

Brown's Royal Gorge Rafting runs guided oar-raft and paddle-raft trips on the Arkansas River. These trips last 1-2 days and range in difficulty from family trips to adventures for experienced paddlers only. On all outings, participants can enjoy the Arkansas' beautiful mountain and canyon scenery and views of mountain sheep, deer, and other wildlife.

Brown's Royal Gorge Rafting's season runs from April to October.

Buffalo Joe River Trips
Pete & Diana Makris
113 N. Railroad St.
P.O. Box 1526
Buena Vista, CO 81211
(719) 395-8757, (800) 356-7984
Arkansas, Dolores Rivers
Max. rapids: III-IV
Colorado River Outfitters Association, Arkansas River Outfitters Association

Buffalo Joe runs guided raft trips of 1/2 day to 3 days from May 1 to Labor Day. They are suitable for beginning to advanced paddlers age 8 or older. Oar and paddle craft are available, along with experienced guides.

Guests can enjoy 14,000-foot peaks, Anasazi ruins, beautiful wilderness, great whitewater, and views of deer, elk, bighorn sheep, herons, eagles, and hawks.

Centennial Canoe Outfitters

Fred Welsh
P.O. Box 440307
Aurora, CO 80044
(303) 755-3501
Yampa, N. Platte, Colorado, Gunnison, White, Green, Dolores Rivers
Max. rapids: I-II
PPA

Centennial rents canoes for guided and unguided trips of 1-6 days on easy-to-paddle sections of little-traveled western rivers. The mountain and canyonland scenery is magnificent, and there are special-interest trips for families, singles, women, and paddlers interested in geology, archaeology, music, and spiritual experiences.

Centennial offers a canoe class before each trip, good food, first-class guides, music, storytelling, and other entertainment. Between unspoiled campsites, paddlers may fish for trout and spot a wide variety of wildlife.

Fly fishing. Courtesy of Dvorak's Kayak and Rafting Expeditions, Inc. Nathrop, Colorado.

Colorado River Runs, Inc.

Joe Kelso
Star Route Box 32
Bond, CO 80423
(303) 653-4292, (800) 826-1081
Colorado River, Eagle River, Arkansas River
Max. rapids: III-IV
Colorado River Outfitters Association, America Outdoors

Colorado River Runs offers guided 1 day raft trips on the Colorado, Eagle, and Arkansas Rivers. The trips, suitable for guests of all ages, offer excitement, isolation, gorgeous Rocky Mountain scenery, and a chance to view deer, eagles, and coyotes.

The company, which has been in business for 20 years, runs trips from May through October.

Echo Canyon River Expeditions

Dave and Kim Burch
45000 US Highway 50 W.
Canon City, CO 81212
(800) 748-2953, (719) 275-3154
Arkansas, Piedra, Gunnison, Lake Fork of the Gunnison, and San Miguel Rivers
Max. rapids: V
Colorado River Outfitters Association, Arkansas River Outfitters Association

Echo Canyon's raft trips range from "mild to wild" and are suitable for people age 6 and older. Trips range in length from 1-3 days and run on five Colorado rivers, offering spectacular scenery, trout fishing, and a chance to view deer and bighorn sheep.

Echo's trips, by oar or paddle boats, run between April and September.

Far Flung Adventures, Inc.
Steve Harris/Mike Davidson
P.O. Box 377
Terlingua, TX 79852
(915) 371-2489, (800) 359-4138
(reservations)
Gunnison River, Dolores River,
Arkansas River
Max. rapids: V+
America Outdoors, Rio Grande Guides
Association

Far Flung Adventures specializes in taking rafters on camping trips through the ruggedly beautiful Big Bend region of Texas as well as in other states in the U.S. and Mexico. Its tours last from 1-7 days in a season running from January to December. It caters to everyone from novices to whitewater experts capable of meeting Class V+ challenges.

The remoteness of the Rio Grande's

Big Bend National Park, its canyons and wildlife combine with good fishing to make these trips unforgettable. Far Flung Adventures offers paddling lessons, camping, fishing, and swimming.

Four Corners Paddling School
Nancy Wiley
Box 379
Durango, CO 81302
(303) 259-3893
Animas River, Dolores River
Max. rapids: III-IV

Four Corners Paddling School offers canoeing and kayaking classes for paddlers of all levels, novice to advanced. Classes are small, with five or fewer students per instructor, and the instructors are well-qualified, each with many years of teaching experience. Also available are rolling clinics, women's clinics,

Rafting on the Arkansas River. Courtesy of Echo Canyon River Expeditions, Canon City, Colorado.

A.C.A. kayak and canoe instructor certification, squirt clinics, slalom-gate training clinics, and hole-playing clinics.

The founder and director of the school, Nancy Wiley, was selected by Canoe Magazine in 1987 as one of the top 10 kayakers in the United States.

Classes are offered for 2-day to 4-day sessions during the June-to-September season. Trips run on the Animas and Dolores Rivers, which flow from high alpine snowfields to deep desert canyons, offering a unique and diverse river experience.

Four Corners Rafting
Karen Dils
Box 1032-PA
Buena Vista, CO 81211
(800) 332-7238, (719) 395-8949
Arkansas River, Dolores River
Max. rapids: V
America Outdoors, Arkansas River Outfitters Association, Colorado River Outfitters Association

Four Corners Rafting runs guided oar- and paddle-raft trips on the Arkansas and Dolores Rivers. Trips on the Arkansas vary widely in difficulty, offering family-class to adventure-class whitewater. The high-mountain setting features spectacular vistas of 14,000-foot mountains and a chance to fish for trout and view deer, bighorn sheep, ouzels, and hawks. All trips are on self bailing rafts.

Three- to six-day trips are available on the Dolores River, which boasts fun whitewater, Indian ruins, and changing, captivating scenery, including red sandstone, evergreens, and desert terrain.

Four Corners' season runs from May to August. The owners also run Arkansas River Tours. (See separate listing.)

Holiday River & Bike Expeditions
544 East 3900 South
Salt Lake City, UT 84107
(801) 266-2087, (800) 624-6323
Colorado, Green, Yampa Rivers
Max. rapids: V+
Utah Guides and Outfitters

Holiday River Expeditions rents canoes and rafts and runs guided canoe, kayak, and raft trips on the Colorado, Green, San Juan, and Yampa Rivers in Utah and Colorado, and the Snake, Main Salmon, Lower Salmon, and Lochsa Rivers in Idaho. These trips last 1-12 days, offer oar and paddle options, and range in difficulty from beginners' runs to expert-level whitewater adventures. Floaters pass through pristine areas with spectacular scenery ranging from arid desert canyons to alpine forests. Along the way, guests can camp, swim, fish for trout, and catfish, and spot deer, bighorn sheep, raptors, otters, and beavers.

Holiday's season runs from April to October.

Joni Ellis River Tours, Inc.
Joni Ellis
Box 764
Dillon, CO 80435
(303) 468-1028, (800) 477-0144
Upper Colorado River, Blue River, Arkansas River
Max. rapids: III-IV
America Outdoors and Colorado River Outfitters Association

Joni Ellis River Tours runs 1-day guided trips on the Upper Colorado River, Blue River, and Arkansas River. The Upper Colorado run is a scenic, introductory whitewater trip that passes through beautiful Little Gore Canyon and includes stops at natural hot springs and historic miners' cabins. The Arkansas River trip through Browns Canyon is one of Colorado's most exciting family whitewater trips. The Blue River tour puts in at 9,000 feet, offering gorgeous alpine scenery and two miles of continuous whitewater, making it an excellent choice for both families and whitewater enthusiasts.

Joni Ellis runs tours from May to September and offers guests the choice of paddle rafts, oar rafts, and inflatable kayaks. Wildlife to see include eagles, hawks, migratory birds, deer, and beavers.

Rafting on the Arkansas River. Courtesy of Echo Canyon River Expeditions, Canon City, Colorado.

Mad Adventures, Inc.
Roger Hedlund/Jack Van Horn
Box 650
Winter Park, CO 80482
(303) 726-5290, (800) 451-4844
Upper Colorado River, Arkansas River
Max. rapids: III-IV
America Outdoors

Mad Adventures runs 1-day guided paddle-raft trips on the Arkansas and upper Colorado Rivers. Trips on the Colorado have mild whitewater and terrific scenery and are well-suited for families. The Arkansas trips, for experienced paddlers only, have challenging whitewater and spectacular canyons with 800-foot-high walls.

Among the wildlife to be seen are deer, elk, beavers, golden eagles, and ospreys. Guests may also fish for rainbow, cutthroat, and brown trout.

Moondance River Expeditions, Ltd.
Nonny and Bear Dyer
310 West First Street
Salida, CO 81201
(719) 539-2113
Arkansas River
Max. rapids: V+
America Outdoors, Colorado River Outfitters Association, Arkansas River Outfitters Association

Moondance runs 1-5 day guided raft trips on a 100-mile stretch of the Arkansas River from north of Buena Vista to Canon City, Colorado. The area is home to hot springs, mountain lions, and spectacular mountain scenery.

Trips run from May to September and are by oar boat, paddle boat, oar/paddle combination boats, or Russian paddle-catamaran. With this selection, Moondance can accommodate guests with all levels of ability and experience, and is proud to offer trips accessible to the disabled, elderly, and young children.

Moondance, appropriately, also offers moonlight float trips. These trips run for five nights each lunar cycle and consist of six miles of Class I and II water.

Courtesy of Dvorak's Kayak and Rafting Expeditions, Inc. Nathrop, Colorado.

Mountain Waters Rafting
Casey D. Lynch
P.O. Box 2681
108 West 6th Street
Durango, CO 81302
(800) 748-2507
Animas River, Piedra River
Max. rapids: V+
America Outdoors, Colorado River Outfitters Association

Mountain Waters Rafting offers guided oar- and paddle-raft trips lasting 1 and 2 days. Runs on the lower Animas are excellent trips for families and novices. Trips on the upper Animas and Piedra are for experts only, with rapids of up to Class V. The upper Animas trips are notable, too, for including a shuttle

aboard the Durango-Silverton Narrow Gauge Railroad.

On all trips, guests can enjoy the high-desert scenery, glimpses of remnants of Durango's wild-west history, and a chance to view deer, beavers, otters, muskrats, eagles, hawks, and other wildlife. The season runs from May to September.

Noah's Ark Whitewater Rafting
Chuck and Lindy Cichowitz
P.O. Box 850
Buena Vista, CO 81211
(719) 395-2158
Arkansas River
Max. rapids: III-IV

Noah's Ark runs 1-3 day guided and unguided raft trips on the Arkansas River. The difficulty of trips varies greatly, depending on the section of river chosen and whether one travels by oar or paddle boat. The easiest trips are fine for families and children age six and up. The toughest trips are challenging for advanced paddlers. On the river, guests have chances to fish for trout and view eagles and deer.

The company also offers a riverfront campground and rock-climbing and rappelling courses.

O.A.R.S.
George Wendt
P.O. Box 67
Angels Camp, CA 95222
(209) 736-4677, (800) 446-7238 (CA), (800) 346-6277 (U.S.)
American, Cal-Salmon, Stanislaus, Tuolumne, Merced, Rogue, Snake, San Juan, Colorado, Salmon and Middle Fork Salmon Rivers.
Max. rapids: III-IV
America Outdoors

O.A.R.S. runs guided dory, raft, and kayak trips in six Western states. In Colorado, trips run on the Colorado River. These outings feature swimming, camping, side hikes, wildlife viewing, and other activities. Tours run from April to October.

Pagosa Rafting Outfitters
Wayne Wells
Box 222
Pagosa Springs, CO 81147
(303) 731-4081
Upper San Juan River, Piedra River, Upper Animas River, Conejos River
Max. rapids: III-IV
Colorado River Outfitters Association, America Outdoors

Pagosa Rafting Outfitters runs 1-3 day oar- and paddle-raft trips of 1-3 days. Trips on the San Juan and Conejos rivers are fine for families, offering inter-mediate whitewater and great views of wilderness, ghost towns, and abandoned historic railroads. Trips on the Piedra and upper Animas are more demanding, restricted to teens and fit adults.

The Piedra run starts high in the mountains of the San Juan National Forest and offers spectacular vistas, craggy canyons, beautiful forests, and some of the most challenging white-water in the Four Corners area. The upper Animas trip has even more chal-lenging whitewater, including stretches of almost continuous Class IV rapids. This trip is exclusively for fit adults who have some river-running experience and are prepared for vigorous paddling.

Pagosa's season runs from April to September. The company also offers horseback and jeep trips and tours of Indian cliff dwellings.

Performance Tours Rafting
Kevin and Mary Foley
P.O. Box 7305
110 Ski Kill Road
Breckenridge, CO 80424
(303) 453-0661, (800) 328-7238
Arkansas River, Blue River, Colorado River
Max. rapids: V+

Performance Tours Rafting offers guided raft trips and raft rentals on the Arkansas, Blue, and Colorado Rivers. Trips last from 1-3 days and run amid the greatest concentration of 14,000-foot peaks in the country. In addition to the beautiful mountain scenery, guests can enjoy blue-ribbon trout fishing and the chance to spot deer, elk, eagles, hawks, bighorn sheep, and mountain lions.

With a choice of rivers and paddle and oar boats, Performance Tours has trips to suit guests of all ages. The company's season runs from May to September.

Raftmeister
Debbie K. Marquez
P.O. Box 1805
Vail, CO 81658
(303) 476-7238
Eagle River, Arkansas River, Colorado River
Max. rapids: III-IV
Colorado River Outfitters Association, America Outdoors

Raftmeister runs guided kayak and raft trips of 1-3 days on the Eagle, Ar-kansas, and Colorado Rivers. On the Arkansas, guests can run the Numbers or Brown's Canyon. The Numbers, for more experienced paddlers, features nu-merous Class IV rapids; Brown's Can-yon, also a great whitewater trip, is slightly less overwhelming. The Eagle offers exhilarating rides for whitewater enthusiasts on its upper stretches, while Lower Eagle provides great adventure for families. Wildlife float trips on the Eagle are also available in the morning when wildlife is particularly abundant. On the Colorado, guests can ride the Upper Colorado, an historic, scenic family trip, or the Shoshone/Glenwood Canyon, a scenic and thrilling run.

With this wide choice of rivers, Raft-meister can accommodate guests of all ages and skill levels. The company's sea-son is from May to October.

Rafting on the Arkansas River. Courtesy of Echo Canyon River Expeditions, Canon City, Colorado.

Raven Adventure Trips
Art and Virginia Krizman
P.O. Box 108
Granby, CO 80446
(303) 887-2141, (800) 332-3381
Arkansas River, Colorado River, North Platte River
Max. rapids: V+
America Outdoors, Colorado River Outfitters Association, Arkansas River Outfitters Association

Raven Adventure Trips runs 1-3 day guided raft and inflatable kayak trips on the Arkansas, Colorado, and North Platte Rivers. The Arkansas, renowned for its exhilarating Class III-IV whitewater, is nestled in central Colorado between the Collegiate Peaks and the Sangre de Cristo Mountains. On Arkansas River trips, guests 8 and older may

choose oar or paddle boats.

The Colorado River trips, with Class II-III rapids, are perfect for first-time rafters, families, and groups of all types. Guests age six and older can enjoy beautiful scenery, historic cabins, and hot springs. Trips on the Colorado are by raft or inflatable kayaks, as are trips on the North Platte River.

The North Platte trips, set in northern Colorado at over 8,000 feet, run through the remote Northgate Canyon, a designated wilderness area. The minimum age for the North Platte trips is 14. On Raven Adventure's trips, which run from May to September, guests can view elk, deer, bears, bighorn sheep, and bald and golden eagles. Fishing is for brown and rainbow trout.

River Runners, Ltd.
11150 US Highway 50
Salida, CO 81201
(719) 539-2144, (800) 525-2081, (U.S.)
(800) 332-9100 (CO)
Arkansas River
Max. rapids: V+
Colorado Rafting Association, Colorado
River Outfitters Association, Arkansas River
Outfitters Association

River Runners' 1-3 day guided trips
are on the Arkansas River. With offices
at the beginning, middle and end of the
"raftable" Arkansas, the company offers
access to many different stretches of
river. Between this selection and guests'
choice of oar-, paddle, and paddle-
assisted boats, the company has trips for
people of all ages.

All trips pass through areas of gorgeous scenery, whether high among the
peaks of the continental divide or deep
within towering canyons. Trips also offer
fishing for brown trout and chances to
view owls, eagles, hawks, deer, elk, and
mountain sheep. The season runs from
May to September.

River Runners runs a riverside campground and offers horseback rides, pack
trips, and scenic jeep tours of ghost
towns.

Rocky Mountain Outdoor Center
Dick Eustis
10281 Hwy 50
Howard, CO 81233
(719) 942-3214, (800) 255-5784
Arkansas, Dolores Rivers
Max. rapids: III-IV
America Outdoors, Colorado River Outfitters
Association

Rocky Mountain Outdoor Center
offers guided raft, canoe and kayak trips
of 1-3 days on what it calls the "best
whitewater in the country."

It sets an 18-year minimum age limit
for the Royal Gorge, which is best for
those who have rafted before. Brown's
Canyon, which provides moderate rapids and breathtaking scenery, is open to
paddlers age 13 and up. For younger

children, the company recommends two
half-day runs.

Seasoned guides accompany each
raft, and paddling lessons are available
for canoeists and kayakers. The scenery
includes the 1,000-foot deep Royal
Gorge and wildlife is plentiful. Camping
is also available during the April-September season.

Western River Expeditions
Larry Lake
7258 Racquet Club Drive
Salt Lake City, UT 84121
(801) 942-6669, (800) 453-7450 (outside
UT)
Colorado River
Max. rapids: III-IV
America Outdoors

Western River Expeditions runs
guided raft trips and rents rafts and inflatable kayaks on the Colorado River in
Colorado, Utah and Arizona; the Green
River in Utah and the Main Salmon in
Idaho. Green River trips, by oar or paddle raft, provide thrilling whitewater and
views of towering red rock cliffs and
arches, deep gorges, frontier cabins, and
Indian petroglyphs. Colorado River
tours offer spectacular scenery in Cataract Canyon, Westwater Canyon or the
Upper and Lower Grand Canyon. Rapids are moderate to large, and paddlers
can swim, take side hikes, and view historic Indian and Old West sites. Finally,
trips on the Main Salmon involve scenic
blue-green waters, pine-covered mountains, stops at hot springs and abandoned mining camps, and camping on
white sand beaches.

All trips are suitable for anyone of
good health above the minimum age set
for each trip, depending on its difficulty.
During Western River's March-September season, some trips can be combined
with a ranch stay.

Whitewater Rafting

Susi Larson
P.O. Box 2462
Glenwood Springs, CO 81602
(970) 945-8477
*Colorado (Glenwood Canyon) and Roaring
Fork Rivers*
Max. rapids: III-IV
*Colorado River Outfitters Association,
America Outdoors*

A family-owned business since 1974,
Whitewater Rafting rents rafts and provides guided raft trips ranging from easy
family floats to whitewater for the adventurous.

A challenging stretch is the Shoshone
whitewater — two miles of continuous
Class IV rapids. The riverbanks are dotted with natural hot springs, and Glenwood Canyon displays millions of years
of geological history. Paddlers can spot
blue herons, mountain sheep, and Canada geese, and fish for rainbow and
brown trout. Camping is also available
during its May-to-Sept season.

Wilderness Aware Rafting

Joe and Sue Greiner
P.O. Box 1550 SP
Buena Vista, CO 81211
(719) 395-2112, (800) 462-7238,
FAX (719) 395-6716
*Dolores River, North Platte River,
Gunnison River, Arkansas River,
Colorado River*
Max. rapids: III-IV
*America Outdoors, Arkansas River
Outfitters Association, Colorado River
Outfitters Association*

Wilderness Aware Rafting runs 1-10
day guided raft trips on rivers in Colorado and Texas, offering "family whitewater to wild water" for adventurers age
6 to 86. Guests may choose either paddle or oar boats. Although 1/2 and 1-
day trips are offered on the exciting
Arkansas River daily, Wilderness Aware
specializes in multi-day trips when
camping gear is carried on the rafts and
camps are made riverside at remote
spots. Also, on some Class II and III

sections during multi-day trips, guests
may try one- and two-person self-bailing
inflatable kayaks. The wildlife seen includes deer, bighorn sheep, otters, and
beavers. Fishing is for brown and rainbow trout.

Wildwater, Inc.

Robert Breckinridge
317 Stover Street
Fort Collins, CO 80524
(303) 224-3379, (800) 369-4165
*Arkansas River, North Platte River,
Colorado River, Poudre River*
Max. rapids: V+
Colorado River Outfitters Association

Wildwater Inc. offers rentals and
kayak trips on some of the best wildwater in the state, including the Poudre,
Colorado's only designated wild and scenic river. Trips range from "mild to wild"
and last from 1-6 days. Canoes, kayaks,
rafts, and tubes are available for rent.
Wildwater's season runs from May to
September, with exceptional big water in
June and early. Wildlife seen include
deer, bears, and bighorn sheep. Guests
also can fish for trout.

Connecticut

Float through the Connecticut hills on a sunlit autumn day when the fall foliage is ablaze and watch migrating birds head south for winter. Take the broad Connecticut River down the middle of the state or the Housatonic's fast water in the Berkshire Hills when the river level is neither too high nor too low. On a calm summer day, take a sea kayak or canoe into the estuaries along the shore of Long Island Sound. Or just set out on a placid pond or lake for a day's cruising and fishing. Connecticut has all these to offer, plus interesting historic sites and museums.

The Connecticut River, formerly badly contaminated by industrial pollution, has been largely cleaned up. Fish have returned to this waterway which in earlier centuries had been famous for salmon and shad spawning. Bird life is abundant, trees line the riverbanks and some handsome old houses may be seen — or even visited — from the water.

North of Hartford, the Connecticut has a series of easy rapids for 4 1/2 miles below Enfield Dam. But most canoeists prefer to skirt them by using the adjacent canal. At Middletown the river widens and deepens as it passes between forested hills. Then come several state parks and forests affording the canoeist plenty of places to picnic and camp. And once it passes Hadlyme the mile-wide river becomes tidal for the rest of its journey past Essex to its sea outlet at Old Saybrook.

The Housatonic in the northwest corner of the state offers paddlers a different experience. It provides various degrees of whitewater — Class IV-V at Bull's Bridge Gorge, where seasonal guided raft trips are available — as well as gentle floating. Another appealing stretch of the Housatonic is the scenic ten miles from the Massachusetts state line southward to the Falls Village Dam. It provides smooth floating through pastures and a treelined Berkshires valley replete with otters and other wildlife.

Below Falls Village, paddlers find a mixture of flatwater and whitewater on another ten-mile section of the river, down to Housatonic Meadows State Park. Several restaurants offer lunch at the well-known Covered Bridge in West Cornwall, and there are various picnic sites. But the water level on this segment of the Housatonic, and on the next section down to Kent School, varies widely with season and rainfall. Outfitters caution that they may have to postpone or cancel trips, or move them to other sections of the river.

The Mystic River in southeastern Connecticut is only a few miles long and largely tidal. But it offers easy canoeing in calm weather and takes the paddler to the Mystic Seaport Museum with its ancient whaling vessels.

Clarke Outdoors
Mark Clarke
Box 163, Route 7
West Cornwall, CT 06796
(203) 672-6365
Housatonic River
Max. rapids: III-IV
PPA, ACA

Clarke Outdoors runs 1-day guided and unguided canoe, kayak, and raft trips on the Housatonic River in the Berkshire foothills from March to November. Canoe and unguided raft trips are 10 miles long, passing under the scenic covered bridge of West Cornwall. These trips have flat water and Class I and II rapids.

Kayak lessons and canoe clinics are also available, as are seasonal Class III and IV guided raft trips through the Housatonic's Bulls Bridge Gorge. Lessons are led by Mark Clarke, a six-time national open canoe champion, and other ACA-certified instructors.

Main Stream Corp.
John & Joseph Casey
Box 448, Rte. 44
New Hartford, CT 06057
(203) 693-6791
Connecticut and Farmington Rivers,
many lakes
Max rapids: III-IV
PPA

Main Stream rents canoes, kayaks, and tubes, and runs guided canoe, kayak, and raft trips from March 15 to November 1. The company has 20 years'

experience and certified guide and paddling instructors. The Farmington River is a designated national wild and scenic river. Trips last 1-2 days, camping is available, and paddlers can fish for trout and bass.

The Mountain Workshop
Sue and Corky Clark
P.O. Box 625
Ridgefield, CT 06877
(203) 438-3640
New England rivers and lakes, Everglades,
Allagash River
Max. rapids: I-II

The Mountain Workshop offers guided 1-12 day canoe and kayak trips on rivers and lakes in New England, the Allagash in Maine, and Florida's Everglades. Trips are best-suited for adventuresome beginners seeking personalized instruction.

North American Canoe Tours
David Harraden
65 Black Point Road
Niantic, CT 06357
(860) 693-6465, (860) 739-0791
Farmington River
Max. rapids: II-III
PPA

North American Canoe Tours offers tube rentals for trips through Satan's Kingdom on the Farmington River between May and September. Tubing trips last two to three hours and pass through scenic countryside, offering a chance to fish for trout and spot birds, deer, and beavers.

Elsewhere in Connecticut, NACT rents canoes and pedal boats at seven state parks, including Hopeville Pond State Park in Griswold, Squantz Pond State Park in New Fairfield, Burr Pond State Park near Torrington, Lake Waramaug State Park in New Preston, and Quaddick Pond State Park in Thompson. Canoes can be rented from an hour to all day, to fish or view the beautiful scenic areas of Connecticut. The NACT also rents canoes, by reservation, for group trips on the Connecticut River near Gillette Castle.

NACT also offers trips in Everglades National Park and on the Suwannee River. (See description under Florida.)

Path & Paddle Adventures, Inc.
Gregory Craig
56 Ivy Lane
Newington, CT 06111
(203) 666-2334
Farmington, Housatonic, Quinebaug Rivers in Conn., Deerfield & Charles Rivers in Mass., Battenkill River in Vt.
Max. None

Path & Paddle runs guided canoe trips and rents canoes for mostly flatwater outings in scenic countryside with mountain ridges and broad valleys. This employee-owned company arranges 1-day and weekend trips for individuals, families, and groups, using quality canoes. Certified instructors give paddling lessons and lead tours.

The emphasis is on providing a warm, friendly, and enjoyable experience for all comers during a May-to-October season. There is good fishing for trout and bass, and paddlers may watch a wide variety of wildlife.

Riverrunning Expeditions
Joan Manasse
85 Main Street
Falls Village, CT 06031
(203) 824-5579
Housatonic River
Max rapids: I-II
PPA

A family business for more than 20 years, Riverrunning Expeditions rents canoes, rafts, and tubes and runs guided canoe and raft trips on the clean waters of the Housatonic. Mild whitewater offers fun and challenge for paddlers of every skill level. Trips are best suited for those who have been in canoes before and know the basic safety rules.

Paddlers in the farmland countryside can spot birds and deer and fish for perch and bass. Camping and paddling lessons are available during the March-to-October season.

Delaware

Paddling in the First State is mostly on tidal waters within marshes and swamps. Canoeists should not be put off by the bloodthirsty names of some of the rivers, like Murderkill, Broadkill and Slaughter Creek. It is in fact a very peaceful and friendly place. More to the point is the need to time each trip in accordance with the tides coursing in and out of Delaware Bay from the Atlantic. Most Delaware streams ebb and flow as they glide eastward into the bay through flatlands and wildlife refuges. But there are rivers in the southern Delaware, notably the Nanticoke, that flow southwest into Chesapeake Bay. Many of the state's 50 small lakes and ponds have good beaches and great freshwater fishing.

From Wilmington, the nearest rivers to paddle are the Appoquinimink and Blackbird Creek in New Castle County. Of these, Blackbird Creek is the prettiest. It passes through attractive unspoiled marshland, where the wall of reeds opens up from time to time to allow vistas of farmland on high ground.

Further south, the Smyrna and Leipsic rivers also take the paddler through vast wetlands, where the view is usually limited by tall reeds. But the Leipsic traverses the Bombay Hook National Wildlife Refuge with its wealth of waterfowl.

Slaughter Creek provides another rewarding bird sanctuary experience as it runs through Prime Hook National Wildlife Refuge. The upper stream starts out amid forests of pine and cedar, then the lower creek winds its way through salt marshes to Cedar Creek.

The Prime Hook refuge has two other canoe trails worth exploring, both on Prime Hook Creek. One is a 10-mile float from Del. Rte. 1 to the refuge headquarters, the other a circuit tour. But it is easy to go astray amid the confusing maze of major ditches and side channels. Prime Hook Creek is mostly sheltered from the wind by trees or reeds, and although it is tidal the ebb-and-flow range is weak and the current is gentle.

Beaston's Marina
Steven D. Beaston
Bayview Park
Bethany Beach, DE 19930
(302) 539-3452
Little Assawoman Bay, Assawoman Canal
Max. rapids: None

Beaston's Marina rents canoes from April to November for outings in the salt-marsh region of Little Assawoman Bay and Assawoman Creek. This is flat water that takes paddlers through a wildlife refuge abounding in waterfowl: ducks, geese, ospreys, herons and egrets. Crabbing and perch fishing are local pastimes.

Beaston's Marina is a small family business catering to individual tourists' needs. Canoes can be rented for up to a fortnight.

Trap Pond State Park
Delaware State Parks
Rte. 2 Box 331
Laurel, DE 19956
(302) 875-5153
Trap Pond, James Branch
Max. rapids: None

Leisurely canoeing through stands of 200-year-old bald cypresses is available at Trap Pond State Park with its 142-site campground. Paddlers in this freshwater pond can enjoy great scenery, wildlife, and birdwatching while fishing for large mouth bass.

The James Branch is a freshwater stream connecting to the tidal Lower Delaware River. Both Trap Pond and the James Branch are regularly cleared of litter and downed trees. Beaver, otter, deer, eagles, and waterfowl may be seen, and other fish in these waters include bluegill, crappie and pickerel. The season runs April-November.

Waples Mill Pond Canoeing
H.H. Plummer
Routes 1 and 5
RD 1, Box 138
Milton, DE 19968-9723
(302) 684-8084
Prime Hook Wildlife Refuge, Prime Hook Creek
Max. rapids: None

Waples Mill Pond Canoeing has been in business for 15 years. Open year-round, it rents canoes for day trips in Prime Hook National Wildlife Refuge, Prime Hook Creek, and nearby areas. Longer trips can be arranged.

Prime Hook Creek is a unique eco-system. Its upper five miles are strictly freshwater before it turns salty close to the sea. Scenery changes from woodland to coastal marshes with tall reeds. Wildlife ranges from whitetail deer and grey foxes to otters, opossum, raccoons, ospreys, and great blue herons. Anglers fish for largemouth bass, crappie, perch, pickerel, and bluegill.

Florida

Land of lazy waters, sparkling springs, abundant wildlife — Florida is a place to float idly into the wilderness and consort with nature. Alligators rather than unrunnable rapids are Florida's hazards to be avoided. Birds are ubiquitous: gleaming white egrets, slender blue herons and keen-eyed kingfishers. The observant paddler may also see rare animal species such as bobcats, wild hogs or even a Florida panther stalking the riverbanks. Armadillos are found in some parts of the state, while otters, raccoons and opossums are common. All told, Florida has more than 1,700 rivers, streams and creeks running to a total length of more than 10,000 miles. Some stem from great springs gushing millions of gallons of translucent, crystal-clear water daily.

The Everglades in the south and Okefenokee Swamp in the north are justly famed as back-country havens of natural beauty. Half land, half water, the 1.4m.-acre Everglades National Park provides a habitat for endangered plants and animals. Essentially a 50-mile-wide slow-moving river, the Everglades consist largely of mangrove swamps and sawgrass marshland. Canoes may be rented in Flamingo, the southernmost point, and Everglades City in the northwestern corner of the park. Several canoe trails are marked, but paddlers are advised to pick up charts of the maze-like waterways and file trip plans before setting out. Okefenokee Swamp, smaller but just as fascinating, is accessible from Waycross, Georgia (see Georgia).

The Withlacoochee River in westcentral Florida — as distinct from its northern namesake which flows into the state from Georgia — is an easy float for paddlers of all ages. Clean and largely undeveloped, the Withlacoochee provides fishing for catfish, largemouth bass and brim, along with glimpses of interesting wildlife on its wooded banks.

Further south in the same area runs the Peace River, an artery which drains much of westcentral Florida into the Gulf at Punta Gorda. An unspoiled stream, the Peace has overhanging trees along its banks. Paddlers find plenty of sandbanks and swimming holes — places to pause and look out for alligators, wild boar, turkey and a wide variety of birds.

On the Alabama state line in the Florida panhandle, the Perdido is a safe and secluded river with white sandy beaches. But one canoeist writer advises paddlers to stick to its lower stretches since he found that its upstream part contained more abandoned bridges, log jams and other obstacles than any river of his experience.

Just a few miles to the east of the Perdido is the Blackwater River State Forest, the largest state forest in Florida. It is the home not only of the Blackwater, with its dark, tannin water, but of Juniper and Coldwater Creeks as well. All three offer cool, unpolluted water amid attractive scenery, with riverbeds of white sand.

A favorite river near Orlando is the Wekiva, a tranquil stream that has been designated Wild and Scenic. Rich in fish and wildlife, it is claimed to have the cleanest water in the state. Equally appealing are the Wekiva's tributaries, the Little Wekiva and Rock Springs Run, which is great for tubing. The run to Blue Springs State Park on the St. John's River (into which the Wekiva flows) is to be avoided at weekends, when it is liable to be mobbed by Orlando trippers.

Elsewhere in Florida, the Loxahatchee River is said to be the only remaining wild and natural river in the southeast part of the state. Situated within Jonathan Dickinson State Park near the coast, the Loxahatchee has been well preserved and it displays abundant wildlife.

Adventures Unlimited
Jack, Esther, Mike, and Linda Sanborn
Route 6, Box 283
Milton, FL 32570
(904) 623-6197, FAX (904) 626-3124
Coldwater Creek, Juniper Creek,
Blackwater River
Max. rapids: None
PPA, Florida Association of Canoe Liveries
and Outfitters

Adventures Unlimited offers canoe, kayak, raft, and inner tube rentals on three Florida wilderness streams: Coldwater Creek, Blackwater River, and Juniper Creek. These spring-fed rivers flow at an average depth of two feet over soft, sandy bottoms through pine and cedar forests of Northwest Florida.

White-sand beaches dot the banks and are perfect for swimming, sunning, and camping. Adventures Unlimited offers trips of 1-3 days, cabin and camping gear rentals, and a chance to spot deer, turkeys, bobcats, bears, and armadillos.

Fishing is for bass, bream, pickerel, and catfish. Adventures Unlimited is open year-round.

Adventures Unlimited-Perdido River
David and Linda Venn
160 River Annex Road
Cantonment, FL 32533
(904) 968-5529
Coldwater River, Perdido River, Blackwater
River, Sweetwater-Juniper
Max. rapids: None

Adventures Unlimited-Perdido River offers 1- and 2-day trips along the Perdido River, renting canoes, kayaks, and inner tubes.

The river is scenic and secluded, with white-sand beaches and clear to tea-colored water. The calm waters are suitable for paddlers of all ages and encourage fishing and wildlife viewing. Fishing is for bass, bream, and catfish, and the wildlife to see includes deer, beavers, otters, and snakes.

Paddling on Coldwater Creek. Courtesy of Carter Photography/Adventures Unlimited, Milton Florida.

Adventures Unlimited also offers cabin rentals and tent and R.V. camping during its April-to-October season.

American Canoe Adventures
Vicky & Wendell Hannum
Rte. 1, Box 9022
White Springs, FL 32096
(904) 397-4178
Suwannee River, Swift Creek
Max. rapids: I-II
PPA

American Canoe Adventures rents canoes, kayaks, rafts, and tubes year-round for outings on clean waters that offer good for fishing and swimming. It has trips of 1/2 day to 7 days for paddlers of all skill levels. Paddling lessons and camping are also available.

Canoeists can catch catfish and bass and observe deer, turtles, wild turkeys, and other birds.

Back Country Tours, Inc.
Alan McGroary
39 Hollis Street
Pepperell, MA 01463
(508) 433-9381, (800) 649-9381 (in MA)
Blackwater River, Sweetwater River, Juniper River
Max. rapids: I-II

Back Country Tours specializes in guided canoe trips and canoe rentals on "lesser known, uncrowded scenic waterways." Its trips run on the Souhegan and Merrimack rivers in New Hampshire; the Sauantacook and Nissitissit Rivers in Massachusetts; the Connecticut and Nashua Rivers in New Hampshire and Massachusetts; the Delaware River in New York, Pennsylvania, and New Jersey; the Blackwater, Sweetwater, and Juniper Rivers in Florida; and nine lakes near Long Pond Mountain in New York's Adirondacks. Several of these excursion are "vacation" trips of 3-7 days that offer lodging at campgrounds, cabins, or bed-and-breakfast inns. All trips are suitable for beginners and experienced paddlers.

Back Country Tours' season runs from July to November.

Biscayne National Underwater Park Co., Inc.
Scott A. Windham
P.O. Box 1270
Homestead, FL 33030
(305) 230-1100, FAX (305) 230-1120
Shoreline of the southern tip of Florida, Biscayne Bay, Biscayne Nat. Park
Max. rapids: None

Biscayne National Underwater Park offers canoe rentals for exploring the longest stretch of mangrove shoreline on Florida's east coast. Hourly, half-day and full-day rates are available. The water is clear, shallow, and calm, making canoeing easy for families and allowing paddlers to view fish, stingrays, and manatees. The park's clean, uncrowded waters are also an excellent place to swim.

Bob's Canoe Rental and Sales
L.L. Plowman
4569 Plowman Lane
Milton, FL 32570
(904) 623-5457
Blackwater River, Coldwater Creek, Juniper Creek
Max. rapids: I-II
Florida Association of Canoe Liveries and Outfitters

Bob's Canoe Rental offers canoe, kayak, pedal boat, and inner-tube rentals year round on Blackwater River, Coldwater Creek and Juniper Creek in Northwest Florida. Good currents and calm waters make paddling easy for families, beginners, and advanced paddlers alike. Trips last 1-3 days and offer views of white-sand beaches, wildflowers, flowering trees, birds, raccoons, and turtles. Fishing is for bass, bream, bluefish, and catfish.

Bob's prides itself on its many years'

experience and friendly personal service. The outfitter also offers a pavilion with grills, tables, game areas, and a white-sand beach.

Canoe Escape, Inc.
Joe and Jean Faulk
9335 East Fowler Avenue
Thonotosassa, FL 33592
(813) 986-2067
Hillsborough River
Max. rapids: None
PPA, Florida Association of Canoe Liveries and Outfitters

Canoe Escape, Inc., runs 1-day, self-guided trips through the cypress swamps and hardwood hammocks of the Hillsborough River. Set in a wilderness park just minutes from Tampa, the river varies from a narrow, twisting stream beneath a tree canopy to a broad, sunlit river. In all, 25 miles of riverfront and 16,000 acres within the park are protected as wilderness, offering habitat for many wading birds, including limpkins, wood storks, ibises, herons, egrets, and birds of prey, as well as deer, wild hogs, river otters, turtles, and alligators. Fishing is for bass, panfish, catfish, and speckled perch.

Downstream paddling on this placid river is easy for paddlers of all ages. Trips run year-round.

Canoe Outfitters of Florida, Inc.
Eric and Sandy Bailey
16346 N. 106th Terrace
Jupiter, FL 33478
(407) 746-7053
Loxahatchee River
Max. rapids: None
PPA, Florida Association of Canoe Liveries and Outfitters

Canoe Outfitters of Florida has 1-day canoe trips on a section of Loxahatchee River designated as part of the Wild and Scenic river system. Trips pass through pristine countryside with 500-year-old cypress trees and other native vegetation sheltering ospreys, eagles, owls, snakes, and turtles.

Trips also offer a chance to camp, see manatees, and fish for bass, brim, snook, and tarpon.

Canoe Outpost - Peace River
Becky Bragg
2816 NW County Rd. 661
Arcadia, FL 33821
(941) 494-1215
Peace River
Max. rapids: None
PPA, Florida Association of Canoe Liveries and Outfitters

Canoe Outpost — Peace River offers canoe and kayak trips along Florida's most popular State Canoe Trail. For the novice or the experienced paddler, the flat blackwater of the scenic Peace River offers opportunities for picnicking, swimming, fossil hunting, fishing, wildlife observation, and camping along its lush banks. Fishing is for bass, catfish, bream, and snook, and paddlers may see alligators, birds, deer, wild hogs, and turkey.

Trips of 1/2 day to 8 days are available. Canoe Outpost, open year-round, offers group discounts.

Canoe Outpost - Suwannee River
David Pharr
Rte. 1, Box 98A
Live Oak, FL 32060
(800) 428-4147
*Suwannee, North Withlacoochee, and
Alapaha Rivers.*
Max. rapids: III-IV
PPA, FACLO

Open year-round, Canoe Outpost
rents canoes and kayaks for trips of 1-20
days. These rivers' clean, black waters
offer easy to moderate paddling and are
good for all skill levels. As they round
sharp bends and dodge occasional
shoals, paddlers can enjoy clear springs,
white sandbars, and limerock cliffs.

Fishing for panfish, catfish, bass, and
perch is good. Local wildlife includes turtles, deer, otters, beavers, and alligators.

Canoe Outpost - Withlacoochee
George Blust
P.O. Box 188
29135 Lake Lindsey Rd.
Nobleton, FL 34661
(904) 796-4343
Withlacoochee River South
Max. rapids: None
PPA, FACLO

Canoe Outpost offers easy, unguided
trips of five to 83 miles on the winding
Withlacoochee, with its state forest
lands and abundant wildlife. These tours
can last up to a week, allowing paddlers
ample time to explore and fish for bass,
catfish, and panfish. Alligators, turtles,
hogs, wild turkeys and numerous birds
may be seen. Camping is available, with
all the necessary gear available for rent.
Canoe Outpost is open year-round.

Canoe Safari
Dan & Susan Neads
3020 NW CR 661
Arcadia, FL 33821
(941) 494-7865
Peace River
Max. rapids: None
PPA, *Florida Association of Canoe Liveries
& Outfitters*

Canoe Safari rents canoes and offers
guided canoe trips to people of all ages
on the aptly-named Peace River, described as the most unspoiled river in
southwestern Florida. These easy floats
last anywhere from 1/2 day to 8 days.

An unusual feature of the river is that
it is rich in shark's teeth, bones, and
other fossils. It also has nice sandy
beaches for camping and swimming. Paddlers find alligators, river otters, turtles
and other wildlife, and enjoy great fishing for bass, bream, and catfish. Canoe
Safari is open year-round.

Cypress Springs
Harold & Linda Vickers
Box 726
Vernon, FL 32462
(904) 535-2960
Cypress Springs, Holmes Creek
Max. rapids: None

This outfitter rents canoes, kayaks
and tubes year-round for paddling on
the crystal-clear waters of Cypress
Springs. Canoes, kayaks, and tubes are
rented for half-day and full-day trips.
Camping and bass fishing are available.
Around 90 million gallons of water flow
from Cypress Springs daily, providing
ideal conditions for swimming and scuba
diving.

Escape Tours Outfitters
Marilyn Laughlin & Carl Reinsch
32422 Red Oak Drive
Eustis, FL 32736-9589
(800) 589-7978, FAX (904) 483-3555
*Many rivers, lakes and ocean locations
around the state*
Max. rapids: None

An all-inclusive tour company, Escape Tours offers both scheduled trips
and customized tours around Florida
and its offshore islands. It does not rent
boats, but provides kayaking trips lasting
up to 10 days, with expert guides who
can escort skilled as well as novice paddlers. Catering to individuals and
groups, Escape Tours organizes trips to
secluded rivers, mangrove islands, white

sandy beaches and the Florida Keys. Paddlers enjoy serenity, beauty, wildlife and all kinds of fishing.

Estero River Tackle & Canoe Outfitters

Paula Stuller
20991 S. Tamiami Trail
Estero, FL 33928
(813) 992-4050
Estero River, Estero Bay and environs
Max. rapids: None
PPA, ACA, Florida Association of Canoe Liveries and Outfitters

Open year-round, Estero River has half-day and full-day canoe and kayak rentals on the Estero River. The river is tidal and spring-fed, suited for leisurely canoeing and excellent saltwater fishing for snook, mangrove snapper, and sea trout.

An acclaimed four-and-a-half mile Florida-designated canoe trail leads to Estero Bay through a picturesque semi-tropical landscape.

Camping is available at the nearby Koreshan State Historical Site.

Gulf Coast Kayaking Co.

Frank Stapleton/Cindy Bear
4882 NW Pine Island Rd.
Matlacha, FL 33909
(941) 283-1125, FAX (941) 283-7034
Matlacha Pass Aquatic Preserve, Pine Is.
Sound Wildlife Refuge
Max. rapids: None
TASK, PPA

Gulf Coast runs guided kayak trips and rents canoes and kayaks year-round for people interested in nature. Suitable for beginners, these outings enable paddlers to relax and enjoy serenity while learning about the ecosystem.

The shallow, clear, brackish waters teem with wildlife amid a subtropical mangrove system. Manatees and dolphins may be seen, along with many shorebirds. Fish include redfish, snook and tarpon.

Huron Kayak & Canoe

Maks Zupan
Box 367
Everglades City, FL 33929
(941) 695-3666
10,000 Islands, Everglades Nat. Park,
all of S. Florida
Max. rapids: None

Run by a former world champion kayaker and canoeist, Huron Kayak & Canoe introduces paddlers to the delights of mangrove tunnels, endless islands and the open Gulf of Mexico. It offers guided canoe and kayak trips as well as rentals for trips of 1-6 days amid dolphins, manatees, pelicans, and white egrets.

Suitable for novices, these trips emphasize technique, fitness, and the joys of the outdoor environment. Camping and swimming are available, and fishing is for snook, grouper, redfish, tarpon, and trout. The season runs Nov. 15-April 15.

Katie's Wekiva River Landing

Katie Moncrief
190 Katie's Cove
Sanford, FL 32771
(407) 322-4470, (407) 628-1482
Wekiva River, Little Wekiva River, Rock Springs Run, St. John's River
Max. rapids: None
PPA

Katie's Landing has guided trips and canoe and kayak rentals on sandy bottomed, spring-fed rivers. The waters are clean, gentle, and suitable for paddlers of all ages.

The rivers are zealously protected, designated as scenic and wild waters, outstanding Florida waters, an aquatic preserve, and a Florida State Canoe Trail. The water is so clear and clean that paddlers can easily see many varieties of aquatic vegetation and fish, including catfish, largemouth bass, and bream. Other wildlife to be seen include deer, raccoons, otters, black bears, alligators, turtles, herons, red-shouldered hawks, ospreys, and bald eagles.

Trips range in length from 1-3 days and are available year-round. Katie's Landing also offers cabin rentals, tent and R.V. sites, and a well-stocked country store.

Key West Kayak Co.
Jim and Ellen McCarthy
P.O. Box 4411
Key West, FL 33040
(305) 294-6494
Atlantic Ocean, Gulf of Mexico, mangrove creeks
Max. rapids: None

Key West Kayak Co. offers guided and unguided sea-kayak trips in the clear, shallow waters of the Atlantic Ocean and back country of the Gulf of Mexico. Trips last a half day or full day and concentrate on finding a wide variety of wildlife for paddlers to see. The clear waters allow easy viewing of sharks, rays, fish, sponges, coral, and other marine life. As they paddle on open water and down mangrove-lined creeks, guests can also see herons and egrets and fish for

tarpon, bonefish, snapper, and barracuda

Key West Kayak's trips, which run year-round, are leisurely, require no previous kayaking experience, and are fine for paddlers of all ages.

Little Manatee River Canoe Outpost
Frank & Jan Lapniewski
18001 US 301 South
Wimauma, FL 33598
(813) 634-2228, (800) 229-1371
Cockroach Bay
Max. rapids: None
PPA, Florida Association of Canoe Liveries

Paddlers of all skill levels can enjoy this outfitter's 1- and 2-day trips in Cockroach Bay, described as "one of the last healthy estuaries on Tampa Bay." Both guided and self-guided canoe and kayak outings are available.

Paddlers enjoy views of deer, hogs, otters, manatees, birds, and exotic vegetation. Camping and black bass fishing are also available during the year-round season.

Paddling on the Santa Fe River. Courtesy of Santa Fe Canoe Outpost, High Springs, Florida.

North American Canoe Tours

David Harraden
P.O. Box 5038
Everglades City, FL 33929
(941) 695-4666
Everglades Wilderness Waterway, 10,000 Islands, Turner River, Suwannee River
Max. rapids: None
PPA, Florida Association of Canoe Liveries and Outfitters

NACT has guided adventures and canoe and kayak rentals in the Everglades National Park, offering guests a chance to see alligators, manatee, bottlenose dolphins, sea turtles, and an abundance of aquatic life. Guided canoe trips are from 1-7 days through the mangrove forest backcountry, sawgrass prairies, and 10,000 Island areas. Adventures include all equipment and meals. Those wanting to explore on their own can rent a canoe and supplies, and receive help in planning their trips. Car shuttles to Flamingo are also available.

NACT provides accommodations at the Ivey House B&B and daily guided activities, including canoe or kayak treks. Adventures and services are available from November through April.

NACT also runs fall trips on the Suwannee River in Georgia and has its headquarters in Niantic, Conn. NACT can be reached in Conn. during the off-season.

Old Spanish Sugar Mill

Patricia Schwarze
P.O. Box 691
DeLeon Springs, FL 32130
(904) 985-5644
Spring Garden Creek (through Woodruff Wildlife Refuge)
Max. rapids: None

Located inside the DeLeon Springs State Recreation Area, Old Spanish Sugar Mill offers guided canoe trips and rents canoes, kayaks, and tubes for paddlers attracted by Florida's beautiful swamps and marshes. Although open year-round, the outfitter says these excursions are most pleasant in the cooler months.

Trips are easy and fun, giving paddlers a view not only of the scenery with its cypresses and maples, but of alligators, bass, otters, and various birds.

Outdoor Adventures, Inc.

Howard Solomon
6110-7 Powers Ave.
Jacksonville, FL 32217
(904) 739-1960
Cumberland Island, Okefenokee Swamp, Suwannee, St. Marys, Silver and Ichetucknee Rivers, other inland and Atlantic coastal waters of northeast Florida and south Georgia
Max. rapids: I-II
America Outdoors, PPA, Florida Association of Canoe Liveries & Outfitters

Outdoor Adventures offers year-round guided tours to some of the most beautiful and remote places in Florida and Georgia, including the Okefenokee Swamp, Cumberland Island, and the Suwannee River. OA also offers North Florida's only A.C.A. certified instruction in both coastal kayaking and canoeing. Professional guides provide expert training and leadership for fully-outfitted day trips and overnight camping. Also available are bicycling tours and hot-air balloon flights.

Ray's Canoe Hide-Away

Richard & Audrey Lawrence
1247 Hagel Park Rd.
Bradenton, FL 34202
(941) 747-3909
Upper Manatee River
Max. rapids: None
PPA, FACLO

Ray's Canoe Hide-Away, open year-round, rents canoes for inexpensive trips lasting from 1/2 day to 4 days. These trips run through a beautiful, jungle-like environment that is increasingly hard to find in Florida.

Sub-tropical waters provide easy family paddling, and canoeists can watch various birds, turtles, and occasional alligators while fishing for catfish and bass.

Santa Fe Canoe Outpost
Jim and Sally Wood
P.O. Box 592
High Springs, FL 32655
(904) 454-2050
Santa Fe, Ichetucknee & Suwannee Rivers
Max. rapids: None
PPA, Florida Association of Canoe Liveries
and Outfitters

Santa Fe Canoe Outpost offers canoe
and kayak rentals for trips of 1-7 days on
the Santa Fe, Suwannee, and Ichetucknee Rivers. These spring-fed waters are
crystal-clear and offer easy paddling and
excellent fishing for bass, mullet, gar,
catfish, and perch. The banks, thickly
wooded with cypress trees, provide secluded sites for wilderness camping and
shelter abundant wildlife, including
alligators, deer, beavers, turtles, snakes,
otters, wild boars, and a wide variety of
birds.

Santa Fe Outpost, open year-round,
also offers custom trips, guided, full-
moon night trips, and complete or partial outfitting for those needing camping
gear. Catered group/corporate outings
are now available.

Paddling in the Everglades from a base
aboard a houseboat. Courtesy of Wilderness
Southeast.

Snook Haven Restaurant & Fish Camp
5000 E. Venice Ave.
Venice, FL 34292
(941) 485-7221, (941) 484-2553
Myakka River
Max. rapids: None

Snook Haven rents canoes year-
round for day trips on the generally calm
waters of the Myakka River, with its
typical Florida woodland scenery and
wealth of wildlife. Since the river has
very little current, it is suitable for
novices, kids, and older citizens. Alligators, turtles, otters, raccoons, and birds
may be seen, while bass, snook, redfish
tarpon, bluegills, crappie and catfish rise
to the fisherman's bait.

Southern Exposure Sea Kayaks
Larry M. Willis
18487 S.E. Federal Hwy.
Tequesta, FL 33469
(407) 575-4530
Intracoastal Waterway, Loxahatchee River
Max. rapids: None
T.A.S.K.

Southern Exposure runs guided and
self-guided sea kayaking trips for everyone from novices to expert paddlers.
The waters range from the primitive
beauty of the Loxahatchee to the Intracoastal Waterway. Paddlers can see alligators, dolphins, and abundant birds
and fish.

The company prides itself on its
knowledge of local flora and fauna,
excellent paddling instruction, safety,
and year-round service.

Southern River Sports

John & Vivian Farnsworth
4836 Bonita Beach Rd. S.W.
Bonita Springs, FL 33923
(813) 495-6676
Everglades and any rivers on Florida's west coast
Max. rapids: None
PPA

South River rents kayaks and runs guided kayak trips year-round for people of all skill levels. The paddling, along the Gulf coast or in backwaters and rivers, is mostly easy. But rough-sea kayaking is also available in season. Paddlers can enjoy a profusion of wildlife, with virtually every migratory bird and hundreds of year-round species. There is also good fishing for grouper, trout, snook, bluefish, and other fresh and saltwater fish.

TnT Hideaway, Inc.

Gretchen E. Evans
527 Coastal Hwy.
Crawfordville, FL 32327
(904) 925-6412
Wakulla River
Max. rapids: None

TnT Hideaway rents canoes year-round for half-day trips on the clean and treelined Wakulla River. It rises at the Wakulla Springs Wildlife Refuge only three miles north of the outfitter's location — a good half-day paddle. Wildlife includes alligators, manatees, turtles, otters, wading birds, eagles, wood ducks, and osprey. Catfish, mullet, bass, sheephead and bream may be caught.

Turner's Camp

Dennis and Alicia Lowe
033 Hooty Point
Inverness, FL 32650
(904) 726-2685
Withlacoochee River, Gum Slough
Max. rapids: None

Turner's Camp offers one-day guided canoe tours and rentals on the Withlacoochee River and Gum Slough. Trips are five or 10 miles long, on placid waters suitable for paddlers of all ages.

The Withlacoochee is a scenic river in a mostly undeveloped setting. Gum Slough is clear, spring-fed, and completely undeveloped. On both waters paddlers can see deer, wild hogs, alligators, otters, bald eagles, ospreys, and anhinga. There is also good fishing for largemouth bass, catfish, and eight varieties of panfish.

Turner's Camp, open year-round, also offers cabin rentals and tent and R.V. camping.

Up The Creek

Robert Samson
6250 N. Andrews Ave., Ste. 204
Fort Lauderdale, FL 33309
(954) 771-7175
Suwannee, Withlacoochee, Peace, Oklawaha Rivers. Most other Florida rivers. Everglades Nat. Park
Max. rapids: None
PPA

Operating year-round, Up The Creek runs customized, professionally-guided canoe trips to many destinations. These are suitable for beginners as well as experienced paddlers. Lasting up to a week, trips take clients to waters ranging from the Everglades to small spring-fed freshwater streams. On longer trips, paddlers may camp or stay in bed-and-breakfast lodgings with all meals and equipment included.

Armadillo, deer, beaver, and raccoons lurk in the woods, while fishing is mostly for bass, bluegill, snook and redfish.

Wilderness Southeast

711 Sandtown Road
Savannah, GA 31410
(912) 897-5108
Everglades - 10,000 Islands, Okefenokee Swamp, Georgia Atlantic Coast
Max. rapids: None

Wilderness Southeast is a nonprofit educational corporation that leads small groups on guided expeditions to teach participants about the natural history of unique wilderness ecosystems. A

4-day sea kayaking trip along Georgia's wild barrier islands allows ample time to explore marshland, beaches, and tidal creeks, and sight dolphins, shorebirds, and other abundant wildlife. Also in Georgia is a 5-day canoe trip through the wilderness of Okefenokee Swamp, which explores the peat prairies, towering cypress forests, and sandy pine islands.

In Florida's Everglades, Wilderness Southeast has 7-day canoe and sea-kayak trips spent exploring wild beaches, isolated coastal islands, and mangrove estuaries. On Everglades trips, guests sleep aboard a moving base of two houseboats.

Withlacoochee River RV Park & Canoe Rental, Inc.
Jim & Sue Nattrass
Box 114
Lacoochee, FL 33537
(904) 583-4778
Withlacoochee River
Max. rapids: None

Withlacoochee R.V. Park and Canoe rental offers 1- and 2-day canoe rentals for trips through lush wilderness on the Withlacoochee in westcentral Florida. Trips pass along placid waters through unspoiled cypress swamps and pine forests, site of ancient campgrounds of the Seminole Indians.

The Withlacoochee is a "blackwater" river, its waters tea-colored from the tannins in the vegetation. Fishing is for bass, brim, and catfish, and the wildlife to be seen includes birds, alligators, turtles, wild hogs, and deer.

Campsites are available for tents and R.V.s at the outfitter's campground, which is open year-round.

A nature-study trip in the Everglades. Courtesy of Wilderness Southeast, Savannah, Georgia.

Georgia

North Georgia's mountainous terrain is superb watersports country, offering a broad selection of rivers that enthrall novices and experts alike. There, for instance, is the Chattooga, whose fabled whitewater divides Georgia from South Carolina (for Chattooga River description see South Carolina). But while rafters brave the Chattooga rapids, less adventurous souls canoe quiet Georgia streams in search of wildlife lurking among mountain laurel and rhododendron. And down in the southeastern corner of the state lies Okefenokee Swamp, a naturalist's delight.

Start in the north with the Chestatee, where an easy day-trip run begins near Dahlonega and ends at Lake Sidney Lanier. It takes floaters through an area which was the scene of America's first gold rush, which began in 1828, 20 years before James Wilson Marshall's historic find at Sutter's Mill in California. Dahlonega itself, with its gold museum, is worth exploring. The lower Chestatee is runnable all year round but the upper Chestatee, with its Class I-III rapids, is much affected by water levels.

Another great stream for beginners — except at high water — is the Etowah, which can be run from Dahlonega to Rome. It is a river of rare beauty, enriched by thickets of mountain laurel, hemlock and rhododendron along its banks, interspersed with high rock bluffs and farmland. In the Chattahoochee National Forest the upper Etowah is little more than a stream, and it can only be run in early spring or after heavy rains. But the scenery is beautiful, there are ledges and rock gardens to enliven the float and plenty of places to camp and fish. The middle stretch of the Etowah has a 10-foot waterfall to portage and numerous Class II rapids. Further downstream the river turns calmer but still contains some easy rapids.

The Amicalola Creek is in fact a full-fledged river, spiced with lively Class II-III rapids and splendid scenery. It derives its name from a Cherokee phrase for tumbling water, and its upper east fork tumbles over Amicalola Falls. The state park named for these falls marks the southernmost end of the Appalachian Trail. Rapids on the Amicalola such as Edge of the World and Off the Wall are quite demanding. But the river is normally only runnable in the spring.

Also in this general area is the Toccoa River, which rises in Union County and flows northward through Blue Ridge Lake and onward into Tennessee. It has gentle Class I-II rapids, excellent scenery, clean water and good fishing. Southwest of the Toccoa runs Talking Rock Creek, which probably gets its name from the echo that comes from its cliffs in response. Talking Rock Creek actually runs through a handsome gorge with sheer walls up to 100 feet high. Access is difficult and water levels fluctuate greatly, so novices are advised to run it only when the water is low to moderate. But the rapids are seldom tougher than Class I-II.

Georgia has two other notable attractions for the canoeist: the Chattahoochee and Okefenokee. Like the Chestatee, the Chattahoochee River starts by running to Lake Sidney Lanier near the northern mountains. But then the Chattahoochee gathers strength and widens to a major artery, heading first for Atlanta and then bordering Alabama on its way southward to cross into Florida on its way to the Gulf of Mexico. Upstream of Atlanta the Chattahoochee provides some enjoyable woodland canoeing, followed by several miles of floating past many of Atlanta's finest suburban homes. But below Atlanta its charms diminish as dams and power boats proliferate. Atlanta's combined sanitary and sewage drain system overflows in heavy rainstorms, discharging up to 100 million gallons of untreated sewage a day into the Chattahoochee.

Okefenokee Swamp, covering an area of more than 600 square miles, is an experience — like Florida's Everglades — not to be missed. The name is a corruption of the Indian word Owaquaphenoga, meaning "trembling earth." Anyone boating in the swamp can see why; one can step "ashore" and find oneself swaying on an mass of densely matted floating vegetation. Some of these "islands" may already be occupied by basking alligators. Four-fifths of the swamp belongs to the Okefenokee National Wildlife Refuge, which allows canoe trips in rented or privately-owned boats. The slow-moving rain water, stained to tea color by tannic acid, is decked with waterlilies, bladderwort and other plants. The surface is so smooth that it reflects cypress, tupelo, oak and other trees with mirror-sharp clarity. Besides alligators, snakes, deer, otters and many varieties of birds turn this great unspoiled wilderness into a nature lover's paradise.

Appalachian Outfitters
Ben and Dana LaChance
Highway 60 South
P.O. Box 793
Dahlonega, GA 30533
(706) 864-7117, (800) 426-7117
Chestatee River, Etowah River
Max. rapids: II-III
PA, ACA

Appalachian Outfitters offers primarily unguided canoe and kayak trips on two Class I-III Georgia rivers. These trips range in length from two hours to two-and-a-half days, and are of varying difficulty, with pastoral beginning sections and challenging ledges, rapids, and rocks gardens to test the skills of experienced paddlers. Shuttle and guide services, paddling instruction and equipment are available.

Trips pass through quiet, beautiful terrain in the Appalachians, with hemlock and pine forests, laurel- and rhododendron-lined banks, and fishing for small and largemouth bass, trout, perch, crappie, bream, red-eye bass, and catfish. Wildlife seen include deer, beavers, otters, great blue herons, ospreys, turtles, and wood ducks.

Beacon Sports Center
Chris & Bill Campbell
Box 327 Hwy 52 East
Ellijay, GA 30540
(706) 276-3600
Cartecay River, also Amicalola, Taccoa,
Ellijay, Coosawatee Rivers
Max. rapids: III-IV
PA

Beacon Sports runs guided kayak trips and rents canoes, kayaks, and tubes for floats on what it calls the prettiest river in southern Appalachia. This is the Cartecay, which has mostly Class I water but some Class III rapids, so it is suitable for all skill levels.

Most of the other rivers used are Class I-IV and are located in state or national forests. Wildlife ranges from bear to bobcat, and the fishing is for all species of trout, bass, bream, and crappie.

Camping and paddling lessons are available during the March-October season.

Flint River Outdoor Center
Jim McDaniel
4429 Woodland Rd.
Thomaston, GA 30286
(706) 647-2633
Big Lazar Creek
Max. rapids: III-IV

This outfitter runs guided canoe and raft trips from April to October on a clean mountain stream amid rocky bluffs, rhododendrons, mountain laurel, and woodland. It also rents canoes and rafts and provides paddling lessons, camping, and fishing for bass, bream, and catfish.

Upstream trips have only Class I-II rapids and are suitable for beginners, while downstream waters are for advanced paddlers. Beaver, muskrat, otter, deer, turkey, and bobcat may be observed.

Raft, GA
Robert A. Reichert
P.O. Box 7363
Marietta, GA 30065
(404) 971-0707, (404) 971-6553 (off-season)
Chattahoochee River
Max. rapids: I-II

Raft, GA offers rentals for day trips on the Chattahoochee near Atlanta. The trips are mostly on flat water with some Class I and II rapids, suitable for paddlers of all ages and levels of experience. Wildlife to see include beavers, snakes, and raccoons. Fishing is for trout and bream Raft, GA's seasons runs from May through September.

River Through Atlanta
Christopher Scalley
3280 Old Alabama Rd.
Alpharetta, GA 30202
(770) 740-8779
Chattahoochee, Jack's, Conasauga,
Hiawassee Rivers
Max. rapids: I-II

This year-round outfitter specializes
in fly fishing for brown, rainbow and
brook trout, bass, and bream close to a
metropolitan area. It offers guided dory
trips and rents canoes, rafts and tubes,
and field trips to mountain streams that
are two hours away at most. The setting
is southern rural Piedmont — pretty
farmland and old stands of forest pine.
Guides offer instruction in both paddling and fishing skills.

S.C. Foster State Park
Georgia Department of Natural
Resources
Route 1, Box 131
Fargo, GA 31631
(912) 637-5274, (912) 637-5325
Okefenokee Swamp, access to
Suwannee River
Max. rapids: None

S.C. Foster State Park offers canoe
rentals for day trips on Billy's Lake in
Okefenokee Swamp and for overnight
camping trips in the Okefenokee National Wildlife Refuge. Paddling is easy
on the swamp's calm waters, which cast
mirror-like reflections and are tea-colored from tannic acid. The swamp is a
slow-flowing river, supporting varied
plant life including water lilies, bladderwort, neverwet, bald cypress, pond
cypress, tupelo, oaks, and pines. There
is fishing for bass, bream, catfish, jack,
and perch, and a chance to see snakes,
alligators, deer, foxes, squirrels, otters,
and many species of birds.

Southeastern Expeditions
50 Executive Park South,
Suite 5016
Atlanta, GA 30329
(800) 868-7238, (404) 329-0433
Ocoee (Tennessee) and Chattooga (Georgia,
South Carolina) Rivers
Max. rapids III-V
America Outdoors

Southeastern Expeditions offers guided
canoe, kayak, and raft trips from March
to October for paddlers age 10 to 80.

The company says its wide diversity o
trips caters to guests of all income
levels. Southeastern's Atlanta headquarters handles reservations; trips start
from its two outposts, on the Ocoee and
Chattooga Rivers.

Wildlife seen along these trips includes deer, opossum, raccoons, foxes,
ospreys, trout, crappie, and blue gill.

Suwannee Canal Recreation Area
Carl Glenn, Jr.
Rte. 2, Box 3325
Folkston, GA 31537
(800) SWAMP-96
St. Marys, Suwannee Rivers and
Okefenokee Swamp
Max. rapids: None

Exploration of beautiful Okefenokee
Swamp, with its unique scenery and
wildlife, is this outfitter's specialty. The
company provides guided trips by canoe
and kayak and rents canoes for trips of
up to 5 days through this maze of paddling trails. Since it is mostly flat water,
such outings are suitable for all ages. In
addition to alligators, bears and other
wildlife, the area abounds in fish rangin₂
from warmouth and bream to catfish
and jackfish.

Wilderness Southeast
711 Sandtown Road
Savannah, GA 31410
(912) 897-5108
Everglades - 10,000 Islands, Okefenokee
Swamp, Georgia Atlantic Coast
Max. rapids: None

Wilderness Southeast is a nonprofit

An alligator seen in the Okefenokee Swamp. Courtesy of Wilderness Southeast.

educational corporation that leads small groups on guided expeditions to teach participants about the natural history of unique wilderness ecosystems. A 4-day sea kayaking trip along Georgia's wild barrier islands allows ample time to explore marshland, beaches, and tidal creeks, and to sight dolphins, shorebirds, and other abundant wildlife. Also in Georgia is a 5-day canoe trip through the wilderness of Okefenokee Swamp, which explores the peat prairies, towering cypress forests, and sandy pine islands. On these trips, paddlers can also see frogs, alligators, owls, river otters, and cranes.

Wildewood Outpost
Anne Gale
P.O. Box 999
Helen, GA 30545
(706) 865-4451
Chattahoochee River
Max. rapids: I-II
PPA

Wildewood Outpost offers guided and unguided canoe and raft trips on the Chattahoochee. This scenic river offers paddlers a chance to view rhododendrons, mountain laurel, beavers, deer, turtles, snakes, and waterfowl. The river's clear waters contain trout, bass, and brim. The company's season goes from April to October.

Wildwater Limited
Jim Greiner
550 Fortson Rd.
Athens, GA 30606
(800) 451-9972
Chattooga, Nantahala, Ocoee,
Big Pigeon Rivers
Max. rapids: V+
America Outdoors

Wildwater Limited operates in Georgia, North Carolina, South Carolina, and Tennessee, offering more than a dozen trip options for paddlers age 8 and over, ranging from novices to experts. The Chattooga is a National Wild and Scenic River, the Nantahala adjoins the Great Smoky Mountains National Park, and the Ocoee has been chosen for the 1996 Olympic whitewater events.

The company has served over 400,000 customers in 25 years of operation, and prides itself on its staff, facilities, and safety record. It rents rafts and kayaks as well as running guided canoe, kayak and raft trips during a March-to-mid-November season.

Hawaii

Jungle rivers and sea kayaking are the twin delights of Hawaii for paddlers. Streams splash out of the verdant mountains on Kauai Island, cascading over waterfalls into deep valleys. Then they slow down and merge into 10 rivers that provide Class I waters ideal for family floating. These mini-rivers are insignificant by world standards but they can be floated year-round and are worth exploring for their scenery alone. Paddlers may find themselves in a pool at the foot of a spectacular waterfall, surrounded by tropical jungle. Looking up, they can admire fluted ridges in the forested hills above.

None of the other islands have canoeable rivers. But sea kayaking can be enjoyed off Kauai, Oahu, Maui, and possibly elsewhere in the Aloha State. Paddlers avoid northern shores when these are battered by heavy winter waves. Nevertheless, experienced sea kayakers contend with Pacific surf equivalent to Class IV whitewater. Some use "surf-skis" for surfing and racing — lightweight ultra-thin kayaks up to eight yards long (for the two-person craft) and less than twenty inches wide.

From June to August one can safely negotiate the 40-mile shoreline from Hana Bay to Kahului on the north coast of Maui in four to eight days. On this route, sea kayakers pass green jungle, small streams with waterfalls and low cliffs as they move from one beach landing to the next.

Amid the mountainous islands, day-trip ocean paddlers can explore caves and remote beaches so shut off by rugged cliffs that they are virtually inaccessible to shore hikers. They can look for whales, seals and turtles, fish for barracuda, or snorkel among reefs sparkling with small multicolored tropical fish.

Go Bananas Kayaks Hawaii
Gary Budlong
732 Kapahulu Ave.
Honolulu, HI 96816
(808) 737-9514
All ocean shorelines of Oahu Island
Max. rapids: None

Personalized sea kayaking trips geared to individuals are the specialty of Go Bananas Kayaks. Open year-round, the company provides guided trips and rents boats. Clients can snorkel and scuba dive in clear tropical waters, fish for papio, tuna, sailfish, and tropical reef ish, or simply admire the beautiful mountain scenery. When conditions are right, they can kayak surf. The company caters to all skill levels and provides lessons for novices.

Kayak Kauai Outbound
Micco and Chino Godinez
P.O. Box 508
Hanalei, HI 96714
(808) 826-9844, (800) 437-3507, FAX (808) 822-0577
10 rivers on Kauai, coastal waters
Max. rapids: III-IV
American Canoe Association. TASK

Kayak Kauai Outiftters offers guided and unguided canoe and kayak trips of 1-6 days along Kauai's jungle rivers and remote coastline. With Class I waters, the river trips are perfect for beginners, families, and anyone seeking a relaxing, scenic trip. These rivers offer stunning views of fluted ridges, green valleys, fern grottoes, and birds. Some rivers provide access to waterfalls, lagoons and wildlife preserves.

Equally scenic but more challenging are 1- to 6-day sea kayaking voyages. These offer sheer cliffs with dark sea caves, plunging waterfalls, remote beaches, and waters dotted with spinner dolphins, flying fish, turtles, and monk seals. In the summer, sea kayak the famed Na Pali coast of Kauai's north shore, considered one of the world's most challenging sea kayak trips, or, in winter, whale watch along Kipu Kai's remote south shore.

Kayak Kauai also offers sea kayak seminars and daily paddling and snorkel tours through the Hanalei National Wildlife Refuge, the Fern Grotto, and to Secret Falls.

Maui Sea Kayaking
Ron Bass
Box 106
Puunene, HI 96784
(808) 572-6299
Coastal waters around Maui
Max. rapids: None
ACA

Maui Sea Kayaking specializes in catering to clients of differing ability, including children and people with disabilities. It never takes out more than four clients on any guided trip and gives lessons to beginners. Paddlers enjoy typical Hawaiian scenery of rolling green jungles and lava flows. Humpback whales may be seen from November to April and dolphins at any time during the company's year-round season.

South Pacific Kayaks & Outfitters
Michael & Melissa McCoy
2439 So. Kihei Rd., 101B
Kihei, Maui, HI 96753
(808) 875-4848, (800) 77-OCEAN
505 Front Street
Lahaina, Maui, HI 96761
(808) 661-8400
Waters surrounding Maui. Cape Kinau,
La Perouse, Hana, Keanae
Max. rapids: None
ACA, Trade Association of Sea Kayaking

South Pacific Kayaks gears most of its sea kayaking trips to first-time paddlers, considering most river paddlers to be novices on the open ocean. The outfitter's new Jungle Coast tour requires previous experience, but trips are geared to all needs.

Open year-round, South Pacific Kayaks offers seaworthy, late-model kayaks for paddlers to enjoy majestic mountain scenery, giant sea cliffs, black lava, and magnificent whale-watching. Snorkel tours enable paddlers to watch tropical fish. Paddling lessons and camping are also available during the December to May season.

HAWAII

Idaho

The Snake, the Salmon, Hells Canyon — these are names to set the city dweller's imagination soaring. Mighty rivers, rugged mountains, Lewis an Clark floating their rafts into the unknown. Anyone entering this Idaho wil derness today can only be awestruck at the daring and endurance of th first white pioneers to cross the Rockies nearly 200 years ago.

Today the adventure is less daunting, but still to be savored. The Middl Fork of the Salmon, the Main Salmon (the original River of No Return) the Lower Salmon, the Snake, Selway, Payette, Lochsa, Owyhee, Moyie an St. Joe rivers — all told they provide hundreds of miles of magnificen floating for rafters of all tastes and abilities.

The Salmon's Middle Fork offers some of the best whitewater in the Wes Rafters may begin their 100-mile journey at nearly 6,000 feet altitude in th crisp cool air of a conifer forest. Then as sidestreams swell the current i churns through more than one hundred rapids, graded Class I-IV. In June when the spring runoff is at its peak, whitewater enthusiasts are in thei element. July and August bring medium flows and warmer weather, allow ing paddlers to relax in the biggest wilderness of the lower 48 states, the 2. million-acre River of No Return Wilderness. Forests and granite cliffs con trast with Alpine meadows ablaze with Indian paintbrush and other wild flowers. Bighorn sheep and mule deer eye passing rafts while eagles soa above. Hot springs enable swimmers to wallow in warm water at the end o the day.

Congress has designated the Middle Fork as a Wild and Scenic River t ensure that it will remain forever free from dams, powerboats, roads an pollution. Six-day river tours start from the tiny frontier town of Stanle with its miners' log cabins and dirt streets. Near the lower end of Middl Fork lies Impassable Canyon, whose craggy cliffs rise higher than the wall of the Grand Canyon. It is indeed virtually impassable except by raft, an its Class IV rapids provide a whitewater climax to the trip.

Shoshone Indians called the Main Salmon Aggipah — big fish water — but never tried to run it in their frail canoes. Nor did even Lewis and Clar dare attempt its formidable miledeep canyon. But today it attracts man rafters, some as early as April-May to admire its big game and wildflowers. Whitewater enthusiasts come in June-July as the melting snow sets the river rampaging over classic rapids like Elkhorn and Big Mallard. Families enjoy the calmer waters of midsummer and fishermen bring their rods in October-November, steelhead season. People stop to study Indian pictographs, examine prospectors' cabins and optimistically pan for gold.

Lower Salmon (or Salmon River Canyons) trips generally begin from Whitebird and take the rafter through volcanic canyons down to the Salmon's confluence with the Snake. Often they take in a section of the Snake as well. Since the Lower Salmon is usually too high to float in June, outfitters tend to run trips from July through September. This is a favorite season for family rafting, with white sandy beaches providing ideal campsites beside 70-degree water for swimming. Yet the Lower Salmon is not without excitement as its rapids still give rollercoaster rides.

The Snake provides the biggest rapids in the Pacific Northwest as it courses through Hells Canyon, flanked by snowcapped peaks 8,000 feet above sea-level. Dividing Idaho from Oregon, it is the deepest canyon in North America and it ranks as another National Wild and Scenic River. Described as a fisherman's paradise, it is rife with trout and smallmouth bass. Outfitters offer 5-6 day trips, sometimes combined with two or three days of horseback riding.

Utterly challenging is the Lochsa River, a raging torrent with the wildest whitewater in Idaho. Its season is May through July and outfitters recommend previous paddling experience. Along its course from the Bitterroot Mountains to its confluence with the Selway and Clearwater rivers, the Lochsa charges through more than 40 major rapids. No Idaho stream offers more continuous whitewater, yet paddlers can relax under the stars on islands amid the white pines and cedars.

Less traveled is the Owyhee amid the desert canyons of southwestern Idaho, raftable only during the spring snowmelt. It is a naturalist's delight with nesting ducks and geese, otter, beaver and desert bighorn sheep that scale the canyon walls. Indian rock carvings and cowboy cabins adorned with old cooking stoves and waterwheels may also be seen. Another river raftable only in springtime is the Moyie, a whitewater stream for beginners as well as experts. The Moyie lies in the northeast corner of the Idaho panhandle and crosses the Canadian border. A little further south is an appealing stream for family rafting, the St. Joe. Near Boise, the state capital, runs the Payette, known for its whitewater as well as its scenery. And the beautiful Clearwater, formed at Three Rivers from the Selway and the Lochsa, is famous for its steelhead fishing.

Tappan Falls on the Middle Fork of the Salmon. Courtesy of Bill Bernt, Aggipah River Trips, Salmon, Idaho.

Adventure Connection, Inc.
Nate Rangel
P.O. Box 475
Coloma, CA 95613
(800) 556-6060, (916) 626-7385
North, Middle and South Forks of the American River, Upper Klamath River, Stanislaus River, Kaweah River, Middle Fork of the Salmon, Sacramento River (canoe trips only)
Max. rapids: IV
America Outdoors, California Outdoors, Friends of the River, American Rivers

Adventure Connection offers luxury river vacations of 1, 2, and 6 days on the finest rivers in California and Idaho. Trips range from easy canoe excursions suitable for children 5 and older, on up to advanced whitewater trips. Special half-price family trips, group discounts, and free trips for group leaders are available.

Adventure Connection offers highly experienced guides, deluxe camping facilities, gourmet food and fine wines and beer served with every dinner.

Aggipah River Trips
Bill Bernt
P.O. Box 425
Salmon, ID 83467
(208) 756-4167
Middle Fork, Lower, and Main Salmon Rivers
Max. rapids: III-IV
Idaho Outfitters and Guides Association

Aggipah River Trips runs paddle-raft, oar-raft, dory, and inflatable kayak trips on the Salmon River. Trips last 3-6 days and allow time for stops to fish, look at old prospector's cabins and Indian pictographs, pan gold, pick berries, and soak in hot springs. During summer trips, guests invariably see bighorn sheep and eagles and often spot deer, minks, and otters. During spring trips, deer, elk, and bighorn sheep are common and it's not unusual to see mountain goats and bears.

Aggipah also offers drift boat fly fishing trips, horseback/float combination trips, and lodge trips in which guests stay in lodges each night. With the various boat and lodging offerings, Aggipah has trips suitable for guests of all tastes and ages.

WILDERNESS WHITEWATER

on Idaho's Salmon River

Middle Fork, Main & Lower Salmon

We offer premium whitewater trips on the Middle Fork, family-focus trips on the Main Salmon, special fishing trips for trout and steelhead, lodge trips with no camping and off-season trips for maximum solitude.

Owner-operated, 25 years on the Salmon

Bill Bernt
Aggipah River Trips
PO 425PA
Salmon, Idaho 83467
208-756-4167
day or evening

American River Touring Association
Steve Welch
24000 Casa Loma Rd.
Groveland, CA 95321
(800) 323-2782, (209) 962-7873
Middle Fork and Main Salmon Rivers, Selway River, Merced River, Tuolumne River, Klamath River, Rogue River, Illinois River, Umpqua River, Green River, Yampa River, Colorado River
Max. rapids: IV
America Outdoors, Oregon Guides and Packers, Idaho Outfitters and Guides, Utah Guides and Outfitters

ARTA offers a total of 16 raft trips in five western states. The trips, in California, Oregon, Utah, Idaho, and Arizona, are by oar rafts, paddle rafts, oar/paddle combination rafts, and inflatable canoes.

Most trips are of Class III difficulty and appropriate for novices and families, as well as those with more experience. Other trips of up to Class V+ challenge even the most advanced paddler. Depending on the location, the trips feature such added attractions as wildflowers, side streams, swimming holes, Indian ruins, warm water, abundant wildlife, good hiking and fishing, and hot springs.

ARTA, a non-profit company, also offers whitewater schools, professional guide training, and family discounts.

Canyons Incorporated
Les and Susan Bechdel
P.O. Box 823
McCall, ID 83638
(208) 634-4303, FAX (208) 634-4766
Middle Fork and Main Salmon Rivers
Max. rapids: III-IV
Idaho Outfitters and Guides Association, America Outdoors

Canyons Incorporated runs 6-12 day guided trips on the Main Salmon River and the Middle Fork of the Salmon. Guests choose the degree of challenge they want: oar rigs, paddle rafts, duckies, hard kayaks, and canoes. With this range of offerings, there's a trip and boat to fit anyone from a complete beginner to an expert. Both the Main Salmon and Middle Fork of the Salmon offer spectacular scenery, clear water, and tremendous fishing. Guests also can view Indian pictographs and remnants of the gold-mining boom.

Lessons are also available, as Canyon's guides are certified canoe/kayak instructors with many years of experience. Owners Les Bechdel and his wife, Susan, have led river expeditions on four continents. Les is a leading authority on whitewater and co-author of the book *River Rescue*. He is also a four-time national champion who has represented the United States in five world championships.

Cascade Recreation
Steve Jones
Route 1, Box 117 A
Horseshoe Bend, ID 83629
(800) 292-7238
Payette River, Main Salmon River
Max. rapids: III-IV
Idaho Outfitters and Guides Association, America Outdoors

Cascade Recreation specializes in guided paddle raft and kayak trips on the Payette River in Boise National Forest. 1-day trips on the Main Payette, South Fork, and North Fork each have their own distinct character, ranging from gentle, scenic trips to exciting runs through steep canyons and Class III-IV rapids. Also available are 2- and 3-day trips on the South Fork of the Payette, a 6-day trip down the Main Salmon, custom tours lasting up to 18 days, and rafting/horsepacking trips.

Cascade Recreation's trips run between May and October and feature good opportunities to fish for rainbow, cutthroat, and brown trout and view bears, moose, elk, deer, otters, beavers, and birds.

Castaway Fly Fishing Shop

Joe Roope
3620 N. Fruitland
Coeur d'Alene, ID 83814
(208) 765-3133
Coeur d'Alene River, St. Joe River
Max. rapids: I-II

Castaway Fly Fishing Shop offers customized trout-fishing trips on the Clark's Fork River in Montana and the St. Joe and Coeur d'Alene Rivers in Idaho. These dory trips last 1-3 days and pass through pristine wilderness with abundant wildlife and excellent fishing for rainbow and cutthroat trout. Among the wildlife to see are elk, deer, bears, beavers, and sheep. Castaway's season runs from May to October.

Davis Whitewater Expeditions

Lyle Davis
Box 86
Winnemucca, NV 89445
(800) 261-9451, (702) 623-2048
FAX (702) 623-5194
Snake, Owyhee, Lower Salmon Rivers
Max. rapids: V

Davis Whitewater Expeditions offers guided kayak and raft trips on the Owyhee River, on the Snake River through Hell's Canyon and in the Gorge of the Lower Salmon. These tours pass through deep, narrow, high-desert canyons, offering pristine wilderness; excellent fishing for trout, bass, catfish, and sturgeon; swimming, and a chance to spot bears, otters, elk, goats, sheep, and raptors.

Trips are small and personal, provide good food and last 3-6 days. Davis expeditions, which run between April and October, vary greatly in difficulty from gentle, scenic excursions to very demanding Class V adventures. Both oar-powered and paddle trips are available.

Eakin Ridge Outfitters

LaMont Anderson, Bud & Gayla Lesley
P.O. Box 1382
Salmon, ID 83467
(208) 756-2047
Main Salmon River
Max. rapids: None
Idaho Outfitters & Guides Association

Eakin Ridge Outfitters offers leisurely guided raft floats, in a beautiful mountain wilderness, for everyone from children to grandparents. Trips normally last 1 or 2 days, and offer fishing, camping, and swimming. The company also offers combined tours that include horseback riding or jet boat trips in addition to rafting.

Paddlers may also spot elk, deer, and bears, and fish for trout, whitefish, and steelhead. The season runs from May to September.

ECHO: The Wilderness Company

Dick Linford and Joe Daly
6529 Telegraph Avenue
Oakland, CA 94609
(510) 652-1600, (800) 652-ECHO
Middle Fork and Main Salmon Rivers
Max. rapids: III-IV
Idaho Outfitters and Guides Association

ECHO runs guided trips on the Main Salmon and Middle Fork in Idaho; the Tuolumne and South Fork American in California, and the Rogue in Oregon. The company has 1-11 day trips available for paddlers at all skill levels. It offers a variety of boats, including inflatable kayaks, oar rafts, paddle rafts, and oar/paddle rafts.

ECHO also offers a large number of special trips, including White (and Red) Wine and Whitewater; Bluegrass on Whitewater; River Trips for Kids, Yoga Workshop and the Rogue String Quartet. ECHO's season runs from April to September.

A five-year-old treasures her first steelhead, caught along the Salmon River. Courtesy of Bill Bernt, Aggipah River Trips, Salmon, Idaho.

Eclipse Expeditions
Wayne and Gloria Ferguson, Dan Clemens
P.O. Box 1043
Salmon, ID 83467
(800) 366-6246
Main Salmon River
Max. rapids: III-IV
Idaho Outfitters and Guides
Association, America Outdoors

Eclipse Expeditions has 3-6 day guided kayak, raft, and dory trips on the Main Salmon in the 2.3 million-acre Salmon River Wilderness Area.

Trips run between May and November, offering personal service for small groups and fine opportunities to fish and view wildlife. Eclipse also offer specialty trips, including photography seminars, continuing education trips, lodge trips, and steelhead fishing.

Epley's Whitewater Adventures
Ted & Karen Epley
P.O. Box 987
McCall, ID 83638
(208) 634-5173
(800) 233-1813
Lower Salmon River (Idaho)
Max. rapids: III-IV
Idaho Outfitters & Guides Association,
North American Outfitters, National Forest
Recreation Association

Epley's Whitewater Adventures offers 1-5 day guided raft trips from May to September for people of all ages. Trips run on the clean, scenic Lower Salmon River, which flows between high canyon walls with varied vegetation. Alternately wide and narrow, the canyon sports large sandy beaches good for camping and picnics.

This full-service company provides complete equipment for its guests, who need bring only personal clothing. Bass and trout fishing are excellent, and the canyon's abundant wildlife includes otters and eagles.

High Adventure River Tours
Randy McBride
P.O. Box 222
Twin Falls, ID 83301
(208) 733-0123
Snake River
Max. rapids: III-IV
Idaho Outfitters and Guides Association

High Adventure River Tours has 1-day guided and unguided trips on two sections of the Snake River. The Hagerman stretch is ideal for beginning rafters, offering Class I, II, and III rapids and fine fishing for rainbow and German trout. For those seeking more adventure, the company offers trips on the Murtaugh stretch, which has Class III and IV rapids and passes through the scenic 400-foot deep Snake River Canyon.

Both stretches boast abundant wildlife, including deer, ducks, and occasional eagles or coyotes.

Holiday River & Bike Expeditions, Inc.
544 East 3900 South
Salt Lake City, UT 84107
(801) 266-2087, (800) 624-6323
Snake River, Main and Lower Salmon Rivers, Lochsa River
Max. rapids: V+
Utah Guides and Outfitters

Holiday River Expeditions rents canoes and rafts and runs guided canoe, kayak, and raft trips on the Colorado, Green, San Juan, and Yampa Rivers in Utah and the Snake, Main Salmon, Lower Salmon, and Lochsa Rivers in Idaho. These trips last 1-12 days, offer oar and paddle options, and range in difficulty from beginners' runs to expert-level whitewater adventures. Floaters pass through pristine areas with spectacular scenery ranging from arid desert canyons to alpine forests. Along the way, guests can camp, swim, fish for trout, and catfish, and spot deer, bighorn sheep, raptors, otters, and beavers.

Holiday's season runs from April to October.

Hughes River Expeditions, Inc.
Jerry Hughes
P.O. Box 217
Cambridge, ID 83610
(208) 257-3477
Snake River, Middle Fork of the Salmon, Main Salmon River, Owyhee River, Bruneau River, Grande Ronde
Max. rapids: V+
Idaho Outfitters and Guides Association, America Outdoors

Hughes River Expeditions specializes in "first-class service on spectacular rivers." Trips last three to seven days and vary in difficulty with the river and type of boat selected. Oar rafts, paddle rafts, drift boats, and inflatable kayaks are available for trips on the Snake River, Middle Fork of the Salmon, Salmon River Canyon, Owyhee, and Bruneau. All trips offer excellent food, scenery, fishing, equipment, and supplies.

Of the rivers, Owyhee and Bruneau are exceptionally pristine, passing through desert canyonlands that are part of some of the country's most remote wilderness. The Bruneau, "an Idaho secret," is a guides' favorite.

Hughes River Expeditions also offers an array of 3-6 day fishing trips. Guests fish for smallmouth bass, cutthroat trout, rainbow trout, steelhead, white sturgeon, and channel catfish.

James Henry River Journeys
James Katz
P.O. Box 807
Bolinas, CA 94924
(415) 868-1836, (800) 786-1830
Main Salmon River
Max. rapids: III-IV
Idaho Outfitters and Guides

James Henry River Journeys runs guided canoe, kayak, and raft trips in California, Arizona, Idaho, Oregon, and Alaska. In California, the outfitter offers trips with Class II-III rapids, of 1-3 days, on the Stanislaus, East Fork of the Carson, and the Lower Klamath. In Arizona, the company runs Grand Canyon trips, with Class IV + rapids, of 6, 8, 9, 13, and 14 days. Trips in Idaho, of 4, 5 or 6 days, run on the Class III-IV Main Salmon. In Oregon, trips of 3, 4, and 5 days run on the Class III Rogue. Finally, in Alaska the company offers a natural history expedition on the Tatshenshini-Alsek Rivers.

Many special-interest trips are also available. These include Salmon River Bluegrass, Country, Folk, and Cajun Music Trips; Whitewater Workshops; Organizational Development and Teambuilding; Wine Tasting and Gourmet Cuisine; Lodge Trips on the Rogue and Salmon; Rogue and Salmon Natural History Trips; Alaska Nature Photography; and Alaska Wilderness Literature.

All trips run through especially scenic wilderness areas and are carefully planned to move at a leisurely pace, allowing ample time for side hikes, fishing, photography, and general relaxation. As a result, participation is open to anyone active and in good health. The company's season runs from May to September.

Kingfisher Expeditions
Steve Settles
P.O. Box 1095
Salmon, ID 83467
(208) 756-4688
Middle Fork and Main Salmon Rivers
Max. rapids: III-IV
Idaho Outfitters and Guides Association

Kingfisher Expeditions runs 1-6 day guided raft and dory trips on the Main Salmon and Middle Fork of the Salmon. Trips feature exciting rapids, good food, and ample time to swim, hike, fish, and soak in hot springs. Guests can also view Indian pictographs, pioneer's cabins, and abundant wildlife.

Kingfisher's trips are great for families and all those age eight and up. Also available are float/horseback packages through the Bighorns Crags and 1-5 day steelhead fishing trips.

Mackay Wilderness River Trips
Brent Estep
3190 Airport Way
Boise, ID 83705
(208) 344-1881, (800) 635-5336
Middle Fork and Main Salmon Rivers
Max. rapids: V+
Idaho Guides and Outfitters Association

Mackay Wilderness River Trips offers kayak rentals and guided trips by kayak and dory on the Middle Fork of the Salmon and the Main Salmon. Trips range in length from 3-11 days and in difficulty from easy to extremely challenging.

As one of the largest and oldest outfitters in Idaho, Mackay features excellent service, experienced staff, and trips and lessons suitable for all ages during its April-to-October season.

Bighorn sheep sighted along the Salmon River. Courtesy of Bill Bernt, Aggipah River Trips, Salmon, Idaho.

Middle Fork Wilderness Outfitters
Gary & Kitty Shelton
P.O. Box 575
Ketchum, ID 83340
(800) 726-0575, (208) 726-5999,
FAX: (208) 726-7086
Middle Fork Salmon River
Max. rapids: III-IV+
Idaho Outfitters and Guides Association

Middle Fork Wilderness Outfitters runs guided kayak, raft, and dory trips on the Middle Fork of the Salmon for guests age eight to 70. These trips last 4-6 days, include both oar-boat and paddle-boat options, and feature gourmet food, clean and comfortable camping, and views of the famous, rugged canyons and wilderness of Idaho's backcountry.

On these trips, which run from June to September, guests can view bighorn sheep and other wildlife and fish for rainbow, cutthroat, and Dolly Varden trout.

Nichols Expeditions
Chuck and Judy Nichols
497 North Main
Moab, UT 84532
(801) 259-3999, (800) 648-8488
Copper River, Green River, Koyukuk River,
Main Salmon River, Sea of Cortez,
Magdalena Bay
Max. rapids: II-IV
Utah Guides and Outfitters, Idaho Guides
and Outfitters

Some of the best whitewater in the lower 48 states awaits Nichols Expedition paddlers on Idaho's Salmon River. Guests help navigate paddle rafts through rollercoaster waves and boulder-studded rapids. These 5-day raft trips are suitable for families with children 7 and older.

A different kind of experience calls people to Nichols' 6-day Green River Wilderness Quest in Utah's Labyrinth Canyon. The trip's "movement and sensory awareness exercises that help tune in the wilderness within ourselves."

Nichols Expeditions also offers sea kayaking in Alaska (see Alaska listings), and Baja, Mexico. Operating year-round, Nichols Expeditions also offers mountain biking and charter combination trips.

Northwest River Co.
Doug Tims
P.O. Box 403
Boise, ID 83701
(208) 344-7119
Selway River
Max. rapids: V+
Idaho Outfitters and Guides Association, America Outdoors

Northwest River Co. offers guided 4- and 5-day raft trips on the Selway River from June 2 to July 21. Early in the season, high water levels make for difficult rapids that challenge experienced paddlers and are too difficult for most beginners. Later trips are great for anyone.

All Northwest River Company's trips on the Selway offer excellent rapids, water quality, and trout fishing in an exceptionally scenic area of granite mountains and virgin stands of pine, cedar, and fir. Wildlife to see includes bears, mountain lions, moose, deer, elk, birds of prey, and waterfowl. Fishing is for cutthroat trout and Dolly Varden.

Orion Expeditions, Inc.
James L. Moore and Emily Johnston
1516 11th Avenue
Seattle, WA 98122
(206) 322-9130, (800) 553-7466
Middle Fork and Lower Salmon Rivers
Max. rapids: V+
Idaho Outfitters and Guides, America Outdoors

Orion Expeditions offers whitewater and calm-water guided trips by raft and kayak on many of Washington's and Idaho's most exciting rivers, such as the Middle Fork Salmon, Lower Salmon, Skagit, Wenatchee, Sauk, Deschutes, and the legendary Skykomish. Some are of Class V + difficulty and strictly for

experts while others are suited to beginners. The landscape varies from Alpine to high desert canyon scenery. Orion's season runs from December to October and its trips, led by experienced and competent guides, last from 1-6 days.

Elk, bighorn sheep, black bears, eagles, and ospreys may be seen, and the rivers contain several species of trout.

Outdoor Adventures
Bob Volpert
P.O. Box 1149
Point Reyes, CA 94956
(415) 663-8300
Middle Fork and Main Salmon Rivers
Max. rapids: III-IV
America Outdoors, Idaho Outfitters and Guides, Oregon Outfitters Association

Outdoor Adventures specializes in guided raft trips and raft rentals on federally designated Wild and Scenic rivers in Idaho, Oregon, and California. In Idaho, 6-day trips are available on the Middle Fork of the Salmon and the Salmon River. Included are all shuttles from Boise, tents and sleeping bags, delicious on-river meals, quality guides, and Avon rafts.

In Oregon, 3- and 4-day trips are available on the Rogue River, featuring lively rapids, wonderful hiking trails, and abundant wildlife. On these trips, the last night is spent at Half Moon Bar, a rustic lodge by the river where paddlers can enjoy hot showers, comfortable beds, and home-cooked meals.

In California, Outdoor Adventures offers 2-day trips on the Tuolomne River, 3-day trips on the Forks of the Kern, and 1-day trips on the Upper Kern. These California trips offer some of the wildest whitewater in the country during the spring run-off in April and May. During this time, wetsuits and previous rafting experience are required. All other Outdoor Adventures trips are fine for families and beginners. The company's season is from June to September.

Ouzel Outfitters
Kent Wickham
Box 827
Bend, OR 97709
(503) 385-5947, (800) 788-RAFT
Lower Salmon River
Max. rapids: III-IV
Oregon Packers and Guides

Ouzel Oufitters specializes in trips of 1-5 days on the "loveliest and liveliest" rivers in the Northwest. These include the Rogue, North Umpqua, McKenzie, Lower and Middle Owyhee, and Deschutes Rivers in Oregon; the Lower Salmon in Idaho; and the Lower Klamath River in California. All trips but the Middle Owyhee runs have class III-IV rapids and are fine for families and guests of all levels of experience to paddle in paddle rafts, inflatable kayaks, or guide-accompanied, "row-your-own" oar-rafts. The Middle Owyhee run, with class IV-V rapids, is a challenging, expedition-like trip for adventurous, experienced rafters only.

Ouzel Outfitters' trips run between May and September. Depending on the river traveled, guests can view bears, deer, eagles, and otters, and fish for bass, trout, steelhead, and salmon.

R & R Outdoors, Inc.
Rob and Rex Black
HC2 Box 500
Pollock, Idaho 83547
(208) 628-3830, (800) 777-4676
Salmon River
Max. rapids: III-IV
Idaho Outfitters and Guides Association

R & R Outdoors, Inc. runs 1-13 day guided raft trips on the Salmon River from June to September, and fishing float trips from February to December. Offering both oar boats and paddle boats, R & R has trips suitable for river runners of all levels of ability.

R & R also offers several vacation packages that include a night in the outfitter's comfortable guest lodge, barbecue, and a "lumberjack breakfast" at the start or end of the trip. On the river,

R & R supplies all meals and tents, and offers guests ample opportunity to fish, view wildlife, and explore wilderness canyons and valleys.

ROW (River Odysseys West), Inc.
Peter Grubb
P.O. Box 579-PA
Coeur d'Alene, ID 83814
(208) 765-0841, (800) 451-6034
Snake River, Middle Fork and Main Salmon Rivers, Lochsa River, Moyie River, Owyhee River, St. Joe River, Selway River
Max. rapids: III-IV
America Outdoors, Idaho Outfitters and Guides Association, Oregon Packers and Guides

ROW, one of the country's best-known outfitters, offers a wide array of trips on Idaho rivers to suit adventurers of all ages and levels of ability. Trips vary in length from 1-17 days and offer wilderness scenery ranging from desert to high alpine terrain.

In addition to its diverse offerings, ROW also takes particular pride in the quality of its guides and its annual "Family Focus" trips, which are designed with special activities for children. On ROW's trips, which run between May and October, paddlers may see bears, moose, bighorn sheep, mountain goats, river otters, deer, elk, and eagles. Fishing is for cutthroat and rainbow trout, smallmouth bass, and sturgeon.

Salmon River Experience
812 Truman
Moscow, ID 83843
(208) 882-2385, (800) 892-9223
Salmon River, Snake River
Max. rapids: III-IV
Idaho Outfitters and Guides Association

Salmon River Experience runs 1-5 day guided trips on the Lower Salmon and Snake Rivers. The 1- and 2-day Salmon trips take in some of the river's most spectacular rapids on scenic stretches lined with white, sandy beaches. The 3-5 day trips run on the lower gorge through steep rock canyons

The upper end of the Middle Fork of the Salmon River in Idaho. Courtesy of Bill Bernt, Aggipah River Trips, Salmon, Idaho.

that are accessible only by water. Fishing is good and wildlife is abundant. Deer, elk, moose, bears, mountain goats, and eagles can be seen.

Excellent meals and guided oar and paddle boats ensure comfort and safety for beginners, but even the most advanced boaters find challenge in inflatable kayaks. SRE's season runs from June to September and includes special trips, such as a "mining history" trip and 2-day and 3-day mountain bike/rafting trips. The mountain bike portion of the latter runs through the Nez Perce National Forest high above the Salmon River, next to the Gospel Hump Wilderness Area, offering breathtaking views, visits to ghost towns, and chances to view wildlife.

Salmon River Outfitters
Steven Shephard
P.O. Box 32
Arnold, CA 95223
(800) 346-6204
Salmon River
Max. rapids: III-IV
Idaho Outfitters and Guides Association
Salmon River Outfitters offers 6-day guided raft and kayak trips on the Salmon River between June and October. By specializing on the Salmon River and running only one trip at time, the company provides knowledgeable, personal service. Salmon River Outfitters also provides all equipment and excellent food.

Silver Cloud Expeditions
Jerry Myers
P.O. Box 1006
Salmon, ID 83467
(208) 756-6215
Salmon River
Max. rapids: III-IV
Idaho Outfitters and Guides Association

Silver Cloud Expeditions provides guided kayak, raft, and dory trips of 1-6 days on the Salmon River. These trips offer beautiful wilderness camps, stunning scenery in the second-deepest canyon in North America, and a chance to view golden eagles, bighorn sheep, river otters, and other wildlife. The Salmon River also offers excellent trout fishing. In addition, guests on these trips can snorkel, pan for gold, hike, swim, soak in hot springs, explore historical sites, eat good food, and enjoy nightly programs on natural history, fly fishing, gold mining, and other topics.

The trips, offered between March and October, vary widely in difficulty. Novices and families with children age seven and up can choose to ride in oar boats rowed by guides; the more adventurous may prefer to paddle rafts or inflatable kayaks.

Solitude River Trips, Inc.
Al and Jeana Bukowsky
P.O. Box 907
Merlin, OR 97532
(503) 476-1876
Middle Fork Salmon River
Max. rapids: III-IV
Idaho Outfitters and Guides Association,
America Outdoors

Solitude River Trips offers guided kayak, raft, and McKenzie drift boat trips of 5 and 6 days on the Middle Fork of the Salmon River. These trips offer challenging whitewater, terrific fly-fishing for rainbow and cutthroat trout, and stunning, varied scenery, which includes alpine meadows, rock-strewn gorges, and desert. These trips, available with either paddle-boat or oar-boat option, are easy enough for people of all ages. Along the way, participants can enjoy swimming, camping, fly-fishing lessons, and a chance to spot deer, elk, sheep, goats, bears, cougars, and eagles. Solitude's season is from June to September.

Sun Valley Rivers Co.
Jon McGregor
P.O. Box 1776
Sun Valley, ID 83353
(208) 726-7404
Middle Fork of the Salmon River
Max. rapids: III-IV
Idaho Outfitters & Guides Association

Sun Valley Rivers offers guided kayak, raft, and dory tours through total wilderness, with top equipment and guides. Trips last from 1-5 days between June 1-September 30. With the spring runoff, the whitewater is best in June and July. Trout fishing begins in July, reaches its peak in August, and continues into September, when bird hunting starts.

Elk, deer, bears, bighorn sheep, and various birds can be seen.

Wapiti River Guides
Gary Lane
Box 1125
Riggins, ID 83549
(208) 628-3523, (800) 488-9872
Salmon River, Grande Ronde River,
Owhyhee River, rivers throughout Alaska
Max. rapids: V+
Oregon Guides and Packers Association,
Idaho Outfitters and Guides Association

Wapiti River Guides, with trips in Idaho, Oregon, and Alaska, specializes in small personalized trips of moderate difficulty "for ages 3 to 103, families, and nature lovers." The outfitter's trips are distinctive, too, for their guides' emphasis on natural history and Native American culture, and for the fine scenery, which includes caves, spires, pictographs, petroglyphs, and historic sites.

Trips, ranging in length from 1-12 days, also allow time for interesting side hikes and viewing elk, deer, bald eagles, bobcats, cougars, bears, bighorn sheep, minks, and other wildlife. Fishing is for steelhead, trout, and bass.

Warren River Expeditions, Inc.
Dave Warren
Box 1375
Salmon, ID 83467
(208) 756-6387, (800) 765-0421
Main Salmon River
Max. rapids: III-IV
Idaho Outfitters and Guides Association

Warren River Expeditions runs 3-8 day guided and unguided trips on the Main Salmon, offering paddlers raging whitewater and the scenic beauty of Idaho's "Frank Church — River of No Return" Wilderness. Guided trips are by canoe, kayak, or raft, with trips available for guests of all ages. All kayak schools and kayak support trips are run in conjunction with regularly scheduled raft trips. This allows kayakers to spend time on the river with non-kayaking family and friends.

All trips include two nights in spectacular backcountry lodges, one the first night and one the middle night. Warren River Outfitters also offers a unique trip in which guests spend each night at a different backcountry guest ranch. These guest-ranch trips generally run in April, May, late August, and September.

During Warren River's April-to-October season, the outfitter also offers kayak lessons and rentals.

Western River Expeditions
Larry Lake
7258 Racquet Club Drive
Salt Lake City, UT 84121
(801) 942-6669, (800) 453-7450 (outside UT)
Main Salmon River, Colorado River, Green River
Max. rapids: III-IV
America Outdoors

Western River Expeditions runs guided raft trips and rents rafts and inflatable kayaks on the Colorado River in Colorado, Utah, and Arizona; the Green River in Utah; and the Main Salmon in Idaho. Green River trips, by oar or paddle raft, provide thrilling whitewater and views of towering red rock cliffs and arches, deep gorges, frontier cabins, and Indian petroglyphs. Colorado River tours offer spectacular scenery in Cataract Canyon, Westwater Canyon or the Upper and Lower Grand Canyon. Rapids are moderate to large, and paddlers can swim, take side hikes and view historic Indian and Old West sites. Finally, trips on the Main Salmon feature scenic blue-green waters, pine-covered mountains, stops at hot springs and abandoned mining camps, and camping on white sand beaches.

All trips are suitable for anyone of good health above the minimum age set for each trip, depending on its difficulty. During Western River's March-September season, some trips can be combined with a ranch stay.

White Otter Outdoor Adventures
Randy Hess
P.O. Box 2733
Ketchum, ID 83340
(208) 726-4331, (208) 838-2406
Main Salmon River
Max. rapids: V+
Idaho Outfitters and Guides Association

White Otter Outdoor Adventures has personable, experienced guides and more than 20 years' experience running trips on wild rivers. The company offers 1-day guided kayak and raft trips and rentals of canoes, kayaks, and rafts. Its trips on the Snake River have Class IV and V rapids and are designed for experienced rafters looking for the best in whitewater excitement.

Trips on the headwaters of the Salmon are calmer, suited for beginners, families, and those seeking more time for fishing, photography, and viewing wildlife. The Salmon is also an excellent river for beginners to learn kayaking in open, inflatable kayaks.

During the season from May to October, White Otter also offers dinner trips, gourmet food, and side trips to the Yankee Fort Dredge, the ghost town of Custer, and a working gold mine.

Whitewater Voyages
William McGinnis
P.O. Box 20400
El Sobrante, CA 94820-0400
(510) 222-5994, (800) 488-RAFT
Colorado River, Kern River, Merced River, Tuolumne River, Cache Creek, American River, Yuba River, Klamath River, Stanislaus River, Trinity River, Middle Fork Salmon River, Rogue River
Max. rapids: III-IV
America Outdoors, American River Recreation Association

Whitewater Voyages offers an extensive array of trips, with guided oar- and paddle-boat runs in California, Arizona, Oregon, and Idaho. Trips by kayak and raft range in length from 1-5 days and in difficulty from Class II to Class V. With runs on nine Wild and Scenic Rivers and on more California rivers than any other outfitter, Whitewater Voyages has trips for paddlers of all level of experience.

The outfitter also has specialty trips, including whitewater schools, family trips, low-cost river-cleanup trips, "team-building" trips and excursions in the former Soviet Union to paddle with Russians as part of project R.A.F.T.

Illinois

Smoothed by ancient glaciers, the land of Illinois is bordered by the Mississippi, Ohio and Wabash Rivers and Lake Michigan. The hills of the Illinois Ozarks in the southern tip of the state mark where the glaciers stopped their planing action. Across the rest of the state, most rivers are slow and meandering. Illinois is not renowned for either whitewater or crystal-clear water; it is after all the home of Big Muddy River, Little Muddy River and Muddy Creek. But one of the great assets of Illinois for the paddler is that the state government is most helpful. Its tourist office publishes a highly informative map of the canoeing rivers, showing put-ins, dams and nearby roads. Alongside the map is a brief description of each river's characteristics, and on the back is a detailed listing of the access sites giving their exact location and stating whether parking is available. Fishermen are also well served: the state puts out a 60-page illustrated fishing guide packed with data on what to catch where on Illinois fishing waters. Both publications may be obtained from the Illinois Department of Commerce and Community Affairs, 620 East Adams Street, Springfield, IL 62701.

The Big Muddy River in southern Illinois meanders slowly through the scenic Shawnee National Forest in its lower reaches and its diverse wildlife makes it — in the words of the state guide — "a year-round delight for the naturalist who isn't in any hurry to get downriver." Lusk Creek in the same Shawnee Forest area is described as one of the state's most picturesque float trips, with its canyons, bluffs, tall trees, wildflowers and wildlife. The 18-mile float down to its confluence with the Ohio at Golconda entails portages at low water but allows good fishing, birdwatching and mushroom gathering.

A prime destination for paddlers from the Chicago area is the Lower Fox River, with its dam-free Historic Fox Valley Canoe Trail starting at Yorkville Dam. This two-day, 35-mile trip, the most popular canoe trail in the state, is full of interest: Maramech Hill, Sauk Ford where Lincoln is said to have camped, Slooper Settlement of Norway, Indian Creek Massacre site, the Spa at Wedron with sulfur springs, and many caves, islands, and rare flora and fauna.

Also close to Chicago is the Kankakee in northern Illinois, claimed to be one of the few natural, unspoiled rivers of the Midwest. Canoeists of all ages enjoy this gentle stream, which was paddled by LaSalle when he explored the region in the late 1600s. It provides good shoreline scenery and great fishing for species ranging from catfish and crappies to bass and walleye.

Due south of the town of Kankakee is the Middle Fork of the Vermilion River, the only National Wild and Scenic River in Illinois. Its run through the pleasantly-named Kickapoo State Park gives paddlers a taste of Class I-II canoeing on clean water over a sand and gravel riverbed. Deer, wild goats, wild turkeys and blue heron may be viewed, while anglers go for small mouth bass, crappie, walleye and bluegill.

The best whitewater in the state is on the Vermilion of the Illinois, often dubbed Big Vermilion, which runs into the Illinois River near Starved Rock. Its six-foot waves are for seasoned canoeists only, but they will love its wild course through forests of flowering trees and between high bluffs topped with white pine and juniper.

Close to the Wisconsin state line runs the Sugar River, flowing rapidly through a secluded landscape. Replete with riffles and deep pools, the Sugar's attractions include a stone bluff where Indians marked the half-way point between Lake Michigan and the Mississippi. Although much of the land has been cleared, enough cover survives for the area to remain a major flyway for migrating ducks and geese.

Immortalized by the poetry of Edgar Lee Masters, the Spoon River in western Illinois is an appealing stream in its own right. Its setting is primitive and it runs through unspoiled old towns. When water is high it can be turbulent and demand experienced paddling.

Elsewhere, paddlers can enjoy waters ranging from the Chicago River, canoeable all the way down to Chicago's Loop, to the Cache River tucked away in the far south near the Kentucky state line. The mysterious Cache wends its way through a maze of bald cypress and tupelo trees in an area resembling Louisiana bayou country. Its hazards include logjams and poison snakes, but it is a naturalist's dream.

Cache Core Canoes
John C. Henderson
RR 1, Box 71AA
Ullin, IL 62992
(618) 845-3817
Lower Cache
Max. rapids: None
Cache Core Canoes rents canoes and runs guided canoe trips for day trips through bayou wetlands adjoining Buttonland Swamp. These outings, amid bald cypresses up to 1,000 years old and water tupelo, are for ecology-minded nature lovers who enjoy easy paddling. Paddlers can observe hundreds of species of plants and spot may spot bears,

otters, herons, and kingfishers. The Lower Cache also offers fishing for bass, perch, bluegill, catfish, and cypress trout.

Long Reach in Bottomland Swamp. Courtesy of Cache Core Canoes, Ullin, Illinois.

Canoe Limited
Max & Sonja Jones
Rte. 1, Box 250A
Greenup, IL 62428-9791
(217) 923-2707
Embarras River
Max. rapids: None
PPA

Canoe Limited rents canoes and kayaks for easy family day trips on the scenic Embarras River, which features a wealth of wildlife and other attractions. The stretch of river covered reaches from Fox Ridge State Park to Lincoln Log Cabin State Historic Site.

Fishing is for catfish, bass and "scrub" fish, while the wildlife includes deer, beavers, muskrats, blue herons, wild turkeys, and bald eagles. Canoe Limited's season runs from May to September.

Chicagoland Canoe Base, Inc.
Ralph C. Frese
4019 N. Narragansett Ave.
Chicago, IL 60634
(312) 777-1489
Dozens of waterways within driving distance of Chicago
Max. rapids: None
PPA

Chicagoland Canoe Base rents canoes year-round to people looking for scenic beauty and historic sites. It directs paddlers to uncrowded rivers for easy trips that feature urban or rural scenery, fossil sites, and unusual biotic communities.

On some of these trips, paddlers can watch deer, beavers, and varied birdlife, and fish for salmon, trout, and muskie.

Country Canoe
Stanley Hayes
824 Jackson
Pecatonica, IL 61063
(815) 239-1246
Sugar River
Max. rapids: None

Country Canoes offers canoe rentals for 1-4 day trips on the Sugar and Pecatonica Rivers, which have clear, fast waters that run through wetlands and swamps, sand hills and bluffs, hardwood forests, prairies, and bogs.

With Class I rapids, the trips are easy enough for beginners. Also, as trips end at the outfitter's headquarters, paddlers can travel at whatever speed they choose without having to worry about being early or late for the shuttle. Country Canoes' season runs from May to November.

Daily Canoe Trips
Patrick E. Daily
One Small St.
Aroma Park, IL 60910
(815) 939-2486
Kawkakee River
Max. rapids: I-II
PPA

Daily Canoe Trips rents canoes for trips of 1-2 days on the Kawkakee, claimed to be the cleanest river in the Midwest. The river has excellent fishing for bass, catfish, and walleye, offers island sandbars where paddlers can picnic and view waterfowl.

Floats are calm except in spring high-water. Daily Canoe Trips' season runs from April 15 to October 15.

Jet Recreations Inc.
(Kickapoo Canoe Rental)
Jim Trask
Box 582
Oakwood, IL 61858
(217) 354-2060
Middlefork River
Max. rapids: I-II

Kickapoo Canoe Rental rents canoes for 1-day trips on the Middlefork River, Illinois' only designated National Scenic

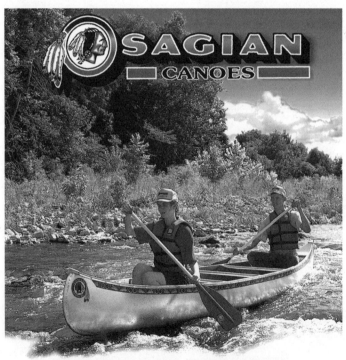

River. The Middlefork runs through unspoiled wilderness and has clean, Class I-II whitewater that offers moderate challenge and smallmouth, crappie, walleye, and bluegill fishing. Paddlers also can spot deer, wild goats, turkeys, and blue herons.

The season runs from April to September.

Kankakee River State Park Canoe Trips

Willie & Fred Floyd
P.O. Box 226
Bourbonnais, IL 60914
(815) 932-0488
Kankakee River
Max. rapids: None
PPA

Kankakee State Park Canoe Trips rents canoes for 1- and 2-day trips, and offers camping and fishing. The company is a full-service outfitter, supplying live bait, fishing licences, ice, and tackle in addition to canoeing equipment. The season runs from April to October.

Lundeen's Landing

Fred & Carolyn Lundeen
Box 182
Barstow, IL 61236
(309) 496-9956
Rock River
Max. rapids: None
PPA

Lundeen's Landing runs guided canoe trips and rents canoes for leisurely paddling on the gentle Rock River, with its many islands and sandbanks suitable for picnicking. On 2-day family camping trips, the guides provide campfire dinners and breakfasts. Deer, beaver, and a variety of birds ranging from blue herons to ducks may be seen, while fishermen go for catfish, smallmouth bass, flathead, and carp. The season runs May 15- October 15.

Reed's Canoe Trips

Orville and Dorothy Reed
907 N. Indiana Avenue
Kanakee, IL 60901
(815) WE CANOE
Kanakee River
Max. rapids: None
PPA

Reed's Canoe Trips offers 1- and 2-day canoe and kayak trips on the Kankakee River, one of the most unspoiled canoeing rivers in the Midwest.

The Kankakee is wide, with flat water, making trips easy for beginners and experienced paddlers alike. Its clean waters and many small islands and sandbars make the river ideal for swimming, picnicking, and exploring, with overnight camping available at private campgrounds, the Kankakee River State Park, and the La Salle State Fish and Wildlife Area.

The river also boasts especially good fishing for bass, walleye, northern pike, catfish, and crappie. The Kankakee consistently produces state-record catches and is widely regarded as one of the best fishing streams in Illinois.

Schmidt's Canoeing Service

Wesley & Carol Schmidt
1232 Ridgeway Ct.
Elgin, IL 60123
(708) 697-1678
Fox River, Nippersink Creek, other local rivers
Max. rapids: None

Schmidt's Canoeing Service rents canoes and offers guided canoe trips through both urban and rural areas with access to stores and restaurants en route. These outings of 1-3 days are suitable for beginners and intermediate paddlers. The company provides personal service and flexibility in scheduling trips.

Guests may spot beavers and blue herons and fish for catfish, bass, walleye, carp, and perch. Schmidt's season runs from April to November.

Indiana

Indiana's Blue River, well-named for its aqua-blue color, runs through some of the most appealing country in the Hoosier State. First explored by Squire Boone, brother of Daniel Boone, it rises in Washington County due north of Louisville and flows southwest to the Ohio. Traces of the Indian tribes that Squire Boone encountered can still be found today. The most spring-fed of all Indiana's streams, the Blue winds through many "half canyons" — cliffs rising on one side or the other. These limestone bluffs are dotted with caves and old quarries in what is known as Indiana's Cave Country. Hardwood forests and hills add to the scenery, so it is no surprise that the Blue was the first river chosen for Indiana's Natural and Scenic Rivers System.

Much of the riverbed is covered in rocks and sediment, and rapids contain gravel bars. But the level drops at a rate of merely four feet per mile so the rapids are rated only at Class I-II. A favorite run is from Milltown to Rothrock Mill, a 13-mile trip that takes about five hours to float. It contains the best rapids on the river but is only runnable from April through June or after heavy rainfall later in the season. Paddlers must be sure to take out at the access site before the Rothrock Mill Dam since the dam is extremely dangerous. There are other good floats above Milltown, especially in springtime. But above Fredericksburg the water level gets too low.

Long the most popular, and probably the most beautiful, stream in the state is Sugar Creek, named by the pioneers for the many sugar maples in the area. This unpolluted river runs 90 miles southwest from Tipton County (north of Indianapolis) to join the Wabash. Its course takes it through or beside several state parks and other public lands well equipped with campgrounds and other recreational facilities. The scenery is an attractive mix of cliffs and pleasant woodland, with covered bridges and plenty of good fishing. Canoeists paddling on their own should check water levels before setting out on Sugar Creek, which can be hazardous when the river is in flood. But at other times it is a gentle Class I-II float. Crawfordsville is a popular put-in.

Another very clean and scenic Indiana river is the Tippecanoe in the north-central portion of the state. It runs through wooded countryside with abundant deer, beaver, heron, duck and geese. Lacking rapids, the Tippecanoe is a good paddling river for anyone. It has strong appeal for fishermen, who can find many varieties of bass, blue catfish, flathead, perch, sunfish and crappie.

Sticklers for accuracy say that the name Whitewater River is a bit of a misnomer. True, this river has many rapids and the steepest gradient in the state — six feet per mile on average — but it does not contain genuine whitewater. Running north-south in the eastern part of Indiana, it flows through farmland in two forks and then in one before heading eastward into Ohio.

Cave Country Canoes
P.O. Box 145
Milltown, IN 47145
(812) 365-2705
Blue River
Max. rapids: I-II
PPA

Cave Country Canoes, Inc., rents canoes, kayaks, and rafts for 1-3 day trips on the Blue River. Most sections of the river are suitable for family canoeing, with Class I-II rapids, but previous paddling experience is required for one section during springtime when water levels are higher. The many springs that feed into the Blue give it its aqua-blue color. Two-hundred-foot limestone bluffs with cave entrances and a canopy of huge sycamore trees shade the river. Paddlers can see deer, muskrats, beavers, and blue herons, and fish for smallmouth and largemouth bass, goggle eye, and bluegill.

Cave Country Canoes prides itself on quality service and promises no long waits for bus shuttles. During its April 1-to-October 31 season, the outfitter offers riverside camp sites for people taking 2-day trips and organized groups, two large bunkhouses for group outings, and hot showers.

Germany Bridge Canoe Trips
Paul and Maxine Bardsley
4201 N. 375 W.
Rochester, IN 46975
(219) 223-2212
Tippecanoe River
Max. rapids: None
PPA

Germany Bridge Canoe Trips offers canoe and tube rentals on the Tippecanoe River for 1-5 day flatwater trips. The river is clean and scenic, passing through wooded country with abundant deer, beavers, ducks, geese, and herons. Fishing is very good, especially for smallmouth bass, channel catfish, and northern pike.

Trips run from April to November and are suitable for paddlers of all ages.

Canoeing on Sugar Creek. Courtesy of Lee Merriman, Turkey Run Canoe Trips, Rockville, Indiana.

Morgan's Brookville Canoe Center
Bob & June Morgan
7040 Whitewater River
Brookville, IN 47012
(317) 647-4904, (800) WE CANOE
Whitewater River
Max. rapids: I-II
PPA

Morgan's Brookville rents canoes, kayaks, rafts, and tubes for trips ranging from three miles to 51 miles, depending on river conditions. The Whitewater is a broad river surrounded by hills and sparsely inhabited countryside. At Morgan's 109-acre base, guests can take paddling lessons, camp, and fish for bass, walleye, bluegill, and crappie.

Outings during the April-to-October season are suitable for families and groups.

Root's Camp & Ski Haus
Jack H. Root
6844 N. Clinton
Fort Wayne, IN 46825
(219) 484-2604
Cedar Creek, St. Joseph River
Max. rapids: I-II

Root's Camp rents canoes and offers guided canoe trips for easy 1-day floats down Cedar Creek and the St. Joseph River. This historic area, redolent of Indian wars and Johnny Appleseed, offers glimpses of deer and many bird species. The company provides quality canoes and good personnel during its April-November season.

Trading Post Canoe Rental
Larry & Susan Acree
Co. Rd. 300 N.
P.O. Box 132
Mongo, IN 46771
(219) 367-2493
Pigeon River
Max. rapids: None
PPA

Trading Post Canoe Rental rents canoes and kayaks for scenic trips of up to 2 days through an unspoiled state fish and wildlife area. Open April through October, the outfitter recommends its waters to beginners, families, and youth groups.

There are no houses on the river for 30 miles — only Canada geese, beavers, and other wildlife. The river also has trout, catfish, pike, bass.

Turkey Run Canoe Trips
Bev Chaplain
311 West Ohio Street
Rockville, IN 47872
(317) 597-2456, (317) 569-6705
Sugar Creek
Max. rapids: I-II

Turkey Run Canoe Trips rents canoes and tubes for 1- and 2-day trips on Sugar Creek, a scenic canoeing stream lined with sandstone cliffs, woods, and sandy beaches. Both the flatwater and mild whitewater trips are fine for families and children age six and older. Along these trips, which run between April and October, paddlers can swim, view deer and turkeys, and fish for smallmouth bass and catfish. Camping at campgrounds enroute is also available.

Iowa

Less than 1,200 feet separate the highest from the lowest elevation in the Hawkeye State, so Iowa's rivers mostly meander idly across the plain. But despite its lack of whitewater, Iowa offers the paddler a wide variety of canoe trails with first-rate fishing in its rivers and lakes. The state puts out an excellent brochure (see below). All Iowa's streams flow into the Missouri or the Mississippi, which respectively form the western and eastern borders of the state. Some, like the Turkey River in the northeast "Little Switzerland" corner of Iowa have a strong current with gentle rapids. Others, like the Boone River, have high rock walls, caves and Indian burial sites. The scenery, while not spectacular, is generally unspoiled and attractive.

Reaching nearly 500 miles, the Des Moines River is the longest in the state. Six miles south of Fort Dodge the Des Moines provides a very attractive float over the eleven-mile stretch from Kalo to Lehigh. Described as an ideal one-day excursion, this trip runs past sandstone bluffs, caves and ravines with plenty of good fishing spots and places to explore. One interesting site is Boneyard Hollow, a deep ravine where prairie Indians slew buffalo, deer and elk by driving them over the cliff and picking their remains for meat, hide and bones.

In Little Switzerland the Upper Iowa River is a popular stream for both canoeists and fishermen, who can wade easily on its gravel bed. The entire 110-mile stretch from Lime Springs, close to the Minnesota state line, to the confluence with the Mississippi can be floated. The Upper Iowa — which is unconnected with the Iowa River — features old mill sites, limestone bluffs, wooded banks and such attractions as the 100-foot-high stone pillars known as Chimney Rocks. April to early June is the recommended season.

A unique experience — portaging through the main street of town — is to be found on the Turkey River when the canoeist reaches the Clayton County seat of Elkader. There is one dam above and one below the town. It must be the only portage in recreational canoeing which offers a grocery store and several eating places along three city blocks. State officials advise those portaging on a Saturday to arrange wheeled transport so as to avoid "totally disrupting business in the town."

The Iowa River, running diagonally southeast across the state to the Miss issippi, is a meandering prairie stream flowing through some historic terri tory. Near the put-in below the Alden Dam is Mormon Bridge, named after a pioneer group which lost many members in the severe winter o 1844-45. Further downstream at Steamboat Rock are the sites of early gold rushes amid forested recreational areas and limestone bluffs. In Hardin County, where the river runs through a greenbelt, it is one of the loveliest floats in Iowa.

The Little Sioux is another typical prairie stream, with a sand, mud and gravel bottom and high mud banks. It flows at barely one mile per hour dropping an average of only two feet per mile. It is rich in wildlife, notably white-tailed deer, raccoon, beaver and otter — which are now being rein troduced after having been hunted nearly to extinction. When floating the westward-flowing Little Sioux in the northwest corner of the state, pad dlers should visit the Sanford Museum at the Cherokee take-out.

Another Iowa river of considerable historic interest is the Wapsipinicon (Wapsi) in the northeast. On it lies the village of Waubeek, settled by New England whaling families in the 1850s who moved to the heartland to remove any temptation for their menfolk to maintain their hazardou seafaring tradition. Their old homes still display harpoons, ships' bells and other emblems from their maritime lifestyle. The most scenic stretches are between Waubeek and Anamosa, and at Pinicon Ridge Park north o Central City.

The Raccoon River offers a good weekend trip through unspoiled tim berland in central Iowa. Although the float runs right down to Des Moines it feels pleasantly remote from civilization. And catfish, smallmouth bass and walleye are plentiful.

For detailed descriptions of Iowa canoe trails, call the state's Department o Natural Resources, tel. (515) 281-5918, and ask for the float trip leaflet covering the river concerned.

ACR Inc.
Tim & Jamie Appleby
RR 3, Box 207A
Monticello, IA 52310
(319) 465-3697
Maquoketa, Wapsipinicon Rivers
Max. rapids: None

Open from Memorial Day to Labor
Day, Appleby Canoe Rental caters especially to families with children. Its trips
are along waters with very slow currents,
allowing paddlers to sit back and relax
as they enjoy the Indian bluffs and other
beautiful sights.

Trips last 1-3 days and enable paddlers to swim, camp, and fish for smallmouth bass, catfish, walleye, and bull
heads amid clean water and sandbars
suitable for picnicking.

Dam Bait Shop
Bob Harms, Joyce Sweet
Box 112B
201 North Main Street
Linn Grove, IA 51033
(712) 296-3611
Little Sioux River
Max. rapids: None

The Dam Bait Shop rents canoes for
leisurely 1/2 day to 7 day trips on the
Inkpaduta Trail of the Little Sioux, with
its great scenery, fishing, and wildlife.
Outings can be organized to allow paddlers to camp either in developed campgrounds or in primitive sites, with access
to their vehicles in either case.

Walleye, crappie, carp and catfish can
be caught in this typical prairie stream.
The company's season runs from April 1
through October.

Turkey River Canoe Trips
Eleanor Gossman
102 South Main
Elkader, IA 52240
(319) 245-1010, (319) 245-1434
Turkey River, Volga River
Max. rapids: I-II

Turkey River Canoe Trips rents canoes for trips of up to 3 days on both the
Turkey and Volga rivers with their attractive uncrowded scenery. Paddlers may
view the historic Motor Mill and Keystone Bridge as they float these streams,
whose rapids rate only Class I-II. Bass,
catfish, trout, and walleye may be found,
and the wildlife includes deer, wild turkeys, and eagles.

Turkey River Canoe Trips' season
runs from May 1-October 21.

University of Iowa Rec Services
Wayne Fett
Touch the Earth
E216 Field House
Iowa City, IA 52242
(315) 335-9293, (315) 335-5256
Upper Iowa River, Wolf River, Red River,
Wisconsin River, Upper Iowa River, BWCA,
Ocoee River, Chattooga River, Nantahala
River, St. Francis River, Poudre River
Max. rapids: I-II

University of Iowa Recreation Services offers guided canoe, kayak, and raft
trips and rents canoes for trips in Iowa
on the upper Iowa River; in Minnesota
in the Boundary Waters Canoe Area; in
Wisconsin on the Wolf, Red, and Wisconsin Rivers; and in the southeast on
the Ocoee, Chattooga, Nantahala, St.
Francis, and Poudre Rivers. These trips,
open to students and the general public,
feature a low student-to-instructor ratio
and are geared for beginning to intermediate paddlers. All trips run through
scenic, remote, and wild areas. Trips last
1-4 days.

The department of recreation services, open year-round, also offers rock
climbing, cross-country skiing, backpacking, and bicycle touring.

Kansas

Rivers meandering through the vast wheatfields of the Great Plains banks lined with willow and cottonwood — this is canoeing in the Sun flower State. But it is not the whole story; in parts of Kansas the paddle finds forests, bluffs, sandhills and wetlands. Official tourist brochures boas that 10,000 miles of Kansas streams are "fishable" and that the state ha ten canoe trails on waters suitable for river-runners of all skill levels.

Kansas rivers flow east or southeast across the rolling Great Plains. Man become unfloatable after long periods of drought. This is especially tru of the Kansas River, otherwise known as the Kaw. Paddlers who intend t float — not drag — their canoes on the 59-mile stretch of the Kaw abov Topeka should first check with the U.S. Army Corps of Engineers at Tuttl Creek (913-539-8511) and Milford Lake (913-238-5714) on outflows from these upstream reservoirs. When waterlevels suffice, sunbathers find idea picnic sites on its large, clean sandbars. But overnight campers will want t seek sheltered spots out of the wind to pitch their tents. Bald eagles may b seen in winter and a wide variety of songbirds, shore birds and waterfowl a other seasons. Deer, coyote, beaver and muskrat can also be observed. Fo a change of pace, some paddlers combine the 17-mile float from Edwards ville to Kansas City with a leisurely riverboat cruise and dinner on the broa Missouri.

Another recommended trip is on the Arkansas River from Raymond, som 35 miles northwest of Hutchison, to the Oklahoma border near Arkansa City. This 150-mile float takes the paddler down a typical prairie rive with braided channels around sandbanks and islands. Wildlife is abundan on the more remote stretches.

The Marais des Cygnes flows through farmland, towns and picturesqu wooded areas in eastern Kansas. As its name (Marsh of Swans) implies, it i a favorite stopover for aquatic birds on their annual migrations. Its mudd banks, lined with oaks, sycamores and willows, provide a habitat for numer ous amphibians and reptiles. The canoeing trail comprises the 14 miles o the river down to the town of La Cygne, plus the ensuing 18 miles to th end of the waterfowl area beside the Missouri state line.

Some of the best scenery and wildlife observation in Kansas is to be found n the Fall River in the southeast corner of the state. It also offers Class I-II hitewater on its upper reaches which can challenge the novice canoeist nd provide fun for the experienced. But it is floatable only in the spring nd after heavy rainfall. It is a great fishing river, well stocked with spotted ass, channel cat, and crappie and white bass in season. Almost all of this 2-mile trail is through land owned by the Corps of Engineers and is open o public access, fishing and hunting. The put-in is at Highway K-99 bridge lose to Eureka.

Southwest of Wichita runs Grouse Creek, another good stream for wild- fe, fishing and scenery. All of the four-mile trail starting just south of ilverdale, next to the Oklahoma state line, is within the Kaw Wildlife Area. t is a clean and lively river running through woods, with catfish a favorite atch.

KANSAS

Wichita Boathouse
Arkansas River Foundation
35 West Lewis
Wichita, KS 67202
316) 267-9235
Big Arkansas, Little Arkansas Rivers
Max. rapids: None

Wichita Boathouse and Arkansas River Museum rents canoes from its downtown location for river paddling ast riverside parks, with their sculpture nd other attractions. Herons, cranes, eese, and ducks may be viewed, and he fishing includes catfish and carp.

The museum displays a winning America's Cup yacht, a replica of the Cup itself, and many other historic ex- ibits. In the summer, the Boathouse uns the RiverKids youth program which eaches children boating skills. Paddling essons are also available for grown-ups luring the April-October season.

Kentucky

Stretching from the Appalachians to the Mississippi, the Bluegrass State has plenty of rain and no shortage of navigable rivers for the paddler to explore. All of the main Kentucky streams, the Cumberland, Green, Kentucky, Licking, Salt and Tennessee, flow northwestward into the great Ohio River. And the Ohio, which forms the state's entire northern border, pours all this Kentucky water into the Mississippi.

Elkhorn Creek is perhaps Kentucky's most popular canoeing stream because of its easy accessibility from big cities, its gentle whitewater and natural beauty. Flowing northwest to its confluence with the Kentucky River north of Frankfort, it is also close to Louisville, Lexington and Cincinnati. Elkhorn Creek has attractive scenery with a mixture of sheer cliffs, tall trees, wildflowers and fertile farmland. Fish include bass and bluegill, while the wildlife ranges from deer to raccoons and muskrats. Rapids are mostly mere riffles or Class I, with the only Class II stretch below Forks of the Elkhorn where the north and south branches converge. The Kentucky River is a broad, slow stream with nothing more difficult than Class I — an invitation to leisurely cruising.

By contrast, the lower Rockcastle River in south central Kentucky offers intense Class III-IV whitewater which demands technical skill. This is an exhausting 17-mile run, and its last six miles, known as the Lower Narrows, is full of twisting blind drops which should be scouted one by one. As Bob Sehlinger puts it in his Canoeing and Kayaking Guide to the Streams of Kentucky, it is whitewater that "lambastes the paddler with every challenge in the book." The time to do it, by canoe or raft, is April through June. The upper sections of the Rockcastle provide 25 miles of easy paddling for families and beginners through forested hills and farmland in the heart of the Daniel Boone National Forest.

The Big South Fork of the Cumberland River comes northward from Tennessee through a remote region — the Big South Fork National Recreation Area (see Tennessee). Access is difficult but it offers several good canoe and rafting trips varying from Class I to Class IV or even Class V at times. Parts of the Big South Fork are best in the fall, when the hills are filled with changing colors. Just above Cumberland Falls the Cumberland offers a 17-mile run which is good for beginners, and below the falls is a five to seven mile run of Class II-III whitewater which includes rapids dubbed Screaming Right-Hand Turn, Stair Steps and the Last Drop. Guided raft trips suitable for families and novices are available through this scenic wilderness.

One of the hairiest whitewater rivers in the East is the Russell Fork of the Levisa through Breaks Interstate Park on the Virginia-Kentucky state line. Long considered unrunnable, the Russell Fork drops an incredible 500 feet in two and one-half miles. One of its Class IV-V rapids, appropriately named El Horrendo, is more of a waterfall than a drop. October is the time to raft this formidable 10-mile run, when water is released from the reservoir dam.

The Licking River is runnable all year below Falmouth, where its South Fork joins the mainstream. Access points are scarce, but the scenery is attractive with hardwood trees lining the banks as the broad, clean river winds gently through hilly valleys to its confluence with the Ohio. Deer, otter and many birds may be observed, while anglers reel in bass, muskie, sauger, crappie and catfish.

The upper North Fork of the Kentucky River provides an interesting insight into traditional mountain lifestyle, with old frame houses, wooden footbridges and porch rockers in riverside communities. The paddling is easy Class I. The Middle Fork is also populated, but the natural scenery is beautiful as the narrow stream winds through the hill country with Class I-II rapids.

Other popular Kentucky streams are the Red River, which flows through a beautiful gorge on its way to join the Kentucky River, the Green River, one of Kentucky's longest, and the Nolin, a tributary of the Green. The Red River mostly runs through extremely attractive countryside and its upper section is normally navigable from December to May. The middle section is just as scenic, but the lower river is less appealing after it emerges from Red River Gorge. The Green River, which empties into the Ohio opposite Evansville, Ohio, has two good canoeing stretches downstream from Green River Lake Dam. Much of the lower reach runs through Mammoth Cave National Park and is rich in natural history, with its riverside caves, forests and wildlife. The Nolin flows through the same park to join the Green and offers similar scenery, although canoeists must portage several dangerous dams. All three rivers have easy rapids except where the old mill dams create Class II+ hazards.

KENTUCKY

"Devil's Jump" on the Cumberland's Big South Fork. Courtesy of Sheltowee Trace Outfitters, Whitley City, Kentucky.

Canoe Kentucky/Elkhorn Outdoor Center (EOC)
Bess, Corey and Ed Councill
7323 Peaks Mill Road
Frankfort, KY 40601
(502) 227-4492, (800) K-CANOE-1,
FAX (502) 227-8086
*Elkhorn Creek, Kentucky, Salt, Green,
Nolin and Red Rivers. Paintsville Lake
Max. rapids: IV
PPA*

Canoe Kentucky is an adventure/paddlesports network of a dozen locations · across the state offering canoeing, kayaking, and rafting (duckies too) on Class I and II scenic, fun and safe streams. Guided trips are also available, both in and out of state, as well as clinics. In co-operation with the EOC, the company can package these outdoor activities with bicycling, horseback riding, fishing, touring (historical, geological and environmental) caving, camping, and hiking.

Also featured is the largest Kentucky paddlesports showroom providing shuttle, repair, trip planning and full livery services.

Green River Canoes
Mike Daugherty
215 Crawford St.
Campbellsville, KY 42718
(502) 789-2956, (800) 413-2266
*Green River, Green River Lake
Max. rapids: I-II
PPA*

Green River Canoes supplies rental canoes as well as running guided canoe trips lasting 1-2 days for clients keen on fishing and relaxing. Deer, beaver, and numerous birds may be seen, camping is available and fish include large and smallmouth bass, bluegill, and walleye. The company's season runs from April until October.

Licking River Canoe Trips
David & Marty Hunter
Rte. 1, Box 516-A
Ewing, KY 41039
(606) 289-4734, (606) 289-4005
*Licking River
Max. rapids: None
PPA*

Licking River Canoe Trips runs both guided and unguided canoe outings on gentle waters with just minor riffles. The rolling landscape includes steep, wooded

cliffs inhabited by deer, turkeys, muskrats, and cranes, and the river holds catfish, bass, carp, white perch and crappie.

The company, based next to the Blue
Lick Battlefield State Park, is associated
with Elk Creek Stables, which offers
horseback riding, camping, hiking, and
cabin rentals. Its season runs April to
November.

Rockcastle Adventures Canoe Livery
Jim Honchell
P.O. Box 662
London, KY 40741
(606) 864-5987, (606) 864-9407
*Rockcastle River, Cumberland River, Buck
Creek, Wood Creek, Laurel Lake,
Cumberland Lake*
Max. rapids: III-IV

Rockcastle Adventures offers canoe
and kayak rentals on the Rockcastle
River, Back Creek, Wood Creek, Laurel
Lake, and Lake Cumberland. Most popular is an 11-mile trip on the upper Rockcastle, which features gentle current and
light rapids, and passes through the
heart of the scenic Daniel Boone Na-

tional Forest. This trip, and the 2- and
3-day trips on the Upper Rockcastle,
are fine for novices and families.

Also popular is a challenging 17-mile
day trip on the Lower Rockcastle, which
passes through spectacular gorges and
boasts tough Class I-IV whitewater. This
trip is for experienced canoeists only.

On these and other trips, paddlers
can camp, spot deer and waterfowl, and
fish for bass, drum, redeye, catfish, and
walleye. During the March-to-October
season, the company also offers hiking
and caving trips.

Sheltowee Trace Outfitters
Richard Egedi, Sr.
P.O. Box 1060
Whitley City, KY 42653
(606) 376-5567, (800) 541-7238
Cumberland River, Russell Fork
Max. rapids: III-V
PPA

Sheltowee Trace Outfitters offers
canoe and tube rentals and guided raft
trips on the South Fork of the Cumberland, Russell Fork, and Cumberland

*Cumberland River below Cumberland Falls. Courtesy of Sheltowee Trace Outfitters, Whitley
City, Kentucky.*

The gorge section of the Big South Fork of the Cumberland River. Courtesy of Sheltowee Trace Outfitters, Whitley City, Kentucky.

Rivers. Family and beginner raft trips on the Cumberland feature exciting Class II and III rapids, scenic canyons, swimming, and views of wilderness waterfalls. Family and beginner trips of one and two days run on the Cumberland River on scenic sections with gentle currents and small rapids.

Wild water raft and canoe trips run on the Russell Fork and South Fork of the Cumberland — some of the most demanding water in Kentucky and Tennessee. These trips feature tight turns, large rocks, narrow chutes, and other challenges to thrill even the most skilled paddlers.

All trips run through wilderness areas with abundant deer, foxes, rabbits, and other small wildlife, and good fishing for bass, walleye, and catfish. During its March-to-October season, the company also offers shuttle service for hikers and backpackers.

Still Waters Canoe Trails
Beth and Dave Strohmeier
249 Strohmeier Road
Frankfort, KY 40601
(502) 223-8896
Kentucky River, Elkhorn Creek
Max. rapids: I-II

Still Waters Canoe Trails offers 1-2 day canoe rentals for trips on Elkhorn Creek and the Kentucky River. Elkhorn Creek is a scenic stream with mostly Class I rapids and quiet pools. Noted for its smallmouth bass fishing, the Kentucky River has Class I rapids and is bounded by tall hills and cliffs. All trips but one five-mile, Class II section of Elkhorn Creek are fine for beginners.

The shores of both streams have colorful wildflowers, stately trees, and abundant wildlife, including deer, raccoons, muskrats, and blue herons. The two streams also have good fishing for largemouth and smallmouth bass, bluegill, and catfish.

Stoner Creek Dock
Hardy & Tamura Dungan
387 Chambers St.
Paris, KY 40361
(606) 987-3625
Stoner Creek
Max. rapids: None

Stoner Creek Dock rents canoes,
paddleboats, and fishing boats for easy
trips for naturelovers and fishermen.
Horse farms flank the creek, sharing the
banks with owls, ducks, raccoons, and
muskrats. Paddlers can also catch a variety of fish during the April-to-October
season.

Thaxton's Canoe Trails
Ann Thaxton and Sue Beagle
RR2, Box 391
Falmouth, KY 41040
(606) 472-2000, (606) 654-5111
South Fork, Middle Fork, Main Fork
of the Licking River
Max. rapids: I
PPA, ACA, USCA, AWA

Thaxton's Canoe Rental rents canoes, kayaks, and tubes for 1-3 day trips
on the Licking River and its tributaries.
The Licking River Valley, first explored
by legendary frontiersmen Simon Ken-
ton and Daniel Boone, is a region rich in
history and teeming with sportfish, birds,
and animals. The Licking River's exceptionally clear waters are ideal for novices
and advanced paddlers. Thaxton's, the
oldest family-owned canoe rental in the
state, was the first to offer guided moonlight floats, tube trips, kayak and sea
kayak rentals, and interpretive floats.
Trips run between April and October.

USA RAFT
Mary Kay Heffernan
P.O. Box 277
Rowlesburg, WV 26425
(800) USA RAFT
North Fork Potomac River, Gauley River,
Cheat River, Tygart River, New River, Upper
Youghiogheny River, Nolichucky River, Ocoee
River, Nantahala River, French Broad River
Max. rapids: II-III
America Outdoors

USA Raft offers outings on 10 of the
best whitewater rivers in the East — the
Russell Fork in Kentucky; the Upper
Youghiogeny in Maryland; the Nolichucky, French Broad, and Nantahala in
North Carolina; the Nolichucky and
Ocoee in Tennessee; and the New,
Gauley, Cheat, and Tygart in West
Virginia. With this selection of trips,
rivers, and outfitters, USA Raft offers
affordable outings to suit paddlers of all
skill levels at locations convenient to
residents throughout the Middle Atlantic and Southeast.

Louisiana

Paddling in Louisiana is chiefly on lazy bayou streams, creeks and lakes. Many local floaters are fishermen or naturalists drawn by the state's rich resources of fish and wildlife. With its great alluvial Mississippi delta, marshlands and prairie to the south and its rolling country to the north, Louisiana is no place for whitewater. The state's highest point is just 535 feet above sea level. But in the so-called "uplands" there are numerous clear and lively streams with sand or gravel bottoms where fishermen may test their skill against cunning spotted bass. State tourist brochures list no fewer than 66 rivers as suitable for canoeing and tubing. But in Louisiana's hot, humid, sub-tropical climate, few paddlers feel particularly energetic. Many just loll in their boats with a cane pole and a box of worms, hoping the catfish and bream will bite.

Among the streams served by canoeing and tubing outfitters are the Amite and Bogue Chitto Rivers and Pushepatapa Creek in the southeast, with the Quiska (Whisky) in the Shreveport region of the northwest. The scenery varies from vast marshlands to forests that cover half the state.

White-tailed deer and wildcats frequent wooded swamps beside the rivers, while muskrats, minks, opossums, raccoons, wild hogs and skunks roam the lowland woods. In the coastal bayous the paddler may see occasional alligators and coypus (beaverlike animals).

Nearly half the wild ducks and geese in North America are said to winter in the state's coastal marshes. All told, more than one hundred bird species, notably the brown pelican, Louisiana's state bird, live there. Close to the coast speckled trout, redfish, crabs, shrimp and oysters abound in the brackish waters of the largest estuary marsh in the nation. Further inland, Louisiana lakes and rivers have been well stocked with striped and hybrid bass. Fish of up to thirty pounds are often caught in Toledo Bend and other lakes.

Atchafalaya Basin Backwater Tours
Jon Faslun
P.O. Box 128
Gibson, LA 70356
(504) 575-2371
Big Bayou Black, Tiger Bayou
Max. rapids: None

Atchafalaya Basin Backwater Tours offers guided powerboat trips and rentals of pirogues (canoe-like dugouts) for exploring the deep swamp country of the Atchafalaya Basin. The waters travelled — the Big Bayou Black and Tiger Bayou — are clean, beautiful, and unspoiled. The bayous are home to 15 kinds of fish, 30 types of animals, and 48 species of birds.

Paddling tours cover five miles roundtrip and are best suited for teens and fit adults. Trips run year-round.

Maine

Maine's great expanses of forests, its mountains and its five thousand streams and rivers enable it to rival the West as wilderness canoeing territory. Down East is a paradise for the New Yorker or Bostonian who wants to escape the hassle and the heat of the city. One can lose oneself in the vast hinterland of Maine and not see another soul for days. Whitewater rivers, slow-moving streams and lakes abound. The bays and rocky coves of the Atlantic coast also beckon.

The best-known of Maine's attractions for river-runners is the Allagash Wilderness Waterway, nearly 100 miles of lakes and river coursing northward with relatively easy rapids. This is a land of quiet and boundless forests alive with beaver, moose, deer and the occasional bear. The fishing is great and the birdlife prolific. The entire trip from Telos Lake in the south to its confluence with the St. John River at Allagash can be canoed comfortably in a week. But the paddler with time to spare can easily spend a second week savoring side trips and studying wildlife along this original federal Wild and Scenic River. A favorite detour is to Allagash Lake, a pristine spot which can only be reached by poling a canoe up six miles of riffles from Chamberlain Lake. Allagash Wilderness Waterway may be paddled anytime between May and October, although the water may be too high in May-June and rather low in late summer. Blackflies are at their most pestilential in June. Outfitters recommend some prior canoeing experience for the Allagash since the Chase Rapids (below Churchill Lake) present nine miles of Class II whitewater. There are four portages en route.

For real whitewater enthusiasts the West Branch of the Penobscot River, claimed to be the most exciting river in the East, offers a 12-mile run that starts with rugged Class V rapids. The trip begins in spectacular Ripogenus Gorge, where the river drops 70 feet per mile for the first two miles. Then it alternates between calm stretches and Class III-IV whitewater as it passes Baxter State Park and Mount Katahdin, Maine's highest peak. The dam-controlled river can be run all summer long, with the greatest flow in May-June.

Novices and others not seeking whitewater enjoy paddling the Upper West Branch of the Penobscot, a four-day, 50-mile trip between the dam at the foot of Seboomook Lake and the start of the rugged West Branch run at Ripogenus. There are no difficult rapids, no portages and half the floating is on lakes.

Definitely not for the faint-hearted is the Dead River, a Class III-V stream that shows it is very much alive by providing the longest stretch of continuous whitewater in the East. This 15-mile run through a remote wilderness canyon begins at Grand Falls and ends near the village of West Forks. It can only be floated when dam water is released; the big releases come in May.

The Kennebec, into which the Dead River flows at The Forks, boasts the largest river gorge in New England and some mighty rapids on its upstream portion. Starting at Harris Dam, adjoining Indian Pond, the Class IV-V rapids along this upper four-mile section are particularly daunting in the spring. But the remaining eight miles of this run are gentle and appealing for families with children, who may skip the upper gorge and start their float at Carry Brook.

Rapid River is one of the fastest streams east of the Mississippi, plunging 100 feet per mile as it flows from Lake Richardson to Lake Umbagog in a wonderfully rustic region of Maine woods. With its Class IV rapids it is a challenging river at all times, but especially when water releases occur. Lake Umbagog is rich in wildlife and — by one recent report — habitat for a nesting pair of bald eagles.

Up north, the large St. John River runs parallel to the Canadian border through magnificent forest wilderness. It offers long stretches of solitude along its 83-mile course down to Allagash Village. Some of the trip involves heavy whitewater and should be attempted only by the experienced. It can only be run from mid-May through mid-June when the run-off is right.

Less energetic canoeists and fishermen can sample Maine's 2,500 lakes which, seen from the air, gleam like jewels in the forest. The largest, of course, is Moosehead Lake, which despite its many tourist facilities is still largely undeveloped and a favorite choice for anglers seeking trout and salmon. There are organized "canoe safaris" for nature photographers in search of moose in the surrounding woods.

Sea kayakers revel in a totally different experience: paddling among dozens of islands off Penobscot Bay amid seals, porpoises and — if they are in luck — various species of whales. Among the many sea birds they see are puffins, gannets, cormorants, fulmars, kittiwakes, and ospreys. All told, this deeply-indented stretch of the Maine coast is one of the best sea kayaking regions in the country.

Canoeing on the 135-mile St. John River Trail. Courtesy of Back Country Tours, Inc., Pepperell, Massachusetts.

Allagash Guide, Inc.
Blaine R. Miller
Box 3210, Rte. 1
Norridgewock, ME 04957
(207) 634-3748
Allagash, St. John & W. Branch of Penobscot in Maine Ashuapmushuan & Nepisiquit Rivers in Canada
Max. rapids: III-IV

Allagash Guide runs guided canoe and raft trips on remote, clean rivers with great scenery and excellent fishing, particularly in Canada. It offers 4-10 day tours on a wide choice of waterways and caters to paddlers of all skill levels. Operating June 15-Sept. 1, the company prides itself on providing good food and excellent equipment, along with paddling lessons and camping. Brook and lake trout may be caught, along with pike and salmon.

Allagash Wilderness Outfitters
Rick and Judy Givens
Box 620-L HCR 76
Greenville, ME 04441
(207) 723-6622
Allagash, Penobscot, St. John Rivers
Max. rapids: I-II
PPA

Allagash Wilderness Outfitters, with some 30 years of experience, offers full or partial outfitting for 3-8 day trips on the Allagash, Penobscot, and St. John Rivers and other area waterways. Both flatwater and moderate whitewater trips are available to suit paddlers of all skill levels. Trips pass through unspoiled spruce and fir forests and offer excellent fishing for trout, perch, and landlocked salmon. Moose, deer, bears, beavers, loons, and waterfowl are also abundant.

The outfitter's season runs from May to September.

Back Country Tours, Inc.
Allan McGroary
39 Hollis Street
Pepperell, MA 01463
(508) 433-9381, (800) 649-9381 (in MA)
Connecticut River, Nashua River
Max. rapids: I-II

Back Country Tours, Inc., specializes in guided canoe trips and canoe rentals on "lesser known, uncrowded scenic waterways." Its trips run on the Souhegan and Merrimack Rivers in New Hampshire; the Sauantacook and Nissitissit Rivers in Massachusetts; the Connecticut and Nashua Rivers in New

Hampshire and Massachusetts; the Delaware River in New York, Pennsylvania, and New Jersey; the Blackwater, Sweetwater, and Juniper Rivers in Florida; the St. John in Maine, and nine lakes near Long Pond Mountain in New York's Adirondacks. Several of these excursion are "vacation" trips of 3-7 days that offer lodging at campgrounds, cabins, or bed-and-breakfast inns. All trips are suitable for beginners and experienced paddlers.

Back Country Tours' season runs from July to November.

Canal Bridge Canoes

Carl & Patricia Anderton
125 Main St.
Fryeburg, ME 04037
(207) 935-2605
Saco River
Max. rapids: I-II
PPA, Saco River Recreation Council

Canal Bridge rents canoes for easy paddling on the clear waters of the Saco River, with its sandy bottom and miles of beaches ideal for camping. The countryside is tree-lined, with occasional mountain views. Deer, moose, and beavers can be seen.

The outfitter offers flexibility in arranging leisurely 1-4 day trips between May and mid-October. Camping and swimming are available, along with fishing for trout, bass, pickerel, and perch.

Crab Apple Whitewater. Inc.

Charles A. Peabody
HC 63, Box 25
The Forks, ME 04985
(800) 553-7238, (207) 663-4491
Kennebec, Dead Rivers
Max. rapids: III-IV

Crab Apple Whitewater runs "moderately difficult" floats, with a guide on every raft, through exciting whitewater in a remote and scenic wilderness area. Guided raft trips are its sole business, and participants need no prior rafting experience. Since the flow is dam-controlled, the whitewater continues throughout the April-to-October season.

Lodging is available at the company's inn on the Kennebec River. Trips are available every day, with no minimum number of rafters required. All told, the company runs seven raft trips in three states. Moose, deer, eagles, and osprey can be spotted, and the rivers contain trout and landlocked salmon.

Downeast Rafting Inc.

Ned McSherry/Rick Haddicott
P.O. Box 119
Center Conway, NH 03813
(603) 447-3002, (800) 677-RAFT
Kennebec River, Dead River, Penobscot River, Rapid River, Swift River
Max. rapids: V+

Downeast Rafting provides guided raft trips on the Kennebec, Dead, Penobscot, Rapid, and Swift Rivers, which run through the Maine woods with their wealth of wildlife. These 1-day trips are offered from mid-April to October. Rafters experience Class III-IV whitewater on some streams and Class V on the technical Penobscot.

Downeast's guides are experienced and personable. All the company's Kennebec and Dead River packages include lodging at its inn or campground, meals, grilled lunch on the raft trip, and a video/slide show of the trip at the end.

Various other package tours, including guided fishing trips and even combined skiing-rafting trips, are available.

Eastern River Expeditions

John Connelly
Box 1173
Greenville, ME 04441
(207) 695-2411, (800) 634-7238
Dead River, Kennebec River, Penobscot River, Moose River, Gauley River
Max. rapids: V+
Maine Professional River Outfitters Association, America Outdoors

Eastern River Expeditions offers guided raft and inflatable-kayak trips on five rivers in Maine, New York, and West Virginia. In Maine, paddlers can choose among whitewater trips on the

Kennebec, Penobscot, and Dead Rivers. Most Maine trips are fine for novice paddlers, combining excellent wilderness scenery with consistent, high-quality Class II-IV whitewater, provided by dam releases.

Advanced rafting experience is a prerequisite for trips on New York's Moose River and West Virginia's Gauley River, which have Class IV-V rapids.

These trips of 1-2 days pass through wilderness offering camping spots, clear water, fishing, and chances to spot deer, loons, moose, ducks, beavers, foxes, great blue herons, and other wildlife.

Explorers At Sea, Inc.
D. Gay Atkinson, II
P.O. Box 469, Main Street
Stonington, ME 04681
(207) 367-2356
Penobscot Bay
Max. rapids: None

Explorers at Sea offers 1/2-5 day sea kayaking trips along the mid-coast of Maine off Stonington, a fishing village with nearly 100 islands just south of town. One- and two-day trips are designed for beginning sea kayakers, while the trips of 3-5 days are geared to paddlers with basic boating skills and camping experience.

The bays traveled are dotted with spruce-clad, granite islands, some of which are public and open for exploring and camping. These trips offer excellent chances to view eagles, ospreys, seals, and porpoises.

Explorers At Sea also offers family adventures. Its season runs from May to September.

Gilpatrick's Guide Service
Gil Gilpatrick
P.O. Box 461
Skowhegan, ME 04976
(207) 453-6959
Allagash River, St. John River, Penobscot River
Max. rapids: III-IV
Maine Professional Guides Association

Gilpatrick's Guide Service offers one-week guided canoe trips on the Allagash, St. John, and Penobscot Rivers. All trips run through pristine wooded wilderness of spruces, firs, and occasional hardwoods. Wildlife is abundant, especially moose, deer, bald eagles, ospreys, geese, and ducks. Also, anglers enjoy fishing for brook trout, lake trout, and whitefish.

Beginners are welcome on guided trips where the outfitter's master Maine guides give lessons enroute. Gilpatrick's season is from June to October.

Libby Sporting Camps
Matt Libby
Drawer V
Ashland, ME 04732
(207) 435-8274, (207) 435-6233
Penobscot River, Upper Allagash River,
Aroostook River
Max. rapids: III-IV
Maine Guides Association, Maine Sporting Camps Association

Libby Sporting Camps runs guided canoe and kayak trips and rents canoes for wilderness trips of 1-10 days for paddlers of all skill levels. Trips run on the Upper Penobscot, Allagash, and Aroostock in Maine and the Atikonak in Labrador. All expeditions run through pristine pine forests and offer striking views of mountains, waterfalls, and abundant wildlife, including moose, deer, bears, otters, eagles, ospreys, and beavers. There is also excellent fishing for landlocked salmon and brook trout.

Magic Falls Rafting Co.
David Neddeau
Box 9
West Forks, ME 04985
(207) -873-0938, (207) 663-2220
Kennebec, Dead, Penobscot Rivers
Max. rapids: III-IV
America Outdoors

Magic Falls Rafting runs a wide variety of 1- and 2-day raft, kayak and fun yak (inflatable kayak) trips from May 1 to October 15. Guests float clean rivers in a large unpopulated area alive with moose and deer. They may fish for trout and salmon, camp and swim. Paddling lessons are also available.

Mahoosuc Guide Service
Polly Mahoney & Kevin Slater
Box 245
Newry, ME 04261
(207) 824-2073, FAX (207) 824-3784
Allagash, St. John, Penobscot (E. Branch & W. Branch) Rivers in ME, Temiscamie River in Quebec. Upper Missouri in MT
Max. rapids: I-II

Traditional-style canoeing in wooden canoes built on the premises is offered by Mahoosuc Guide Service amid the forests of Maine. Clean water, mountain scenery, and myriad wildlife from moose and black bear to fox and porcupine enhance the experience.

The company has Cree Indians as co-guides and runs trips from May-October lasting up to 10 days. It offers white-water paddling lessons and rents canoes as well providing guided trips. Camping is available, and fish include brook trout, walleye lake trout, salmon, and northern pike.

Maine Island Kayak
Tom Bergh
70 Luther St.
Peaks Island, ME 04108
(800) 796-2373, (207) 766-2373
Gulf of Maine, Nova Scotia, Lake Superior
Max. rapids: None
TASK, ACA

Sea kayaking among wild outer islands is the specialty of Maine Island Kayak. Attractions include historic fishing villages, seals, porpoises, and 70 species of fish. Trips vary from 1/2-14 days, and are suited mostly to athletic and advanced paddlers, but lessons are available. The summer season runs May-September.

Maine Outdoors
Don Kleiner
P.O. Box 401
Union, ME 04862
(207) 785-4496
Saint George River, a variety of canoe routes in northern and western Maine
Max. rapids: None
Maine Professional Guides Association

Maine Outdoors offers full-day, half-day, and evening canoe trips in mid-coast Maine. All trips are led by a registered Maine guide and naturalist. Wildlife abounds on these trips; paddlers see ospreys, beavers, and the occasional eagle. These trips are well suited for both novice and veteran paddlers.

Maine outdoors, a short drive from Camden, Rockland, and Boothbay, also offers extended canoe trips through northern and western Maine. These trips are a chance to relax and enjoy wild country, wildlife, and beautiful scenery while someone else does the cooking and tends to other details. Custom trips are also available.

Maine Sport
Stuart and Marianne Smith
Route 1
Rockport, ME 04856
(207) 236-7120, (207) 236-8797
Penobscot Bay, St. Georges River, St. Croix River, Penobscot River, Kennebec River
Max. rapids: III-IV
PPA, ACA

Maine Sport offers guided canoe, kayak, and raft trips and canoe and kayak rentals for trips on Penobscot Bay, Georges River, West Branch Penobscot, Kennebec River, and many lakes. Raft trips last 1 day and canoe trips from one to three days. All excursions are of little to moderate difficulty, suitable for beginners as well as experienced paddlers.

What is distinctive about many of these trips is that waterways are interconnected, allowing paddlers to travel rivers, lakes, and tidewaters on a single trip. Also, the wilderness areas traveled feature abundant birds, deer, moose, seals, and other wildlife, depending on location. Fishing is good, too, for both freshwater and saltwater species.

Maine Sport, which offers trips from April to October, also operates a well-stocked paddle store with a wide array of canoes, kayaks, and paddle gear.

Maine Whitewater, Inc.
James A. Ernst
P.O. Box 633
Gaddabout Gaddis Airport
Bingham, ME 04920
(207) 672-4814, (800) 245-MAIN
Dead, Penobscot, Kennebec Rivers
Max. rapids: V+

Maine Whitewater, Inc., runs 1-day guided rafting trips on the Penobscot, Kennebec, and Dead Rivers. These dam-controlled rivers offer consistently good Class III-V whitewater from May to September. State-licensed guides are chosen for their "love of adventure and outgoing personalities."

Both the Penobscot and Kennebec trips begin in gorges. The Penobscot River winds along the base of Mount Katahdin and the Kennebec trip features a stop at 90-foot Mukie Falls. Moose, deer, ospreys, and bald eagles may be seen along these rivers.

Matagamon Wilderness
Donald & Alan Dudley
Box 220
Patten, ME 04765
(207) 528-2448
Webster Lake, Webster Stream, East Branch Penobscot River, Matagamon Lake
Max. rapids: III-IV
Maine Campground Owners Association, Maine Guides Association

Located in the wilds as its name suggests, Matagamon Wilderness offers excellent fishing and challenging waters in an uninhabited mountainous area. Moose, deer, bears, and eagles are common.

The outfitter rents canoes and provides guided canoe trips of up to 5 days, with lessons, camping, and swimming

available. The season runs from May through August. Paddlers should be in good physical shape for the wilderness trips. There is excellent fishing for brook and lake trout, salmon, and whitefish.

Mount Pleasant Canoe & Kayak
Don Peckham
P.O. Box 86
W. Rockport, ME 04865
(207) 785-4309
Penobscot West Branch, St. Croix Rivers, Maine coast
Max. rapids: I-II

Novice paddlers who enjoy leisurely birding, camping, and wildlife are typical customers of Mt. Pleasant Canoe & Kayak. The outfitter offers guided canoe and sea kayak trips of 1/2 day to 3 days.

During the May-to-October season, kayakers may view schooners and sailboats against a mountainous backdrop, with abundant wildlife, including seals, porpoises, moose, and ospreys.

North Country Guide Service
Steve Roderick
RFD #1, Box 2840
McFalls, ME 04256
(207) 539-8483
Allagash River
Max. rapids: I-II
Maine Professional Guides Association

North Country Guide Service runs guided trips of 6 or 7 days on the Allagash Wilderness Waterway and Allagash River. These trips, with Class I-II rapids, are easy, relaxing, and fine for people of all ages. All canoes are equipped with motors, which give paddlers a rest when they want one. As a result, guests can be assured of travelling greater distances. 6-day trips, for instance, cover 98 miles.

On these trips, paddlers can enjoy clean waters, protected wilderness, and certain success at spotting moose and deer at close range. Ducks, geese, eagles, and osprey are also abundant. Fishing for brook trout, lake trout, salmon, and whitefish is excellent. North Country's season runs from May to September.

North Country Rivers
Jim Murton
P.O. Box 47
E. Vassalboro, ME 04935
(207) 923-3492, (800) 348-8871
Penobscot, Kennebec, Dead Rivers
Max. rapids: V+
America Outdoors

North Country Rivers offers guided canoe, kayak, and raft trips on the Penobscot, Kennebec, and Dead Rivers. With these rivers to choose from, all paddlers, from beginners to experts, can find a trip to suit their skills. On all trips, guests can enjoy Maine's vast, pristine wilderness, with good fishing for trout and landlocked salmon, and a chance to spot moose, bears, deer, eagles, and ospreys. North Country Rivers' season is from April to October.

Northern Outdoors
Wayne and Suzie Hockmeyer
P.O. Box 100, Route 201
The Forks, ME 04985
(207) 663-4466, (800) 765-RAFT (7238)
Kennebec River, Moosehead Lake
Max. rapids: III-IV
America Outdoors, Raft Maine Association

Northern Outdoors offers guided raft trips on the Kennebec and Penobscot Rivers from two outfitting locations, the Forks Resort Center and Penobscot Outdoor Center. The West branch of the Penobscot is a steep, turbulent, ledge-drop river, which is extremely challenging and best-suited for paddlers with some rafting experiences. Trips on the Penobscot also offer spectacular scenery and abundant wildlife, including moose, deer, and bald eagles.

Trips on the Kennebec pass through the biggest river gorge in New England. Guests may elect to run either a 12-mile trip with whitewater that is among the biggest in the East, or a lower eight-mile

"The Cribworks" rapid on the Penobscot River, Maine. Photo by Jan Lorimer, North Country Rivers, Inc., Vassalboro, Maine.

trip, which is gentler and very safe. The river also boasts pristine wilderness scenery and views of moose, deer, and bald eagles. During its April-to-October season, Northern Outdoors also offers good bass, trout and salmon fishing, inflatable-kayak trips, camping, cabins, and deluxe lodge rooms.

North Woods Ways
Alexandra & Garrett Conover
RR2, Box 159-A
Guilford, ME 04443
(207) 997-3723
St. John, Allagash, West Branch of Penobscot, other rivers in ME, Grand River in Labrador
Max. rapids: I-II
   North Woods Ways runs guided canoe trips of 5-14 days to some of the wildest places in Maine, Quebec and Labrador, using traditional equipment and travel skills. Paddlers float rivers with pure, drinkable water and watch wildlife such as bear, moose, deer, coyote, and birds. Trout and landlocked salmon may be caught during the May-October canoe season.

Pelletier's Campground
Norman L'Italien
Box 67
St. Francis, ME 04774
(207) 398-3187, (207) 834-6118
Allagash Waterway, St. John River
Max. rapids: I-II
   Pelletier's Campground rents canoes from May-September for easy floats on the Allagash and more challenging springtime paddling on the St. John. Lessons are available, and these 2-8 day trips are suitable for all who know the basics of camping and canoeing.
   The company calls the Allagash "a place of solace and refuge," with clean water and primitive, well-maintained campsites. Moose, deer, ducks and other waterfowl may be seen. Salmon and different trout species can be caught.

Moose drinking. Courtesy of Northern Outdoors, The Forks, Maine.

Penobscot River Outfitters
Richard LeVasseir
P.O. Box H
Medway, ME 04460
(207) 746-9349, (800) 794-KAMP (Maine only)
Penobscot River, Allagash River
Max. rapids: III-IV
   Penobscot River Outfitters offers guided and unguided canoe and kayak trips of 1-7 days on the East or West Branches of the Penobscot River and the Allagash Wilderness Waterway. Trips vary in difficulty, with runs to suit beginners and experienced paddlers. The scenic East Branch of the Penobscot has great fishing, is little-traveled, and has some challenging stretches of whitewater. The West Branch, also very scenic, is clean and has good fishing for salmon, trout, bass, and pike. Paddlers on all trips have a good chance of spotting moose, deer, eagles, beavers, otters, and bears.
   Penobscot River Outfitters' trips run from May to October.

A paddler negotiates Ledge Falls on the Kennebec River. Courtesy of Northern Outdoors, The Forks, Maine.

Ray's Guide Service
Ray Reitze
RFD 2, Box 2757
Canaan, ME 04924
(207) 426-8138
Allagash, St. John, West Branch of Penobscot, Moose, Aroostook, Big Black Rivers
Max. rapids: III-IV

Ray's Guide Service runs canoe trips of up to 10 days through the beautiful mountain scenery of Maine's remote woodland. Ray Reitze, a native of the area, knows the wildlife, teaches wilderness survival, and is credited with a pleasant Down East sense of humor.

His trips cater to young and old, novices, and experts, featuring clean water, swimming, camping, fishing for trout and salmon, and watching moose, loons, eagles, and other wildlife. The season runs from May to October.

Saco Bound Inc.
Ned McSherry
P.O. Box 119
Center Conway, NH 03813
(603) 447-2177, (603) 447-3801
Max. rapids: None
PPA, Saco River Rec. Council

The Saco River is a perfect stream for family floating, and Saco Bound is ideally placed for enabling paddlers to relish it. Saco Bound rents canoes and kayaks from May 1-October 15 for periods of 1/2 day to 3 days, with ample campsites available on beaches and sandbars along a 43-mile route. The company runs guided day trips with barbecue lunches on Tuesdays and Thursdays in July and August.

During the summer months the crystal-clear stream is warm and levels average three to four feet, with deeper holes for swimming. Early October is the time to experience brilliant fall foliage, when the White Mountains are ablaze with color.

**Sunrise Country Canoe
Expeditions, Inc.**
Martin Brown
Cathance Lake
Grove Post, ME 04657
(207) 454-7708, (800) RIVER-30
St. Croix, St. John, Machias Rivers
Max. rapids: III-IV
PPA, Maine Professional Guides Association,
America Outdoors, American Rivers

For over 20 years, Sunrise Country
Canoe Expeditions has run canoe expeditions, specializing in whitewater technique and offering lessons, rentals, and
guided trips. In Maine, the outfitter runs
excursions on the St. Croix, Machias,
and St. John Rivers. These trips have
rapids of Class I-III, last 4-10 days, and
are set in remote, unspoiled wilderness.
The St. Croix and St. John trips have
easy to moderate rapids and are suitable
for novices as well as experienced paddlers. Trips on the Machias are more
difficult, offering fine technical whitewater over the course of an extended
wilderness journey.

Sunrise Country Expeditions also offers trips on three rivers in Quebec,
Arctic expeditions to Baffin Island,
Ungava in Arctic Quebec and Iceland,
and paddling amid the deserts of the
American Southwest. The season runs
from March to mid-October.

Unicorn Expeditions
Jay Schurman
P.O. Box T
Brunswick, ME 04011
(207) 725-2255, (800) UNICORN
Kennebec, Penobscot, Dead Rivers
Max. rapids: V+
America Outdoors

Unicorn Expeditions offers guided
canoe, kayak, and raft trips and canoe
rentals for trips of 1-6 days on the Kennebec, Penobscot, and Dead Rivers in
Maine; the Hudson and Moose Rivers in
New York; and the Deerfield River in
Massachusetts. These trips range widely
in difficulty to suit all skill levels from
beginner to expert. Moose River trips

have some of the wildest whitewater in
the Northeast; the dam-controlled
Penobscot and Kennebec Rivers ensure
Class V whitewater all summer long;
and the Hudson's spring high water
offers 16 miles of exhilarating Class III
and IV rapids.

Among the wildlife to see on these
trips are moose, bald eagles, bears, deer,
and ospreys. There is also fishing for
bass, salmon, and trout. During its April-
to-October season, Unicorn also offers
"getaway" packages, which include rafting and lodge or inn accommodations.

Voyagers Whitewater
John P. Kokajko
Route 201
The Forks, ME 04985
(207) 663-4423
Kennebec River, Dead River, Penobscot River
Max. rapids: III-IV
America Outdoors

Voyagers Whitewater runs raft trips
of 1- and 2-days on the Kennebec River,
Dead River, and West Branch of the
Penobscot. These trips offer exciting
whitewater on clean wilderness rivers.
No prior rafting experience is required,
but participants should be in good
health and capable of vigorous physical
activity. On these trips, which run between May and October, paddlers can
also fish for trout and look for moose,
deer, bears, foxes, and other wildlife.

Wilderness Expeditions
John Willard
Box 41
Rockwood, ME 04478
(207) 534-2242, (800) 825-9453
Kennebec, Penobscot, Dead, Moose,
Allagash, St. John, Moosehead Rivers
Max. rapids: V+

Wilderness Expeditions runs guided
canoe, kayak, and raft trips and rents
canoes and kayaks for trips of 1-7 days
on Moosehead Lake, the Allagash Wilderness Waterway, and the Kennebec,
Penobscot, Dead, Moose, and St. John
Rivers. With this range of offerings, the

outfitters has organized trips for paddlers at all levels, from novice to expert, which feature wilderness scenery and moose, deer, bears, eagles, ospreys, beavers, and other wildlife. And for those who prefer to set their own dates and trip schedules, the company provides full or partial outfitting and helpful route suggestions. Boating runs from April to October.

As part of the Birches Resort, Wilderness Expeditions also offers horseback riding, ice fishing, and "cabin tent" and cottage rentals.

Wilds of Maine
Michael Patterson
2 Abby Lane
Yarmouth, ME 04096
(207) 846-9735
All of Maine's canoeing rivers
Max. rapids: I-II
ACA

Wilds of Maine lays on both regular and customized guided canoe trips to suit everyone from families with young children to whitewater enthusiasts. The company will take clients to any river of their choice, with fresh food cooked on open fires and all services and gear provided. Camping, swimming, paddling-lessons and exposure to Maine's wilderness are offered during the May-October season. Trips vary from 3-14 days and fishing is plentiful.

Woodland Acres, Camp N'Canoe
Chris and Sue Gantick
RR 1, Box 445
Brownfield, ME 04010
(207) 935-2529
Saco River
Max. rapids: I-II
PPA, Saco River Livery Association

Woodland Acres Camp N'Canoe offers shuttles and canoe rentals for 1-3 day trips on the Saco River in the foothills of the White Mountains. The river, which runs under several covered bridges, has clean water and lots of sandbars for camping, swimming, and picnics. Moose, loons, beavers, raccoons, and deer can be seen along its banks. Fishing is for brown trout, smallmouth bass, and pickerel.

Canoe trips on the Saco are suitable for "novices, families, and lazy people," but more accomplished paddlers can take longer trips with some Class II rapids. Rentals are available from May 15 to October 15.

Maryland

Where Maryland's northwestern panhandle reaches up into the Appalachians, it takes in a famous stretch of the Youghiogheny River known as the "Upper Yough." Whitewater experts call it one of the world's most difficult commercially rafted rivers. It begins to get hairy at Bastard Falls, dropping an average of 116 feet per mile. Along one 3.5 mile section of the river alone, the Upper Yough has more than 20 Class IV and V rapids sporting such odd names as Snaggle Tooth, Meat Cleaver, Powerful Popper, Lost-n-Found, Cheeseburger and Double Pencil Sharpener.

The Savage River, flowing through Savage River State Forest elsewhere in the panhandle, rivals the Upper Yough as a whitewater stream. Its five miles of Class III-IV rapids (Class IV-V at high water) fed by dependable reservoir releases have made it a favorite venue of national slalom and whitewater racing. It was the scene of the 1972 Olympic trials, the 1989 World Championships, and the 1992 U.S. Olympic Whitewater Slalom Team trials.

By contrast, the Pocomoke River at the other end of the state meanders placidly through the coastal flats of the Delmarva (Delaware-Maryland-Virginia) peninsula between Chesapeake Bay and the Atlantic. With its wealth of blue herons, ospreys, eagles, ducks, and fish, its appeal is strictly to birdwatchers and anglers.

Like its neighbors to the north and south, Maryland encompasses three great geological divides: the Appalachian mountains, the Piedmont's rolling plateau and the coastal plain bestriding Chesapeake Bay and extending to the Atlantic. The Potomac traverses all three as its winding course divides Maryland from Virginia.

The Potomac has a great asset for paddlers who like to step ashore and see the sights: much of its left bank belongs to the C & O National Historical Park. Its famous 185-mile towpath was heavily damaged in the floods of early 1996 and largely closed for reconstruction. Nevertheless, canoeists can see disused locks and admire the work of those tough Irish immigrants who built the Chesapeake and Ohio canal in the 19th century. They can tour Antietam battlefield (see below), maybe take in a stretch of the

Shenandoah (see West Virginia), and explore historic Harpers Ferry, where the two rivers converge. The Potomac can be paddled year-round and i cleaner than its reputation. It supports bass and other cleanwater fish, and even around Washington, D.C. it is said to be safe for swimming. The bes whitewater and perhaps the finest scenery are to be found on the ten mile stretch upstream from the capital to Great Falls. These falls themselve should be portaged. So should Little Falls and Brookmont Dam, an inno cent-looking two-foot weir that has, in the words of one authority, "a rever sal that will stop you and never let you go."

Due south of Hagerstown, Antietam Creek provides a closeup view o Antietam Battlefield, scene of the Civil War's bloodiest single-day encoun ter. This easy 12-mile float, starting from Devils Backbone Park, is best run in spring and autumn when water levels are high. Bordering the Maryland panhandle is the North Branch of the Potomac, which is also floatable in late summer and early fall after dam releases from Bloomington Lake. Close to Baltimore but only runnable in winter and spring after heavy rain is a three-mile trip down Gunpowder River through Gunpowder Falls Stat Park.

Adventure Bound, Inc.
Len Bostian
1440 Jarrettsville Rd.
Jarrettsville, MD 21084
(410) 557-7116
Susquehanna, Juwiata, Potomac, Cacapon Rivers
Max. rapids: I-II

Adventure Bound offers guided canoe trips and rents canoes to beginners and others for easy trips of 1-10 days on clean rivers with excellent fishing. Amid beautiful mountains and valleys, paddlers can glimpse deer, bears, raccoon, skunk, and otters. These rivers also boast good fishing for bass, muskie, and pike.

Trips are varied, and camping, swimming, and paddling lessons are available. Adventure Bound's season runs from April to October.

Assateague Island National Seashore
National Park Service
7206 Nat. Seashore Lane
Berlin, MD 21811
(410) 641-1441
Chincoteague Bay, behind Assateague Island National Seashore
Max rapids: None

The National Park Service runs unique two-hour canoe tours of the wetlands of a minimally developed Atlantic coast barrier island from June 25 to August 22. Participants also can camp, swim, watch wading birds, and study the biodiversity of marine wetlands. There is no fishing in the bayside canoeing area, which is a fish nursery. But fishermen can surfcast in the ocean. A concessioner rents canoes weekends in the spring and fall, and daily in the summer. The park service has a brochure describing four backcountry bayside canoe-in campsites.

Harpers Ferry River Riders, Inc.
Mark Grimes
P.O. Box 267
Knoxville, MD 21758
(301) 834-8051, (800) 326-7238
Shenandoah River, Potomac River,
Tygart River
Max. rapids: III-IV

Harpers Ferry River Riders offers 1-day guided raft and tube trips and canoe and kayak rentals on the Shenandoah, Potomac, and Tygart Rivers. Trips on the Potomac and Shenandoah, with Class I-III rapids, are fine for beginners and offer scenic views of historic Harpers Ferry, wooded mountains, and abundant wildlife, including great blue herons, egrets, nesting bald eagles, turtles, geese, deer, and ducks. The two rivers also feature good fishing for smallmouth and largemouth bass, catfish, panfish, and carp.

The Tygart River, also scenic, has more challenging whitewater with up to Class V rapids. The outfitter's season is from April to October.

Historical River Tours
Eric & Peggy Neilson
Box 183
West Friendship, MD 21794
(304) 535-6649
Shenandoah, North Branch Potomac Rivers
Max. rapids: II-III
America Outdoors

Historical River Tours offers guided kayak and raft trips to historic Harpers Ferry and both river and bike trips along the C. & O. Canal, with its disused locks and other early structures. In addition, the company runs guided floats on both the Potomac and Shenandoah, with spectacular cliffs, wildlife, and fishing for smallmouth bass and pike.

Easily reachable from Washington, D.C. and Baltimore, the outfitter caters especially to family, church and youth groups, with "good, clean, family fun." Paddling lessons are available during the April-October season.

Laurel Highlands River Tours
Mark and Linda McCarty
P.O. Box 107
Ohiopyle, PA 15470
(412) 329-8531, (800) 4 RAFTIN
Upper Youghiogheny River
Max. rapids: V+
America Outdoors

Laurel Highlands River Tours, one of the oldest whitewater companies in the East, claims to have the largest fleet of equipment anywhere. It operates on the Cheat River as well as the Lower, Middle, and Upper Youghiogheny from bases in Albright, W.Va., Ohiopyle, Pa. and Friendsville, Md. In a season running from March to October, it offers guided raft trips and rents both rafts and canoes for floats on both rivers. All are 1-day trips.

The "Yough" has the most popular whitewater in the East and the Cheat is famed for its spring thrills. Canoeing and kayaking instruction is available and accommodations range from camping to luxury motels.

Light White Canoe Floats
C. Fenner Goldsborough
1008 Union Ave.
Baltimore, MD 21211
(410) 889-9585
Tributaries of the Susquehanna River:
Gunpowder, Deer Creek, Little Falls
Western Run, Muddy Creek
Max. rapids: I-II

Light White Canoe Floats rents canoes for day trips from May 1 through October on clean waters with swimming holes and good fishing for trout, crappie, and sunfish. Paddling lessons are available on these outings, which are suitable for novices and nature lovers. Paddlers can see geese, swans, herons, ducks, and trout.

Rafters brave the fierce rapids of the Upper Youghiogheny. Courtesy of Laurel Highlands River Tours, Ohiopyle, Pennsylvania.

Mountain Streams and Trails Outfitters
Michael and Ralph McCarty
P.O. Box 106, Route 381
Ohiopyle, PA 15470
(800) 245-4090
Upper Youghiogheny River
Max. rapids: V+
America Outdoors

Mountain Streams and Trails operates on all three sections of the Youghiogheny as well as the Class III-IV Cheat, the challenging Tygart, isolated Big Sandy Creek, and the Class III-VI Upper and Lower Gauley rivers. It runs guided raft and kayak trips in addition to renting canoes, kayaks, and rafts, tailoring its trips to suit the needs of every paddler.

The company has skilled guides, trained in first aid and equipped with radios. They take guests through the spectacular panorama of maples, pines, and rhododendrons that blanket the walls of the Middle and Lower Yough River canyon, habitat for deer, beavers, bears, ospreys, herons and an occasional wildcat. 1-day and 2-day tours are offered during a March-October season.

Passages to Adventure
Benjy Simpson
P.O. Box 71
Fayetteville, WV 25840
(304) 574-1037, (800) 634-3785
Upper Youghiogheny
Max. rapids: V+
America Outdoors, Outdoor Recreation Coalition of America

Passages to Adventure provides guided canoe, inflatable kayak and raft

rips as well as renting canoes and inflat-
ble kayaks on the Cheat, New, and
Gauley Rivers in West Virginia and the
Upper Youghiogheny in Maryland.

With this variety, the company caters
to all paddlers, from beginners to experts. The wild Cheat River has challenging, technical rapids that come in
quick succession down a majestic canyon. The Lower New River offers huge
rolling waves, giving a "rollercoaster"
ride that is the company's most popular
trip. The Upper New is wide, scenic,
and has Class II rapids — ideal for
families and first-time rafters. The
Upper Gauley has superb whitewater
that requires previous paddling experience. The Lower Gauley has huge waves
but doesn't require prior experience.
Finally, the Upper Yough is famous for
its extremely technical Class IV-V+
rapids.

Pocomoke River Canoe Co.

Barry R. Laws
312 N. Washington Street
Snow Hill, MD 21863
(410) 632-3971
Pocomoke River, Nassawango Creek
Max. rapids: None

Pocomoke River Canoe Co. offers
guided canoe trips and canoe rentals
of 1-3 days on the Pocomoke River and
Nassawango Creek. These trips are
especially good for novices, nature lovers, and bird watchers, offering views of
unspoiled regions on the Eastern Shore
and particularly abundant wildlife, including great blue herons, eagles, otters,
ospreys, and ducks. Fishing is for bass,
gar, and other freshwater fish.

Precision Rafting Expeditions, Inc.

Roger Zbel
Box 185
Friendsville, MD 21531
(301) 746-5290, (800) 477-3723
Upper Youghiogheny, Cheat, Big Sandy,
Gauley & Russell Fork Rivers
Max. rapids: V+

Precision Rafting offers guided and
unguided rafting and kayaking on some
of the most unspoiled rivers in the East.
These day trips range from total flatwater to hair-raising Class V adventures. A
small company with a personal touch,
Precision Rafting boasts an outstanding
safety record and sets a high standard
for all its trips. The Big Sandy is pristine
and has several beautiful waterfalls,
while the Yough is a wild and scenic
river canyon. Wildlife includes deer,
bear and birds of prey, along with trout
and bass.

Rainy Day, Inc.

Donald and Mabel Rogers
11238 Adkins Road
Berlin, MD 21811
(410) 641-5029
Pocomoke River, Sinepauxent Bay
Max. rapids: None

Rainy Day, Inc., rents canoes for flatwater, scenic trips on Pocomoke River
and in the bay behind Assateague Island
at the Assateague Island National Seashore. These trips, which require no
paddling experience, offer a peaceful
way to explore wetlands and coastal
waters; fish for flounder, spot, sea bass,
and crabs; gather clams; and spot Assateague wild ponies, sika deer, and
abundant waterfowl. Camping and
swimming are also available.

Rainy Day's season is from April to
October.

River & Trail Outfitters
Lee Baihly
604 Valley Road
Knoxville, MD 21758
(301) 695-5177
Shenandoah River, Potomac River,
Antietam Creek
Max. rapids: None

River & Trail Outfitter runs guided and unguided canoe and raft trips on the Shenandoah and Potomac Rivers. An excellent beginners' raft trip and intermediate canoe trip is the "Staircase," a six-mile run down the Shenandoah to its confluence with the Potomac at Harpers Ferry. Highlights of this Class I-III trip include a mile-long series of rapids and ledges that demands attentive paddling. A more challenging raft trip is a seven-mile run on the North Branch of the Potomac. This guided trip has Class I-III rapids in close succession, with waves and rollers up to six feet high. Canoe and kayak lessons and several other canoe trips are available. These include "Taylor's Landing," an 11-mile flatwater trip on the upper Potomac; the "Needles," a 1/2-day run on the Potomac that includes a challenging mile-long rock garden with Class I-II rapids.

1-3 day trips on the calm waters of the lower Shenandoah are also available. Many of these trips boast excellent bass fishing and a chance to spot herons, ospreys, bald eagles, and deer. River & Trail's season runs from April to November.

Upper Yough Expeditions
Gary Davis and Dave Martin
P.O. Box 158
Friendsville, MD 21531
(301) 746-5808, (800) 248-1UYE
Upper Youghiogheny River
Max. rapids: V+
NAPSA

Upper Yough Expeditions runs thrilling half-day whitewater trips on the Upper Youghiogheny. Trips, in guided four-man, self-bailing rafts, are 11 miles long and include dozens of spectacular rapids. The 3.5-mile "heart" of the Upper Yough is virtually one huge rapid in itself. This stretch alone has more than 20 Class IV and V rapids. Experienced rafters are preferred on these trips and the Class V trips the outfitter offers on the Top Yough, Russell Fork, Big Sandy, North Branch of the Potomac, and Savage Rivers.

Upper Yough Expeditions' season runs from March to November. Russell Fork dam releases are on October weekends only.

USA RAFT
Mary Kay Heffernan
P.O. Box 277
Rowlesburg, WV 26425
(800) USA RAFT
North Fork Potomac River, Gauley River,
Cheat River, Tygart River, New River,
Upper Youghiogheny River, Nolichucky
River, Ocoee River, Nantahala River,
French Broad River
Max. rapids: II-III
America Outdoors

USA Raft offers outings on ten of the best whitewater rivers in the East — the Russell Fork in Kentucky; the Upper Youghiogeny in Maryland; the Nolichucky, French Broad, and Nantahala in North Carolina; the Nolichucky and Ocoee in Tennessee; and the New, Gauley, Cheat, and Tygart in West Virginia.

With this selection of trips, rivers, and outfitters, USA Raft offers affordable outings to suit paddlers of all skill levels at locations convenient to residents throughout the Middle Atlantic and Southeast.

Whitewater Adventures, Inc.

Robert and Shirley Marietta
P.O. Box 31
Ohiopyle, PA 15470
(412) 329-8850, (800) WWA-RAFT
(992-7238)
Upper Youghiogheny River
Max. rapids: V+
America Outdoors

Whitewater Adventures runs guided raft and kayak trips on the Lower, Middle, and Upper Youghiogheny as well as renting canoes, kayaks, and rafts from March to November. Paddlers can take their pick; the dam-controlled Yough is rated Class V on its upper section and Classes III and II on its lower and middle stretches, respectively. Trips are suitable for "folks from 12-100 who are willing to paddle a bit and have a good time."

A highly professional staff and the best modern equipment are mainstays of the company, which offers lessons and provides a guide for every raft on the steep and technical Upper Yough. Trout, walleye, and bass can be caught on the Yough as it winds through the Laurel Highland Mountains.

In West Virginia, Whitewater Adventures of Cheat River Canyon runs "very thrilling" guided raft trips from March to July through Class IV-V rapids on the free-flowing Cheat River. The stream cuts through a very steep canyon in an historic part of West Virginia. It has beautiful wildflowers and mountain laurel, along with deer, wild turkeys, and grouse.

One of the oldest outfitters on the Cheat river, the company has skilled guides and the latest equipment. Rafts generally hold eight people and the day trips cover a 12-mile distance.

Rafters on the Lower Yough. Courtesy of Wilderness Voyageurs, Ohiopyle, Pennsylvania.

Massachusetts

P addling may be enjoyed in the Mayflower State anywhere from the coast lowlands and islands around Cape Cod to the wooded Berkshire Hills i the west. The four thousand miles of rivers in Massachusetts include th great Connecticut River that flows north-south across the state and th wide Merrimack that swings through the northeast corner past Lowel Historic sites and fall colors greatly enhance the state's sightseeing appeal

Some of the best canoe trails in Massachusetts are on the Deerfield Rive which runs through the rolling Berkshires to join the Connecticut Rive at Greenfield. But it is essential to time it right: the Deerfield varies fror a rampaging stream at high water to a placid float. There is Class IV wil water and equally wild scenery on the upper river as it comes in from Ver mont. From Shelburne Falls downstream the river is less hazardous bu its levels can still change very swiftly, depending on dam releases and rain fall or sudden thaws. The Deerfield is described as the last wilderness rive in southern New England. Its fish include trout and bass and its wildlif ranges from beaver and bear to hawks and eagles.

The Nashua, which flows northwards across the New Hampshire stat line to its confluence with the Merrimack in Nashua, has been much cleane up in recent years. Fish and wildlife are returning. Flocks of great blue her ons are seen at Pepperell Pond, a beauty-spot rich in animal and plant life A gentle paddle on the Nashua can reveal tracks of raccoon, deer, beave muskrat, and turtles. Another great Massachusetts river for the naturalis is the Ipswich, in the northeast corner of the state, which passes through a Audubon bird sanctuary.

Paramount among all the rivers in southern New England is the Con necticut. By the time it reaches Massachusetts it is already a broad waterwa runnable at all water levels and well supplied with campsites. One attrac tive section of the river is the 21 miles of flatwater upstream from Nortf ampton. Here the scenery is rural and unsullied by civilization except fc power boats at intervals. Between Northampton and Holyoke the stream cu through the Holyoke Range, with Mt. Nonotuck and Mt. Tom on the right an Mt. Holyoke on the left. It then turns urban through Holyoke and Springfielc

The Merrimack, also swollen to a wide river before it enters Massachusetts from New Hampshire, is navigable at all times. It runs through a mixture of woodland and towns as it parallels the state line to the sea and becomes tidal after it passes through Lawrence.

The Blackstone River flows southwards from Worcester, with scenic stretches between milltowns. Parts of the canal built to connect Worcester and Providence are still intact and the area around Rice City Pond is a state recreation area. The river has some whitewater but many dams which must be portaged.

For a different kind of experience altogether, paddlers visit Cape Cod, where canoeists and kayakers can explore both fresh and salt water habitats of many kinds of wildlife. These include lakes, streams, estuaries, salt marshes and bays, where paddlers can find harbor seals, gray seals, ospreys, many kinds of fish and even an occasional whale.

Adventure Learning Center
John & Nancy Halloran
57 Bear Hill
Merrimac, MA 01860
(508) 346-9728, (800) 649-9728
Atlantic Coast north of Boston and
MA & NH river estuaries
Max. rapids: None
TASK

Sea kayaking in interesting areas abounding in shore birds is provided by Adventure Learning from May through September. Day trips with paddling lessons are available as well as tours for seasoned paddlers. Experienced guides take clients to islands and waters which seem wild although close to cities. Whale-watching trips are scheduled. The company also rents canoes and kayaks.

Back Country Tours, Inc.
Allan McGroary
39 Hollis Street
Pepperell, MA 01463
(508) 433-9381, (800) 649-9381 (MA)
Connecticut River, Nashua River
Max. rapids: I-II

Back Country Tours, Inc., specializes in guided canoe trips and canoe rentals on "lesser known, uncrowded scenic waterways." Its trips run on the Souhegan and Merrimack Rivers in New Hampshire; the Sauantacook and Nissitissit Rivers in Massachusetts; the Connecticut and Nashua Rivers in New Hampshire and Massachusetts; the Delaware River in New York, Pennsylvania, and New Jersey; the St. John in Maine; the Blackwater, Sweetwater, and Juniper Rivers in Florida; and nine lakes near Long Pond Mountain in New York's Adirondacks. Several of these excursion are "vacation" trips of 3-7 days that offer lodging at campgrounds, cabins, or bed-and-breakfast inns. All trips are suitable for beginners and experienced paddlers.

Back Country Tours' season runs from July to November.

Barton Cove Canoes & Campground
Bill Gabriel
49 Millers Falls Rd.
Northfield, MA 01360
(413) 659-4470 (winter), (413) 863-9300 (summer)
Connecticut River
Max. rapids: None
PPA

Barton Cove rents canoes for 1- and 2-day trips on the quiet, scenic Connecticut River with its great fishing for bass, pickerel, and shad. Bald eagles and deer may be viewed. The company caters to families, Scout and church groups, with camping available. Its season runs May-October.

Cape Cod Coastal Canoeing
Fred & Shirley Bull
36 Spectacle Pond Dr.
E. Falmouth, MA 02536
(508) 564-4051
Coastal salt marshes, bays, inlets, barrier spits & estuaries
Max. rapids: None
PPA

This company runs guided canoe and sea kayak trips lasting 3-4 hours in clean tidal waters. Knowledgeable guides take small groups on naturalist interpretive tours of salt marshes, places of quiet serenity filled with varied flora and fauna. Suitable for novice and experienced paddlers alike, these trips are ideal for families, clubs, individuals and hobbyists such as birders and photographers.

Charles River Canoe & Kayak Center
Larry Smith
2401 Commonwealth Ave.
Newton, MA 02166
(617) 965-5110
Boston Harbor, Massachusetts coast, Charles, North & Sudbury Rivers
Max. rapids: None
PPA

Paddlers may enjoy rural beauty in an urban setting when they rent canoes and kayaks or take guided canoe and kayak trips from the Charles River Canoe & Kayak Center. Canoe trips are suitable for beginners, but kayakers must have previous experience or take lessons at the Center before setting out.

Canoeists take local 1-day river outings; kayakers may explore the eastern Massachusetts coast and Boston Harbor. The company's season runs from April through September.

Crab Apple Whitewater, Inc.
Charles A. Peabody
P.O. Box 295
Charlemont, MA 01339
(800) 553-7238, (413) 339-6660
Deerfield River

Crab Apple Whitewater, a family business, runs guided raft trips from April to October through a wilderness area in the Berkshire Mountains of western Massachusetts. The Fife Brook section of the Deerfield River offers easy Class II-III whitewater, a great introduction to rafting for families with children age 8 and up. The Monroe Bridge stretch presents technical, challenging whitewater for experienced paddlers.

Along the Deerfield, a catch-and-release trout stream, paddlers may spot beavers and otters.

Essex River Basin Adventures
Richard Osborn, Tom Ellis
66 Rear Main St., Box 270
Essex, MA 01929
(508) 768-ERBA, (800) KAYAK-04
Essex River, coastal islands
Max. rapids: None
PPA

Guided kayak trips on the protected waters of the Essex River estuary are provided by this outfitter from May to November. In addition, it runs trips with more experienced kayakers to explore offshore islands. Several guides accompany each tour, so that paddlers of varying skills can be accommodated. A favorite destination is Crane's Beach, a four-mile unspoiled barrier beach. Hog Island and other islands along the protected marshland of the Essex River also make this a special place. Ospreys, herons, cormorants and shorebirds may be seen, and fishing is for striped bass.

Nashoba Paddler

Neal Menscher
Rte. 225 at Nashua River, Box 228
W. Groton, MA 01472
(508) 448-8699
*Nashua, Squannacook, Deerfield Rivers
(MA), St. Croix River (ME), Merrimack
River (NH), Tully Lakes (MA)*
Max. rapids: I-II
PA

Nashoba Paddler runs guided canoe trips and rents both canoes and kayaks for outings from May to October on a variety of New England rivers. The company offers personal service and emphasizes relaxed enjoyment of the streams, with their forested banks and natural beauty. Lessons are available on both flatwater and whitewater to improve paddling technique. Trips last up to five days, with camping and swimming available. Wildlife includes blue heron, turtle, beaver, mink, otter and deer. Striped bass are abundant on the Nashua and Squannacook.

The Outdoor Centre of New England

10 Pleasant Street
Millers Falls, MA 01349
(413) 659-3926
Millers, Deerfield, Ashuelot, West Rivers
Max. rapids: III-IV

The Outdoor Center of New England (OCNE) claims to be the best technical paddling school in the Northeast. The school has a broad array of paddling classes for all levels, beginner to expert, in canoeing and kayaking. Instruction is available in solo and decked canoes, and kayaking. Workshops include rolling clinics, squirt clinics, over-40 classes, and "kids" classes.

The OCNE, open April to October, conducts whitewater playboating classes on the Millers, Deerfield, Ashuelot, and West Rivers. The school specializes in private instruction for both individuals and small groups, tailored to meet students' needs and ability.

Palmer River Canoe & Kayak

Ray & Mary Brierly
206 Wheeler St. (mailing & canoe store)
Rehoboth, MA 02769
Deans Plaza (Taunton River location)
Rte. 44
Raynham, MA 02767
(508) 336-2274
Palmer, Taunton, Running, Nemasket Rivers
Max. rapids: II
PPA

Palmer River Canoe & Kayak offers both guided and unguided canoe and kayak trips on the flatwater Palmer River. These are suitable for families who enjoy rural countryside and fishing for trout, bass, pickerel, and perch. It also has Class II floats on the Taunton River by canoe, kayak, and raft. These may last from 1 1/2 hours to overnight and offer views of bald eagles. Paddling lessons are given by certified instructors. The season runs April-October.

Zoar Outdoor, Inc.

Bruce Lessels
Mohawk Trail, Box 245
Charlemont, MA 01339
(800) 532-7483
Deerfield River, West River
Max. rapids: III-IV
America Outdoors

Zoar Outdoor, Inc., rents canoes and kayaks and leads guided trips by canoe, kayak, and raft on the Deerfield and West Rivers. Its 1-day trips vary in difficulty to suit paddlers of all levels, from beginner to expert.

All trips pass through the rolling wooded hills of the Berkshires, offering excellent scenery, and a chance to spot beavers, deer, bears, coyotes, foxes, hawks, and eagles. The rivers also offer good fishing for trout and bass. Zoar's season runs from April to October.

Michigan

Michigan is a favorite state for recreation, with fishing rivaling winter sports as the most popular outdoors pastime. Fishermen find brook, brown and rainbow trout on rivers throughout the state. But those who prefer just to paddle and float find plenty of opportunities for good canoeing, kayaking and tubing.

The Sturgeon River just south of Mackinac Strait no longer lives up to its name as a source of caviar. But it is an excellent trout stream and the fastest river in the Lower Peninsula. To call it "challenging" is an exaggeration, but with its brisk current, hairpin turns and other obstacles it is not recommended for novices, non-swimmers or small children. The nearby Pigeon River, designated as one of Michigan's Wild and Scenic streams, flows through Pigeon River State Forest. A clear river, it is home to the only elk herd east of the Mississippi and other wildlife including beaver, muskrat, turkey, porcupine, turkey, fox and heron.

A little further south, near the town of Grayling, the well-known Au Sable begins its journey eastward to Lake Huron flanked by its North and South Branches. The name Grayling harks back to happier days for fishermen some 150 years ago, when the abundance of grayling in the Au Sable attracted anglers from far and wide. Since then, the grayling has become extinct in the river's waters, but brook, brown and rainbow trout are still plentiful. Although several dams interrupt the river's flow, the Au Sable is an ideal stream for family canoeing. Portages are clearly marked, the water is clean and much of the river runs through unspoiled territory where primitive camping is free. Average water depth on the 32-mile stretch below Mio Dam — the National Scenic River section — is between one and three feet and guaranteed by the dam. Beaver, deer, ducks, otter, wild mink and bald eagles may be enjoyed during a leisurely float.

The Muskegon is the longest of Michigan's rivers and navigable almost from its source near Houghton Lake in the middle of the Upper Peninsula to its outlet into Lake Michigan at Muskegon. The Muskegon has only one difficult stretch, at Big Rapids, and one strenuous portage, at Hardy Dam. Otherwise it rates as another good family paddling stream. Much of the and it traverses is state property and many campgrounds line its 170-mile course. The fishing varies from place to place: the best trout are upstream near Evart and there are good runs of salmon and steelhead from Muskegon up to Croton Dam.

Another long river is the Manistee, which flows more than 150 miles southwest from the Otsego Lake area to its mouth at Manistee on Lake Michigan. With its remoteness, campgrounds, and clean water, it is described as one of the Lower Peninsula's finest rivers for expedition canoeing and camping. Here, again, the fishing is varied and excellent, ranging from salmon downstream to walleyes, smallmouth bass and northern pike above Tippy Dam and brown or brook trout upstream.

Very popular among canoeists is the Pine River, which flows into the Manistee at Tippy Dam Pond. It gets so crowded on Saturdays that some outfitters urge customers to come on Sundays or weekdays. The Pine is claimed to be Michigan's best fast water canoeing river. It runs through the Manistee National Forest, and in order to keep the river banks unspoiled, camping is forbidden within a one-quarter mile corridor each side of the stream except at developed campgrounds.

Further south within Manistee National Forest, the Pine River runs parallel to the Muskegon into Lake Michigan. Its lower section, covering past 60 miles before the river delta begins, is an appealing run. It offers good fishing, many interesting wildlife species — notably turtles — and a glimpse of the high rollways that were used during the lumber boom of the 19th century to pile and store logs.

Finally the Upper Peninsula, where the most celebrated stream is the Big Two Hearted River, made famous by Ernest Hemingway when he used it for the title of his short story about the Fox River. It is the only Wilderness River in Michigan and claimed to be one of the top ten trout streams in America. But it is plagued by black flies in early summer and logjams year-round. Although there is an easy 4-6 hour float down the lowest stretch of the river, several portages are needed to skirt logjams further upstream.

For the Lake Superior sea kayaker, the colorful sandstone cliffs, white and and pebble beaches of the Pictured Rocks National Lakeshore provide a joyous paradise. During the summer season, paddlers step ashore from the lake's clear blue waters to explore caves and natural rock formations. The put-in is at Sand Point, near Munising, and camping is available at designated sites.

MICHIGAN

Alcona Canoe Rental, Inc.
Kevin Ornatowski
6351 Bamfield Road
Glennie, MI 48737
(517) 735-2973, (800) 526-7080
Au Sable Rivers
Max. rapids: None
RCA, PPA

Alcona Canoe Rental runs canoe, tube and kayak trips on the Au Sable River. All trips on this national wild and scenic river are easy enough for beginners and families and offer great trout, walleye, and bass fishing. Paddlers can also spot whitetail deer, bald eagles, mink, beaver, otter, ducks, and geese.

Trips offered through this wooded wilderness are 2 1/2- hour, 5-hour and overnight excursions which pass through federal land where camping is free. During its April-to-October season, Alcona also offers cabin rentals, primitive campsites, hot showers and a camp store.

Anchor Bay & St. John's Marsh Canoe & Boat Livery
Walter & Kris Dombrowski
7427 Dyke Rd.
Algonac, MI 48001
(810) 725-0009
Anchor Bay to North Channel to Lake St. Clair, St. John's Marsh
Max. rapids: None
PPA

Located next to the St. John's Marsh wildlife sanctuary, this outfitter rents canoes, kayaks, and peddle boats for trips of up to a week. On these easy floats, paddlers can see rich wildlife, including swans, ducks, turtles, and bald eagles. Fishing is for bass, pike, walleye, smelt, and panfish.

AuSable Canoes
John H. Cammin
217 Alger
Grayling, MI 49738
(517) 348-5851
Au Sable River
Max. rapids: None
Michigan Recreational Canoeing Association
PPA

AuSable Canoes rents canoes and kayaks and provides guided trips on the clean, calm Au Sable from April to October. Paddlers can angle for trout while admiring a wide array of wildlife including minks, beavers, deer, bears, otters, and eagles.

Trips, which range from less than three hours to a full week, are very easy, ideal for families and groups. Camping is available in the state and national forest of mixed pines and hardwoods.

Baldwin Canoe Rental
P.O. Box 269
Baldwin, MI 49304
(616) 745-4669
Pere Marquette, Pine Rivers
Max. rapids: I-II
Recreational Canoeing Association, PPA

"We treat people like we would want to be treated" has been the motto of Baldwin Canoe Rental for the past 25 years. It rents canoes and rafts for periods of 1-5 days from April to mid-October for trips on two National Scenic Rivers: the Pine and the Pere Marquette. The countryside is very scenic, with steep banks, clear, spring-fed waters, and abundant wildlife. Camping is available.

Carl's Canoe Service
Mark and Val Miltner
7325 West 50 Mile
Cadillac, MI 49601
(616) 862-3471, (800) 71-RIVER
Pine River
Max. rapids: I
RCA, PPA, ACA

Carl's Canoe Service rents canoes for 1-3 day trips on the Pine River. Quietwater, moving water and Class I white-water floats are available.

The Pine River runs clean and cold through undeveloped woodland that is 75 percent state and national forest. Passing through the Pine's deep river valley, paddlers can glimpse deer, raccoons, minks, beavers, muskrats, ducks, and otters. Trout fishing is especially good, as the river is a natural trout stream. During the April-to-November season, camping is also available at state, federal and private campgrounds along the river.

Note: The owners of Carl's Canoe Service also operate Marrik's Pine River Paddlesports Center. Both liveries can be reached at the same phone number.

Double R Ranch

Richard Reeves
424 Whites Bridge Road
Smyrna, MI 48887
(616) 794-0520
Flat River
Max. rapids: None

Double R Ranch rents canoes for 1-day trips on the Flat River. This flat-water river is good for novices and those seeking a peaceful, scenic trip. The river also offers good fishing for smallmouth bass and pike, and a chance to spot blue herons, turtles, and other wildlife.

The livery's season runs from May to October.

Grand Rogue Campgrounds — Canoe and Tube Livery

Wendell Briggs
5400 West River Drive
Belmont, MI 49306
(616) 361-1053
Grand River, Rogue River
Max. rapids: None
RCA

Grand Rogue Campground offers canoe trips on the Grand River and tubing on the Grand and Rogue Rivers. Trips last from one to four hours and are easy enough for beginners and families with small children. The Grand is a wide, slow-moving scenic river. The Rogue River, also scenic, is faster. Along both rivers floaters can spot ducks, deer, cranes, raccoons, and turtles and fish for bass, trout, pike, and walleye.

Guests can also enjoy Grand Rogue's modern campground with tent and R.V. camping, washroom, laundry, and camp-store. The season runs from May to October.

Happy Mohawk Canoe Livery

735 Fruitvale Road
Montague, MI 49437
(616) 894-4209
White River
Max. rapids: None
RCA

Happy Mohawk Canoe Livery rents canoes, rafts, and tubes for 1- and 2-day trips on the White River, through the Manistee National Forest. Trips wind through scenic, wooded wilderness inhabited by abundant wildlife, including deer, raccoons, minks, muskrats, waterfowl, and many types of turtles.

The flatwater river can be canoed safely by anyone, and has especially clean water, with good fishing for salmon, steelhead, pike, bass, bluegill, and perch. During the May-to-October season, camping is also available at the modern, fully equipped White River campground.

Heavner Canoe Rental

Alan Heavner
2775 Garden Rd.
Milford, MI 48381
(810) 685-2379
Huron River, Proud Lake, Kent Lake
Max. rapids: None
PPA

Heavner rents canoes for easy but beautiful trips in the Proud Lake Recreation Area, less than an hour's drive from Detroit. During an April-October season, guests can enjoy camping, swimming, and trout fishing.

Hiawatha Canoe Livery
Michael and Carol Quinlan
1113 Lake Street
Roscommon, MI 48653
(517) 275-5213, (800) 736-5213
Au Sable River
Max. rapids: I-II

Hiawatha Canoe Livery offers guided and unguided canoe and tube trips on the Au Sable River, through the scenic, unspoiled Mason Wilderness. Trips on the Au Sable last from one to seven days, are easy enough for beginners, and feature excellent fishing for trout and bass.

Hiawatha's season runs from April to November.

Hinchman Acres, Inc.
Sam Giardina
702 N-M-33
Mio, MI 48647
(517) 826-3267
Au Sable River
Max. rapids: None
Michigan Recreational Canoeing Association

Hinchman Acres rents canoes and tubes for 1-14 day trips on the Au Sable River. Paddling is easy and the wilderness setting offers fine trout fishing and a chance to view deer, beavers, ducks, otters, minks, and bald eagles. Campgrounds are available at many spots along the river and, on the stretch between Mio and Oscoda, paddlers can set up camp wherever they want.

Horina Canoe Rental
James Horina
Highway M-37, Route 1
Wellston, MI 49689
(616) 862-3470
Pine River
Max. rapids: I-II
RCA, PPA

Horina rents canoes for 1-3 day trips on the fastest sections of the Pine River. These runs have Class I and II rapids and are for intermediate and advanced paddlers only. Trips run through the protected Manistee National Forest, which

treats paddlers to scenic views of woodlands, high sandbanks, beautiful clay formations, and plentiful wildlife, including deer, geese, ducks, beavers, minks, and otters.

The cool, shady Pine River also boasts excellent fishing for brown, rainbow, and brook trout. Horina's season runs from April to October.

Indian Valley Campground
Bill Mulder
8200 108th St.
Middleville, MI 49333
(616) 891-8579
Thornapple, Coldwater Rivers
Max. rapids: I-II
MAPCO, MARVAC, RCA

Indian Valley Campground rents canoes and tubes for trips of 1- and 2-days on the Thornapple and Coldwater Rivers. Outings are suitable for beginners, who can enjoy swimming, camping, fishing for bass and northern pike, and watching deer, various birds, and other wildlife. The season runs from April to November.

Marrik's Pine River Paddlesports Center
Mark and Val Miltner
7325 West 50 Mile
Cadillac, MI 49601
(616) 862-3471, (800) 71-RIVER
Pine, Big Manistee Rivers
Max. rapids: I
RCA

Pine River Paddlesports Center, nestled in the heart of of the Manistee National Forest, offers canoe and kayak floats on quietwater, moving water and Class I whitewater. These trips on the Pine and Ministee Rivers last 1-3 days. Camping, mountain bikes and a paddlesports store are available.

The owners of PRPC also operate Carl's Canoe Service on the Pine River — see separate description.

Mead's Canoe Livery
Tony Quinlan
11724 Steckert Bridge Road
Roscommon, MI 48653
Au Sable River — South Branch
Max. rapids: None
RCA

Mead's Canoe Livery rents canoes for 1-day trips on the South Branch of the Au Sable, a flatwater wilderness river. Trips are easy, well-suited for beginners and families, and offer camping, fishing for trout and pike, and views of deer, wild turkeys, beavers, and eagles. Mead's season runs from May to November.

Northland Outfitters
Tom and Carma Gronback
Highway M-77
P.O. Box 65
Germfask, MI 49836
(906) 586-9801
Manistique River, Manistique Lake, Fox River, Big Island Lake Complex
Max. rapids: None

Northland Outfitters rents canoes and kayaks for 1-8 day trips on Manistique River, Fox River, Manistique Lake, and the Big Island Lake Complex. All trips run through the scenic wilderness of the Hiawatha National Forest, the Seney National Wildlife Refuge, or both. Paddlers on these trips can enjoy wilderness camping; fishing for trout, bass, muskie, pike, and perch; and viewing the abundant wildlife, including deer, bears, moose, bald eagles, and more than 200 species of birds. A particularly good fishing-canoeing trip can be had at Big Island Lake Complex, whose 12 islands are ideal settings for fishing base camps. Northland's season is from May to October.

Old Log Resort
Mark and Jeanette Knoph
1070 M-115
Marion, MI 49665
(616) 743-2775
Muskegon River
Max. rapids: None
RCA

Old Log Resort rents canoes and kayaks on the Muskegon, a flatwater river easy enough for first-time paddlers. Trips last 1-4 days and pass through scenic wilderness, offering a chance to camp, view eagles, bears, deer, otters, bobcats, beavers, and muskrats, and fish for pike, smallmouth bass, and walleye. The season runs from April to November.

Paddle Brave Canoe & Campground
Paul & Karen Walper
10610 Steckert Bridge Rd.
Roscommon, MI 48653
(517) 275-5273
South Branch of the Au Sable River
Max. rapids: None
PPA, Michigan Campground Owners Association

Paddle Brave rents canoes and tubes for trips of 1 hour to 5 days on the clear and unspoiled Au Sable River, where paddlers can spot trout in the water. This livery is at the edge of the river's wilderness area, and is the only privately owned campground on the South Branch.

Paddlers can enjoy 17 miles of river without any cabins — "just the way Mother Nature made it." Trips are easy, with a 4 mile-per-hour current and a depth ranging from one to four feet. Deer, foxes, and bald eagles frequent the river. The rental season runs from May to September.

Penrod's Canoe Trips
Jim Humes
100 Maple, P.O. Box 432
Grayling, MI 49738
(517) 348-2910
Au Sable River
Max. rapids: None
RCA, PPA

Penrod's Canoe Trips rents canoes and kayaks on the Au Sable River for 1-7 day trips. Paddling is easy, as the river has a swift current, few obstructions, and an average depth of only 18 inches for the first 25 miles. Trout fishing is good and wildlife is plentiful, expecially deer, otters, minks, muskrats, beavers, and ducks.

Camping is available at state forest, state park, and private campgrounds along the river. Penrod's also rents comfortable riverside cabins on wooded sites. The season is from April to October.

River Raisin Canoe Livery
Charles and Cherry Haddix
P.O. Box 136
Carleton, MI 48117
(313) 269-2004
Raisin River
Max. rapids: None

River Raisin Canoe Livery rents canoes and kayaks for 1- and 2-day trips on the River Raisin, a gentle wilderness river. The river offers good fishing for walleye, pike, bass, and bluegill and a chance to spot deer, foxes, raccoons, minks, and muskrats. Also distinctive are the grapevines that hang from trees along the banks. The season runs from May to October.

River's Edge Campground
Bill Mudget
P.O. Box 189
Holton, MI 49425
(616) 821-2735
White River
Max. rapids: None
RCA

River's Edge Campground rents canoes, kayaks, and tubes for easy family trips on the flatwater White River. The river is clear, has a sandy bottom, and offers good fishing for pike, salmon, trout, and bass. Trips last 1-3 days and pass through wooded wilderness with plentiful deer, beavers, raccoons, and other wildlife. The season runs from May to October.

River's Edge also offers primitive "pumps and privies" camping.

Riverside Canoe Trips
Tom and Kathy Stocklen
5042 Scenic Highway
Honor, MI 49640
(616) 325-5622, (616) 882-4072
Platte River
Max. rapids: None
Michigan Recreational Canoe Association,
PPA

Riverside Canoe Trips rents canoes, kayaks, rafts, and tubes for trips of two hours to a day on the Platte River. Trips on the Lower Platte are gentle, scenic, and ideal for families. Runs on the Upper Platte feature, fast, clean, spring-fed waters. This stretch has no rapids but does have narrow sections with quick turns and overhanging branches, requiring prior paddling experience. On all trips, paddlers who leave early or late in the day have a good chance to see deer, beavers, muskrats, wild turkeys and other wildlife. In addition, the Platte River, Platte Lake, Loon Lake, and Lake Michigan offer good fishing for salmon, trout, bass, and other species.

During its May 1-Oct. 15 season, Riverside also offers sunset canoe trips, a general store, and camping at nearby sites.

River View Campground & Canoe Livery
Alfred G. Schmid
P.O. Box 225
Sterling, MI 48659
(517) 654-2447, FAX (517) 654-2318
Rifle River
Max. rapids: None
PPA

Tubers prepare for a trip on the Muskegon River. Courtesy of Sawmill Canoe Livery, Big Rapids, Michigan.

RVC rents canoes, kayaks, and tubes for trips of 2 hours to 3 days, featuring fishing, camping, and swimming. It offers friendly service and well-maintained equipment. The Rifle River is a clean, natural waterway with trout and salmon fishing and wildlife galore. Seasonal sites are available.

The company's season runs from April 15 through October.

Russell Canoes and Campgrounds
Robert Russell
146 Carrington Street
Omer, MI 48749
(517) 653-2644, (800) 552-4928 (MI)
Rifle River
Max. rapids: None
RCA, PPA

Russell Canoes and Campgrounds rents canoes and tubes on the scenic, flatwater Rifle River. Trips last 1-5 days and are safe and fun for novices and families, as well as more advanced canoeists. The stretches paddled are through clean, wooded, wilderness terrain, with lots of wild deer, turkeys, eagles, and turtles. Fishing, too, is good, especially for trout, bass, suckers,

salmon, and walleye.

During the May-to-October season, tent and R.V. camping is also available. The 140-site campground has modern washrooms, laundry facilities, and a camp store.

Salmon Run Campground & Vic's Canoes
Annette Alvis
8845 Felch Ave.
Grant, MI 49327
(616) 834-5494
Muskegon River
Max. rapids: None
PPA, Mich. Recreational Canoe Association

Salmon Run Campground & Vic's Canoes offers easy canoeing on a wide, peaceful river. The company rents canoes, rafts, and tubes from May 1 until Oct. 15 to paddlers of all ages and levels of experience. The emphasis is on customer service, with professional staff and modern equipment.

The clean Muskegon, with its sandy bottom and wooded bluffs, offers excellent trout, walleye, and bass fishing. Blue herons, swans, turtles, beavers, deer, and woodchucks are among the local wildlife.

Sawmill Tube and Canoe Livery
Donn and Lori Trites
230 Baldwin Street
Big Rapids, MI 49307
(616) 796-6408
Big Muskegon River
Max. rapids: I-II
RCA

Sawmill Tube and Canoe Livery offers guided and unguided canoeing and tubing trips on the Muskegon River. The river is wide and gentle, well-suited for novice and intermediate paddlers. The Muskegon also offers exceptionally good fishing for trout, bass, northern pike, crappie, walleye, and perch.

Trips last from 1-7 days and pass through unspoiled areas with abundant wildlife, including eagles, deer, blue herons, beavers, otters, geese, and ducks. Sawmill's season runs from April to October.

Sawyer Canoe Company
Robert D. Gramprie
234 S. State Street
Oscoda, MI 48750
(517) 739-9181
Au Sable River
Max. rapids: None

Sawyer Canoe Company rents canoes on the scenic, flatwater Au Sable River. Trips run for 1-7 days and are fine for beginners. Paddling is easy, as the Au Sable has a steady four-to-six mph current and is free of rapids and obstructions. A wilderness river, the Au Sable runs through unspoiled forests and sandhills, and offers views of deer, otters, beavers, muskrats, squirrels, and rabbits. Paddlers also enjoy good fishing for bass, brook trout, walleye, lake trout, steelhead, and salmon. Sawyer's season runs from May to October.

Skip's Huron River Canoe Livery
Skip and Jan McDonald
3780 Delhi Court
Ann Arbor, MI 48103
(313) 769-8686
Huron River
Max. rapids: I-II
RCA, PPA

Skip's Huron River Canoe Livery rents canoes and open kayaks for beginner and intermediate trips on the Huron River. With gentle rapids and small rock dams, the Huron offers some challenge in addition to its acclaimed scenery and smallmouth-bass fishing. Trips last 1/2 day and run between April and October. Camping is also available.

Sportsmans Port Canoes & Campground
Mary Barber
RR #1, Pine River
Wellston, MI 49689
(616) 862-3571
Pine River
Max. rapids: I-II
PPA, RCA

Sportsman's Port runs guided and unguided canoe trips on the Pine River, one of the most challenging rivers of Michigan's lower peninsula. Trips, best suited for paddlers with some canoeing experience, run through wooded wilderness featuring clay hills, clean water, and abundant wildlife, including deer, otters, beavers, wild turkeys, and eagles.

During the May-to-October season, the company also offers shuttle service and camping at its campground, which is equipped with hot showers and a store.

Sturgeon and Pigeon River Outfitters

Scott Anderson
4271 S. Straits Highway
Indian River, MI 49749
(616) 238-8181, FAX (616) 238-4500
Sturgeon River, Pigeon River
Max. rapids: I-II
Michigan Recreational Canoeing Association, PPA

Sturgeon and Pigeon River Outfitters rents canoes, kayaks, and tubes on the Sturgeon and Pigeon Rivers. Both rivers are crystal-clear and premier trout streams. The Sturgeon is the fastest, most challenging river in the lower peninsula. Canoeists on the Sturgeon must have basic paddling and maneuvering skills, The Pigeon is gentler, requires no prior experience, and is designated a Michigan Wild and Scenic River. The Pigeon runs through the Pigeon River State Forest, home of the only elk herd east of the Mississippi. Both rivers have abundant wildlife, including deer, elk, beavers, muskrats, blue herons, turkeys, and foxes.

The season runs from May to October.

Sylvania Outfitters, Inc.

US Highway 2 West
Watersmeet, MI 49969
(906) 358-4766
Ontonagon River System
Max. rapids: III-IV
Michigan Recreational Canoeing Association, PPA

Sylvania Outfitters rents canoes and kayaks for 1-6 day trips on the Ontonagon River. Some of the trips are fine for novices; other have Class III-IV rapids and are for advanced paddlers only. All trips are through unspoiled wilderness with plentiful deer, otters, raccoons, eagles, loons, and ducks. Fishermen also enjoy good fishing for trout, smallmouth and largemouth bass, northern pike, and walleye. Sylvania's season runs from April to October.

T.C. Paddlers

Bill Queen
Summer: 1327 S. Shore Rd.
E. Frankfort, MI 49635
(616) 352-7093
Winter: 415 W. Madison
Ann Arbor, MI 48103
(313) 995-9161
Lake Michigan, Lake Superior, Crystal Lake, Herring Lake
Max. rapids: None

T.C. Paddlers offers guided kayak trips to customers interested in paddling along the bluffs and dunes of crystal-clear Lake Michigan. They can also discover historic villages and explore sheltered, woodland lakes with outlets to the Great Lakes.

The outfitter can tailor trips to customers' needs, providing paddling lessons, giving environmental classes for students in grades 5 through 12 and other groups, or combining paddling with biking. The afternoon or evening kayaking trips are suitable for beginners, and the season runs from May 30-October 1.

Tomahawk Trails Canoe Livery

A. Anderson
P.O. Box 814
Indian River, MI 49749
(616) 238-8703
Sturgeon River, Pigeon River
Max. rapids: I-II
Recreational Caoeing Association

Tomahawk Trails rents canoes, kayaks, and tubes for 1- and 2-day trips on the Sturgeon and Pigeon Rivers. Trips on the Sturgeon are challenging, requiring previous paddling experience. The Pigeon is a scenic "family river," good for beginners and children. Both rivers have good trout fishing and offer chances to glimpse elk, deer, beavers, turtles, and eagles. Tomahawk's season runs from May to November.

Troll Landing Campground & Canoe Livery
Mike & Janice Golda
2660 Rifle River Trail
West Branch, MI 48661
(517) 345-7260
Rifle River
Max. rapids: I
RCA

Troll Landing rents canoes, kayaks, and tubes for trips of 1-3 days on the Rifle River. Paddling on the flatwater Rifle River is not difficult, as the river is clear and shallow, with a steady seven-mile-per-hour current. Paddlers of all ages can enjoy these scenic trips as they wind through pine and hardwood forests on the lookout for deer, ducks, and beavers. During the April-to-October season, guests can also fish for brown trout and steelhead.

Two Hearted Canoe Trips, Inc.
Richard and Kathy Robinson
Rainbow Lodge
P.O. Box 386, Co. Rd. 423
Newberry, MI 49868
(906) 658-3357
Two Hearted River
Max. rapids: I-II
RCA

Two Hearted Canoe Trips rents canoes for 1-3 day trips on the Two Hearted River in the scenic wilderness of northern Luce County. 1-day trips are easy but the longer runs are somewhat strenuous, requiring two or three portages of a couple hundred feet.

The scenery in this remote, unspoiled area is beautiful, with large white pines, hardwoods, and abundant wildlife, including bears, deer, moose, raccoons, otters, beavers, and eagles. Trout fishing is also very good.

During its April-to-November season, the livery also offers primitive campsites, motel rooms, and a well-stocked camp store.

Uncommon Adventures
Michael Gray
P.O. Box 6066
East Lansing, MI 48826
(800) 482-0220
Lake Michigan, Lake Huron, Lake Superior, Georgian Bay, Florida's 10,000 Islands, Belize, Honduras
Max. rapids: None
RCA, PPA

Uncommon Adventures offers guided coastal kayak tours and first class instruction on U.S. inland seas in summer and warm water destinations like Florida and Belize in winter. Since 1984, the company has provided thoughtfully guided trips complemented by great food and a sense of stewardship towards land and sea. Trips are fully outfitted, 1-10 days long, and tailored for individuals, families and corporate groups.

U-Rent-Em-Canoe Livery
Michael J. Hawthorne
685 W. State Street
Hastings, MI 49058
(616) 945-3191
Thornapple River, Kalamazoo River, Gun River
Max. rapids: I-II
PPA, *Michigan Recreational Canoeing Association*

U-Rent-Em-Canoe Livery runs guided canoe trips and rents canoes, kayaks, rafts, and tubes on the Thornapple River and all nearby fishing lakes. Trips on the Kalamazoo River and Gun River are also available by request. River trips wind through wooded wilderness with abundant deer, waterfowl, and birds. Paddling is easy enough for novices, yet small rapids and other minor obstacles keep things interesting. 1- and 2-day trips are available.

All trips are on clean waters offering good fishing for bass, pike, panfish, trout, and muskie. The livery's season is from April to October.

Vic's Canoes
8845 Felch Ave.
Grant, MI 49327
(616) 834-5494
Muskegon River
Max. rapids: None
RCA, PPA

Vic's rents canoes, tubes, kayaks, and rafts for 1- and 2-day trips on the Muskegon, a wide river with gentle rapids, suited for beginners and experienced paddlers alike. Trips pass through pine and birch woods, offering views of deer, eagles, small game, ducks, herons, and other wildlife. The river's clean water also makes for good fishing for rainbow trout, smallmouth bass, steelhead, salmon, and walleye.

All trips begin or end at Salmon Run Campground, which offers comfortable tent and R.V. camping with hot showers, laundry rooms, a camp store, and swimming pool. The season is from April to October.

Whispering Waters Campground & Canoe Livery
Roger & Uta Vilmont
1805 North Irving Rd.
Hastings, MI 49058
(616) 945-5166, FAX (616) 948-9584
Thornapple River
Max. rapids: None
MAPCO, RVIC, RCA

Whispering Waters rents canoes and tubes for 1-day trips on the exceptionally clean Thornapple River, with its undeveloped shoreline and excellent smallmouth bass fishing. These outings are suitable for beginners to intermediate paddlers during the summer. Winter and spring trips are for experienced paddlers only.

The company prides itself on offering full service at its 26-acre wooded campground with hot showers. Its 118 campsites range from rustic to full hook-up pullthroughs. Deer, beavers, muskrats, and many interesting birds, including sandhill cranes may be observed.

White Birch Canoe Livery & Campground
Bob and Pat Holt
5569 Paradise Road
Falmouth, MI 49632
(616) 328-4547
Muskegon River, Dead Stream Swamp
Max. rapids: None

White Birch Canoe Livery & Campground rents canoes for 1-hour to 14-day trips on the Muskegon River, West Branch of the Muskegon, and Dead Stream Swamp. The outfitter has routes for everyone from senior citizens to marathon paddlers.

The Muskegon River passes through protected state land, making it ideal for camping and viewing deer, raccoons, otters, beavers, herons, ducks, ospreys, sandhill cranes, eagles, and wild turkeys. Also, the river's clear, clean water offers excellent fishing for pike, bass, panfish, and walleye.

Wolynski Canoe Rental, Inc.
2300 Wixom Trail
Milford, MI 48381
(810) 685-1851
Huron River
Max. rapids: None
RCA, PPA

Wolynski Canoe Rental rents kayaks and canoes for relaxed trips on the gentle Huron River. Guests park free, ride hay wagons to the river, and enjoy good personal service. The wooded landscape contains turtles, wildflowers, Canada geese, blue herons, and other birds. The Huron contains trout, bass, bluegill, and carp.

Minnesota

Mention canoeing in Minnesota and most paddlers immediately think of the Boundary Waters Canoe Area. This million-acre wilderness of forested lakes has a unique appeal. Here along a 150-mile stretch of the Canadian border, roads peter out and travelers must move by water. Along 1,200 miles of canoe routes linking a thousand lakes by way of streams and portages, the silence is broken only by the dip of paddles, the splash of fish, the rustling of aspen leaves, and the haunting call of the loon. Since motorboats are generally banned from BWCA waters, no engines sully the air and shatter the calm of most of the lakes in this federally protected region. Amid the pines and birches along the shoreline lie 2,000 designated campsites. And deep in the forest lurk moose, bear, wolves, deer, beavers, and otters.

To the canoeist, lured perhaps by the writings of local naturalist Sigurd Olson, this is paradise. We see the pristine waterland very much as the Ojibwe Indians and the French voyageurs found it centuries ago. Minnesotans call it the world's greatest canoe country.

Those BWCA lakes where motorboats are allowed are mostly at the access points on the fringes of the area: the Gunflint Trail at the eastern end and the Ely area in the west. Gunflint Trail, site of many canoe liveries, leads northward from Grand Marais on Lake Superior. Ely is about a two hour drive north of Duluth.

Adjoining the BWCA to the west is the Voyageurs National Park, a smaller area open to motorized boats as well as canoes. Here canoeists must share the 34 lakes with everything from houseboats to cabin cruisers. And the bigger lakes, like Rainy Lake astride the Canadian border, can be treacherous for canoeists in rough weather. But the only way to explore Voyageurs, too, is by boat. Visitor centers, a renovated 1913 hotel, campsites, and skilled naturalist and fishing guides are all available.

Both inside and outside the boundary waters Minnesota has 23 rivers offering everything from whitewater to lazy floats. Nineteen of them, including those mentioned below, are state-designated canoe streams.

Great for wildlife viewing, for example, is the Big Fork, which runs northward toward the Canadian border to empty into the Rainy River at Smokey

Bear State Forest. Its middle stretch, from Big Fork to Big Falls, is punctuated with Class I and II rapids. It is known as a pleasant wilderness trip for novices who are cautious, prepared to portage, and have backcountry skills. The Big Fork also has good walleye and muskie fishing.

The upper reaches of the Cloquet, which runs into the St. Louis near Brookston, is said to be one of the state's most pristine rivers. It has Class I, II, and II rapids as it passes through deep forests of pine, birch, and aspen.

The crystal-clear Crow Wing, flowing from a lake near Akeley in the middle of the state, is a popular float for novices. It glides through Crow Wing State Park, with many campsites and reminders of Indians and fur traders as it heads for its confluence with the Mississippi.

Where the St. Croix marks the state line close to the Twin Cities, this National Scenic Riverway requires only novice to intermediate skills. The most popular section is below Dalles, where the river widens and flows through a wooded valley with steep stone bluffs. But Class II-IV expertise is needed near St. Croix Falls Dam, which itself requires a mile-long portage.

Whitewater skills are also necessary on the Class II-IV section of the scenic Kettle River from Banning State Park to Sandstone, roughly half-way between the Twin Cities and Duluth.

Fuller details of these and other Minnesota rivers are given in leaflets available from the state's Office of Tourism, 121 7th Place East, 100 Metro Square, St. Paul, MN 55101-2112, tel. 1-800-657-3700 or (locally) 612-296-5029. Paddlers can obtain free river maps showing access points, campsites, rest areas, portages, dams, waterfalls, and white water, from the Department of Natural Resources, 500 Lafayette Road, Box 40, St. Paul, MN 55146, tel. 612-296-6157 or 1-800-766-6000 (Minnesota callers only). Call these numbers also for weekly water level reports.

Arrowhead Canoe Outfitters
Kim Holzman
HC 1, Box 3299
Ely, MN 55731
(218) 365-5614, (800) 245-5614
BWCA
Max. rapids: None

Arrowhead Canoe Outfitters offers guided and unguided canoe trips of 1-30 days in the Boundary Waters Canoe Area and Quetico Provincial Park. This vast wilderness features beautiful forests, thousands of crystal-clear lakes, excellent fishing, and abundant wildlife, including loons, ospreys, bald eagles, moose, wolves, coyotes, red foxes, raccoons, black bears, minks, weasels, and beavers. Anglers can fish for walleye, pike, trout, bass, crappie, and perch.

Arrowhead's routing service gives paddlers the choice of a leisurely course or a fast trip through many lakes. Guests also can choose between basic and deluxe outfitting packages, which feature top-quality boats and food. Guided trips are available for those interested in archaeology, history, photography, or just a smoother, more enjoyable trip. Arrowhead's season is from May to November.

Bear Track Outfitting Co.
David and Cathi Williams
Box 937
Grand Marais, MN 55604
(218) 387-1162, (800) 795-8068
BWCA, Isle Royale National Park
Max. rapids: None

Bear Track Outfitters runs guided and unguided canoe and sea kayak trips of 3-30 days in the Boundary Waters Canoe Area. Guests can choose among a wide array of equipment, including eight types of tandem canoes and six types of solo canoes. Also available are towing service across Saganaga and Seagull Lakes, camping gear rentals, provisions, lodging in rustic cabins, fly-in canoe tours, and guided fishing trips.

Bear Track, open year-round, also offers backpacking, snowshoeing, and cross-country skiing trips. On these various trips, guests can see moose, bears, wolves, deer, beavers, otters, and minks; and fish for walleye, northern pike, bass, and lake trout.

Borderland Lodge & Outfitters
G.W. Resorts, Inc.
7480 Crane Lake Rd.
Crane Lake, MN 55725
(218) 993-2233, (800) 777-8392
Crane, Sand Point, Namakan, Kabetogama, Loon, La Croix Lakes
Max. rapids: None

Borderland runs guided canoe trips and rents canoes for wilderness trips in the BWCA and Voyageurs National Park with their abundance of fish and wildlife. It provides shuttles to help paddlers reach remote areas where they may view pictographs and animals ranging from wolves and bears to moose. Fish include walleye, bass, crappies, and trout. Camping is available and the company is open year-round, with snowmobiling in the winter.

Boundary Waters Canoe Outfitters
Marty Lakner
1323 E. Sheridan St.
Ely, MN 55731
(218) 365-3201, (800) 544-7736
BWCA, Quetico Park
Max. rapids: None
PPA

In business since 1959, Boundary Waters Canoe Outfitters runs guided canoe trips and rents canoes for up to 15 days to paddlers exploring this great wilderness region. The company offers reasonable rates, top-quality equipment, tasty meals, and personal service.

Camping is available, and there is good fishing for walleye, bass, northern pike, and trout. Other wildlife includes deer, bears, moose, wolves, otters, mink, and eagles.

Canadian Border Outfitters
Patrick and Chickie Harristhal
Box 117, Moose Lake
Ely, MN 55731
(218) 365-5847, (800) 247-7530
BWCA
Max. rapids: None
Ely Outfitters Association

Canadian Border Outfitters offers guided and outfitted canoe trips in the Boundary Waters Canoe Area and Quetico Provincial Park. Trips last from 3-10 days, are suited for paddlers of all ages, and leave from all entry points in the Ely area. Canadian Border's base is at Moose Lake, 18 miles northeast of Ely. The base offers tow boats, fishing licenses, tackle, maps, meals, motel rooms, and a bunkhouse.

All trips give paddlers a chance to spot moose, bears, eagles, deer, minks, otters, ospreys, and loons. Anglers can enjoy excellent fishing for northern pike, walleye, smallmouth bass, lake trout, and panfish. The outfitter's season is from May to October.

Canadian Waters, Inc.
Jon and Dan Waters
111 East Sheridan Street
Ely, MN 55731
(218) 365-3202, (800) 255-2922
(reservations)
BWCA
Max. rapids: None
PPA

Canadian Waters offers guided and outfitted canoe trips in the Boundary Waters Canoe Area and Quetico Provincial Park. Trips last from 3-20 days, with 7-day trips being the most popular. Canadian Waters takes particular pride in its canoes, claiming to have the world's largest outfitting fleet of light, Old Town Oltonar canoes. The outfitter also offers several special services, including towing, guide service, motorboat fishing, and airport shuttle service.

On all trips, guests can enjoy wilderness scenery; a chance to view moose, deer, bears, eagles, ospreys, minks, otters, and beavers; and fishing for smallmouth bass, walleye, northern pike, and lake trout. Canadian Waters' season runs form May to September.

Canoe Country Escapes
Brooke and Eric Durland
194 South Franklin Street
Denver, CO 80209
(303) 722-6482
BWCA
Max. rapids: I-II
PPA

Canoe Country Escapes offers guided and unguided canoe trips in the Boundary Waters Canoe Area and Quetico Park. Trips, which last 5-10 days, are tailored to suit a wide range of paddlers. Most popular are the pampered lodge-to-lodge trips in which guests spend four nights in comfortable lodges and three at well-tended campsites set up before guests' arrival. Also available are traditional guided and outfitted trips, family trips, and trips for seniors. Out-

fitting and lodge accommodations at the start and end of Canoe Country's tours are provided through Gunflint Northwoods (see separate listing).

Canoe Country Outfitters
Robert R. Olson
629 East Sheridan St.
P.O. Box 30
Ely, MN 55731
(218) 365-4046
BWCA
Max. rapids: None

Canoe Country Outfitters offers guided and unguided canoe trips in the Boundary Waters Canoe Area and Quetico Provincial Park. Trips last from 3-30 days, are fine for paddlers of all ages, and boast excellent fishing for walleye, northern pike, smallmouth bass, and lake trout. Guests also can view moose, bears, deer, loons, and wolves.

Canoe Country has two bases, one in downtown Ely and one at Moose Lake. Between the two, the outfitter claims to serve all major entry points, providing customers with "the best route selection, scenery, fishing, and seclusion." Also available are fly-in canoe trips, camping, and cabins at the Ely and Moose Lake bases, airport pickup, and a choice of "light" or "ultralight" outfitting. The outfitter's season runs from May to October.

Cascade Kayaks
John Amren & Jennifer Stoltz
Box 141
Lutsen, MN 55612
(218) 387-2360, (800) 720-2809
Lake Superior
Max. rapids: None
TASK

Sea kayaking on the nation's largest freshwater lake is Cascade Kayaks' specialty, with guided and unguided trips lasting from a few hours to 8 days. The owners guide all trips, which are suitable for beginners through intermediate paddlers. Groups are small — six clients or

A canoe on Gillis Lake. Courtesy of Gunflint Northwoods Outfitters, Grand Marais, Minnesota.

less — and the scenery varies from islands, cliffs, and caves to waterfalls and sandy beaches. The lake is clean and wildlife includes bald eagles, moose, bear, deer, otter, and duck.

Clearwater Canoe Outfitters & Lodge
Robert E. Marchino
HC 64, Box 355
Grand Marais, MN 55604
(218) 388-2254, (800) 527-0554
BWCA, Quetico
Max. rapids: III-IV

Clearwater Canoe Outfitters and Lodge offers guided and outfitted trips in the Boundary Waters Canoe Area and Quetico Provincial Park. These pristine wilderness trips last 5-10 days and require no previous kayaking experience. The company uses quality equipment and has knowledgeable guides.

All trips offers abundant wildlife, including moose, beavers, otters, eagles, foxes, and mountain lions. Also, anglers can enjoy excellent fishing for walleye and trophy trout. Clearwater's season runs May-October.

Gunflint Northwoods Outfitters
Bruce and Sue Kerfoot
750 Gunflint Trail
Grand Marais, MN 55604
(800) 362-5251
Boundary Waters Wilderness
Max. rapids: III-IV
PPA

Gunflint Northwoods Outfitters runs guided and unguided canoe and kayak trips of 2-8 days in the Boundary Waters Canoe Area and Quetico Park. With primarily flatwater, canoeing trips are suited for all ages and anyone interested in multi-day trips in the world's largest canoeing wilderness. The outfitting company particularly prides itself on its extensive canoe and equipment offerings, breads and homemade snacks, and careful trip planning.

During Gunflint Northwoods' May-to-October season, the outfitter also offers lodging in its bunkhouse and modern cabins. On its trips, paddlers can view moose, beavers, bald eagles, otters, and loons, and fish for walleye, smallmouth bass, lake trout, and northern pike.

A cosy campsite in the BWCA. Courtesy of Gunflint Northwoods Outfitters, Grand Marais, Minnesota.

Headwaters Canoe Outfitters
Andy Kuik
12404 Land End Lane, SE
Bemidji, MN 56601
(218) 751-2783
Mississipi River, Turtle River
Max. rapids: III-IV

Headwaters Canoe Outfitters offers guided trips and canoe rentals on the Mississippi, Turtle, Big Fork, and Little Fork Rivers. Trips last 1-7 days and range in difficulty from beginners' runs to trips for experts only. The areas traveled are clean, scenic, require few portages, and offer a good chance to spot eagles, deer, beavers, otters, and muskrats. Also, anglers can enjoy fishing for walleye, nothern pike, perch, and bass.

Headwaters' season runs from May to October.

Hungry Jack Outfitters
Dave & Nancy Seaton
434 Gunflint Trail
Grand Marais, MN 55604
(800) 648-2922, (218) 388-2275
BWCA, Quetico Park
Max. rapids: None
PPA, Gunflint Trail Association, Minn.
Resort Association

Taking its name from Hungry Jack Lake, this outfitter rents canoes for trips of 3-10 days or more. Custom-planned to suit each paddler's needs, these floats are lake-to-lake flatwater trips, suitable for beginners and experts alike.

The scenery includes old-growth pine trees and rocky cliffs. The wilderness is full of wildlife ranging from moose and black bears to bald eagles. There is excellent fishing for walleye, smallmouth bass, lake trout, northern pike, and stream trout. Hungry Jack's season is from May 1 to October 1.

Huntersville Outfitters
F.A. and Dorothy Kennelly
RR 4, Box 317
Menahga, MN 56464
(218) 564-4279
Crow Wing River
Max. rapids: I-II

Huntersville Outfitters outfits canoe trips of 1-12 days on the Crow Wing River. The river is remarkably clear, with sandy beaches and excellent swimming areas. All trips are fine for beginning and advanced paddlers alike, as the intermittent rapids are exciting but not dangerous. The river also boasts historical sights, such as boat landings used by the Hudson Bay Company, and excellent fishing for walleye, northern pike, and bass. This wilderness area has abundant wildlife, too, including deer, foxes, coyotes, eagles, ducks, beavers, and otters.

Huntersville's season runs from May to October.

Ketter Canoeing
Betty L. Ketter
101 79th Avenue N
Minneapolis, MN 55444
(612) 560-3840, (612) 561-2208
Mississippi River, Rum River, Crow Wing River, Elk River
Max. rapids: I-II

Ketter Canoeing rents canoes and kayaks for trips on the Mississippi, Run, Crow Wing, and Elk Rivers. The outfitter also offers shuttle service for those who bring their own boats.

La Croix Outfitters
Box 475
Cook, MN 55723
(218) 666-2842
Western BWCA, Quetico Park, Vermilion, Little Fork Rivers
Max. rapids: I-II

La Croix Outfitters rents canoes for up to 10 days and provides full trip orientation and planning for its guests. Its personal service aims to enable paddlers to soak up the sun and beauty of the landscape without worrying about find-

ing their way. The water is pure enough to drink, the walleye and bass fishing is some of the best in the country, and animal wildlife is abundant. The season runs May 1-Oct. 1.

LaTourell's Moose Lake Outfitters
Bob LaTourell
Box 239
Ely, MN 55731
(800) 365-4531, (218) 365-4531
BWCA, Quetico Park
Max. rapids: None
PPA

Three generations of experience, plus a location closest to the BWCA and Quetico Park, enable this outfitter to offer its customers unusual service. Its guided and unguided trips range from easy to difficult, mostly involving portages varying from very short to nearly a mile. Lasting up to 14 days, these outings take guests through unspoiled wilderness abounding in animals and fish. Camping and swimming are available during the company's May-October season.

Marine Landing Boat & Canoe Service, Inc.
John A. Burrill
P.O. Box 142, 10 Elm St.
Marine on St. Croix, MN 55047
(612) 433-2864
St. Croix River
Max. rapids: None

Marine Landing offers guided and unguided canoe trips, suitable for all ages, on the clean waters of the St. Croix National Wild and Scenic Riverway. These trips last 1-2 days and provide opportunities for camping, swimming, and fishing for walleye, bass, and muskee. Deer, bald eagles, trumpeter swans, and otters are among the local wildlife.

Midwest Mountaineering

Rod Johnson, Steve Gougeon,
Craig Johnson
309 Cedar Ave. South
Minneapolis, MN 55454
(612) 339-3433

Midwest Mountaineering is a retail store in Minneapolis that has an extensive canoe and kayak department, including rentals.

Moose Lake Wilderness Canoe Trips

Tom and Woods
P.O. Box 358
Ely, MN 55731
(800) 322-5837
BWCA
Max. rapids: None
PPA

Moose Lake Wilderness Canoe Trips offers guided and outfitted canoe trips in the B.W.C.A. and Quetico Provincial Park. The outfitter says its specialty is "the finest equipment and facilities at reasonable rates." Trips run between May and October, boast excellent fishing for walleye, bass, northern pike, and lake trout, and offer a chance to spot moose, bears, wolves, eagles, and beavers.

Northwest Passage

Rick Sweitzer
1130 Greenleaf Avenue
Wilmette, IL 60091
(847) 256-4409, (800) RECREATE,
FAX (847) 256-4476
Current River, Rio Grande, Chicago River, BWCA, Lake Michigan, Lake Superior
Max. rapids: III-IV

Northwest Passage offers guided raft trips on the New and Gauley Rivers in West Virginia; canoe trips on the Current River in Missouri, the Rio Grande in Texas, and the Boundary Waters Canoe Area in Minnesota. It also has sea kayak trips on Lake Michigan in both Illinois and Door County, Wisconsin; and on Lake Superior in Michigan. Most of these trips, which last 1-7 days, are designed for beginners; some require prior experience. Depending on the location, these trips offer excitement, challenge, remoteness, and beauty.

An adventure travel company, Northwest Passage also offers skiing, hiking, cycling, backpacking, dogsledding, and rock climbing. Outings run year-round in the U.S., Canada, the Arctic, Greenland, Switzerland, New Zealand, Costa Rica, Belize, Crete, Tanzania, southern Africa and Antarctica.

Nor'wester Outfitters

Carl and Luanna Brandt
Gunflint Trail
Grand Marais, MN 55604
(218) 388-2252, (800) 9912-4FUN
BWCA
Max. rapids: None

Nor'wester Lodge outfits canoe trips of 3-14 days in the Boundary Waters Canoe Area. Trips, leaving from 15 entry points, all offer excellent wilderness scenery; and a chance to spot moose, beavers, minks, and bald eagles, and fish for trout, walleye, bass, and northern pike. Nor'wester's season is from May to October.

Outdoor Adventure Canoe Outfitters

Doug & Linda Jordan
Box 576
Ely, MN 55731
(218) 365-3466, (800) 777-8574
BWCA and Quetico Park
Max. rapids: None
PPA

Outdoor Adventure runs guided and unguided canoe trips of up to 24 days on the matchless Boundary Waters. The company prides itself on providing quality equipment and service. It uses lightweight, compact gear and spends ample time with each party before every trip.

Since most trips involve portaging from lake to lake, guests should be physically fit. But some outings need few or no portages, and are suitable for people of nearly all ages. The wilderness offers 15,000 square miles of clean lakes with outstanding fishing for walleye, northern pike, smallmouth bass, and lake trout.

Paddlers can admire deer, moose, bears, beavers, and other wildlife, amid the evergreens and snow-white paper birch trees. The company's season runs from May 8 to October 1.

Rockwood Outfitters
Rick Austin
625 Gunflint Trail
Grand Marais, MN 55604
(218) 388-2242, (800) 942-2922
BWCA and Quetico Park
Max. rapids: None
PPA, Minnesota Resort Association

Rockwood Outfitters rents the finest ultra-light canoes and camping equipment for personalized trips of 3 days to 2 weeks in the nation's largest wilderness canoe area. It also offers meals at Rockwood Lodge, a handbuilt log lodge dating from the 1920s, and accommodation in modern cabins spaced along the lakeshore.

Trips are easy to moderately difficult, with a wide variety of canoe trails through pure lakes flanked by towering pines. Moose, bears, wolves, and other wildlife frequent the shore, and the lakes offer great fishing for walleye, smallmouth bass, and trout. Rockwood's season runs from mid-May through September.

Root River Outfitters
Lawrence E. Charlebois
P.O. Box 357
Lanesboro, MN 55949
(507) 467-3400
Root River
Max. rapids: I-II
Root River Trail Tours

Root River Outfitters rents canoes, kayaks, and tubes for leisurely paddling through beautiful deep bluff country with clean water and great fishing for trout, bass, pike, sunfish, and catfish. Wildlife includes wild turkeys, with many smaller species.

Trips of 4 hours to 4 days run during the April-to-October season. The company also offers shuttle service.

Sawbill Canoe Outfitters, Inc.
Cindy & Bill Hansen
Box 2127
Tofte, MN 55615
(218) 387-1360
Boundary Waters Canoe Area Wilderness
Max. rapids: None
PPA

With 38 years' experience, Sawbill Canoe Outfitters offers skilled route planning and instruction and fine lightweight canoes and equipment. The outfitter rents canoes from May 1 to October 30 for periods of 2-20 days. Paddlers may make their trips as easy or difficult as they wish, pausing to swim, camp, and fish in the incomparable BWCA water wilderness.

Amid the solitude, canoeists may spot moose, loons, otters, beavers, black bears, and wolves. Anglers pursue lake trout, northern pike, walleye pike, and smallmouth bass.

Seagull Canoe Outfitters
Debbie Mark and Roger Hahn
920 Gunflint Trail
Grand Marais, MN 55604
(218) 388-2216, (800) 346-2205(reservations)
Boundary Waters Canoe Area
Max. rapids: I-II
PPA, Minnesota Canoe Assocation

Seagull Outfitters offers guided and outfitted canoe trips in the Boundary Waters Canoe Area and Quetico Provincial Park. Trips last from 3-10 days and are of minimal to moderate difficulty, with most routes suitable for anyone in good health. All trips offer pristine wilderness scenery; a chance to spot moose, bald eagles, otters, and loons; and excellent fishing for walleye, smallmouth bass, northern pike, and lake trout.

Seagull specializes in deluxe, ultra-light outfitting and also offers special-interest packages, fly-in trips to remote areas, towing, partial outfitting, and a complete store. The outfitters, whose season runs from May to October, has discounts for children under 16, repeat customers, and those who begin their trips in May or September.

Superior-North Canoe Outfitters
Earl & Anita Cypher
HC64, Box 965P
Grand Marais, MN 55604
(218) 388-4416
BWCA, Quetico Park
Max. rapids: None
PPA

Superior-North rents ultra-light canoes for people of all ages to explore many islands and deep lakes of the Canadian Shield. Quality equipment and food are provided, the lakewater is drinkable, and fishing is for walleye, smallmouth bass, northern and lake trout. Bear, moose, loon and bald eagle may be seen. Camping and swimming are available during the May 15-Sept. 10 season.

Tofte Lake Resort
Norman A. Saari
5421 Fernberg Trail
Ely, MN 55731
(218) 365-4691
Basswood Lake and other wilderness lakes in the BWCA
Max. rapids: None
Minnesota Resort Association

A small business with 32 years' wilderness guiding experience, Tofte Lake Resort rents canoes and runs guided canoe trips in the unspoiled Northwoods of the Boundary Waters Canoe Area. Tours are easy to challenging. The company arranges trips for fishermen, couples, families, and women.

Pure water, sparkling waterfalls, ancient pine trees, island-dotted Canadian Shield lakes and abundant wildlife characterize this wilderness. Trips, which last up to 14 days, offer excellent fishing and camping. The company's season runs from May to September.

Tom & Woods' Outfitters
Box 358
Ely, MN 55731
(800) 322-5837, (218) 365-5837
BWCA, Quetico Park
Max. rapids: None
PPA

With over 30 years' experience, Tom & Woods' Outfitters offers a wide range of trips suitable for individual needs. These range from easy to very challenging, bringing paddlers into a 2m. acre wilderness with over 2,000 interconnected lakes. The company rents canoes as well as guiding trips during its May-September season. Camping is available, fishing is good, and clients may view wildlife including moose, bear, deer, fox, eagle and loon.

Top of the Trail Outfitters
Jeff Drew
1001 Gunflint Trail, Saganaga Lake
Grand Marais, MN 55604
(800) 869-0883
BWCA & Quetico
Max. rapids: I-II

Top of the Trail offers direct water access (no portages) for canoe trips into Minnesota's Boundary Waters Canoe Area and Canada's Quetico Provincial Park. Trips vary in difficulty and last from 3-14 days. All trips take paddlers through unspoiled wilderness and give them an opportunity to observe moose, deer, otters, beavers, eagles, loons, ospreys, and other wildlife. Fisherman can enjoy fishing for walleye, smallmouth bass, northern pike, and lake trout.

Top of the Trail is a full-service outfitter offering both complete and partial outfitting, but specializing in ultra-lightweight outfitting, including 40-pound kevlar canoes. The outfitter offers numerous special interest packages, including fly-in/paddle-out and fly-in/fly-out canoe trips that allow paddlers to begin their trip in the remote interior of the wilderness. Canoe transport service to all points on Saganaga Lake is also avail-

able. Discounts are available for those who begin their trip in May or September. Additional discounts are offered for students, children under 12, those who can begin their trips mid-week, repeat customers, and groups of eight or more.

Tuscarora Canoe Outfitters
Kerry Leeds
Gunflint Trail, Box 870
Grand Marais, MN 55604
(218) 388-2221, (800) 544-3843
Entire BWCA and Quetico Provincial Park
Max. rapids: None
PPA

Tuscarora rents canoes to paddlers exploring the lakes and rivers in the great wilderness straddling the Canadiar border — two million acres without roads, motors, buildings, or planes. Paddlers have a personalized trip-planning session with a guide intimately familiar with the 50 canoe routes served. Tours of 3-18 days can be arranged to suit anyone from novices to ambitious adventurers.

Paddlers may observe moose, beavers otters, bears, and birdlife, and enjoy excellent fishing for smallmouth bass, walleye, northern pike, and lake trout. The season runs May 5 to October 5.

Canoeists pause for a rest in the BWCA. Courtesy of Top of the Trail Outfitters, Grand Marais, Minnesots.

Vermilion River Canoe Outfitters
Richard & Paulette Dahl
494 Co. Rd. 422
Buyck, MN 55771
(218) 666-2444
Vermilion River, BWCA
Max. rapids: None

Vermilion River Canoe Outfitters rents canoes to people of all skill levels for trips of 1-30 days on the scenic Vermilion River with its rocky cliffs, trees, and wildlife. The outfitter instructs its customers to portage the rapids, some of which are Class V. The company prides itself on good equipment and personal service.

The region has good fishing is for walleye, northern pike, and bass, and offers

chances to view deer, eagles, beavers, otters, and moose. The rental season runs from May-October.

Voyageur Canoe Outfitters
Sue & Mike Prom
990 Gunflint Trail
Grand Marais, MN 55604
(218) 338-2224, (800) 777-7215
Lake Saganaga, in the BWCA and Quetico Provincial Park
Max. rapids: V+
PPA, MACO, NRPA, MCRUA

Voyageur rents canoes and runs guided canoe trips for periods of 2-14 days in the wilderness, where no motors are allowed and the number of vacationers is limited. These customized floats are for people of all abilities, who can enjoy drinkable water; camping and swimming; great scenery; wildlife ranging from moose and black bears to eagles and waterfowl; and fishing for walleye, bass, northern pike, and lake trout. The season runs from May 1 to mid-October.

Voyageur North Outfitters
John and Lynn O'Kane
1829 East Sheridan
Ely, MN 55731
(218) 365-3251, (800) 848-5530
BWCA
Max. rapids: None

Voyageur North Outfitters offers guided canoe trips and canoe and kayak rentals in the Boundary Waters Canoe Area and Quetico Provincial Park. Trips last from 2-14 days, offering chances to spot moose, otters, loons, and eagles. Fishing is also excellent, given the area's plentiful trout, northern pike, walleye, bass, crappie, and sunfish.

Voyageur North specializes in careful trip planning and in providing quality, ultra-light equipment. During its April-to-October season, the outfitter also offers bunkhouse accommodations, a Finnish sauna, guided fishing trips, and fly-in trips for fishing or canoeing.

Way of the Wilderness
Bud Darling
947 Gunflint Trail
Grand Marais, MN 55604
(218) 388-2212, (800) 346-6625
BWCA & Quetico Park
Max. rapids: None
PPA

Way of the Wilderness rents canoes for trips of up to 3 weeks for trips on the fabled Boundary Waters with their clear glacial lakes and granite outcroppings. These tours involve easy lake paddling with some portaging between lakes. Moose, deer, bears, beavers, otters, loons, and eagles may be seen.

Camping and chalet bunkhouse accommodation are available. The lakes also boast excellent fishing for walleye, smallmouth bass, northern pike, and lake trout. The family-owned company's season is from May through September.

Wilderness Adventures
Loy Householder
943 East Sheridan Street
Ely, MN 55731
(800) THE-BWCA
BWCA
Max. rapids: V+
Ely Area Outfitters Associaiton

Wilderness Adventures is a small, quality outfitter specializing in personal service and the latest lightweight equipment." The outfitter offers guided and unguided trips of 2-30 days in the Boundary Waters Canoe Area and Quetico Provincial Park. Trips range from very easy to difficult, depending on the distances covered and the number and difficulty of portages. All trips offer a chance to spot moose, bears, eagles, beavers, otters, and wolves, and to fish for walleye, northern pike, bass, and panfish. Wilderness Adventures' season run from May through September.

Wilderness Outfitters, Inc.
Jim Pascoe & Gary Gotchnik
1 East Camp St.
Ely, MN 55731-1290
(218) 365-3211, (800) 777-8572
BWCA and Quetico Park
Max. rapids I-II
PPA

Wilderness Outfitters, which has been outfitting paddlers since 1921, rents canoes and provides guided canoe trips throughout the Boundary Waters with their breathtaking scenery and pure water. The company offers the latest equipment for canoeing, camping, and fishing. Its trips last from 3-30 days during a May-to-October season. Lessons are also available.

Novices and experienced paddlers alike can enjoy the wilderness with its great sandy beaches and excellent fishing. Wildlife includes deer, bears, moose, beavers, otters, eagles, and waterfowl.

Mississippi

Since Mississippi's highest point is just 806 feet above sea level, nobody comes to the Magnolia State in search of whitewater. But canoeists enjoy a broad skein of rivers, lakes and ponds well supplied with fish and other wildlife. Scenery varies from the Piney Woods country to the bayous and beaches of the Gulf of Mexico. Here and there a museum or archaeological site reminds visitors that more Indian tribes lived in Mississippi than in any other southeastern state. And many reminders exist of the state's more recent past: antebellum homes, the Natchez Trace, and impressive Civil War battlefields.

For fishing and sheer boating convenience — in terms of boat ramps, camping, picnicking and rest stops along the way — it is hard to beat the Pearl River and its main tributaries. The Pearl drains a large part of southern Mississippi and is rich in bass, catfish, perch, bream and crappie. As it meanders slowly past the state capital city of Jackson and down to the Gulf, it widens and develops sandbars at its bends. Deer, beaver, opossum, raccoon, fox, and wild turkey lurk along its banks under stands of mixed hardwood, loblolly, sycamore, and willow. Hundreds of different wildflowers color the woods from spring until fall. The Pearl River Basin Development District has created 17 water parks to date, strategically spaced along a "pleasure boatway" from Neshoba County to the coast. The facilities are all there for floaters to relax and enjoy the river's beauty.

But perhaps the most popular float in Mississippi is Black Creek. And despite its summer crowds, this river-for-all-seasons also has a strong appeal to those who want to escape civilization. From its headwaters in Lamar County, it enjoys a Wild and Scenic designation as it passes through the one-half million acre De Soto National Forest. Many sections of Black Creek are remote, picturesque and full of wildlife. Paddlers find plenty of places to camp overnight, surrounded by trees and flowering shrubs. But elsewhere much of the land is privately owned and boaters should get written permission from landowners before pitching tents and lighting fires.

Between Black Creek and Pearl River flows another delightful stream, Wolf River, noted for its clean water and its white sandy beaches overhung by magnolias, cypresses and live oaks. It empties into the Bay of St. Louis where stately mansions in the towns of Long Beach and Pass Christian over look the Gulf.

Many other Mississippi streams can be canoed with enjoyment. Ten of Mississippi's twenty-seven state parks offer rental canoes and most have fishing boats for hire. But state authorities warn paddlers to take care. "Nav igable streams in Mississippi are deceptively slow and gentle," Pearl River Basin officials caution in a bright red handout to floaters. "Water levels are unpredictable ... dangerously low levels exist during summer and fall months."

Black Creek Canoe Rental

Pat and Terry Gibbs
P.O. Box 414
Brooklyn, MS 39425
(601) 582-8817
Black Creek
Max. rapids: None
PPA

Black Creek Canoe Rental rents canoes for trips of 3 hours to 3 days on Black Creek. These trips offer relaxing floats through remote, scenic areas, clean water, good fishing for bass, catfish and bream, and chances to see deer, wild turkeys, wood ducks, owls, great blue herons, and beavers. Most trips are suitable for families with children.

A wide stream with broad white sand-bars that are perfect for camping, Black Creek is one of the most popular float trips in the state. One stretch of the stream, which flows through the half-million-acre DeSoto National Forest, is designated wild and scenic.

Black Creek Canoe Rental prides itself on personal attention to clients' needs and the variety of floats available. The outfitter's season runs from March 1 to October 31.

Bogue Chitto Water Park

Pearl River Basin Development District
Route 2, Box 223P
McComb, MS 39648
(601) 684-9568
Bogue Chitto River
Max. rapids: None

The Bogue Chitto Water Park is a state park where paddlers can take scenic tube and canoe trips year-round. These outings run on the Bogue Chitto River through woodlands where floaters can spot deer and wild turkeys, fish for catfish and bass, and stop at large sand-bars to swim or picnic. Canoe and tube rentals are available from three private liveries that serve the park's waters: Ryal's Rentals (684-4948), Riverview Grocery (249-3670) and Choo Choo (no phone).

Bogue Chitto Water Park also offers trailer sites with water and electricity, primitive camping, boat launching, picnic grounds, a nature trail, and bathhouses.

Black Creek. Courtesy of Black Creek Canoe Rental.

Red Creek Canoe Rental
Kevin Gibbs
Box 414
Brooklyn, MS 39425
(601) 928-7007
Max. rapids: I
Red Creek

Red Creek Canoe Rental rents canoes for one-half to 3-day trips on the clear, red tannin-colored water of aptly-named Red Creek. The stream is ideal for canoeing, fishing and swimming. Around every bend one finds scenes of tranquil beauty — dark, deep pools contrasting with snow-white sandbars. The creek runs gently, enlivened by some riffles and chutes. It may be enjoyed year-round.

Wolf River Canoes
Joseph Feil
21652 Tucker Road
Long Beach, MS 39560
(601) 452-7666
Wolf River
Max. rapids: I

Wolf River Canoes, Inc. offers guided and unguided canoe trips of 1-5 days on the gentle, meandering Wolf River. Day trips are safe and fun for anyone age 7 to 70. On longer trips, paddlers encounter small rapids, but these stretches, too, are easy to negotiate, even for beginners.

The Wolf River is very clean and undeveloped. The river banks boast magnolia, cypress, and live-oak trees and many beautiful, white-sand beaches. Paddlers also can spot deer, raccoons, beavers, owls, and great blue herons, and fish for bass, catfish, gar, and sunfish. Wolf River Canoes, open year-round, also offers shuttle service and a bathhouse.

Missouri

Amid the forested hills of the Ozarks flow spring-fed rivers famed fc
their natural beauty and crystal-clear water. It was here, in the heart c
southeastern Missouri, that the National Park Service established the na
tion's first scenic riverway. It spans 134 miles of the Jacks Fork and Currer
Rivers, and rangers boast that these Class II streams remain "nearly as wil
as the day Indians lightly trod the Ozark trails." This park, the Ozark Na
tional Scenic Riverways, lies 175 miles south of St. Louis and 250 mile
southeast of Kansas City.

One of the best floats in the park is on the Jacks Fork from Buck Ho
low, where Mo. 17 crosses the river, to Alley Spring. This is where the par
is at its best: wild and scenic. You can do it all year if you can read the cu
rents and don't mind some bumps and scrapes. But the best time is in th
spring when the water is high. It's a fast, long one-day trip or a lazy two-da
jaunt.

John Boats — flat-bottomed craft that many people prefer for fishing –
may be rented as well as canoes, rafts, kayaks and tubes. Limestone cliff
some with caves to explore, enliven the wooded riverbanks. Big Spring, nea
Van Buren, is the nation's largest single-outlet spring, gushing 277 millic
gallons of water on an average day. Many paddlers prefer to float the upp
reaches of the Jacks Fork and Current Rivers in winter or spring to avoi
portaging around exposed gravel bars in the summertime.

Yet these bars provide cool and relatively mosquito-free campsites. Floate
should watch out for trunks and roots of fallen trees, especially in the sprir
flood season. Rampant poison ivy as well as the occasional copperhead c
other nasty snake are riverbank hazards. But fishermen will find trout an
bass lazing in treeshaded pools.

Further west, in south central Missouri, Eleven Point River meanders gen
ly through a different section of the Ozark hills. Another spring-fed strea
in the Class II category, it winds through steep bluffs, forested valleys ar
low-lying pastures. About half the lands within the Eleven Point River Na
tional Scenic River area belong to the National Forest System; the rest a
private but dotted with scenic easements. An excellent river for cano

amping, the Eleven Point is especially appealing along a 45-mile stretch ownstream from Thomasville.

Near Steelville, some 90 minutes southwest of St. Louis, are popular vaation resorts offering a wide range of activities, including floating on the pper Meramec and Huzzah Rivers. Two hours south from St. Louis is the lack River, claimed by locals to be the clearest stream in the Ozarks. Its ast Fork offers Class III-IV whitewater in the spring but summer floaters ay be confined to the mainstream. Around Lebanon in the Springfield rea is the unspoiled Niangua River with its gentle waters and profusion of sh and wildlife. Access to the Big Piney River, rated one of the best fishing vers in Missouri, may be found 10 miles west of Licking on Rte. 32. It of-rs a slow and easy float.

What about the mighty Missouri and Mississippi, you may wonder? A ate tourist official says that "some adventurous people do float the Misssippi and Missouri rivers but, to my knowledge, have to provide their own raft, do their own shuttling, etc." He also says that some floating no doubt ccurs on the slow-moving, often muddy streams of north Missouri. But he nows of no canoe outfitters to serve them. Nor is he aware of any outfit-rs specializing in lakeside rentals, although doubtless canoes and other oats are available at resorts and marinas.

For more information, the Missouri Division of Tourism warmly recom-ends *Missouri Ozark Waterways*, a $2.00 book by Oscar Hawksley, pub-shed by the state's Department of Conservation, Public Affairs Section, O. Box 180, Jefferson City, MO 65102-0180.

MISSOURI

kers Ferry Canoe Rental
ene and Eleanor L. Maggard
CR 81, Box 90
alem, MO 65560
14) 858-3224, (800) 333-5628
pper Current River
lax. rapids: I-II
PA, Missouri Canoe Association,

Akers Ferry Canoe Rental rents anoes and tubes for trips of 1-9 days on e upper Current River, which has rystal-clear waters, numerous springs nd caves, along with good trout and ass fishing. Paddlers on these trips can lso enjoy camping, swimming, and a hance to spot deer, beavers, minks, and rkeys. The livery's trips, available year-ound, are fine for all paddlers.

The owners of Akers Ferry Canoe Rental also operate two other liveries near Salem: Wild River Canoe Rental (858-3230) and Round Spring Canoe Rental (858-3224).

Bass' River Resort
Stephan & Robert Bass
Box BB
Steelville, MO 65565
(800) 392-3700, (314) 786-8517,
FAX (314) 786-BASS
Courtois, Huzzah Rivers
Max. rapids: I-II
PPA

Operating on two crystal-clear streams, Bass' River Resort rents canoes, kayaks, rafts, and tubes as well as running guided canoe and jon boat trips. Families and intermediate paddlers enjoy these waters during the May 15-Oct. 15 season. Currents are moderate, but root wads, strainers, and sharp curves add challenges to the 1-4 day outings. Camping, swimming, and fishing for bass, bluegill, and perch are all available. The Ozark mountain scenery is wooded and laced with wildlife ranging from whitetail deer to eagles and herons.

Big Elk Camp & Canoe
John Tinsley
Rte. 2, Box 2548
Pineville, MO 64856
(417) 223-4635
Big Sugar, Indian Creek, Elk River
Max. rapids: I-II

Big Elk rents canoes, rafts, and tubes for easy to exciting floats on clear waters flanked by wooded banks, caves, and huge bluffs. The outfitter promises excellent service during a season that runs from March 1 to December 1. Its trips are suitable for beginners and experienced paddlers alike. Local wildlife includes beavers, muskrats, minks, and deer. Paddlers can also fish for smallmouth, largemouth, and goggle eye bass.

Big Spring Canoe & Tube
Rhonda & Tom Corbett
P.O. Box 574
Sycamore St.
Van Buren, MO 63965
(314) 323-4550
Current, Jacks Fork Rivers
Max. rapids: I-II
PPA

Big Spring rents canoes and tubes for trips of one-half to 5 days or more on clean, spring-fed waters with great smallmouth bass fishing. Paddlers float between
beautiful bluffs dotted with many caves. Turtles, deer, and eagles enliven the landscape.

Trips are designed for everyone from beginners to experts, and include shuttle service. The rivers offer good camping, swimming, and fishing. The company's season runs April 15-Oct. 30.

Fast-water canoeing on the Black River. Photo by Jack Kiser, courtesy of Black River Floats, Lesterville, Missouri.

Bird's Nest Lodge & River Resort

Stephen L. Gottschalk
Birds Nest Rd.
Steelville, MO 65565
(314) 775-2606. (800) 707-7238
Upper Meramec River
Max. rapids: None
PA

Easy day trips are the mainstay of this company, which runs guided canoe, raft and dory trips as well as renting canoes, kayaks, rafts and tubes. It prides itself on its customer service. Floats may last up to 4 days on this gentle Ozark stream, with its rolling hills, wooded cliffs and numerous gravel bars. Deer, turkey, eagles and herons can be seen, and the fishing is for trout and bass. Camping is available and the season runs March-November.

Black River Floats

Carmen Shaffer, Larry Morgan
P.O. Box 1
Centerville, MO 63654
(314) 637-2247, (314) 223-7473
Black River
Max. rapids: None

Black River Floats rents canoes, rafts, and tubes for 1- and 2-day trips on the Black River, a scenic Class I and II river safe for beginning canoeists. Abundant wildlife includes deer, turkeys, and beavers. Also, anglers can enjoy fishing in the Black River's clear water for smallmouth bass, goggle eye, and perch. Black River Floats' season runs from April to October. However, off-season boats are available if reserved in advance.

Blue Springs Ranch and Meramec Canoe Rental

Doyle Isom, Jr.
P.O. Box 57
Sullivan, MO 63080
(314) 468-6519, (800) 333-8007
Upper Meramec River
Max. rapids: I-II
Mid Missouri Canoe Liveries Association

Blue Springs Ranch and Meramec Canoe Rental offers guided canoe and raft trips and canoe, raft, and tube rentals on the Upper Meramec River. Trips last 1-5 days and offer "easy, recreational floating" for families, groups, and fishermen. The stretches floated are scenic, with crystal-clear water, bluffs, wooded hillsides, caves, and plentiful blue herons, deer, wild turkeys, and other wildlife. Paddlers also can enjoy good fishing for trout and bass.

The campground offers tent and R.V. camping, cabin rentals, cookouts, hayrides, trail rides, and a store. The season runs March to November.

Boiling Springs Resort & Canoe Rental

James & Alicia Swindell
HCR 7, Box 124
Licking, MO 65542
(314) 674-3488
Big Piney River
Max. rapids: None

Boiling Springs Resort rents canoes for leisurely trips of 1-5 days on the uncrowded and scenic Big Piney River. These are easy trips for beginners, who may spot deer, beavers, wild turkeys, and other wildlife, and fish for bass, goggle eye, and sunfish. The company's season runs from March to November. Cabins and camping are available.

Carr's Canoe Rental

Gary and Carol Smith
HCR-1, Box 137
Eminence, MO 65466
(314) 858-3240, (314) 226-5459 (home)
Current River
Max. rapids: I-II

Carr's Canoe Rental rents canoes for 1-10 day trips on the Current River. Camping is available along the river and at nearby Round Spring Campground. Carr's is owned by the proprietors of Current River Canoe Rental, located six miles north. See the separate listing in this chapter for further details.

180   *Paddle Ameri*

Cherokee Landing
Gary and Cheryl Stephens
Route 4, Box 303
Bonne Terre, MO 63628
(314) 358-2805
Big River
Max. rapids: None

Cherokee Landing rents canoes and
tubes for 1-day trips on less-traveled
stretches of the Big River, a placid,
scenic river fun for beginners and experienced paddlers alike. The trips feature views of cliffs, caves, and abundant
wildlife, including deer, beavers, and
raccoons. The clear waters also boast
good fishing for bass, catfish, bluegill,
and crappie.

Cherokee Landing's trips run from
April to October.

Clearwater Stores, Inc.
Jim Wohlschlaeger
Route 3, Box 3592
Piedmont, MO 63957
(314) 223-4813
Black River
Max. rapids: I-II

Clearwater Stores, Inc., rents canoes
for 1- and 2-day trips on the scenic
Black River in the East Ozarks. An
excellent stream for beginners as well as
experienced floaters, the Black River
offers fine hill-country scenery; views of
turkeys, deer, beavers, ducks, and blue
herons; and fishing for bass, walleye, catfish, and perch. Tent and R.V. camping
is available at Clearwater Lake, adjacent
to the outfitter's base. Paddlers also can
camp free along the river. Clearwater
Stores' season runs from March to
October.

**Courtois Canoe Rental &
Campground**
Marvin Hanks
P.O. Box 122
Steelville, MO 65565
(314) 786-7452
*Courtois Creek, Huzzah Creek, Meramec
River*
Max. rapids: I-II

Courtois Canoe Rental rents canoes,
kayaks, rafts, and tubes for trips of 1-4
days on the Courtois Creek, Huzzah
Creek, and the Meramec River. All
trips are gentle, scenic floats of minimal
difficulty that are safe and fun for paddlers young and old. Of particular
appeal are the crystal-clear, spring-fed
waters and the unspoiled Ozark wilderness offering scenic views of bluffs,
oak forests, and wildlife. Fishing is good
too, for smallmouth and largemouth
bass.

Courtois Canoe Rental, open year-
round, operates a secluded, riverfront
campground with a modern bathhouse,
general store, and restaurant.

Current River Canoe Rental
Gary and Windy Smith
HCR 62, Box 375
Salem, MO 65560
(314) 858-3250 (summers),
(314) 226-5517 (winters)
Current River
Max. rapids: I-II

Current River Canoe Rental rents
canoes and tubes for 1-7 day trips on
the Current River in the heart of the
Ozark National Scenic Riverways. Classified as a Class I, or occasionally as a
Class II river, the Current is fun for beginners as well as experienced canoeists
The river is crystal clear and especially
scenic, offering views of cliffs and bluffs
and several large caves, one of which
takes two hours to explore on tours led
by the National Park Service. Wildlife
to see includes turkeys, deer, otters,
squirrels, rabbits, birds, turtles, and fish
— smallmouth bass, trout, and goggle
eye.

During Current River's May-to-October season, R.V. and tent lodging is available at Pulltite Campground at the outfitter's base.

evil's Back Floats
olores Swoboda
109 Noser Mill Rd.
eslie, MO 63056
314) 484-3231
ourbeuse River
Max. rapids: I-II

Year-round canoe rentals are provided y this company on the clean and calm ourbeuse River, with its attractive forsted scenery. Amid the bluffs, paddlers ay spot wild turkey and deer while fishg for bass, catfish, perch, catfish, and oggle eye.

Camping is available, and trips may st up to 30 days. They are suitable for eginners and people of all ages.

)ube's Three River Campground, Inc.
ames & Donald Dube
ox 697
ineville, MO 64856
417) 223-4746
ig Sugar Creek, Indian Creek, Elk River
Max. rapids: I-II

Canoe rentals at low prices with timely pickups and very clean facilities are offered by this outfitter. Scenery includes beautiful bluffs, spring flowers, and gravel bars. The water is clean and fishing is great for large- and smallmouth bass, crappie, catfish, and bluegill. During the April-September season guests can camp, swim and float waters suited to beginners as well as experienced paddlers. Deer, eagles, turtles, snakes, and herons can be spotted.

Eagles Nest Campground & Canoe Outfitters
Bill & Lori Hanes
Rte. 2, Box 42A
Noel, MO 64854
(417) 475-3326
Elk River, Indian Creek, Big Sugar Creek
Max. rapids: I-II

Day canoe rental trips amid the scenic limestone bluffs and rolling hills of the Ozarks are this outfitter's specialty. The large, clean campground is at the take-out point for most of these trips, so there is no waiting for a shuttle at the end of the day. Fishing is for small- and large-mouth bass, goggle-eye, catfish, and sunfish. Wildlife includes beaver,

amily floating on the Current River. Courtesy of Eminence Canoe Rental.

armadillo, turtle, and deer, along with many kinds of birds. The company rents tubes as well as canoes during its April-November season.

Eminence Canoes, Cottages & Camp
Wes and Patti Tastad
P.O. Box 276, Hwy. 19 N.
Eminence, MO 65466
(314) 226-3642, (800) 224-2090
Current River, Jack's Fork River
Max. rapids: I-II
PPA, Missouri Canoe Association

Eminence Canoes, Cottages & Camp offers private shuttles or canoe, kayak, and tube trips on the Jacks Fork and Current Rivers in the Ozark National Scenic Riverways Park. Trips last from 1-7 days and are suited for all paddlers, novice to expert, depending on the time of year and section of river selected. The season runs year-round and the scenery includes forests, bluffs with the largest concentration of caves and springs in the United States. Among the wildlife to see are bobcats, mountain lions, deer, beavers, minks, eagles, and buzzards. The fish to catch include smallmouth and largemouth bass, trout, and goggle eye.

Eminence Canoe also offers cottages and a private R.V. and tent campground with a modern washroom.

Fagan's Canoe & Raft Rental
Linda and Joe Fagan
P.O. Box 796
Steelville, MO 65565
(314) 775-5744, (314) 885-2947 (winter)
Meramec River
Max. rapids: I-II
Mid-Missouri Liveries Association, State of Missouri Floaters Association

Fagan's Canoe & Raft Rental offers guided and unguided canoe and raft trips on the Meramec River. Trips last from 1-5 days, are fairly easy, and are best suited for fishermen, families, single canoeists, and large groups. The area is distinctive for its scenic bluffs, caves, springs, and abundant wildlife, including

deer, turkeys, birds, muskrats, minks, and squirrels. Fishing in the Meramec's cool, clear water also is exceptional, especially for brown trout but also for bass perch, drum, goggle eye, and suckers.

Fagan's is open year-round, but winter trips require advance reservation.

Franklin Floats
Bob and JoAnn Franklin
Route 1, Box 9
Lesterville, MO 63654
(314) 637-2205
Black River, Taum Sauk Lake
Max. rapids: II-III

Franklin Floats rents canoes and tubes for 1-3 day trips on all forks of the Black River and on Taum Sauk Lake. A high water the East Fork of the Black River has exciting rapids to challenge advanced paddlers. Otherwise, all trips are fine for anyone, including novices. All paddlers can enjoy the Ozark countryside with its springs, caves, bluffs, and abundant deer, turkeys, and herons. The waters also offer good fishing for smallmouth and largemouth bass, crappie, catfish, bluegill and goggle eye.

Lodging is available in riverfront cabins and at camp sites along the river Franklin Float's season is from April to October, but off-season trips are available by request.

Gasconade Hills Resort
Bob & Pat Sutcliffe
28425 Spring Rd.
Richland, MO 65556
(573) 765-3044, (800) 869-6861
Upper Gasconade River, Osage Fork of the Gasconade
Max. rapids: I-II

This outfitter rents canoes, rafts, and tubes for trips of up to 30 days on a quiet southern Missouri stream, perfect for groups and beginners. Guests may fish for small- and largemouth bass, rock bass, catfish, and perch as they admire the scenery and wildlife. Camping and swimming are available during the company's April 15-Nov. 30 season.

Fall canoeing on the Eleven Point River. Photo by Carole Nance, courtesy of Hufstedtler's Canoe Rentals, Alton, Missouri.

Griffin's Canoe & Campground

James Griffin
Route 16, Box 1010
Lebanon, MO 65536
(417) 588-3353
Niangua River
Max. rapids: I-II

Griffin's Canoe & Campground, open year-round, rents canoes for 1- and 2-day trips on the scenic Niangua River in the Ozarks. These gentle float trips, fine for young and old, range in length from two-and-a-half to 40 miles. The Niangua offers wilderness scenery; views of deer, turkeys, and other wildlife; and excellent fishing for trout and bass.

Griffin's Campground features tent and R.V. camping, hot showers, and a spring-fed fishing pond stocked with bass, bluegill, and catfish.

Hi-Lo Campground & Canoe Rental

Linda A. Skains
Route 1, Box 176G
Tecumseh, MO 65760
(417) 261-2590, (417) 261-2368
Bryant Creek, White River — North Fork
Max. rapids: I-II

Hi-Lo Campground & Canoe Rental rents canoes, kayaks, and tubes for 1-3 day trips on Bryant Creek and the North Fork of the White River. Trips range in difficulty, with stretches to suit paddlers of all levels of experience. On both the Bryant and North Fork, paddlers can enjoy views of wooded banks, springs, 19th century water mills, and wildlife, including deer, blue herons, otters, and wild turkeys. Also, the North Fork offers trout fishing and the Bryant has fishing for bass, rock bass, channel catfish, walleye, trout, and bluegill. Camping also is available during the April-to-November season.

**Hufstedler's Canoe Rental &
Campground**
Mike Brooks
Riverton Rural Branch
Alton, MO 65606
(417) 778-6116
Eleven Point River
Max. rapids: III-IV
*Missouri Canoe Outfitters and Liveries
Association*

Hufstedler's Canoe Rental and Campground offers canoe and tube rentals and guided canoe and dory trips on the Eleven Point River, a designated National Wild and Scenic River. Trips of eight to 44 miles run through pristine wilderness with towering 300-foot bluffs, clear water, and abundant wildlife, including deer, coyotes, mountain lions, beavers, turkeys, owls, bats, and bald eagles. Fishing for rainbow trout, bass, and pike is excellent.

Hufstedler's, open year-round, also has a large, wooded campground with a modern bathhouse and free firewood.

Huzzah Valley Resort
The Cottrell Family
HC 87, Box 7480
Steelville, MO 65565
(314) 786-8412, (800) 367-4516
Huzzah, Courtois, Meramec Rivers
Max. rapids: I-II
MCOA, NCOA, PPA

Huzzah Valley provides canoe, kayak, raft, and tube floats for people of all ages on crystal-clear waters from March until Nov. 15. Its campground has grassy, shaded campsites beside the river, which contains trout, smallmouth and largemouth bass, perch, goggle eye, and bluegill. Paddlers can observe deer, wild turkeys, raccoons, and other wildlife. Bunkhouses and other indoor accommodations are available, along with horseback riding.

Indian Springs Lodge
Greg Schmucker
P.O. Box T
Highway 8 West
Steelville, MO 65565
(314) 775-2266, (800) 392-1110
Meramec River
Max. rapids: I-II

Indian Springs Lodge rents canoes, kayaks, and tubes for 1-day trips on the Meramec River. This slow, easy river is fine for paddlers of all ages and offers wilderness scenery; good fishing for trout, bass, catfish, and sucker; and a chance to view deer, bald eagles, great blue herons, turtles, and trout.

Paddling on the spring-fed Meramec is available year-round. In addition, Indian Springs offers a campground, bar, live bands, hiking trails, a pool, cabins, motel rooms, a restaurant, tennis, horse shoes, and other recreation.

Jack's Fork Canoe Rental
Gene and Eleanor L. Maggard
P.O. Box 188
Eminence, MO 65466
(314) 226-3434, (800) Jacks Fork
Current River, Jack's Fork River
Max. rapids: I-II

Jacks Fork Canoe Rental offers guided canoe and johnboat trips and rents canoes, rafts, and tubes on the Current and Jacks Fork Rivers. These trips last 1-14 days, pass through a scenic wilderness of woods and high bluffs, and offer excellent bass and trout fishing. Paddlers can also enjoy camping, swimming, and views of deer, turkeys, minks, and beavers.

Jacks Fork Canoe Rental's season is from April to November.

Jeff's Canoe Rental
Jeff Vroman
Box 204A
Annapolis, MO 63620
(314) 598-4555
Black River
Max. rapids: I-II

Jeff's Canoe Rentals rents canoes,

afts, and tubes for 1-3 day trips on the scenic, crystal-clear Black River. Trips are easy enough for beginners and boast fine views of rocky bluffs, springs, and wildlife, including deer and wild turkeys. Anglers also can enjoy fishing for small-mouth bass, catfish, bluegill, and goggle-eye.

All trips start upriver and end at the outfitter's base at the Highway K Bridge. Jeff's Canoe Rental's season runs from Memorial Day to Labor Day.

K-Mark Canoe Rental
Dee and Sue Rayfield
Box 186
Annapolis, MO 63620
(314) 598-3399
Black River
Max. rapids: I-II

K-Mark Canoe Rental offers guided and unguided canoe trips of 1- and 2-days on the gentle, scenic Black River in the Ozark foothills. On K-Mark's trips, paddlers can enjoy wilderness scenery, abundant wildlife, and excellent fishing for bass, crappie, catfish, and perch.

During the April-to-October season, the outfitter also offers shuttle service.

The Landing & Rosecliff Lodge
Tom & Della Bedell
1 Big Spring Rd.
Van Buren, MO 63965
(314) 323-8433, 323-8156
Current River
Max. rapids: I-II

The Landing rents canoes and tubes year-round for 1-5 day trips on the crys-tal-clear Current River. These relaxed outings are suitable for beginners and intermediate paddlers, who can enjoy fishing for smallmouth bass and watch-ing for eagles, wild turkeys, and deer. Guests may camp overnight or stay in the 19-room Rosecliff Lodge overlook-ing the river.

Meramec Canoe Rental
Doyle and Vicki Isom
P.O. Box 57
Sullivan, MO 63080
(314) 468-6519, (800) 334-6946
Meramec River
Max. rapids: I-II
Missouri Canoe Association

Meramec Canoe Rental rents canoes, rafts, and tubes at Meramec State Park for trips of 1-5 days on the Meramec River. These scenic trips offer views of caves, bluffs, and wildlife, including deer and wild turkeys. Group discounts are available.

The state park, open from March to November, also offers cabin rentals, barbecues, and a restaurant.

Muddy River Outfitters, Inc.
Robert Hoenike
4307 Main Street
Kansas City, MO 64111
(816) 753-7093
Big Piney River and rivers statewide
Max. rapids: I-II

Muddy River Outfitters offers 1- and 2-day guided and unguided canoe and kayak trips on the clear, calm waters of all rivers of the state. A favorite is the Big Piney River. These trips, suited for beginners and advanced canoeists, are organized from the tour company's head-quarters in Kansas City. The guided trips feature camping on a ridge above the river, a break to explore a mammoth cave, and a stop on the drive back to Kansas City at either an Ozark winery, an outdoor flea market, or at Arrow Rock, a restored historic town.

Muddy River also offers several out-of-state tours, including trips to the Grand Canyon, Yellowstone, the Bad-lands and Alaska.

Neil Canoe Rental and Campground
Martha Gossett
Highway M, P.O. Box 396
Van Buren, MO 63965
(314) 323-4447
Current River
Max. rapids: I-II

Neil Canoe Rental & Campground
rents canoes, johnboats, and tubes on
the Current River. Canoe trips last 1-5
days, offering easy paddling, crystal-clear
water, good fishing for bass and goggle
eye, and beautiful views of large bluffs,
dense forest, and abundant wildlife.
Among the wildlife to watch for are
deer, wild turkeys, raccoons, rabbits,
and birds. The river also has many
gravel bars that make good places to
stop to picnic or swim.

Neil Canoe Rental's season is from
April to October.

Northwest Passage
Rick Sweitzer
1130 Greenleaf Avenue
Wilmette, IL 60091
(847) 256-4409, (800) RECREATE
Current River, Rio Grande, Chicago River,
BWCA, Lake Michigan, Lake Superior
Max. rapids: III-IV

Northwest Passage offers guided raft
trips on the New and Gauley, Rivers in
West Virginia; canoe trips on the Current River in Missouri, the Rio Grande
in Texas, the Chicago River, and the
Boundary Waters Canoe Area in Minnesota. It has sea kayak trips on Lake
Michigan, both in Illinois and in Door
County, Wisconsin, and on Lake Superior in Michigan. Most of these trips,
which last 1-7 days, are designed for beginners; some require prior experience.
Depending on the location, these trips
offer excitement, challenge, remoteness
and beauty.

An adventure travel company, Northwest Passage also offers skiing, hiking,
cycling, backpacking, dogsledding, and
rock climbing. Outings run year-round
in the U.S., Canada, the Arctic, Greenland, Switzerland, New Zealand, Costa

Rica, Belize, Crete, Tanzania and southern Africa.

Ozark Outdoors
Robert Bass & Fred Sanders
Rte. 1, Box 120
Leasburg, MO 65535
(800) 888-0023, (314) 245-6437,
FAX (314) 245-6839
Meramec, Courtois, Huzzah Rivers
Max. rapids: I-II
PPA

Ozark Outdoors runs guided canoe
and jon boat fishing trips and rents canoes, kayaks, rafts, and tubes. Although
popular, the waters and scenery are very
clean and unspoiled. Granite and limestone bluffs reach 200 feet while the
river valleys are full of native oaks, walnut, and sycamores. Smallmouth and
largemouth bass may be caught, along
with bluegill and catfish.

The company takes youth groups as
well as intermediate paddlers during its
April 15-Oct. 15 season. Camping is
available and trips last up to 6 days.

Ozark Springs Resort
David Hughes
26880 Rochester Rd.
Richland, MO 65556
(314) 765-5223
Gasconade River
Max. rapids: None

Ozark Springs Resort offers guided
and unguided canoe trips on clean,
uncrowded waters with excellent fishing.
The scenery has beautiful bluffs and the
wildlife includes deer, beaver, turkey,
and waterfowl. Camping and swimming
are available.

Ozark Sunrise Expeditions, Inc.
Guy M. Thomas
Route 4, Box 10 C
Joplin, MO 64804
(417) 782-5272
Shoal Creek, Buffalo River, Mullberry River,
Frog Bayou
Max. rapids: I-II

Ozark Sunrise Expeditions, Inc., offers guided and unguided canoe trips on Shoal Creek, Buffalo River, Mulberry River, and Frog Bayou. All trips are relatively easy and offer excellent Ozark scenery, including bluffs, caves, and views of deer, turkeys, beavers, and eagles. Trips also feature many good spots to camp and fish for bass, panfish, and catfish.

Open year-round, OSE offers tent and R.V. camping, moonlight canoe trips, dark-night tube parties, sunrise breakfast floats, and "adventure programs" such as orienteering and rappelling, and guided hunting and fishing trips. Rafts are also available.

R&W Canoe Rental & Campground
Rick and Wanda Beasley
Route 16, Box 884
Lebanon, MO 65536
(417) 588-3358
Niangua River
Max. rapids: I-II

R&W Canoe Rental and Campground rents canoes for 1- and 2-day trips on the scenic, gentle Niangua River. Paddlers can spot birds, deer, muskrats, turtles, beavers, and otters among the lush greenery on the Niangua, and fishermen can enjoy angling for shasta, brown, and rainbow trout, goggle eye, bass, bluegill, and perch. Gravel bars along the river provide good stopping points for swimming in the Niangua's clear, spring-fed waters.

R&W also offers a riverfront campground. The season runs from March through October.

The Rafting Co.
Paul & Cheryl Wilkerson
Box 906
Steelville, MO 65565
(314) 775-2628
Upper Meramec River
Max. rapids: None
PPA

The Rafting Co., a camping and RV resort, rents canoes and rafts for "casual and mellow" family trips suitable for young and old. The outfitter prides itself on its prompt service. Paddlers pass a beautiful cave with a spring and they may spot turkey, deer, beaver, muskrats, and geese amid the Ozark scenery. Trophy smallmouth bass fishing is available, along with camping and paddling lessons during the April-November season.

Ray's Canoe Rental
Route 1, Box 754
Steelville, MO 65565
(314) 775-5697
Upper Meramec River
Max. rapids: I-II
Missouri Canoe Association

Ray's Canoe Rental rents canoes and tubes for trips of 1-5 days on the upper Meramec River. The challenge on this Ozark stream comes in negotiating narrow stretches. The Meramec also offers fine wilderness scenery along its wooded banks, views of Meramec Spring and abundant wildlife, and excellent trout and bass fishing in its clear, spring-fed waters. Ray's, open from March to November, offers camping and a rustic cabin.

Ray's Riverside Resort
John and Joe Ann Wilder
Route 7, Box 418
Licking, MO 65542
(314) 674-2430
Big Piney River
Max. rapids: I-II

Ray's Riverside Resort runs guided and unguided trips of 1-6 days on the clean, clear, spring-fed Big Piney River. Trips are of little or moderate difficulty and offer pretty wooded scenery and views of limestone bluffs, rabbits, deer, and wild turkeys. Guided trips are by canoe or raft, and unguided trips are by canoe, raft, or tube. Riverfront camping and fishing for smallmouth bass and rock bass are also available.

Richard's Canoe Rental
Karen Richard
Route 2
Alton, MO 65606
(417) 778-6186
Eleven Point River
Max. rapids: I-II

Richard's Canoe Rental offers guided and unguided canoe and raft trips of 1-7 days on the Eleven Point River, a scenic river easy enough for beginners. Trips pass through protected national forest land with wilderness scenery and plentiful beavers, bears, turtles, minks, and other wildlife. The river's clear water also has excellent fishing, with abundant trout, bass, goggle eye and perch. Rentals and guided trips are available year-round.

River Maddness
Tom Lewis, Gene Schoenhoff
1339 S. Glenstone
Springfield, MO 65804
(417) 883-5089
Most Ozark streams
Max. rapids: I-II
PPA

River Maddness runs guided canoe and raft trips as well as renting both canoes and rafts for trips of up to 6 days throughout the scenic Ozarks. Flanked by high bluffs and hardwood trees, these pristine mountain streams are rich in fish. With a combined total of 50 years' experience in Ozark paddling and guiding, the proprietors know where to find blue ribbon smallmouth bass, panfish, trout, and catfish.

Riversedge Campgrounds
Box 76, Peola Road
Lesterville, MO 63654
(314) 637-2422
Black River
Max. rapids: None

Riversedge Campgrounds rents canoes, tubes and rafts for 1-day trips on the Black River, a crystal-clear "family" river offering good swimming, scenery, and fishing for bass, goggle eye, and catfish. Canoe trips of eight and 15 miles are available. The shorter and more popular trip ends at the campground, which has 110 campsites, one-half mile of beachfront, modern bathhouses and covered horse stalls. The campground also offers hayrides, trail rides, and weekend specials that include camping, a float trip, and a barbecue. Riversedge's season runs from April to October.

Riverside Canoe Rental
Allen & Susan Maxey
HCR68, Box 172
Caulfield, MO 65626
(417) 284-3043
N. Fork of White River, Bryant Creek
Max. rapids: I-II
PPA

Easy floats on good troutfishing waters are the mainstay of Riverside's business, with trips arranged to suit customer's needs. The company rents canoes and tubes, which carry floaters through countryside adorned with high bluffs and woods. Weekend and day trips are the specialty during the Memorial Day-Labor Day season.

Blue herons, golden eagles, turtles, mink, and muskrat may be viewed. Camping is available.

Shady Beach Family Campground
Jeff & Janet Scott
P.O. Box 473, Hwy. 59N
Noel, MO 64854
(417) 475-6483, Reservations:
(800) 745-6481
Indian Creek, Big Sugar Creek, Elk River
Max. rapids: I-II

Shady Beach Campground rents canoes, kayaks and tubes for pleasant 1- and 2-day family trips with some exciting rapids. Depending on the time of year and rainfall, paddlers from novices to experts will enjoy these runs. The company runs a family-oriented campground with strict quiet hours and 24-hour security.

As they float, guests can enjoy the bluffs and rocky beaches. Alert paddlers may spot deer, beavers, cranes, turtles, and golden eagles. There is also excellent smallmouth bass fishing on the clean Elk River and its tributaries.

Sunburst Ranch Inc.
Albert S. Eckilson
HCR 68, Box 140
Caulfield, MO 65626
(417) 284-3443
White River — North Fork
Max. rapids: III-IV

Sunburst Ranch rents canoes for 1- and 2-day trips on the North Fork of the White River. Trips run between April and November, with Class III rapids in the spring and Class II rapids in the summer and fall. Paddlers can enjoy fine Ozark scenery of bluffs, springs, caves, and abundant wildlife. The White River is also a trophy trout stream with outstanding fishing for rainbow and brown trout, smallmouth bass, and goggle eye.

Paddlers can also "rough it in style" at a campground halfway along a 2-day trip.

Montana

Montana's Rockies give rise to some of the finest canoeing, rafting and fishing rivers in the world. The Big Sky State is a place to rejoice in the wilderness, to commune with nature, to recall the wild and wooly West and retrace the routes taken by early explorers. Here are the sources of the mighty Missouri and its great tributary, the Yellowstone. These two rivers drain six-sevenths of the state and flow majestically across the great arid plain that comprises more than half of Montana. Their headwater streams the Big Hole, the Beaverhead, the Jefferson, the Madison, the Gallatin, the Smith and the Bighorn, provide some of the best floating in the state. And there is more good paddling on the western side of the continental divide, where the Bitterroot, the Blackfoot and the three-pronged Flathead converge on the Clark Fork. The Clark Fork, navigable throughout its course through Montana, then joins the massive Columbia bound for the Pacific.

Start in the west with the Bitterroot, which Lewis and Clark originally named "Clark's River." They called it a handsome stream with clear water and a gravel bed. Unfortunately it is no longer pristine today: much of its downstream section towards Missoula has been spoiled by riprapping with rocks and old car bodies to protect mobile homes in the floodplain. But further upstream the Bitterroot is rich in wildlife and the entire river is flanked by the scenic Bitterroot Range to the west and the Sapphire Range in the east.

Also very popular with Missoulans is the Blackfoot River, especially in its lower stretches. One favorite outing is a six-mile trip at Johnsrud State Park. It has Class III rapids in May-June but can be run all summer long. The most difficult whitewater on the Blackfoot is further upstream, above the confluence with the Clearwater.

The Clark Fork itself has been much cleaned up since the grim fish kill caused by pollution in earlier years. Its trout and other aquatic life have returned in strength, and the river has become another popular float in western Montana. The 22-mile run starting at Alberton Gorge in Mineral County — again not far from Missoula — is a good Class II-III trip runnable all year.

round except when the river is frozen. It is tricky at peak water levels, when the rapids come close to Class V, but quite safe in July and August.

Further north, on the fringe of Glacier National Park, the Flathead offers varied paddling on its Main Stem, Middle Fork, and North Fork. The Main Stem has a Class III six-mile run just below Flathead Lake for which a permit is needed from the Flathead Indian Reservation. This is a scenic journey between high cliffs that provide nesting sites for birds of prey. Following this Buffalo Rapids stretch, the entire lower portion of the river is gentle floating on clear water past rocky bluffs, badlands and wildflowers, with many species of birds.

The Middle Fork of the Flathead is reputedly Montana's wildest river. Its remote upper section is too rugged for most floaters in May, when its flow may surge from a low level of 900 cubic feet per second to more than 11,000 cfs. But in June and July it poses a tempting Class III-IV challenge for experienced rafters. Access to this wilderness grizzly-bear region is by plane to the Schaefer Meadows airstrip. Further downstream, the non-wilderness section of the Middle Fork is more frequented because of its easy access. This, too, has rapids that demand expertise, notably in the John Stevens Canyon run where the narrow stream drops thirty-five feet per mile along a five-mile stretch.

Southward from Canada runs the North Fork of the Flathead, offering rich wildlife and spectacular views of peaks rising from adjoining Glacier National Park.

Among the headwaters of the Missouri, the Big Hole is a much-loved and famous river. It sets out as a narrow stream near the Continental Divide and flows into the Jefferson near Twin Bridges. Clear and cold, it curves through 150 miles of wide valleys and narrow canyons. For the fisherman, perhaps its chief attraction is that it contains grayling as well as more common species of trout.

The Madison takes the floater through Bear Trap Canyon, a whitewater wilderness run which includes Kitchen Sink, a Class IV rapid. This is great fishing territory, and at the end of the day the paddler can wallow in the water of the Bear Trap Hot Springs. Also heading northward from Yellowstone National Park to join the Missouri is the Gallatin, with its deep canyon and continuous Class III whitewater.

The Yellowstone, the longest undammed river in the lower 48 states, is famous both for its history in pioneer days and its fishing. The upstream stretch from Gardiner, where the river leaves the Yellowstone Park, down to Livingston is known as Paradise Valley. It runs between the jagged Absaroka Mountains and the Gallatin Range and is alive with trout, Canada geese, eagles and deer. One of its highlights is Yankee Jim Canyon, a four-

MONTANA

mile whitewater stretch that attracts many summer rafters. Less crowded is the next section between Livingston and Big Timber, where the river begins to braid. Then the Yellowstone changes gradually to a warm prairie river, earning its name from the yellowish bluffs on its flanks and attracting a wide range of wildlife.

The only section of the Missouri to have been included in the National Wild and Scenic Rivers system is the 150-mile stretch between Fort Benton and the James Kipp Recreational Area. This is untouched by the many dams that check Mighty Mo's progress through Montana. It attracts paddlers and fishermen from far afield and its rapids rate no more than Class I.

Finally, there are three more great Montana fishing rivers. The Jefferson, a Missouri tributary, abounds in trout and is said to provide some of the West's finest fly fishing. The Beaverhead, which flows into the Jefferson, is claimed to be Montana's best trophy trout stream. And the Smith, which runs into the Missouri above Great Falls, provides not only great trout fishing but also a 60-mile float through a beautiful limestone canyon with walls up to a thousand feet high. Fly fishermen on the Smith can view golden eagles, mule deer, elk, black bear, mink and otter feeding on the river banks.

10,000 Waves - Raft & Kayak
Deb Moravec
Box 7924
Missoula, MT 59807
(800) 537-8315, (406) 549-6670
Blackfoot, Clark Fork, Bitterroot Rivers
Max. rapids: III-IV
America Outdoors

With quality equipment and a focus on safety, this outfitter runs guided raft and kayak trips on three scenic rivers abounding in wildlife. The company has highly-trained professional guides and serves gourmet meals. Its rafting trips are easy and suitable for all over the age of five. Inflatable and sit-on-top kayak floats are not difficult and suited to anyone 12 and over. Kayak lessons and camping are available during the May-Sept. season.

Paddlers can admire argillite canyons, and see bald eagles, osprey, deer, bear, moose, elk, hawks, and kingfishers.

Adventure Whitewater, Inc.
Marek S. Rosin
Box 636
Red Lodge, MT 59068
(406) 446-3061
Stillwater, Yellowstone Rivers
Max. rapids: III-IV

Exciting and challenging floats suitable for families as well as seasoned paddlers are offered by this outfitter on some of Montana's best waters. Adventure Whitewater runs guided raft and inflatable kayak trips on wild and undammed rivers amid mountain scenery, with clean rapids and excellent trout fishing. Its one-man "cat-yaks" have been featured on television and in magazine articles. Black and brown bears, elk, deer, eagles and osprey may be seen. The season runs May 31-Sept. 15.

Whitewater in Alberton Gorge on the Clark Fork River. Photo by Jill King, courtesy of 10,000 Waves - Raft & Kayak Adventures.

Al Gadoury's 6X Outfitters
Allen Gadoury
P.O. Box 6045
Bozeman, MT 59715
(406) 586-3806
Nelson's Creek, Armstrong Creek, DePuy Spring Creek, Yellowstone River, Missouri River
Max. rapids: III-IV

Al Gadoury's 6X Outfitters offers guided dory trips for fly fishermen on Nelson's, Armstrong's, and DePuy's Spring Creek and on the Yellowstone and Missouri Rivers. Gadoury floats these blue-ribbon trout streams in a 15-foot McKenzie-style drift boat equipped with swivel bucket seats and casting yokes fore and aft. Day trips on these catch-and-release waters run from March to November, and offer Class III-IV rapids and views of waterfowl, deer, blue herons, sandhill cranes, and minks.

Al Wind's Trout Futures
Al Wind
P.O. Box 485
Twin Bridges, MT 59754
(406) 684-5512
Big Hole River, Beaverhead River, Jefferson River, Madison River
Max. rapids: III
Fishing Outfitters Association of Montana, Trout Unlimited

Al Wind specializes in guided oar-boat trips for people who enjoy beautiful river scenery and the challenge of fly fishing for trout. Trips last 1-5 days and include expert fly-fishing instruction and descriptions of the area's entomology, trout biology, and wildlife. Trips run on six rivers, all in distinctive country ranging from 7,000 to 2,000 feet in elevation. On some rivers, it's not uncommon for the terrain to go from meadow to forest to canyon in a single day.

During Wind's May-to-October season, guests can fish for brook, rainbow, brown, and cutthroat trout, grayling, and bass. The wildlife to see include eagles, ospreys, herons, ducks, bighorn sheep, deer, moose, and elk.

Bar RL Outfitters
R. J. Luchall
2230 Emory Road
Ronan, MT 59864
(406) 675-4256
Clark Fork River, Bitterroot River
Max. rapids: I-II
Montana Outfitters and Guides Association

Bar RL Outfitters runs 1-5 day guided raft and dory trips on the Clark Fork and Bitterroot Rivers. With Class I and II rapids, these trips are not difficult and are well-suited for families with children age 12 and older. The company also offers trips into the Selway Bitterroot Wilderness Area for paddling and fishing on four high Alpine lakes "teeming with fish of all sizes." Rainbow, brown, and cutthroat trout can be caught.

Of the scenery Bar RL says, "Montana rivers and lakes are all beautiful and pristine — ours are no exception." Wildlife viewing is excellent, too, with chances to see mountain sheep, elk, deer, bears, and mountain goats. The season runs from May to September.

Bar Six Outfitters
1975 Sullivan Lane
Dillon, MT 59725
(406) 683-4005
Big Hole River, Smith River, Beaverhead River
Max. rapids: I-II
Montana Outfitters and Guides Association

Bar Six Outfitters runs guided and unguided raft trips on the Big Hole, Smith, and Beaverhead Rivers, which offer great scenery, fishing, and fun, gentle rapids. Trips pass through beautiful and varied terrain consisting of towering limestone cliffs, caves, timbered mountains, and green meadows. Abundant wildlife can be seen, too, including beavers, minks, deer, elk, bears, otters, hawks, and eagles.

Trips, which last 1-5 days, also feature exceptional fishing for grayling and brown, rainbow, and cutthroat trout. The season runs from May to July.

Big Timber Fly Fishing
Channing W. Welin
HC 89 Box 4316
Big Timber, MT 59011
(406) 932-4368
Yellowstone River, Boulder River
Max. rapids: III-IV
Fishing Outfitters Association of Montana

Big Timber Fly Fishing runs guided fly-fishing trips in dories on the Yellowstone River and walk/wade trips on the Boulder River. Both rivers are large and relatively under-fished. Trips last 1-3 days and pass through scenic terrain where the mountains meet the plains. Trout and Rocky Mountain white fish are the main types of fish caught during the July-to-October season.

The company also offers tubing trips and fishing on select private lakes. Among the wildlife to see are waterfowl, raptors, deer, and many non-game species.

The Canoeing House
Al Anderson
RR 1, Box 192
Three Forks, MT 59752
(406) 285-3488
Jefferson, Madison, Gallatin, Missouri, Yellowstone, Big Hole Rivers, all other SW Montana rivers
Max. rapids: I-II

The Canoeing House offers canoe rentals and guided canoe and riverboat trips on six rivers. The rivers all boast excellent trout fishing and Rocky Mountain scenery. Trips run from 1-5 days and, with gentle Class I and II whitewater, are fine for novices. One particularly scenic trip the company offers, from Divide to the "Headquarters of the Missouri," was the same 125-mile stretch selected as a Sierra Club National Float Trip.

All trips offer good opportunities to spot eagles, beavers, minks, deer, antelopes, herons, and cranes.

Castaway Fly Fishing Shop
Joe Roope
3620 North Fruitland
Coeur d'Alene, ID 83814
(208) 765-3133
Clark's Fork River
Max. rapids:

Castaway Fly Fishing Shop offers customized trout-fishing trips on the Clark's Fork River in Montana and the St. Joe and Coeur d'Alene Rivers in Idaho. These dory trips last 1-3 days and pass through pristine wilderness with abundant wildlife and excellent fishing for rainbow and cutthroat trout. Among the wildlife to see are elk, deer, bears, beavers, and sheep. Castaway's season runs from May to October.

Castle Mountain Fly Fishers
Shane Dempsey
Box 370
White Sulphur Springs, MT 59645
(406) 547-3366
Smith River, Yellowstone River, Whitetail Lake
Max. rapids: I-II

Castle Mountain Fly Fishers offers guided canoe and raft trips and rents canoes and rafts for fly fishermen, families, and anyone seeking a wilderness experience. Trips run on the Smith River, Yellowstone River, and Whitetail Lake through scenic areas with limestone cliffs and unspoiled wilderness. On these trips, of 1-6 days, guests can camp, swim, view wildlife, and fish for brown trout, rainbow trout, native trout, brook trout, and whitefish. Among the wildlife to see are muskrats, ducks, whitetail deer, mule deer, elk, antelope, and black bears.

During Castle Mountain Fly Fishers' April-to-October season, the company also offers fly-fishing lessons, fishing on private streams, and lodging before and after trips.

Fly fishing on the Smith River, one of Montana's many terrific trout streams. Courtesy of Brian D. Nelson/Diamond N Outfitters, Missoula, Montana.

Diamond N Outfitters
Brian D. Nelson
P.O. Box 20193
Missoula, MT 59801
(406) 543-3887
*Clark Fork River, Bitterroot River, Blackfoot
River, Rock Creek, Missouri River, Big Hole
River, Beaverhead River*
Max. rapids: III-IV
*Fishing Outfitters Association of Montana,
Trout Unlimited, West Montana Fish and
Game Association*

Diamond N Outfitters runs guided
oar-boat fishing expeditions on seven
rivers. The guides are excellent teachers
of beginning and advanced fly-fishing
techniques, and run trips of 1-7
days.

Set in the heart of the northern
Rockies, expeditions run through scenic
terrain of canyons, mountains,
meadows, and forests. The rivers boast
excellent fishing for rainbow, brown, and
cutthroat trout on trips between March
and November. Wildlife viewing is good,
too, with chances to see deer, elk, bears,
eagles, minks, beavers, and otters. Custom
trips are also available.

Diamond R Expeditions
Pete and Tanya Rothing
3108 Linney Road
Bozeman, MT 59715
(406) 388-1760
*Madison River, Gallatin River, Jefferson
River, Yellowstone River, Missouri River*
Max. rapids: None

Diamond R Expeditions offers 1-7
day guided canoe trips on five scenic
rivers. These flatwater trips are well-
suited for novices and families. All trips
feature blue-ribbon trout fishing, beautiful
scenery, and abundant wildlife, including
waterfowl, beavers, ospreys,
deer, herons, and cranes.

During its June-to-October season,
Diamond R also offers horseback riding
and pack trips, drift fishing, and a special
combination package consisting of a
4-day pack trip in the Gallatin National
Forest, 2 days floating on area rivers,

and a 1-day mini-tour of Yellowstone
National Park.

E.W. Watson & Sons
Edwin W. Watson
152 Springville Lane
Townsend, MT 59644
(406) 266-2845, (800) 654-2845
*Missouri River, Canyon Ferry Lake,
Madison River*
Max. rapids: None
Montana Outfitters and Guides Association

E.W. Watson & Sons Outfitting runs
guided canoe and raft trips on the
Missouri River, Madison River, and
Canyon Ferry Lake. These flatwater
trips are easy enough for beginners and
feature clear, clean water, beautiful
mountain scenery, and excellent fishing
for brown and rainbow trout. Trips
last 1-6 days and can include a combination
of paddling and horseback
riding when packing up to secluded
camps at high mountain lakes. Among
the abundant wildlife to see on these
trips are deer, elk, blue herons, ospreys,
and eagles.

E.W. Watson's season is from July to
September. The outfitter also offers trail
riding, camping, and hunting trips.

Fishing Headquarters, Inc.
Dick Sharon and B. Thibeault
426 North Montana Street
Dillon, MT 59725
(406) 683-4634, (406) 683-6660
*Beaverhead River, Big Hole River, Jefferson
River, Madison River, Yellowstone River, Red
Rock River*
Max. rapids: I-II

Fishing Headquarters, Inc. runs
guided raft and dory trips and rents
tubes on the Beaverhead, Big Hole,
Jefferson, Madison, Yellowstone, and
Red Rock Rivers. Trips last 1-2 days and
are geared for anyone who can fish or
wishes to learn. These rivers offer scenic
views of high mountains, riverside cliffs,
and abundant wildlife, including deer,
moose, elk, and bighorn sheep. The
fishing, especially on the Beaverhead

and Big Hole Rivers, is exceptional, with excellent chances to land grayling, and brown, rainbow, brook, and cutthroat trout. Fishing Headquarters' season runs from May to October.

Flowing Rivers Guide Service
D.L. Tennant
1809 Darlene Lane
Billings, MT 59102
(406) 252-5859
Bighorn River, Missouri River, Yellowstone River
Max. rapids: I-II
Fishing Outfitters Association of Montana

Flowing Rivers Guide Service offers guided drift-boat trips and canoe rentals on the Bighorn, Missouri, and Yellowstone Rivers. Don Tennant, who has more than 40 years' experience floating, fishing, and working on rivers as a professional biologist, leads all guided trips himself. Fishing for brown and rainbow trout is superb. On guided trips, Tennant offers the guarantee "no fish — no pay."

Canoe rentals offered on rivers with mild whitewater are fine for anyone age nine to 90. All trips boast terrific scenery, fine fishing, and excellent wildlife viewing of deer, beavers, minks, muskrats, eagles, ospreys, geese, ducks, and numerous songbirds. The season runs from April to November.

Glacier Raft Co.
Darwon Stoneman, Onno Wieringa, Sally Thompson
6 Going to the Sun Rd.
West Glacier, MT 59936
(406) 888-5454, (800) 332-9995
Flathead River (Upper, Middle & North Forks), Lochsa River (in Idaho)
Max rapids: III-IV
America Outdoors, National Tour Association

Glacier Raft Co., claimed to be Montana's oldest and largest outfitter, has catered to 250,000 people on Montana and Idaho rivers since 1976. It is the only livery in the state with a permit to operate in the Great Bear Wilderness.

The company rents rafts and offers professionally guided raft trips suitable for novices and experienced paddlers. Tours of a one-half to 6 days run from May to mid-September, with camping and fishing for trout and whitefish. Wildlife in these waters bordering Glacier National Park includes elk, deer, bears, eagles, and ospreys.

Glacier Sea Kayaking
Bobbie Gilmore
390 Tally Lake Rd.
Whitefish, MT 59937
(406) 862-9010
Flathead Lake
Max. rapids: None

This outfitter provides sea kayaking combined with gourmet fare on the largest freshwater lake west of the Mississippi. Naturalist guides take paddlers to view mountain-rimmed lakes, Indian pictographs and wildlife. They also point out active bald eagle and osprey nests and help fishermen catch trout, salmon, whitefish, and perch. Camping trips last up to 7 days. Double kayaks are available to accommodate kids, timid paddlers, non-paddlers and wildlife photographers. The season runs May-October.

Hawk, I'm Your Sister
Beverly Antaeus
P.O. Box 9109
Santa Fe, NM 87504
(505) 984-2268
Missouri River
Max. rapids: I-II
Worldwide Outfitter & Guide Association

Hawk, I'm Your Sister of Santa Fe specializes in women's wilderness canoe and raft trips. Its year-round program is geared to "women of all ages, shapes, sizes and skill levels" with guided trips in five states and three foreign locations. Its aim is to "teach you the language of the forests, canyons, deserts and waterways" in a safe and non-competitive environment. It takes paddlers on Heron Lake in New Mexico and on the Green

Rainbow trout caught on the Kootenai River. Courtesy of Kootenai Angler.

River in Utah, with other excursions as far afield as Mexico, Peru, and Russia.

Jack River Outfitters
Jim Allison
Box 88
Ennis, MT 59729-0088
(406) 581-3062, (406) 682-4948
Madison, Big Hole, Yellowstone, Jefferson Rivers
Max. rapids: None

One-day fly fishing trips on gentle waters are the specialty of Jack River Outfitters, open from April to November. The company runs guided dory outings suitable for all comers. While fishing for brown and rainbow trout, clients enjoy clean water, rugged scenery, and look for moose, antelope, deer, otter, and eagle.

Jerry Malson Outfitting
Jerry and June Malson
22 Swamp Creek Road
Trout Creek, MT 59874
(406) 847-5582
Northwestern Montana rivers
Max. rapids: I-III
Montana Outfitters and Guides Association

Jerry Malson Outfitting offers dory fishing trips and scenic float trips on the rivers of northwestern Montana. These trips, which run from late spring to early fall, are set in a beautiful mountainous area that resembles Glacier National Park. In addition to the scenery, guests on these trips can enjoy fishing for bass, trout, and pike and viewing deer, elk, bears, moose, and other wildlife. Dory trips last 7-14 days. Jerry Malson also offers hunting trips and an outfitting and guide school.

John Maki Outfitters
John Maki
655 Granite
Helena, MT 59601
(406) 442-6129
Smith, Big Hole, Blackfoot, Clark Fork, Missouri Rivers
Max rapids: III-IV

John Maki offers fully guided fly-fishing raft trips of 1-7 days from May to October. The company has been in business for 15 years, offering good equipment, upscale camping, fine food, clean waters, and fine Montana scenery.

Rainbow and brown trout lurk in the waters, while elk, bears, deer, ospreys, eagles, and many other birds may be observed.

Kootenai Angler
David Blackburn
13546 Hwy 37
Libby, MT 59923
(406) 293-7578
Kootenai, Fisher Rivers
Max. rapids: III-IV

Kootenai Angler promises solitude and terrific fishing for Kootenai's rainbow trout, reputedly the strongest fighting fish in any Montana stream. The company rents rafts and runs guided raft and dory fishing trips of 1-4 days from April to November.

Fishermen benefit from guides' instruction and local expertise, enjoy the largest wild rainbow fishery in Montana, and may spot moose, ospreys, eagles, and, possibly, black or grizzly bears.

Lazy T4 Outfitters
Spence Trogdon
P.O. Box 116
Victor, MT 59875
(406) 642-3586
Bitterroot, Big Hole, Clark Fork, and Jefferson Rivers.
Max. rapids: None
Montana Outfitters & Guides Association

Lazy T4 Outfitters provides guided raft trips on exceptional, crystal-clear trout waters amid Rocky Mountain scenery. During its March-to-October season, fishermen can angle for trout and grayling. Deer, moose, bighorn sheep, eagles, ospreys, and other wildlife may be seen during 1-3 day tours. Paddling and fishing instruction is also available.

Magellan Guide Service
Barry Morstad
P.O. Box 6132
Bozeman, MT 59714
(406) 388-1675
Yellowstone River, Madison River, Jefferson River, Gallatin River
Max. rapids: I-III
Fishing Outfitters Association of Montana

Magellan Guide Service runs guided oar-boat fishing trips on several rivers in southwestern Montana, including the Madison, Yellowstone, Jefferson, and Gallatin. These rivers, known for their fine trout fishing, boast sparkling water, pass through broad valleys amid high mountain peaks. Wildlife viewing is excellent, with good opportunities to spot deer, elk, bald and golden eagles, waterfowl, muskrats, and otters.

Magellan also offers a 1-week "Ultimate Angling Tour," which includes fishing on several fine rivers and lakes and lodging in the famous Gallatin Gateway Inn, one of Montana's finest historic railroad hotels.

Missouri River Canoe Co.
Don Sorensen, James Griffin
HC67, Box 50
Loma, MT 59460
(800) 426-2926, (406) 378-3110
Upper Missouri River
Max. rapids: None

This outfitter offers guided and unguided canoe outings lasting up to 12 days on National Wild and Scenic waters explored by Lewis and Clark. These trips are relatively easy and suitable for families with children as well as out-of-shape adults. Paddlers can enjoy white sandstone cliffs as they fish for catfish, pike, and sturgeon. They may stay before and after trips in restored homestead towns with bed-and-breakfast inns and cabins. The season runs April-October.

Missouri River Outfitters, Inc.
Larry J. Cook
Box 762
Fort Benton, MT 59442
(406) 622-3295
Upper Missouri, Marias Rivers
Max. rapids: None

Missouri River Outfitters offers guided and unguided canoe trips lasting up to 12 days on the calm Missouri River and its Marias River tributary. Designated Wild and Scenic, this stretch of the Missouri is a special place, with rock pinnacles and sandy river bottoms full of interesting flora and fauna. During family camping trips, fishermen may go for walleye, sturgeon, catfish, and buffalo fish while looking for bighorn sheep, eagles, and hawks. The company's season lasts from March to November.

Montana High Country Tours
Russ Kipp
1036 East Reeder
Dillon, MT 59725
(406) 683-4920
Smith River, Beaverhead River, Big Hole River, Pioneer Mountain lakes
Max. rapids: III-IV
Montana Outfitters and Guides Association

Montana High Country Tours offers guided float trips on three of Montana's best trout streams, the Beaverhead, Big Hole, and Smith Rivers. An extended 51-mile, 6-day trip through the remote Smith River Canyon is a specialty and an excellent family vacation. The trip features great fishing, towering limestone canyon walls, and abundant wildlife, including deer, elk, bears, moose, sheep, mountain goats, and antelopes. The company also offers jeep, horseback, and llama trips to alpine lakes in the Pioneer Mountains. The season is from May to September.

Montana Raft Company and Glacier Wilderness Guides
Randy Gayner
Box 535PA
West Glacier, MT 59936
(406) 888-5466, (800) 521-RAFT
Flathead River – Middle Fork, Flathead River – North Fork, Glacier National Park waters
Max. rapids: III-IV
Montana Outfitters and Guides

Montana Raft Company & Glacier Wilderness Guides leads guided oar-boat and paddle-raft, and two-person inflatable kayak trips on the Middle and North Forks of the Flathead River. These trips, of 1-8 days, pass through beautiful mountain wilderness along the boundary of Glacier National Park. On these ex-

cursions, guests can fish in the Flathead's pristine waters for cutthroat and rainbow trout. Guests can also view deer, elk, black bears, grizzly bears, mountain goats, and other animals and birds. These trips, offered from May to September, range in difficulty to suit both beginning and intermediate river runners.

The company also offers combination hiking/rafting trips, fishing outings, day hikes, backpacking trips of 4-6 days, and equipment rentals.

Montana River Outfitters
R. Craig Madsen
1401 5th Ave. South
Great Falls, MT 59405
(406) 761-1677, (800) 800-8218,
FAX (406) 452-3833
Smith, Missouri, Blackfoot, Yellowstone, Clark Fork, Flathead Rivers
Max. rapids: III-IV
Montana Outfitters & Guides Assn., Fishing & Outfitters Assn. of Montana

Montana River Outfitters offers guided raft and canoe trips and rents canoes and rafts for trips of up to a week in beautiful, unspoiled wilderness and the wild and scenic Missouri. It caters to families, fly fishermen, and groups, promising world-class trout fishing and "the best service in the business."

Remote mountains, clean waters, spectacular scenery, interesting history, and a rich array of wildlife — including deer, bear and elk — add to the adventure. The company's season runs from April to October. Paddling lessons and camping are available.

Montana Trout Guide Service
Monte Meredith
7385 Pine View Rd.
Custer, MT 59024
(406) 947-2471
Big Horn River, Big Spring Creek
Max. rapids: None

Montana Trout Guide Service offers guided, 1-day fly-fishing trips on the Big Horn River and Big Spring Creek. These dory trips run year-round and feature terrific fishing for rainbow and brown trout on blue-ribbon trout streams where the average fish caught is between 16 and 18 inches. The dories pass through an historic and scenic area with abundant wildlife, including pheasants, deer, ducks, geese, herons, and eagles.

Montana Whitewater
Bill Zell
Box 1552
Bozeman, MT 59771
(406) 763-4465, (800) 799-4465
Gallatin, Yellowstone Rivers in Montana, Nahanni River in Yukon & NW Territories in Canada
Max. rapids: III-IV

Montana Whitewater provides guided raft and canoe trips ranging from scenic to challenging Class III-IV. Trips are suited for everyone from families to experienced rafters. The company gives extra time to novice paddlers and runs a canoe and kayak school. It tries to get to know every guest and provide the best possible experience.

Both the Gallatin and the Yellowstone rivers are undammed and uncrowded. The Gallatin is a narrow, fast-flowing river with near-continuous Class II-IV whitewater. It flows through the narrow, rocky walls of the lower Gallatin Canyon. The Yellowstone offers unsurpassed vistas of Paradise Valley, surrounded by 11,000-foot peaks.

Pioneer Outfitters
Cliff and Chuck Page
Alder Creek Ranch
Wise River, MT 59762
(406) 832-3128
Big Hole River, Beaverhead River, Pioneer Mountain lakes
Max. rapids: I-II

Pioneer Outfitter specializes in float fishing on the Big Hole and Beaverhead Rivers on day trips or by the week. The emphasis is on trout fishing, as both rivers are blue-ribbon streams with excellent fly hatches between May and September. Trips are by oar boat through gentle Class I and II rapids and are perfect for older children and adults.

The company also offers high-country pack trips into remote, roadless areas of the Pioneer Mountains. These trips also boast excellent fishing, scenery, and wildlife viewing.

Point of Rocks Guest Ranch
Max Chase
Rte. 1, Box 680
Emigrant, MT 59027
(406) 333-4361
Yellowstone River, Missouri River, Spring Creek
Max. rapids: None

Point of Rocks runs guided fishing trips and rents tubes on Spring Creek and the Yellowstone and Missouri Rivers. This region, just north of Yellowstone National Park, is exceptionally beautiful and offers excellent fishing for brown, cutthroat, and rainbow trout. Guests on these trips, which run year-round, can also enjoy viewing deer, antelopes, elk, bears, and other wildlife.

Randy Rathie Outfitter
Box 471
Ennis, MT 59729
(406) 682-4162
Madison River, Big Hole River
Max. rapids: None
Montana Outfitters and Guides Association, Trout Unlimited, Ducks Unlimited

Randy Rathie, an outfitter for more than 25 years, runs guided oar-boat fishing trips on scenic flatwater rivers in southwestern Montana. Trips last 1-day, are not demanding, and are well-suited for both beginning and experienced trout fishermen. Wildlife to see include deer, elk, bears, eagles, hawks, and waterfowl. Rathie also offers horseback trips, tubing, lake trips, wildlife photography trips, and camping at high mountain lakes.

Rimrock Outfitting
Robert Stroebel
520 Foothill Drive
Billings, MT 59105
(406) 248-4861
Bighorn River, Yellowstone River, Missouri River, Madison River, Gallatin River, Smith River
Max. rapids: V+
Montana Outfitters and Guides Association

Rimrock Outfitting is a small company that specializes in customized guided trips and rentals to suit guests' needs. Guided whitewater and fishing trips, by canoe, raft, or dory, are available on six rivers, as are rentals of canoes, rafts, and tubes.

Trips last 1-4 days and pass through prairie and mountain country. All trips offer superb fishing for walleye, northern pike, and especially trout. Also, deer, elk, moose, bighorn sheep, turkeys, and antelope can often be seen during Rimrock's May-to-November season.

Rocky Mountain Whitewater
Patrick Doty
905 Ola Drive
East Missoula, MT 59802
(406) 728-2984
Clark Fork, Bitterroot, Blackfoot Rivers
Max. rapids: III-IV
Fishing & Floating Outfitters Association of Montana

Rocky Mountain Whitewater provides 1-day guided raft trips suitable for everyone, including seniors and handicapped people, except during high water. At that time — in late May and June — the rapids are extremely big and challenging.

Although the put-in for the popular Alberton Gorge trip is only 35 miles from Missoula, the scenery is beautiful and well away from roads. There are also half-day floats just outside Missoula. Wildlife includes deer, moose, eagle, ospreys, beavers, and an occasional bear. Four species of trout inhabit the rivers served. The season runs from April to October.

Roy Senter
726 North D Street
Livingston, MT 59047
(406) 222-3775
Yellowstone River
Max. rapids: None

Roy Senter offers float fishing and scenic trips on the Yellowstone River. These dory trips, offered between April and October, pass through a beautiful mountainous region with excellent trout fishing and plentiful birds and other wildlife.

Royal L - Bighorn Lodge
Joe Caton
Bighorn River, MT 59075
(406) 666-2340, (406) 666-2389
Bighorn River
Max. rapids: I-II
Bighorn River Foundation

Royal L - Bighorn Lodge runs 1-5 day guided and unguided raft and dory trips on the Bighorn River. With only gentle Class I and II rapids, the runs are enough for guests of all ages and boast "sensational" fishing for rainbow and brown trout.

The areas also offers unspoiled wilderness and a chance to view deer, bears, and numerous types of birds. The company's season runs from April to October.

Spring Creek Outfitters
Bob Bouee
P.O. Box 328
Big Timber, MT 59011
(406) 932-4387
Yellowstone River, Boulder River
Max. rapids: III-IV
Montana Outfitters and Guides Association

Spring Creek Outfitters runs 1-7 day oar-boat trips for blue-ribbon trout fishing on Spring Creek and the Yellowstone and Boulder Rivers. Trips include personalized fly-fishing instruction and a chance to view abundant wildlife, including deer, elk, bears, and antelope. Scenery is excellent, too, with all floats passing through the middle of Gallatin

National Forest and the Absoraka Bear-tooth Wilderness.

Spring Creek also offers customized horsepack trips for Alpine fishing, camping, and photography.

S.W. Montana Fishing Co.
Dave Marsh
13 Tuke Lane
Sheridan, MT 59749
(406) 842-5364, (800) DRY-FLYS
Beaverhead, Big Hole, Jefferson, Madison,
Ruby Rivers
Max. rapids: I-II

This outfitter runs expertly guided trout fishing trips amid beautiful scenery from April to October. These day outings aboard rafts and dories are not difficult and can be enjoyed by everyone. They provide delicious food and give paddlers an opportunity to view bighorn sheep, deer, and antelope amid the grand mountain landscape. Paddling lessons are available.

Sundown Outfitters
Lyle Reynolds
Box 95
Melrose, MT 59743
(406) 835-2751
Big Hole River, Beaverhead River, Jefferson
River
Max. rapids: None

Sundown Outfitters runs oar-boat fly-fishing trips for beginners and experts alike. A wide array of fish can be caught, especially on the Big Hole River, where it is possible to catch brown, rainbow and brook trout and grayling all in one eight-hour float. Float trips last 1 day, with two fishermen and a guide per boat.

Surrounded by the Lost Pioneer and Highland Mountains, trips offer terrific scenery and a chance to view moose, bighorn sheep, and deer. Sundown's season runs from May to September.

Taylor Outfitters
Paul E. Taylor
Box 991
Dillon, MT 59725
(406) 681-3166
Big Hole River, Beaverhead River, Madison
River, Ruby River
Max. rapids: I-II

Taylor Outfitters offers guided and unguided canoe and raft trips on the Jefferson, Madison, Beaverhead, and Big Hole Rivers. With Class I and II rapids, these trips are relatively easy, allowing beginners and experts time to fish for trout, whitefish, and grayling, enjoy the mountain scenery, and view elk, deer, moose, geese, and ducks. Trips last from 1-7 days and run between June and October.

Taylor Outfitters has an unusual and scenic headquarters. It is based at a ranch on the Jefferson River, where the owners raise elk and play host to abundant deer and waterfowl.

The Montana Fisherman
Carl A. Mann
234 Ridgeway
Lolo, MT 59847
(406) 837-5632, (406) 273-6966
Clark Fork River, Bitterroot River, Flathead
Lake
Max. rapids: None
Montana Outfitters and Guides Association

The Montana Fisherman offers oar-boat raft trips on placid waters of the Clark Fork River, Bitterroot River, and Flathead Lake. Trips last 1 or 2 days and run between April and October.

The company takes pride in organizing relaxing, scenic trips with excellent fishing for rainbow trout, cutthroat trout, lake trout, and white fish. Guests also enjoy mountain landscape and seeing deer, eagles, ducks, geese, ospreys, and blue herons.

4-lb. brown trout caught on the Missouri River. Courtesy of Jerry Nichols, Western Waters, Missoula, Montana.

Tom's Sport Shop and Guide Service
Tom Bugni
210 Harrison Avenue
Butte, MT 59701
(406) 782-6251, (406) 723-4753
Big Hole River, Lower Madison River, Lower Gallatin River, Jefferson River, Yellowstone River, Missouri River, Beaverhead River
Max. rapids: None
Floaters of Montana

Tom's Sport Shop and Guide Service runs drift-boat fishing trips of 1-3 days on the Big Hole, Lower Madison, Lower Gallatin, Jefferson, Yellowstone, Missouri, and Beaverhead Rivers. These guided trips run through the heart of the Rockies, offering beautiful scenery; abundant elk, geese, ducks, and other wildlife; and excellent fishing for rainbow, brown, brook, and cutthroat trout. Tom's season runs from May to September.

Western Rivers
Fred Tedesco
P.O. Box 772
East Helena, MT 59635
(406) 227-5153
Smith River, Missouri River system, Clark Fork River system, Flathead Lake
Max. rapids: None

Western Rivers runs guided and unguided raft trips on the Smith River, Missouri River, Clark Fork River, and Flathead Lake. These trips offer excellent trout fishing, pure waters, good campsites, and spectacular views of limestone canyons, mountains, and deer, elk, beavers, and eagles. Western Rivers' season is from April to October.

Western Waters
Gerald R. Nichols, Jr.
333 Knowles Street
Missoula, MT 59801
(406) 728-6161
Clark Fork River, Madison River, Missouri
River, Big Hole River
Max. rapids: III-IV
Fishing and Floating Association of Montana

Western Waters is a family-run white-water and fishing guide service. White-water trips by oar boat run on the Clark Fork River, which offers big water and wild rides between May and June. During this time, trips are limited to guests age 12 and older. From July to October, the age limit is six and older. Trips last from 1-3 days and can accommodate anyone from novices to experts. The Clark Fork River is particularly scenic, with gorgeous canyons and abundant wildlife, including deer, bears, moose, elk, ospreys, eagles, and ducks.

Fishing trips run on the Madison, Missouri, and Big Hole Rivers. All three are clean and famous for their trophy trout fishing.

During its May-to-November season, Western Waters also offers horseback riding, sightseeing trips, and hikes to mountain lakes.

Wildlife Adventures, Inc.
Jack, Shirley & Rick Wemple
1765 Pleasant View Drive
Victor, MT 59875
(406) 642-3262, 642-3462, (800) 955-8505
Bitterroot River
Max. rapids: None
Montana & Idaho Outfitters and Guides
Associations

In business for over 30 years, Wildlife Adventures offers easy guided 1-day raft trips from June to September amid the scenic Bitterroot mountains. The clean Bitterroot river offers good swimming and abundant rainbow, cutthroat, and brown trout. Lucky paddlers may spot whitetail deer, black bears, and an occasional elk.

Wild River Adventures
Bob Jordan
P.O. Box 272
West Glacier, MT 59936
(406) 387-9453, (800) 826-2724
Middle Fork and North Fork Flathead River
Max. rapids: III-IV

Wild River Adventures specializes in oar- and paddle-raft trips on exceptionally scenic rivers bordering Glacier National Park. Trips on the Middle Fork of the Flathead range from mild to wild, with the greatest challenge coming in the high-water months of May to July. From July until the end of the season in September, rapids are more mild, making trips suitable for families with small children.

Trips on the North Fork of the Flathead are relaxing and scenic, offering fine trout fishing and good views of wildlife and Glacier's peaks. Wild River Adventures also offers guided fishing trips and horseback trips though the Great Bear Wilderness.

Wild Rockies Tours
Matt Thomas, Gail Gutsche & Dan Ward
P.O. Box 8184
Missoula, MT 59807
(406) 728-0566
Missouri, Clark Fork, Yellowstone, Bitterroot
and Blackfoot Rivers
Max. rapids: I-III
ACA

Wild Rockies Tours runs guided canoe trips of up to 8 days in beautiful scenic western and central Montana. Paddlers can select among trips ranging from Class I to Class III rapids. The company uses quality equipment and emphasizes safety and comfort. Custom trips are available.

Guests can swim, view wildlife, take paddling lessons, and hike. The company's season runs from May to October.

Rus Willis & Associates

Rus Willis
10 Bull River Rd.
Noxon, MT 59853
(406) 847-5597/5523
Bull, Kootenai, Clark Fork Rivers, Lake Pend
Orielle (ID), Lake Koocanusa, many
mountain lakes and streams
Max. rapids: None
Montana Outfitters & Guides Association

Rus Willis rents canoes and offers guided trips in canoes and McKenzie river boats to paddlers looking for great scenery, smooth streams, gentle rapids, and excellent lodge accommodations. Fly-fishing lessons help anglers sharpen their skills in pursuing six species of trout, kokonee, bass, and pike.

The Bull River valley lies between two wilderness areas with mountains rising to 8,700 feet. A wide variety of wildlife can be seen. Trips last 6 hours and are led by knowledgeable guides. The season runs from May to October.

Yellowstone Raft Company

Julia Page, Peter White
Box 46
Gardiner, MT 59030
(406) 848-7777
Yellowstone River, Gallatin River, Madison
River
Max. rapids: III-IV
America Outdoors, American Rivers

Yellowstone Raft Company runs 1-day guided trips on the Yellowstone, Gallatin, and Madison Rivers. Guests can opt for oar rafts, paddle rafts, or inflatable kayaks to suit the level of excitement they seek. The scenery is beautiful on all trips, especially those that run along the boundary of Yellowstone National Park, offering striking mountain views to the north and south. Among the wildlife to be seen are deer, antelope, bears, merganser, mallards, ospreys, and great blue herons.

During the May-to-September season, the company also offers tubing, trout fishing excursions, and riverside barbecues.

Nebraska

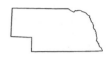

Nobody heads for the prairies in search of whitewater. But the canoei finds much to enjoy on Nebraska's many rivers. These include the Nor Platte and Platte which cross the state like a broad blue belt from Scott bluff near the Wyoming border to where their waters merge with the Mi souri just south of Omaha. There is a put-in on the North Platte right besi the Wyoming state line for a 61-mile trail to the Bridgeport State Recre tion Area. It traverses some spectacular scenery and affords a great view Scottsbluff National Monument and other rocky outcroppings along the wa

On the Platte itself, the Nebraska Game and Parks Commission recor mends a 55-mile stretch at the eastern end of the state, from Fremont to point just short of the confluence with the Missouri. But the commission war that river flows vary considerably, especially along this lower segment, and su gests early spring and late fall as the best paddling seasons. Energetic c noeists can start their Platte River trip by paddling 75 miles down the El horn River, its tributary. This, too, is an appealing float as the Elkhorn win between willows and cottonwoods, then through steep, high bluffs cover in cedars and hardwoods. The ideal time for the Elkhorn is March throu early July, although there is often enough water in September-October.

More challenging is a 70-mile section of the Dismal River near the ce ter of the state. This trip, officially described as "definitely not for the no ice," passes the Nebraska National Forest to Dunning. Wildlife enthusias will enjoy the Calamus River in north central Nebraska, with its abundan of ducks, herons, prairie chickens, pheasants, beaver, muskrats, turtles, ar other species. The 50-mile Calamus trail starts as a narrow and largely tre less stream, with more vegetation further down. Timber is so scarce that cam ers are advised to bring their own charcoal if they plan to cook. Ranche have put up many fences across the river, some of which must be portage

Last but not least is the Niobrara River with its clean water and rugg bluffs forested with pine, birch and oak. Here in the Valentine region of nort ern Nebraska the canoeist can find fast, dependable water during a seaso which runs from April through June. Dubbed "the prettiest prairie riv in the United States," the Niobrara runs from Wyoming to the Missou ithout a single major reservoir. Bobcats, buffalo, mink, elk, otter, beaver, nd wild turkey can be seen, while catfish and trout may be landed early nd late in the year.

For river level information on the North Platte call the Game and Parks Commission at Alliance, 308-762-5605; for the Lower Platte, call the Two Rivers State Recreation Area at Valley, 402-359-5165, and for the Elkhorn call the Fremont SRA, 402-727-3290.

Brewers Canoers
Sandy and Rich Mercure
P.O. Box 14
Valentine, NE 69201
(402) 376-2046, (402) 376-3548
Niobrara River
Max. rapids: None

Brewers Canoe runs guided and unguided canoe trips of 1-2 days on the gentle, scenic Niobrara River. The Niobrara, easy enough for novices, flows through canyons, lush river valleys, and birch woods. It offers fishing for catfish and trout and chances to spot deer, turkeys, eagles, buffalo, and elk.

Brewers Canoe's season runs from May to October.

Dryland Aquatics
Louis E. Christiansen
Box 33C
Sparks, NE 69220
(402) 376-3119, (800) 337-3119
Niobrara River
Max. rapids: I-II
PPA

Easy paddling on a fast-flowing river through a canyon with many small waterfalls is supplied by Dryland Aquatics from April to November. With service as its watchword, the company runs guided canoe trips and rents canoes and tubes for 1-2 day trips, with camping available. Six ecozones meet in this area, and the wildlife includes turkey, deer, porcupine, mink, and very many birds. The floats are suitable for beginners but enjoyable also for experts.

NEBRASKA

Class I rapids on the Niobrana River. Courtesy of Alan Stokes/Rocky Ford Outfitters, Valentine, Nebraska.

Graham Canoe Outfitters
Douglas and Twyla Graham
HC-13, Box 16-A
Valentine, NE 69201
(402) 376-3708
Niobrara River
Max. rapids: I-II

Graham Canoe Outfitters runs guided and unguided canoe trips of 1-2 days on the Niobrara River. This prairie river is swift but gentle, offering easy paddling for novice and experienced canoeists alike. Trips run through the heart of the sand hills in a scenic river valley featuring views of cliffs, pine and deciduous woods, and abundant wildlife, including deer, turkeys, eagles, hawks, beavers, raccoons, and ducks. The Niobrara's clean waters also offer fishing for catfish and trout.

Graham Canoe Outfitter's season is from April to November.

Little Outlaw Canoe & Tube Rental
Rich Mercure
214 W. Hwy 20
Valentine, NE 69201
(402) 376-1822, (800) 238-1867 (NE, SD, IA only)
Niobrara, Snake Rivers
Max. rapids: None

Little Outlaw rents canoes and tubes for outings on the exceptionally clean Niobrara River, amid beautiful scenery. These trips are ideal for novices, since the current runs at an average speed of only four to seven miles per hour and is between 18 and 24 inches deep.

The company is a complete outfitter offering full service packages with bus service or car shuttling available. Tipis may be rented at the campsite. The season runs from May 1 to October 15. Paddlers can fish for catfish and carp, and may spot wild turkeys, deer, elk, and eagles.

Oregon Trail Wagon Train
Kevin Howard
Route 2, Box 502
Bayard, NE 69334
(308) 586-1850
North Platte River
Max. rapids: None

Oregon Trail Wagon Train rents canoes for 1/2-day trips on the North Platte River, a clean, gentle river suited for paddlers of all ages. These relaxing float trips offer a chance to paddle old fur-traders' routes; fish for catfish, trout, pike, and carp; and watch for deer, wild

Swimming and paddling downriver on the Niobrara. Courtesy of Alan Stokes/Rocky Ford Outfitters, Valentine, Nebraska.

...noeists explore the shoreline along the North Platte River. Courtesy of Oregon Trail Wagon ...ain, Bayard, Nebraska.

...keys, coyotes, ducks, and geese.

During its May-to-October season, ...regon Trail also offers chuck-wagon ...okouts and wagon train treks in ...thentic-style covered wagons.

...cky Ford Outfitters

...lan and Mary Stokes
...x 3
...lentine, NE 69201
...02) 497-3479 (summers),
...12) 642-4422 (winters)
...iobrara River
...ax. rapids: I-II

Rocky Ford Outfitters offers guided ...noe trips and canoe and tube rentals ...n the Niobrara River. Trips last 1-5 ...ays and are easy enough for beginners. ...he river has clean, fast-flowing water ...d offers scenic views of high canyon ...alls forested with pine, birch, and ...ks. Paddlers can body surf through ...utes, fish for catfish and trout, and ...impse deer, wild turkeys, bobcats, ...inks, otters, and beavers.

Rocky Ford also offers camping, a ...thhouse with showers, family cabins, ...bunkhouse, and a camp store. The ...ason is from April to October.

Sunny Brook Camp and Canoe Outfitters

Roy E. Breuklander
HC13, Box 36P
Sparks, NE 69220
(402) 376-1887
Niobrara River
Max. rapids: I-II
PPA

Sunny Brook supplies canoes for rent and guided trips down the knee-deep Niobrara, with its 7 m.p.h. current and a few fun rapids at the lower end of the float. Beginners have time to learn to handle their canoes before reaching the rapids. The river runs through a 300-foot deep wooded canyon with wildlife including deer, turkey, mink and bobcat. Trips last 1-2 days, paddling lessons and camping are available, and the company operates year-round.

Nevada

The driest state in the Union with an average annual rainfall of le than eight inches, Nevada is known more for its deserts than its rivers. An indeed there is very little rafting or canoeing in the state. Most Nevad rivers run literally into the sand. Only a few have outlets to the sea: tl Virgin and Muddy rivers join the Colorado in the southeastern corner the state, while the Owyhee, Bruneau and Salmon Falls flow northward Idaho's Snake River. All the others run into depressions (known as sink or closed lakes. The snow-fed Humboldt River, for instance, flows 300 mil southwestwards from the mountains in the northeast, only to vanish in tl Humboldt Sink.

Such canoeing as exists is chiefly on the lakes — notably Lake Tahoe c the California state line, Pyramid Lake to the north and maybe Lake Mea behind Hoover Dam on the Colorado River. But the vast majority of lal fishermen use power boats.

Immediately below the Hoover Dam paddlers can enjoy a 12-mile ru through the Black Canyon of the Colorado River. It takes its name from i massive black cliffs, which compress the river and provide side canyons explore. Few boats are allowed in the canyon, and the desert wildlife ad to the sense of wilderness.

Elsewhere, rafts can be rented on the Truckee River near Fanny Bridg close to the point at which it leaves Lake Tahoe, for a leisurely float on tl quiet stream.

In good years there is some whitewater on the East Fork of the Carsc River. But one National Forest Service ranger said that if there was any ra rental business left on this river "it has dwindled away almost to nothing.

Nevada claims to be the most mountainous state in the Union, in tern of the number of mountains and ranges within any given area. But aft six years of drought in the 1980s, streams became so shallow that rafting preferable to canoeing even on their lower reaches. Their headwaters a mostly too narrow for either rafting or canoeing. Rafting outfitters based Nevada tend to operate chiefly on California or Idaho rivers just across tl border.

olorado River Outfitters

arry Thompson, Joe Hernandez
>49 Hwy. 95, Ste. 49
ullhead City, AZ 86442
20) 763-2325
ake Mohave, Lake Mead, Havasu Wildlife
efuge on the Lower Colorado River
ax. rapids: I-II
PA

Casinos are featured as well as
anyons on the canoe and kayak trips of-
red by Colorado River Outfitters. The
ompany runs both guided and un-
uided trips through desert waterways
ith lots of wildlife, including mountain
eep and beaver. On the Nevada side
f the river paddlers also pass high-rise
otels and casinos. Fishing is for trout,
atfish, striped bass, smallmouth bass,
nd crappie. The water quality is excel-
nt and hot springs may be found in the
anyons. Camping and paddling lessons
re available during the January-January
eason.

Laughing Heart Adventures

Dezh Pagen
Trinity Outdoor Center
P.O. Box 669
Willow Creek, CA 95573
(916) 629-3516, (800) 541-1256
Colorado River
Max. rapids: I
PPA, ACA

The Black Canyon section of the
Lower Colorado, located below Hoover
Dam and Lake Mead, has outstanding
canoeing opportunities and the greatest
assortment of hot springs in any river location. Laughing Heart Adventures conducts trips during Thanksgiving week
and prepares a barbecue turkey with all
the trimmings. Also during Easter vacation guests can enjoy hot springs nestled
between towering canyon walls with
unique views of the sun and stars. There
are also hot waterfalls and a "sauna
cave" to ease any tired muscles after a
day of canoeing and birding.

NEVADA

New Hampshire

With over 100 inches of snowfall a year, New Hampshire's mountai spawn some excellent whitewater streams. The snag is that many of the are only runnable when the snow thaws in the spring or after heavy rair The gung-ho whitewater enthusiast must seize the moment, which is som times hard to catch. But less adventurous canoeists can paddle almc anytime on slower rivers fed by periodic dam releases. What could be mo blissful than floating a clear stream amid brilliant fall foliage with the Wh Mountains soaring in the background?

One of the most popular paddling rivers in New Hampshire is the A droscoggin along a 30-mile stretch from Errol to Berlin. It is the only run the state that combines summer-long canoeing over a good distance wi enjoyable Class I-II whitewater. Between its three sets of rapids this sectio of the Androscoggin has long spells of flatwater and several campsit accessible by both car and canoe. Due to lakes and dams, the river's cle; water maintains a fairly steady flow all summer long.

Another dependable stream for summer canoeing is the Pemigewasse which has a short 2.5-mile whitewater run starting at Bristol Gorge. It rated Class II-III and Class IV at high water. Upstream, the East Branch the Pemigawasset has a six-mile Class IV run down to North Woodstock th provides a hairy adventure in April. But it is also runnable in May and aft heavy rains. The name Pemigawasset is an Indian term that has been ev catively translated as "valley of the winding water among the mountain pine:

The long Connecticut River divides New Hampshire from both Qu bec to the north and Vermont to the west before heading down throug Massachusetts to the sea. The actual state line follows the low water ma; along the Vermont side, so the full river's breadth belongs to New Ham shire. Paddlers on the broad and stately Connecticut can still see traces the river's earlier use as a waterway to float logs downstream to lumber mil These include log cribs — massive artificial islands built of logs and bou ders — and iron rings in the rocks to which log-boom chains were attache Floaters of today can marvel at the toughness of the river men and the teams of horses who kept the logs moving past the icy rapids.

The Mad River, which runs into the Pemigawasset north of Plymouth, is ne of those whitewater streams that experts have to catch during the few eeks a year when it is runnable. True to its name, the Mad River comes imbling like crazy out of the White Mountains when the snows melt in pril. It provides 8-12 miles of nearly continuous Class III-IV whitewater 5 it roars down the attractive Waterville Valley toward Campton Upper illage.

For a change of pace, the Saco River is a great cruising stream, with its ean water, scenic beauty, and abundance of free and open campsites on s sandy beaches and sandbars. Canoeists can make the 40-mile eastbound ip from Weston's Bridge across the Maine state line to Hiram in three days nd there are several access points for shorter floats.

Near Conway in eastern New Hampshire the Swift River provides good hitewater rafting during its short season from April until mid-May. Crash-ig out of the heart of the White Mountains, the Swift offers eleven miles f Class III-IV rapids as it parallels the Kancamagus Highway, both above nd below the Lower Falls scenic area. When it is up, the stream demands onsiderable technical skill from paddlers negotiating its ledge drops and eep descents.

NEW HAMPSHIRE

ack Country Tours, Inc.
llan McGroary
) Hollis Street
:pperell, MA 01463
·08) 433-9381, (800) 649-9381 (MA)
lerrimack River, Connecticut River,
ashua River, Souhegan River
lax. rapids: I-II

Back Country Tours, Inc., specializes guided canoe trips and canoe rentals n "lesser known, uncrowded scenic wa-rways." Its trips run on the Souhegan ıd Merrimack rivers in New Hamp-iire; the Sauantacook and Nissitissit ivers in Massachusetts; the Connecti-ıt and Nashua Rivers in New Hamp-iire and Massachusetts; the Delaware iver in New York, Pennsylvania, and ew Jersey; the Blackwater, Sweetwater, ıd Juniper Rivers in Florida; and nine ıkes near Long Pond Mountain in New ork's Adirondacks. Several of these ex-ursion are "vacation" trips of 3-7 days ıat offer lodging at campgrounds, cab-ıs, or bed-and-breakfast inns. All trips

are suitable for beginners and experi-enced paddlers.

Back Country Tours' season runs from July to November.

Balloon Inn Vermont Vacations
Scott Wright
RR 1, Box 8
Fairlee, VT 05045
(802) 333-4326, (800) 666-1946
Connecticut River
Max. rapids: I-II

Balloon Inn Vermont rents canoes from May-October for self-guided trips on the Connecticut River between Woodsville, N.H., and Orford, N.H. These trips, of 1-3 days, include lodging at historic inns along the river. With only Class I-II rapids to contend with, paddling is only moderately difficult, even for beginners. Along the way, float-ers can enjoy the natural beauty of the river valley, and fishing for trout, pike, bass, and walleye. The company also of-fers bicycling, hiking, and balloon trips.

Canoeing the gentle Saco River. Courtesy of Downeast Rafting, Center Conway, New Hampshi

Connitic Headwater Tours
Thomas & Jeremy Pichierri
Box 95
Pittsburg, NH 03592
(603) 246-3489
Connecticut River, 1st, 2nd & 3rd Lakes,
Lake Francis
Max. rapids: I-II
PPA

Relaxed paddling on fast-moving water is offered by Connitic Headwater Tours, a family business that runs campgrounds with music and camaraderie. The canoe, kayak, and raft floats are for all skill levels and take paddlers through scenic pastoral countryside. Guided trips are available as well as rental boats for 1-3 day outings on the clean headwaters of the Connecticut River and nearby lakes.

Trout and salmon may be fished, and the wildlife includes moose, deer, beaver, and loons. The season runs from June to Sept.-Oct.

Downeast Rafting Inc.
Ned McSherry/Rick Hoddinott
P.O. Box 119
Center Conway, NH 03813
(603) 447-3002, (800) 677-RAFT
Kennebec River, Dead River, Penobscot Rive
Rapid River, Swift River
Max. rapids: V+

Downeast Rafting provides guided raft trips on the Kennebec, Dead, Penob scot, Rapid, and Swift Rivers, which rur through the Maine woods, with their wealth of wildlife. These 1- day trips are offered from April to October. Rafters experience Class III-IV rapids on some streams and Class V on the technical Penobscot.

Downeast's guides are experienced and personable. All the company's Kennebec and Dead River packages include lodging at its inn or campground, meals, grilled lunch on the raft trip, and a video/slide show of the trip at the end Various other package tours, including guided fishing trips and even combined skiing-rafting trips, are available.

Northern Waters Inc.
Ned McSherry
P.O. Box 119
Center Conway, NH 03813
(603) 447-2177, (603) 447-3801
Androscoggin River, Lake Umbagog
Max. rapids: III-IV
PPA

Northern Waters rents canoes and runs paddling clinics on the Androscoggin and Magalloway rivers, which have everything from flat water to Class III rapids. This remote region of northern New England is noted for its excellent scenery, fishing, and camping. But camping is limited to designated sites.

Northern Waters does not rent kayaks for whitewater and will only rent canoes to experienced paddlers for whitewater runs. Whitewater paddling classes are available. The season lasts from mid-June to Labor Day.

Saco Bound Inc.
Ned McSherry
P.O. Box 119
Center Conway, NH 03813
(603) 447-2177, (603) 447-3801
Max. rapids: None
PPA, Saco River Recreational Council

The Saco River is a perfect stream for family floating, and Saco Bound is ideally placed for enabling paddlers to relish it. Saco Bound rents canoes and kayaks from May 1-October 15 for periods of one-half to 3 days, with ample campsites available on beaches and sandbars along a 43-mile route. The company runs guided day trips with barbecue lunches on Tuesdays and Thursdays in July and August. During the summer months the crystal-clear stream is warm and levels average three to four feet, with deeper holes for swimming. Early October is the time to experience brillant fall foliage.

Canoeing the Class II and III rapids of the Androscoggin River. Courtesy of Downeast Rafting, Center Conway, New Hampshire.

Saco Valley Canoe
Allen Russell
P.O. Box 74, Rte. 302
Center Conway, NH 03813
(800) 447-2460
Saco, Kennebec, Penobscot Rivers
Max. rapids: III-IV
PPA

Saco Valley runs guided canoe, kayak, and raft trips and rents canoes, kayaks, rafts, and tubes for trips on crystal-clear waters. Here in the forested valleys of the White Mountains, paddlers find many sandy beaches, a sandy bottom, and excellent fishing for trout, salmon, bass, and pickerel.

Camping and swimming are also available on these mostly flatwater outings, which last up to 3 days. Deer, moose, and raccoons can be spotted during the outfitter's May-to-October season.

New Jersey

To many paddlers, canoeing in New Jersey means the Pine Barrens. This 2,000 square-mile area in South Jersey is actually more a land of bush and brush than pines. But it is sparsely populated and its flat, sandy soil is laced with streams, swamps and marshes. Some rivers are 40 feet wide, but the typical stream is only half as broad and some are so narrow that there is barely room for two canoes to pass. Since the water is tinted by tannic acid from the cedars, paddling in the pinelands is often called "brown water" canoeing. Local wildlife includes beaver, otter, Pine Barrens tree frogs, eagles and osprey, along with some unusual plants.

The Wading River is the most popular in the Pine Barrens, with its various campgrounds and outfitters, easy canoeing and convenient access. On summer weekends there may be hundreds of canoes on its winding waters. Another popular stream is the Batsto, which stems from marshland and then, like the Wading, flows through the Wharton State Forest. The nearby Mullica River has extensive savanna marshes and its sandy banks are great for picnicking and swimming.

Toms River, probably named after a Thomas Luker who settled among the Indians around 1700, is the most frequented river in the area outside Wharton State Forest. Cruising the stream in 2-3 days, the paddler finds stands of holly, pine and deciduous trees.

Just south of the Toms River estuary is a birdwatchers' paradise, Island Beach State Park on the barrier sandspit guarding Barnegat Bay. The park offers naturalist-led canoe tours and keeps the northern one-third of the island in pristine state.

Also unspoiled is Cedar Creek, designated Wild and Scenic by the state of New Jersey. It passes an old iron forge, former cranberry bogs and marshes before turning into a fast-flowing stream rife with interesting wildlife.

Much farther north, only ten miles from busy Newark Airport, lies what sounds like one of the unlikeliest canoeing sites in the country. Yet the locals at Cranford in Union County say that the Rahway River offers tranquil canoeing past old mansions and mills. It is stocked regularly with freshwater trout and also offers carp and catfish.

Last but far from least is the mighty Delaware River which divides th
state from Pennsylvania and attracts thousands of boaters on summer weel
ends. Floating in canoes, kayaks, tubes and rafts, they enjoy spectacular view
notably at the Delaware Water Gap. In this recreation area not far fror
the New York state line, the wooded Tammany and Minsi Mountains ris
steeply to about 1,200 feet above the river. Paddlers wishing to escape th
crowds on this stretch may explore a hidden section of the Delaware name
Walpack Bend, just downstream from Bushkill, Pennsylvania, and acces:
ible only by canoe. It provides both smooth and white water as the riv
follows its rocky streambed. (See also Pennsylvania.)

Further south, novices should watch out for dangerous rapids at Fou
Rift, one mile below Belvedere Bridge, and the hazards in the Lumbervill
Lambertville area. But local whitewater enthusiasts in search of continuoi
adventure will not find it in New Jersey. They must seek it in Pennsylvani
or New York.

Adams Canoe Rentals, Inc.
Robert Wayne Adams
1005 Atsion Road
Shamong, NJ 08088
(609) 268-0189
Mullica River, Batsto River
Max. rapids: None

Adams Canoe Rentals rents canoes
and kayaks for 1- and 2-day trips on the
Mullica and Batsto Rivers. These gentle,
clean, flatwater streams offer easy paddling, beaches for swimming and scenic,
wooded banks. Wildlife is abundant and
there's fishing for pike, catfish, and some
smallmouth bass. The livery's season
runs from April to November.

Al & Sam's Canoe & Boat Rentals
Alfred, Sanford & Frances Fox
1940 Coles Mill Rd.
Franklinville, NJ 08322
(609) 692-8440, (609) 694-0657
Maurice, Menantico Rivers, Willow Grove,
Union Lakes, Menantico Ponds
Max. rapids: None
PPA

Claiming the lowest prices in southern New Jersey, this outfitter offers
guided and unguided canoe and kayak

trips on calm waters suitable for everyone. A family business catering to
families, it uses quality canoes and
emphasizes environment, education
and instruction.

Floats include the "wild and scenic"
designated Maurice River and pristine
lake waters. Paddling lessons, camping
and swimming are available, largemouth
bass and pickerel may be fished, and the
season runs April-October.

Bel Haven Canoes
William Bell
RD 2, Box 107
Egg Harbor, NJ 08215
(609) 965-2205, (800) 445-0953
Wading, Oswego, Mullica, Batsto Rivers
Max. rapids: None
PPA

Bel Haven Canoes rents canoes,
kayaks, and tubes from March through
November for easy trips in a wild and
unspoiled area. Here, within easy reach
of New York City and Philadelphia,
paddlers find native cedar swamps and
cultivated cranberry bogs.

Although the water may be darkened
by surface iron ore and cedar trees, the

rivers are clean, offer fishing for pickerel, and help support turtles, blue herons, deer, beavers, and other wildlife. Trips last 1-2 days and are suitable for people of all ages.

Cedar Creek Campground

Debra Fleming
1052 Route 9
Bayville, NJ 08721
(908) 269-1413, FAX (908) 269-0455
Cedar Creek
Max. rapids: None

Cedar Creek Campground offers relaxing 1-day trips on Cedar Creek, designated "wild and scenic" by the state of New Jersey. These easy floats are fine for beginning canoeists and anyone wanting a tranquil, scenic trip. Paddlers pass through the heart of the New Jersey Pine Barrens and offer views of cedar groves, cranberry bogs, deer, beavers, shorebirds, and waterfowl. Along the way, they can also fish for catfish and pickerel.

The campground, just ten miles from the Atlantic Ocean and Bernegat Bay, offers wooded tent and R.V. sites, modern restrooms, a swimming pool and hot tub, and a fully-equipped convenience store and deli. The season runs from April-November.

Cranford Boat and Canoe Co.

Frank Betz
250 Springfield Avenue
Cranford, NJ 07016
(908) 272-6991
Rahway River
Max. rapids: None

Cranford Boat & Canoe Company rents canoes and kayaks for 1-day trips on the Rahway River, a tranquil, scenic stream, which meanders through the township of Cranford and the Union County Park system. These trips offer views of old mansions, mills, deer, and many bird species.

The Rahway's clean waters also offer carp, catfish, and trout fishing. The season runs from March to December.

Indian Head Canoes

Anthony Brunovsky
RD3 7 Hampton Downs
Newton, NJ 07860
(800) 874-2628, (201) 579-2942
Delaware River
Max. rapids: I-II
PPA

Indian Head Canoes rents canoes, kayaks, rafts, and tubes from April to October for trips lasting 1-7 days on relatively easy waters. This family business has over 20 years' experience and prides itself on offering excellent equipment and facilities at competitive rates. Customers enjoy both calm and whitewater paddling on the upper reaches of the Delaware as it cuts through two mountain ranges.

Hemlocks, oaks, and maples flank the river, along which paddlers can camp, swim, and fish for bass, trout, and shad.

Mick's Canoe Rental, Inc.

Wayne A. Wilson, Carl R. Zirkel
Rte. 563, Box 45
Chatsworth, NJ 08019
(609) 726-1380
Oswego and Harrisville Lakes, Oswego and Wading Rivers
Max. rapids: None
PPA, New Jersey Canoe Livery & Outfitters

Mick's runs guided canoe trips and rents canoes for flatwater trips on clean, clear water. Streams are narrow and pass under canopies of pine and oak, with occasional cedar swamps. Outings last from 1/2 day to 2 days and are suitable for beginners and experienced paddlers.

Camping is also available, and paddlers can fish for pickerel, sunfish, and catfish, and watch for deer, raccoons, beavers, ducks, geese, swans, and raptors. Mick's season runs from April through October.

Canoeing the Egg Harbor River. Courtesy of Winding River Campground, May's Landing, New Jersey.

Paradise Lake Campground
Walter D. Lohman
Route 206, P.O. Box 46
Paradise Lake Road
Hammenton, NJ 08037
(609) 561-7095
Robinson's Creek, Mullica River
Max. rapids: None

Paradise Lake Campground offers canoe rentals on Robinson's Creek and the Mullica River. These flatwater trips pass through the protected scenic pine and oak woods of Wharton State Forest. On these trips, paddlers can swim, camp, and fish for bass, pickerel, catfish, sunfish, and perch. They can also spot occasional deer, otters, beavers, and raccoons.

During its April-to-October season, Paradise Lake Campground also offers tent and R.V. camping with hot showers.

Pineland Canoes, Inc.
Ed Mason
26 Whitesville Rd. (Rte 527)
Jackson, NJ 08527
(908) 364-0389, (800) 281-0383 (in NJ)
Upper Toms River
Max. rapids: None
PPA, NJ Canoe Livery & Outfitters

Pineland Canoes rents kayaks and canoes for trips of 2 hours to 2 days on the Toms River, a winding woodland river. Trips on the Toms are not difficult, but the river's brisk current requires good canoe control. The company has good equipment and radio-dispatched shuttle vehicles for prompt service.

The typical South Jersey Pineland scenery includes a wide variety of trees, shrubs, and flowers. The water is clean, with a gravel and sandy bottom. White-tail deer, otters, beavers, turtles, and many birds may be seen during the outfitter's April 15 to October 31 season.

Professional River Instruction
Wayne Sundmacher
17 Terrill Ave.
Mercerville, NJ 08619
(609) 586-8366
Delaware River, Tohickon Creek, Nescopeck Creek, other tributaries of the Delaware
Max. rapids: III-IV
PPA

Professional River Instruction offers canoeing, kayaking, and rafting lessons for beginners, intermediate, and advanced paddlers on waters ranging from easy riffles to challenging rapids. All instructors are certified by the ACA, and are dedicated to providing a safe and enjoyable experience. Canoe and kayak rentals are also available.

During its April-November season, PRI offers trips of 1-5 days through clean and scenic areas convenient to New York and Philadelphia.

Winding River Campground
James A. Horsey
6752 Weymouth Road
Mays Landing, NJ 08330
(609) 625-3191
Great Egg Harbor River
Max. rapids: None

Winding River Campground rents canoes and tubes for day trips on the Egg Harbor River, a scenic, wooded flatwater river. Trips are easy and allow plenty of time for leisurely fishing for pickerel, eel, and catfish, and watching for turtles, deer, ducks, geese, and other wildlife. During the May-to-September season, the campground also offers tent and R.V. camping, cabin rentals, a heated pool, and a general store.

Children tubing on the Egg Harbor River. Courtesy of Winding River Campground, May's Landing, New Jersey.

New Mexico

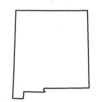

New Mexico is the land of the Rio Grande, a monarch among rivers. The second longest river in the nation, the "Great River" rises on the Continental Divide in the southern Colorado Rockies and flows southward through the middle of the New Mexico desert. Then it forms the boundary between Texas and Mexico before discharging into the Gulf of Mexico at Brownsville. Only the Missouri-Mississippi system surpasses its nineteen-hundred-mile length.

Most people think of New Mexico as dry and parched. But during the May-June spring runoff the Upper Rio Grande in the north rages with a fury to tax the skills of the most daring river runner. Some of its rapids are unrunnable and paddlers must struggle along steep portage trails. The Rio Grande Gorge starts just north of the Colorado-New Mexico state line and continues for fifty miles to Taos Junction. A charter member of the National Wild and Scenic Rivers system, the Gorge offers sheer rock walls up to two hundred feet high, rising to eight hundred feet at the Red River confluence. One 12-mile stretch of the Gorge contains thunderous whitewater that ranks as Class VI and extremely hazardous. Guided raft trips traverse the so-called Taos Box well south of this dangerous area but still within the Gorge. It is an exciting 16-mile trip with Class III-IV rapids, 600-foot vertical cliffs and impressive canyon scenery. One outfitter promises a "frisky" run certain to get everyone wet.

The Lower Rio Grande Gorge offers the Pilar Canyon run, a popular family frolic through five miles of Class III rapids. The season for these Rio floats runs from April to early July.

West of the Rio Grande in northern New Mexico lies the Rio Chama, another Wild and Scenic river. The upper section from Plaza Blanca to El Vado Lake is an interesting day trip past meadows in a deep canyon. Its rapids are chiefly Class III and may involve some portaging; rafting on El Vado Lake is inadvisable because of strong winds. More popular is the 33-mile run from El Vado Dam to Abiquiu Lake, a two-day trip that runs through vivid red sandstone canyons with plenty of forests and wildlife. Here the rapids are rated Class I-III and the time to go is usually from late April to early July.

A beautiful trip in southwestern New Mexico is the Wilderness Run on the Gila River, some 32 miles of paddling through wide green canyons with springs, lots of wildlife, and Class II-III rapids. But the water flow is usually either too much or too little so that the paddling season may be only a week or two in some years. Check with the National Weather Service or the U.S. Geological Survey for flow levels if you want to run this one on your own.

East of Santa Fe the Pecos River changes from a turbulent mountain stream to a pastoral float as it runs from Cowles to Villanueva State Park. The last 25 miles of this stretch passes several picturesque Spanish Colonial villages as the Pecos flows through rocky canyons. It is runnable in May-June during rainy years. Although it rates only Class I-II, its hazards include many dangerous fences, low bridges and several dams that must be portaged.

Bighorn Expeditions
P.O. Box 508
Junction, TX 76849
(915) 475-2118
Rio Grande, Pecos, Devils, and Gila Rivers
Max. rapids: III-IV
America Outdoors, Utah Guides and Outfitters

Bighorn Expeditions offers 2-8 day guided oar-boat trips on the Devils, Pecos, and Rio Grande Rivers in Texas and the Gila River in New Mexico. Unlike most outfitters offering oar-boat trips, Bighorn encourages guests to do the rowing. The company provides 11-foot, one-person rafts that are lively and river-worthy but small enough for easy handling. Trips include thorough lessons and begin on calm stretches, so they are fine for those with no rowing experience. Those wishing to row, however, should be in good physical condition. If you are unsure of your conditioning or prefer to concentrate on photography or bird-watching, you can elect to ride on one of the company's larger, guide-operated rafts.

Bighorn's trips run from March to November through scenic canyon terrain and offer good instruction in whitewater boating and wilderness ethics.

Bill Dvorak's Kayak and Rafting Expeditions
Bill and Jaci Dvorak
17921 U.S. Highway 285
Nathrop, CO 81236
(719) 539-6851, (800) 824-3795
Arkansas River, Colorado River, Green River, Gunnison River, North Platte River, Dolores River, Middle Fork and Main Salmon River, Rio Grande, Salt River
Max. rapids: V+
America Outdoors, Colorado River Outfitters Association, Utah Guides and Outfitters, New Mexico River Outfitters Association

Dvorak's runs a wide array of guided and unguided trips through 29 canyons on a total of 10 rivers in Colorado, Utah, and New Mexico. Scenery ranges from Alpine to desert, and whitewater ranges from Class I to Class V. Guests also have a choice of touring by canoe, kayak, or raft. With this selection of locations and trips, Dvorak's has offerings to suit any individual or group.

Trips run for 1-13 days between March and October and permit time for trout fishing and viewing deer, elk, bears, eagles, beavers, and coyotes.

Far Flung Adventures, Inc.
Steve Harrison/Mike Davidson
P.O. Box 377
Terlingua, TX 79852
(915) 371-2489, (800) 359-4138 (reservations)
Rio Chama
Max. rapids: Rio Grande
America Outdoors, Rio Grande Guides Association

Far Flung Adventures specializes in taking rafters on camping trips through the ruggedly beautiful Big Bend region of Texas as well as in other states in the U.S. and Mexico. Its tours last from 1-7 days in a season running from January to December. It caters to everyone from novices to whitewater experts who can meet Class V+ challenges.

The remoteness of the Rio Grande's Big Bend National Park, its canyons and wildlife combine with good fishing to make these trips unforgettable. Far Flung Adventures offers paddling lessons as well as camping, fishing, and swimming.

Hawk, I'm Your Sister
Beverly Antaeus
P.O. Box 9109
Santa Fe, NM 87504
(505) 984-2268
Heron Lake
Max. rapids: I-II

Hawk, I'm Your Sister of Santa Fe specializes in women's wilderness canoe and raft trips. Its year-round program is geared to "women of all ages, shapes, sizes and skill levels" with guided trips in five states and four foreign locations. Its aim is to "teach you the language of the forests, canyons, deserts and waterways" in a safe and non-competitive environment. It takes paddlers on Heron Lake in New Mexico and on the Missouri River in Montana, with other excursions as far afield as Mexico, Peru, and Russia.

Kokopelli Rafting Adventures
Jon Asher
541 W. Cordova Rd.
Santa Fe, NM 87501
(505) 983-3734, (800) 879-9035
Rio Grande, Chama Rivers
Max. rapids: III-IV
America Outdoors

Kokopelli Rafting Adventures offers half-day, full-day and overnight adventures for individuals, groups, and families. Its friendly staff combines rafting, kayaking, hiking, and backpacking to create memorable outdoor experiences that focus on nature, geology, and archaeology. The company's season runs from March through November. Spring runoff conditions create the best whitewater in May, June, and early July.

New Wave Rafting Co.
Steve and Kathy Miller
Route 5, Box 302A
Santa Fe, NM 87501
(505) 984-1444
Rio Grande, Rio Chama
Max. rapids: III-IV
New Mexico River Outfitter Association

New Wave Rafting of Santa Fe offers 1/2-day to 3-day guided raft trips on the Rio Grande and Rio Chama for "anybody with a sense of adventure." They run through great scenery: high desert country and the Rio Grande volcanic gorge. Beavers and muskrat can be seen, and anglers may hook brown and rainbow trout.

The full-day Taos Box trip on the Rio Grande traverses sixteen miles of wilderness gorge with "rapids guaranteed to get you wet." This exciting trip, with its Class IV+ whitewater, is not for the timid. Less demanding are the Class II-III rapids on the Rio Chama, where floaters spend 2 nights and 3 days paddling 30 miles through canyons of vividly colored sandstone.

Wolf Whitewater
Jack O'Neil
P.O. Box 666
Sandia Park, NM 87047
(505) 281-5042
Rio Grande – Upper Taos Box, Rio Grande –
Lower Pilar Canyon
Max. rapids: III-IV
America Outdoors

Wolf Whitewater of Sandia Park
has a "very frisky" full-day whitewater
rafting trip on the Rio Grande Gorge
(Taos Box) for people aged 12-60. It
also offers 1/2-day runs in the five-mile
Pilar Canyon stretch of the same gorge
for family floaters aged 8-80, in both
paddle and oar rafts. In addition, the
company provides skilled canoe and
kayak instruction.

The scenery on this Wild and Scenic
River is superb, with 600-foot canyon
walls along a seventeen-mile chasm.
Muskrat, beavers, and birds of many
species may be found. Paddlers can also
fish for trout.

New York

Endowed with an abundance of mountain streams, rivers and lakes, New York has it all. Up in the southern Adirondacks the headwaters of the mighty Hudson provide great scenery and rugged whitewater. In the southwestern Adirondacks the Moose River system combines grand wilderness with rapids that even experts treat with respect. Less than two hours drive from New York City flows the Delaware, with its scenic 76-mile run from Hancock to Port Jervis (see Pennsylvania). In the Catskills, not far from the Delaware's headwaters, slalom races are held the first weekend in June on Esopus Creek's exciting whitewater. Out at the western end of the state the Genesee cuts across from Pennsylvania and empties into Lake Ontario at Rochester, offering attractive paddling through Genesee Valley.

The Hudson is the first river that comes to mind when one thinks of New York waterways. The Hudson River Gorge provides 16 miles of almost continuous whitewater as the river rushes through a vertical-cliff canyon. Outfitters offer one-day rafting trips from the end of March until the beginning of June, resuming from Labor Day to Columbus Day. The Gorge rapids are roughest in April-May after the snowmelt and spring rains, some reaching into the Class IV+ category. With such thrills at hand, it is no surprise that the Gorge trip attracts more than twenty thousand rafters a year. Some are also drawn to the area by the excellent trout, pike, and bass fishing, and by the abundant wildlife ranging from loons and hawks to bears and beaver.

For the rugged outdoorsman prepared to face the rigors of April in the Adirondacks, the Moose River offers some of the toughest rapids in the East. At least two of them, Tannery and Mixmaster, are Class V and definitely not for the novice. Wet suits and extra woolens are needed for protection against the cold since April is the only month the river is runnable. Rafts frequently overturn amid these complex rapids with their wide ledges and massive boulders.

Esopus Creek in the Catskills is another exciting stream set in mountain grandeur. The 25-mile canoe trail above Ashoken Reservoir depends after the April-May runoff upon water releases from upstream dams. So paddlers should check with the New York City Board of Water Supply in Prattsville before planning summer trips. At high water, the Esopus is a trip for seasoned rapid-runners.

The Genesee meanders through a pastoral landscape in the foothills of western New York State and offers the birdwatcher much to view through his binoculars. The stretch to paddle is from Genesee, just across the Pennsylvania line, to Portageville — a well-named spot since the waterfalls just downstream in Letchworth State Park are strictly for riverbank sightseeing. But the park's 600-foot-deep gorge of shale and sandstone also contains a six-mile stretch with gentle rapids that makes a great raft trip for families. These tours begin in early April and run through October.

Long Islanders with a penchant for fishing, wildlife and easy canoeing can take a five-mile float on the Nissequogue River, in the middle of the island's North Shore near the town of Kings Park. It offers saltwater fish such as flounder in its estuary as well as trout and striped bass upstream.

Not to be omitted in any listing of New York's aquatic delights are the innumerable lakes, especially in the Adirondacks. Many choose the 45-mile run (with portages) down the Raquette River from Long Lake to Upper Saranac Lake. One of our favorite canoeing spots is Cranberry Lake, in a particularly unspoiled area west of Tupper Lake. But the choice is so wide that everyone can take his pick.

NEW YORK

Adirondack Canoes & Kayaks
Harry Spetla
96 Old Piercefield Rd.
Tupper Lake, NY 12986
(518) 359-2174, (800) 499-2174
Bog, Racquette, Oswagatchie Rivers, Tupper, Saranac Lakes, St. Regis Canoe Area
Max. rapids: I-II
PPA

This outfitter rents canoes, kayaks and rafts as well as operating guided canoe and kayak trips on a wide variety of waters in a vast mountain wilderness. While some floats are rigorous, most are suitable for novices and families. The company has experienced personnel, competitive rates and varied craft.

Black bear, deer and coyotes may be seen in the rugged wilderness, while fishermen go for bass, pike and trout. The season runs April-October.

Adirondack River Outfitters
Box 563
Watertown, NY 13601
(800) 525-RAFT
Hudson River, Moose River, Black River, Scandaga River
Max. rapids: V+

Adirondack River Outfitters runs guided whitewater raft trips on the Hudson, Moose, Black, and Scandaga Rivers. From one of its four outposts, ARO also rents inflatable kayaks and from another it rents canoes.

Trips on the Hudson feature rapids over a mile in length, with waves cresting 10 feet high. This 17-mile course is the most popular spring run in the Adirondacks. Although rated class IV, the Hudson thrills paddlers but is not as demanding as the Moose or Black Rivers.

Trips on the Moose have intimidating rapids resembling small waterfalls. Rated as Class IV-V, Moose trips are best suited

"Rocket Ride" on the Black River. Courtesy of Adirondack River Outfitters, Watertown, New York.

for rafters with prior whitewater experience.

The most challenging of all Adirondack whitewater runs is the "Big Water Black," a spring high-water trip that has a continuous and potentially dangerous three-mile rapid. Paddlers on this Class IV-V trip must have prior whitewater experience. Later in the season, the "Summer Black" trip offers a challenging whitewater run of towering waves and foaming hydraulics. With 14 sets of rapids packed into seven miles of river, this Class IV trip boasts more action per mile than any other New York whitewater run.

Finally, ARO offers trips on the Class III Scandaga, which has gentle, forgiving waves that are ideal for novice rafters and families with children.

ARO's paddle trips last 1 day and are available between May and October. From September to November, the company also offers oar-boat salmon-fishing trips on the Black.

Adventure Calls
Terry Shearn
20 Ellicott Avenue
Batavia, NY 14020
(716) 343-4710
Genesee River
Max. rapids: III-IV

Adventure Calls has guided raft trips over Class III-IV rapids on the remote Cattaragus Creek and the Genesee River. Although these floats are of medium difficulty, they can be enjoyed by anyone in good health. The season starts as early as March and runs until October.

Floaters ride through a 600-foot-deep gorge and heavily wooded countryside, with a great variety of undisturbed flora. The wildlife includes deer, beavers, hawks and vultures, while the fishing covers bass, trout and salmon. Camping is available.

Adventure Sports Rafting Co., Inc.
John Starling
P.O. Box 775
Indian Lake, NY 12842
(518) 648-5812, (800) 441-RAFT
Hudson River, Moose River
Max. rapids: V+

Adventure Sports Rafting runs guided raft trips on both the Hudson and the Moose rivers, through wilderness countryside accessible only by raft. It has a double season, from March to June and again from Labor Day to Columbus Day.

The Hudson River Gorge trip provides 16 miles of almost continuous whitewater between vertical cliffs rising from the river's edge. No experience is necessary, although the rapids range from Class III-IV to Class V+. Customers must, however, be aged at least 16.

Deer, frogs, eagles, ospreys and ravens may be spotted in this remote region. Bass and several species of trout tease the angler.

Kayaker runs "Hole Bros" rapid on the Black River. Courtesy of Adirondack River Outfitters.

Battenkill Sportsquarters
Walter & Veronica Piekarz
RD 1, Box 143
Cambridge, NY 12816
(518) 677-8868
Battenkill River
Max. rapids I-II
PPA, CONY

Battenkill rents canoes, kayaks, and tubes for easy paddling on the clean and scenic Battenkill River. Trips are suitable for novices and semi-novices, who may enjoy trout fishing as they glide past farms and pinewoods.

The company prides itself on its service and good equipment. It also offers lessons during its season, which lasts from mid-July to mid-October.

Belfast Canoe Rental
Judith Barber
37 West Hughes St.
Belfast, NY 14711
(716) 365-8129
Genessee River, Cuba & Rushford Lakes
Max. rapids: I-II
PPA

This company rents canoes for family-style easy paddling on clean and uncongested waters amid attractive rural surroundings. Fishing and camping may be enjoyed during the May-October season, and the outfitter prides itself on providing personal service. Birdlife includes raptors and waterfowl.

Blue Mountain Outfitters
Ernie & Kim LaPrairie
Box 144
Blue Mountain Lake, NY 12812
(518) 352-7306, (518) 352-7675
Lakes & rivers of Central Adirondacks
Max. rapids: None
PPA

Blue Mountain operates guided canoe and unguided canoe and kayak trips on wilderness flatwater, suitable for groups and families of all experience levels. Guests come away with knowledge of plants, trees, and wildlife including deer, bear, otter, and ducks. Camping trips last up to a week and paddling lessons may be taken. Fish include bass, trout and whitefish. The season runs May 1-Oct. 15.

Bob's Canoe Rental, Inc.
Bob Koliner
P.O. Box 529
Kings Park, NY 11754
(516) 269-9761
Nissequogue River, all Long Island waters
Max. rapids: None
PPA, ACA

Bob's Canoe Rental, which describes itself as the oldest and finest canoe livery on Long Island, offers both guided canoe trips and rental canoes. The company is located on the Nissequogue River, an unspoiled river corridor in the midst of Long Island's North Shore. Group tours go to all Long Island waters.

During the season, which runs from St. Patrick's Day to Thanksgiving, canoeists can fish for saltwater fish such as bluefish, fluke and flounder in the estuaries as well as trout and bass in the headwaters. Shorebirds, foxes, raccoons, opossums and turtles are among the local wildlife.

Canoe Center
Brian Hart
5884 Griswold Rd.
Byron, NY 14427
(716) 548-7146, (315) 866-6075
Black Creek, Tonawanda Creek, Genesee River, Oak Orchard Creek, Mohawk River, West Canada Creek
Max. rapids: I-II

From May through September, Canoe Center rents canoes and kayaks on six rivers that offer good bass, pike, and trout fishing. Floating on the quiet, winding rivers, paddlers can look for deer and a variety of other animals and birds among the trees and fields. No rapids are rated harder than Class I-II.

Campsites are available and Canoe Center also provides quality instruction in canoeing and kayaking.

Champaign Canoeing, Ltd.
Ann & Keech LeClair
Brayton Park
Ossining, NY 10562-3201
(914) 762-5121
Weekends: Croton River, Esopus Creek, Housatonic and Farmington Rivers.
Weekdays: Rouge and Jacques Cartier Rivers, Quebec, Canada.
Max. rapids: III-IV
AWA, ACA, Appalachian Mountain Club

Ann and Keech LeClair, certified ACA instructors and holders of many whitewater championship titles, offer weekend instruction from May to September and week-long trips in beautiful parts of Quebec during July and August.

Champaign Canoeing supplies canoes and tents as part of the package, along with excellent food and guides. Weekend instruction is given at the novice, intermediate and expert levels. Experienced whitewater paddlers can choose between a Class II-IV trip on Canada's Rouge River and a Class III-V trip on the Jacques Cartier River. Local scenery includes small towns amid rural farmland.

Eastern River Expeditions
John Connelly
Box 1173
Greenville, ME 04441
(207) 634-7238, (800) 695-2411
Moose River, Gauley River, Kennebec River, Penobscot River, Dead River
Max. rapids: V+
Maine Professional River Outfitters Association, America Outdoors

Eastern River Expeditions offers canoe rentals and guided raft and inflatable-kayak trips on five rivers in Maine, New York, and West Virginia. In Maine, paddlers can choose among whitewater trips on the Kennebec, Penobscot, and Dead Rivers. Most Maine trips are fine for novice paddlers, combining excellent wilderness scenery with Class II-IV whitewater. Trips on the Dead and Penobscot Rip Gorge, however, require excellent conditioning. Penobscot Rip

Small waterfalls feed into the Black River. Courtesy of Adirondack River Outfitters, Watertown, New York.

Gorge also requires intermediate or advanced paddling skills. Advanced rafting experience is a prerequisite for trips on New York's Moose River and West Virginia's Gauley River, which have Class IV-V rapids.

All trips, of 1-2 days, pass through wilderness, offering camping spots, clear water, fishing, and chances to spot deer, coyotes, loons, ducks, beavers, foxes, great blue herons, and other wildlife.

Hudson River Rafting Co.
Pat Cunningham
1 Main Street
North Creek, NY 12853
(518) 251-3215, (800) 888-RAFT
Hudson River Gorge, Black, Moose and Sacandaga Rivers
Max. rapids: V

Hudson River Rafting runs guided raft trips and rents rafts, canoes, and tubes for varied trips of up to a full day. Anyone over age 6 is welcome to float the Sacandaga. The "very challenging" Black River and the scenic Hudson Gorge, with its continuous Class IV rapids, are open to paddlers age 12 and older. The Moose is restricted to experi-

enced rafters because of its extreme Class V whitewater.

Trips may be taken any time from April 1 to Columbus Day, and the outfitter prides itself on its skilled guides.

Lander's River Trips
Richard Lander
1336 Route 97
Narrowsburg, NY 12764
(914) 252-3925, (800) 252-3925
Upper Delaware River
Max. rapids: I-III
PPA, NAPSA

Lander's River Trips rents canoes, kayaks, rafts, and tubes for trips of 1-4 days on the upper Delaware River. This scenic river, of which 72 miles lie within a National Park, offers wilderness scenery and views of deer, bears, eagles, ospreys, herons, and beavers. The Delaware's clean waters also offer excellent fishing for bass, trout, shad, walleye, perch, sunfish, suckers, and eels.

The outfitter offers trips along calm stretches for beginners, and through whitewater for experienced river runners. Also, as the company operates four conveniently spaced campgrounds, paddlers on overnight trips can avoid having to carry camping equipment on the river. Rentals are available between April and October, with group discounts and getaway packages.

Loric Sports & Canoe Rental
Lorraine & Richard Reid
912 U.S.9
Staatsburg, NY 12580
(914) 889-4320
Hudson River and all other lakes and rivers in upper New York State
Max. rapids: None
PPA

Loric Sports rents canoes and kayaks for paddling, fishing, and camping trips down the scenic Hudson River valley and elsewhere in upper New York State. The outfitter has trips for everyone, and is located opposite a beautiful state park where people can camp, rent cabins, fish, and launch their canoes.

The Hudson is a clean, flatwater river in a beautiful mountainous region with great fishing for bass, perch, catfish, and muskie.

Loric Sports also runs trips in Florida's Everglades during the winter.

Middle Earth Expeditions
Wayne Failing
HCR 01 Box 37
Lake Placid, NY 12946
(518) 523-9572
Hudson River Gorge, any lakes or rivers in the Adirondacks
Max. rapids: V+
New York State Outdoor Guides Association, Hudson River Professional Outfitters Association

Middle Earth Expeditions provides guided whitewater rafting trips through the Hudson River Gorge up to Class V+ in difficulty. Daytrips, overnights, and float fishing trips are available. It also runs wilderness canoe and fishing trips through all the major canoe routes in the Adirondack Park. The scenery, wildlife, food, and fishing are superb. A small, low-volume company, it seeks to

meet the individual needs of each customer from beginner to expert. Trips can run from 1-10 days, with the season lasting from April 1 to October 15.

Oak Orchard Canoe Experts
Bill, Todd & Mary Lynn Finley
2133 Eagle Harbor Rd.
Waterport, NY 14571
(716) 682-4849
Oak Orchard Creek, Erie Barge Canal
Max.rapids: I-II
GRMTA

Oak Orchard Canoe Experts rents canoes and kayaks from its Waterport location for Oak Orchard Creek trips and provides hourly rentals from another location at 40 State St. in Pittsford for outings on the Erie Canal.

The Waterport rentals are for half-day or full-day trips in sparkling clean waters through dense woods. Oak Orchard Creek is a twisting, challenging stream with many fallen trees. Local wildlife includes deer, ducks, turtles, bass, and pike. The season runs from April to November. Both stores are open all year for canoe and kayak sales, repairs, and accessories.

Port Jerry Marina
Rich and Mary Kolver
HCR Box 27
Bolton Landing, NY 12814
(518) 644-3311
Lake George
Max. rapids: None

Port Jerry Marina on beautiful, crystal-clear Lake George rents canoes which customers can paddle in May-September to state-owned camping islands in the lake. Experienced canoeists, for whom the lake is best suited, can view deer, beavers, otters, turtles and many different kinds of birds. Fishing is for small and largemouth bass, northern pike and lake trout. Camping is available, and the lake is good for swimming.

Raquette River Outfitters, Inc.
Carol Kennedy/Rob Frenette
P.O. Box 653
Tupper Lake, NY 12986
(518) 359-3228
All Adirondack canoe routes
Max. rapids: None

Raquette River Outfitters services all the Adirondack canoe routes with guided canoe trips and rentals of both canoes and kayaks. It plans custom trips to fit paddlers' vacation needs and schedules, varying in difficulty from leisurely to challenging.

Customers enjoy clean waters with good fishing amid grand mountain scenery. On the hillsides the canoeist may see whitetail deer and black bears while eagles and ospreys circle overhead. Otters and loons swim on the surface and anglers hook smallmouth bass, lake trout, brook trout, walleye, pike and salmon. Camping is available and the season runs from May to October 15.

Shelter Island Kayak
Jay Damuck
Box 360
Shelter Island, NY 11964
(516) 749-1990
Cocles Harbor and other small creeks on Shelter Is.
Max. rapids: None
PA

Owner Jay Damuck personally conducts all his company's guided kayak trips through the beautiful marshland of Shelter Island's protected creeks. He can thus cater to each paddler's personal pace and schedule. Local sights include an old working boatyard and huge Ice Age boulders. Osprey, egret, geese, duck, and tern are among the birdlife, while bluefish can be caught. Damuck also rents kayaks during his May-October season.

St. Regis Canoe Outfitters
Dave & Kathy Cilley
P.O. Box 318
Lake Clear, NY 12945
(518) 891-1838, FAX (518) 891-6405
St. Regis Wilderness Canoe Area, Raquette, Oswegatchie Rivers, Saranac Lake, Low's Lake, etc.
Max. rapids: I-II
PPA

A full-service outfitter, St. Regis offers guided and unguided canoe and kayak trips in the Adirondacks from May to October. These trips go through heavily forested wilderness, with well-marked portages linking the many lakes left by retreating glaciers. Paddlers can choose between family outings and extended backcountry camping excursions.

Lessons, camping, swimming, and fishing for trout, pike, bass, and perch are available. Alert paddlers may spot bobcat, deer, bears, otters, and migratory waterfowl in the region.

St. Regis also offers guided tours of the Florida Everglades in the winter.

Tickner's Adirondack Canoe Outfitters
Dan & Beth Tickner
P.O. Box 267, Riverside Dr.
Old Forge, NY 13420
(315) 369-6286
Moose River, Adirondack Canoe Route
Max. rapids: None
PPA

Tickner's canoe livery caters to paddlers of all levels of ability. It rents canoes and kayaks for self-guided trips, enabling customers to explore as much or as little of the 90-mile Adirondack Canoe Route as they wish during trips of up to 10 days. They find mountains and wilderness dotted with historic camps and towns.

Camping, swimming, and fishing for trout and bass are available during the outfitter's May-October season. Local wildlife includes bears, deer, otters, mink, beavers, loons, ospreys, and herons.

Town Tinker Tube Rental
Harry G. Jameson, III
P.O. Box 404, Bridge Street
Phoenicia, NY 12464
(914) 688-5553
Esopus Creek
Max. rapids: I-II
American Rivers, NYSHTA

Town Tinker Tube Rental has rented its tubes to over 350,000 customers during its 16 years in business beside Esopus Creek. Tubers ride the rapids in a clean stream that takes them through five miles of beautiful wooded scenery in the Catskill Mountains. The upper half of the stretch is for experienced tubers who revel in Class I-II whitewater.

Wildlife and fish are abundant, with the Esopus famous for its trout. The season runs from May 1 through September and camping is available.

Unicorn Expeditions
Jay Schurman
P.O. Box T
Brunswick, ME 04011
(207) 725-2255, (800) UNICORN
Hudson River, Moose River
Max. rapids: V+
America Outdoors

Unicorn Expeditions offers guided canoe, kayak, and raft trips and canoe rentals for trips of one to six days on the Kennebec, Penobscot, and Dead Rivers in Maine; the Hudson and Moose Rivers in New York; and the Deerfield River in Massachusetts. These trips range widely in difficulty to suit all skill levels from beginner to expert. Moose River trips have some of the wildest whitewater in the Northeast; the dam-controlled Penobscot and Kennebec Rivers ensure Class V whitewater all summer long; and the Hudson's spring high water offers 16 miles of exhilarating Class III and IV rapids.

Among the wildlife to see on these trips are moose, bald eagles, bears, deer, and ospreys. There is also fishing for bass, salmon, and trout. During its April-to-October season, Unicorn also offers "getaway" packages, which include rafting and lodge or inn accommodations.

Whitewater Willie's Sales & Rental Inc.
William O. Elston
7 West Main Street
Port Jervis, NY 12771
(800) 233-RAFT
Delaware River
Max. rapids: I-II
PA

Whitewater Willie's Sales and Rentals has canoes, rafts and tubes for rent by paddlers interested in fishing and exploring Hawks Nest Gorge on the Delaware River. The fishing is excellent, including shad, trout, bass, pike and eel. Floaters may view a very wide variety of wildlife as they negotiate Class I-II rapids.

The company offers paddling lessons, and campsites are available. Whitewater Willie's season runs from May 1-October 12.

Whitewater World
Douglas Fogal
Route 903
Jim Thorpe, PA 18229
(717) 325-3656
Hudson River, Moose River, Cheat River
Max. rapids: V+
America Outdoors

Operating in the Adirondacks during spring and fall, Whitewater World runs 1- and 2-day guided raft trips on the Hudson, Moose, and Cheat Rivers. These are clean, scenic streams with Class V+ rapids, coursing through a remote mountain wilderness area.

Whitewater World uses the latest self-bailing rafts and has a new assembly area. It describes its Adirondack runs as "extremely pretty and wild for the East." Bears, moose and deer can be seen, while the fish include trout and bass.

Wild and Scenic River Tours
Jules Robinson
166 Rte. 97
Barryville, NY 12719
(800) 836-0366, (914) 557-8783
Upper Delaware River
Max. rapids: I-II

Wild and Scenic River Tours rents canoes, kayaks, rafts, and tubes for trips of 1-3 days on the Upper Delaware, a designated wild and scenic river with exceptional fishing. Its placid pools and churning rapids run through lush mountains and rural countryside with picturesque villages and historic sites. The trips are suitable for families, schools, camps, and novice whitewater boaters. Paddlers may fish for trout, bass, walleye, and shad, and observe abundant wildlife including black bears, deer, and blue herons.

Expert instruction is also provided during the April-October season.

North Carolina

North and South Carolina belong together like Siamese twins, bound by a shared river system flowing from the Blue Ridge Mountains in the west toward the Atlantic in the east. Tumbling in youthful exuberance through steep gorges with waterfalls and rapids, these rivers slacken their pace as they develop middle-age spread, cross the rolling Piedmont hills and descend to the coastal plain. Headwaters of the 341-mile Savannah River arise in the western mountains of North Carolina to form the waterway that divides South Carolina from Georgia. The Broad, Catawba and Yadkin Rivers also originate in the Blue Ridge, with the Yadkin flowing into the mighty Pee Dee. As they run southeast these rivers connect the Carolinas like arteries linking vital bodily organs. And further east the Cape Fear and Black Rivers follow a similar course before disgorging their waters at Wilmington.

In its western mountains North Carolina has many thrills to offer the river runner, especially among the surging waves and high waters of spring and early summer. Among favorite rivers is the dam-controlled Nantahala just south of the Great Smoky Mountain National Park. Raftable from March to October, the Nantahala Gorge is a beautiful float which provides easy paddling for families and novices. The chasm is deep and forested with rhododendron and mountain laurel. Outfitters offer guided and unguided half-day trips on the eight-mile run, which is mostly rated Class II. At the end the exciting plunge through Nantahala Falls provides a Class III climax to test beginners' newly-learned skills. Small wonder, then, that over 100,000 rafters run the Nantahala every season.

The French Broad River provides good family rafting as it, too, churns through spectacular gorges in the Pisgah National Forest. In places, the mountains rise more than 1,000 feet above the river. Its water flow, however, is not as dependable as the Nantahala's in the summer. On the eight-mile stretch between Barnard and Hot Springs the French Broad has Class II-IV rapids alternating with placid pools.

The free-flowing Nolichucky has a great one-day Class III-IV springtime float across the Tennessee state line through what is claimed to be the deepest gorge in the Southeast. Mountains of the Pisgah and Cherokee National orests rise fully 2,000 feet above the water. Guided "ducky" (inflatable ka-ak) trips are popular when the water level drops in the summer.

Big Laurel Creek has exciting spring rafting for whitewater connoisseurs lose to its confluence with the French Broad near Hot Springs. When in ull spate, this is a very fast river with Class IV rapids and big ledge drops. t one point it drops eighty feet in a half-mile stretch of furious rapids.

Lovers of nature who enjoy more placid waters like to bask in the upper eaches of the New River in the northwestern corner of North Carolina. he North and South Forks which converge just south of the Virginia state ine provide 100 miles of gentle paddling through forested mountains and astoral valleys, enlivened by deer, wild turkey, wild duck and heron.

The Haw River, a favorite Piedmont float for citydwellers in central North arolina, provides great scenery, canoeing and wildlife. It offers easy rapids n its rocky course through a narrow valley before it runs into Lake Jordan lose to Durham.

In the coastal plain of eastern North Carolina are the great rivers that low into Albemarle and Pamlico Sounds: the Neuse, the Pamlico — with s highly scenic Tar River tributary — the Roanoke and the Chowan. Pad-lers on the Roanoke should watch for great fluctuations in flow when am waters are released. There is much fishing on the Roanoke just below ake Gaston when the rockfish (striped bass) are spawning.

For those who yearn for a complete escape from urban civilization, cracoke Island on North Carolina's Outer Banks offers naturalist-guided rips in open kayaks. These take the paddler along the island's Pamlico Sound hore and inlets with their wealth of sea birds, turtles, otters, fish, shellfish nd saltmarsh wildlife. Since almost the entire island belongs to the Cape Iatteras National Seashore, this is sea kayaking in a wonderfully unspoiled etting. But take bug repellent in July and August.

NORTH CAROLINA

dventurous Fast River Rafting
olan Whitesell
4690 Nantahala Gorge
ryson City, NC 28713
704) 488-2386,
Nantahala, Little Tennessee Rivers, Lake ontana
Max. rapids: III-IV
North American Paddle Sports Association
   Adventurous Fast River Rafting offers uided and unguided canoe, kayak, and aft trips on the Nantahala River. The tretches paddled have clean water with

continuous Class II and III whitewater. Paddlers on Class III waters must by Forest Service rules weigh at least 60 lbs. and canoeists must be whitewater certified. All paddlers can enjoy the spectacular mountain scenery as the Nantahala winds its way through a deep, heavily forested gorge with views of hardwoods and abundant birds and small game. The river also offers good fishing for brown and rainbow trout. The season runs year-round.

Kids ride up front for the best view of excitement on this Carolina Wilderness trip on the Nolichucky River. Photo courtesy of Whitewater Photography, Marshall, North Carolina.

Blue Ridge Outing Company
Bob and Cindy Mattingly
7397 US Hwy 74W
Whittier, NC 28789
(704) 586-3510, (800) 572-3510
Tuckasegee River
Max. rapids: I-II
PPA

Blue Ridge Outing Co. offers guided raft trips and rents inflatable duckies and tubes on the Tuckasegee River. Trips last 1 day and are of easy to moderate difficulty, with some runs suitable for all ages, including young children. The Tuckasegee, a clean mountain river, runs through a scenic gorge and offers paddlers a chance to spot fish, birds, beavers, and turtles. The river also has excellent fishing for trout, smallmouth bass, and catfish.

The season runs from April to October.

Brookside Campground & Rafting
Robert & Kathie Wojdylo
Box 93
Topton, NC 28781
(704) 321-5209
Nantahala River
Max. rapids: III-IV

A small company providing personal service, Brookside runs relaxing guided and unguided raft trips in a National Forest environment. Its Nantahala River floats are not difficult and suitable for families. Trout fishing and camping are available during the outfitter's April-December season.

Carolina Outfitters
Billy W. Dills
2121 Hwy 19 West
Bryson City, NC 28713
(800) GOT-RAFT, (704) 488-6345
Nantahala River
Max. rapids: III-IV
America Outdoors, PPA

Carolina Outfitters rents rafts and runs 1/2-day guided raft trips for family groups and advanced paddlers alike through the scenic splendor of the Nantahala National Forest near Great Smoky Mountains National Park. The river is clean and cold, with exciting

whitewater. No experience is necessary, and certified guides are available.

During an April-October season, the company provides friendly service and competitive prices. Vacation lodging, camping, and trout fishing are available.

Carolina Wilderness
Glenn Goodrich
P.O. Box 488
Hot Springs, NC 28743
(800) 872-7437
French Broad, Nolichucky, Pigeon Rivers
Max. rapids: III-IV

Carolina Wilderness offers guided raft

Paddlers enjoy a group outing on the French Broad River. The trip is by Carolina Wilderness; the photo by Whitewater Photography, Marshall, N.C.

trips on the French Broad River, No-lichucky River, and Pigeon River. The French Broad River trips, easy enough for beginners, pass through a scenic forest gorge. The Nolichucky trips, which are more challenging, travel through the deepest gorge in the Southeast. The Pigeon River is a great sampler near Gatlinburg, TN.

Carolina Wilderness, with three river-side outposts, also offers hot showers, inflatable "funyak" trips, and hot barbe-cue lunches on full-day guided trips. The outfitter's season runs from March to November.

French Broad Rafting Company
Ron and Sandy West
1 Thomas Branch Road
Marshall, NC 28753
(704) 649-3574, (800) 842-3189 or
(800) 572-RAFT
French Broad River
Max. rapids: III-IV
French Broad River Rafting Company offers guided 1/2-day or full-day raft trips on the French Broad River. These trips, with Class III-IV rapids, are excit-

ing but not strenuous and are fine for paddlers aged eight and older, as the company always includes a guide in eac of its rafts. It also provides calm water floats for families with children aged six and up who are not yet old enough for whitewater rafting. All trips offer chal-lenging water, the striking mountain scenery of Pisgah National Forest, and a chance to spot herons, deer, ospreys, and muskrats. The river also has excel-lent fishing for bass, catfish, muskie, anc gar.

The outfitter's season runs from March to November.

Great Smokies Rafting Co.
Ray McLeod, Manager
3 Highway 19 West
Bryson City, NC 28713
(800) 277-6302
Nantahala River
Max. rapids: III-IV
Great Smokies Rafting Co. offers guided and unguided raft trips on the Nantahala River, an especially clear river with excellent scenery, trout fish-ing, and Class II-III whitewater. Trips

st a 1/2-day and are fine for families ith children age seven and older.

The company's trips run through the eautiful Nantahala Gorge, which fea-ures brook, rainbow, and brown trout, nd birds, deer, occasional turkeys, and ther wildlife. The company's season is om April to October.

Headwaters Outfitters
avid Whitmire
O. Box 145
osman, NC 28772
704) 877-3106
rench Broad River
ax. rapids: I-II
?A

Headwaters Outfitters offers easy, 1-ay canoe trips in the scenic headwaters f the French Broad River, which fea-ures superb water quality and fishing for out, brim, bass, and catfish. The com-any prides itself on its experience and quipment. It provides both guided and nguided canoe tours.

These are ideal waters for novice pad-lers, families, and groups. The region is ome to beavers, foxes, mink, muskrats,

and bald eagles. The company's season lasts from May to October.

High Mountain Expeditions
Dave and Jacquelyn Jonston
P.O. Box 1299
Blowing Rock, NC 28605
(704) 295-4200
Nolichucky River, Watauga River,
Wilson Creek
Max. rapids: V+
America Outdoors

High Mountain Expeditions runs guided raft and inflatable kayak trips of 1-2 days on the Nolichucky River, Wa-tauga River, and Wilson Creek. Trips range from easy to wild, with runs to suit all ages and experience levels. The "sec-tion 5" Watauga trip is ideal for families with very small children, offering fast-moving water, Class I-II rapids, pastoral scenery, and abundant Canada geese and ducks. The "section 3" Watauga trip is a small-raft or "funyak" trip on a nar-row, Class III stretch of the river in a beautiful forested setting. Watauga Gorge is a heart-pounding Class V trip for experienced, energetic paddlers only.

An inflatable kayak gives a paddler an exciting ride through "On the Rocks Rapid" on the Nolichucky River during a trip run by High Mountain Expeditions. Photo by Johnny Meeks, courtesy of Blue Ridge Mountain Images.

Wilson Creek is a creek-rafters treat, running through a narrow gorge with steep granite walls and Class III-IV whitewater in one of the country's deepest gorges east of the Grand Canyon.

High Mountain Expeditions, open year-round, also offers caving, backpacking, and hiking trips.

Nantahala Outdoor Center
41 U.S. Highway West
Bryson City, NC 28713
(704) 488-2175, (800) 232-RAFT
Nantahala River, French Broad River, Ocoee River, Nolichucky River, Chatooga River
Max. rapids: III-IV
America Outdoors

Nantahala Outdoor Center (NOC) runs guided and unguided trips of 1-21 days on five rivers in North Carolina, South Carolina, and Tennessee. Trips are by canoe, raft, or inflatable kayak.

Nantahala River trips, run near Great Smoky Mountain National Park, offer an excellent whitewater experience for beginners and families. Runs on the French Broad River, another ideal river for family rafting, wind through a spectacular gorge in the Pisgah National Forest. The Ocoee is a favorite of whitewater enthusiasts, with big waves and constant action on its course through Cherokee National Forest. The Nolichucky offers high-water excitement in spring, gentler rafting and kayak trips in late spring and early summer, and stunning scenery at any time. The Chattooga boasts some of the finest whitewater in the Southeast as it tumbles through the Chattahoochee and Sumter National Forests. NOC has Chattooga trips to match any paddler's skill, beginner to advanced. NOC also offers lessons during its March-to-November season.

New River Outfitters
Randy Revis
P.O. Box 433
Highway 221 S
Jefferson, NC 28640
(919) 982-9192
New River
Max. rapids: I-II

New River Outfitters offers guided canoe trips and canoe and tube rentals for trips of 1-6 days on the New River, a designated Wild and Scenic River. Most trips have Class I rapids, making them ideal for beginners, families, groups, and canoe campers. Set in the mountains, the stretches paddled offer views of cliffs, pasture land, and deer, wild turkeys, ducks, herons, and other wildlife. The New River also offers excellent fishing for smallmouth bass, trout, and rock bass. New River Outfitters rents camping gear and operates an historic general store offering food, supplies, mountain crafts, and regional specialties. The season runs from April to October.

Pro Canoe of Raleigh, Inc.
Robert Levine
5710 Capital Blvd.
Raleigh, NC 27604
(919) 872-6999
Dan, Neuse, New, Cape Fear Rivers, N.C. Coast, Dismal Swamp
Max. rapids: I-II

River canoe trips and sea kayaking are Pro Canoe's offerings along a wide swath of the North Carolina coast. It is a scenic area full of history, and the company's trips last up to 3 days with overnight camping and gourmet meals. Paddling lessons are available during Pro Canoe's March-December season, but the river waters are easy and suitable for all. Bass and trout may be caught, while the wildlife includes deer and numerous bird species.

...apids on the French Broad River draw grins all round on trip by Carolina Wilderness, Hot ...rings, North Carolina. Courtesy of Whitewater Photography.

...ide the Wind
...ony Sylvester
...ox 352
...cracoke, NC 27960
...19) 928-6311
...mlico Sound and estuary waters
...ax. rapids: None

Ride the Wind offers guided and ...nguided sea-kayak trips on Pamlico ...ound and estuary waters along Cape ...atteras National Seashore. Trips last ...om one-half to two days, are suitable ...r beginners and veteran sea kayakers, ...nd offer a chance to explore scenic, ...nspoiled marshland and spot many ...ecies of fish, birds, crustacea, mol-...sks, and plants. In these shallow ...aters paddlers also can stop to fish ...nd gather clams, oysters, scallops, or ...abs. And on guided trips, paddlers can ...ceive kayaking instruction and learn ...out the area's natural history.

During its April-to-November sea-...n, Ride the Wind also offers guide-...oks, apparel, and supplies at its ...cracoke headquarters.

River Runners' Emporium
H.M. DuBose
201 Albemarle Street
Durham, NC 27701
(919) 688-2001
Haw River and other North Carolina rivers
Max. rapids: III-IV

River Runners' Emporium rents ca-noes and kayaks year-round for trips on local rivers, principally the Haw River.

Rock Rest Adventures
Joe Jacob
747 Rock Rest Rd.
Pittsboro, NC 27312
(919) 542-5502
Haw, Cape Fear, Black, Neuse, New, Roanoke, Scuppernong Rivers, Outer Banks coast of NC; Kachemak Bay, Prince William Sound in Alaska; Cape Canaveral and Everglades in Florida
Max. rapids: III
PPA

Rock Rest Adventures provides canoe and sea kayak instruction and guided trips in a way that raises environ-mental concern for the protection of coasts, lakes, and rivers. Canoe and sea kayak courses are offered for the beginner through advanced paddler. Trips include day, weekend, and week-long adventures. All equipment is provided except tents and sleeping bags. The company also offers a canoe livery, guide service and outfitted trips on the Swan Lake and Swanson River canoe trails within the Kenai National Wildlife Refuge, Alaska. Its Kenai Wilderness Outpost is at Box 2348, Soldotna, AK 99660.

Rolling Thunder River Company
Ken and Dina Miller
P.O. Box 88
Almond, NC 28702
(704) 488-2030, (800) 344-5838
Nantahala River, French Broad River, Nolichucky River, Ocoee River, Chattooga River
Max. rapids: III-IV
America Outdoors

Rolling Thunder River Co. runs guided canoe, kayak, and raft trips and rents canoes, kayaks, rafts, and "funyaks" on five rivers in North Carolina, Tennessee, and South Carolina. Trips on the Nantahala have Class II-III rapids, are easy enough for beginners and families, and pass through the beautiful Nantahala Gorge. Full-day, wild-water raft trips are available on the Ocoee. These trips, with Class III and IV rapids, are suitable for anyone age 12 and older. Private canoe and kayak instruction on the Ocoee is also available.

On the Chattooga, Rolling Thunder offers an exciting overnight whitewater canoe trip with Class II-IV rapids, spectacular scenery, and abundant wildlife. No experience is necessary on this guided trip. Finally, a combination French Broad River-Nolichucky River raft trip is available. This 2-day expedition includes a night of camping at one of the company's base camps.

Rolling Thunder's season runs from April to October.

Southern Waterways
David & Melanie Donnell
1450 Brevard Rd.
Asheville, NC 28806
(704) 665-1970
French Broad and Green Rivers
Max. rapids: I-II
PPA

Southern Waterways rents canoes, kayaks, and rafts from April to October for 3-5 hour trips through the celebrate Biltmore Estate. These are excellent floats for families, groups, and people of all ages. During the easy paddle, clients can enjoy a great view of Biltmore House, set amid the rolling hills of the Pisgah National Forest.

Deer, bobcat, wild turkeys, and other wildlife may be visible. Paddlers can also fish for muskie, bass, and catfish.

Turtle Island Ventures
Michael & Virginia Robinson
Box 10563
Wilmington, NC 28405
(910) 686-9011
Salt marsh creeks to undeveloped barrier islands, Cape Fear, Black, Lumber Rivers, Lockwood Folly
Max. rapids: I-II
PPA

Paddling through a salt marsh wilderness teeming with life including over 250 bird species is this outfitter's appeal. Naturalists versed in salt marsh ecology guide kayakers through a maze of creek pointing out 200-year-old cypress trees, spartine grass, herons, egrets, alligators, dolphins, sea urchins, and colorful sponges.

Camping trips may last up to 4 days. Paddling lessons may be taken during the company's year-round season.

SA RAFT

ary Kay Heffernan
). Box 277
owlesburg, WV 26425
00) USA RAFT
*orth Fork Potomac River, Gauley River,
heat River, Tygart River, New River, Upper
ughiogheny River, Nolichucky River, Ocoee
ver, Nantahala River, French Broad River
ax. rapids: II-III
merica Outdoors*

USA Raft offers outings on ten of the
est whitewater rivers in the East — the
ussell Fork in Kentucky; the Upper
oughiogeny in Maryland; the Noli-
ucky, French Broad, and Nantahala in
orth Carolina; the Nolichucky and
coee in Tennessee; and the New,
auley, Cheat, and Tygart in West
irginia.

With this selection of trips, rivers,
d outfitters, USA Raft offers afford-
le outings to suit paddlers of all skill
vels at locations convenient to resi-
nts throughout the Middle Atlantic
d Southeast.

Wildwater Limited

Jim Greiner
P.O. Box 430
Bryson City, NC 28713
(800) 451-9972
*Chattooga, Nantahala, Ocoee, Big Pigeon
Rivers
Max. rapids: V+
America Outdoors*

Wildwater Limited operates in Georgia, North Carolina, South Carolina,
and Tennessee, offering more than a
dozen trip options for paddlers age 8 and
over, ranging from novices to experts.
The Chattooga is a National Wild and
Scenic River, the Nantahala adjoins the
Great Smoky Mountains National Park,
and the Ocoee has been chosen for the
1996 Olympic whitewater events.

The company has served over
400,000 customers in 25 years of operation, and prides itself on its staff, facilities, and safety record. It rents rafts and
kayaks as well as running guided canoe,
kayak and raft trips during a March to-
mid-November season.

North Dakota

Land of Sitting Bull, Lewis and Clark, Custer and Teddy Roosevelt, t state of North Dakota epitomizes the West. Through it glides the mighmissouri in the west and the Red River in the east, dividing it from Minn sota. These two river systems drain most of North Dakota. Out of the we ern Badlands run the Little Missouri, the Knife, the Heart, the Cannonb and Cedar Creek, all emptying into the Missouri on its southbound jou ney. Tributaries of the Red River, which runs northward to Canada's Hu son Bay, include the Pembina, the Goose, the Park and the Sheyenne. T Souris also flows north, from the center of the state, and the James ru from eastern North Dakota into South Dakota.

The prairie state has no whitewater, even in the Badlands where the hig est butte tops 3,500 feet. But the scenery varies widely, from agricultu plains and river bluffs to wooded slopes and rugged hills. Many of Nor Dakota's canoeing waters are seasonal, so paddlers should check wat levels with the state tourism office in Bismarck (1-800-HELLO-ND) befc making plans.

North Dakota's only State Scenic River is the Little Missouri, whid offers a panoramic view of buttes and prairie badlands. This stream can, ho ever, only be paddled in the spring. It provides many recreational opport nities within Theodore Roosevelt National Park and Little Missouri Sta Park, including camping and horseback riding. Dangerous bison roam t Roosevelt park along with mule deer, coyote, red fox and bobcat, while t occasional golden eagle or prairie falcon soars above the river valley.

For those who prefer to canoe later in the season, the Sheyenne is a go bet. Runnable from May through July, this river cuts through rolling hil wide bottomland forests, open prairie, and agricultural land. Lake Ashtabu is well known for its fishing and the scenic river below its dam is especia popular with canoeists, as is the neighboring James.

In the northeast corner of the state, the Pembina meanders through valley full of woodland tranquillity. Pembina Gorge, extending from W halla to the Canadian border, is known to biologists as a meeting-pla of North America's central grasslands and forests. It provides a habitat many unusual plant and animal species. The Pembina's mild white water attracts paddlers for canoeing, rafting and tubing in the spring and early summer. Ashore, moose and elk thrive in the forest.

The Red River along the Minnesota border cuts through farmland and small tracts of prairie rich in native grasses and wildflowers. Fishing is popular among anglers from cities along its route, but canoeing, in May and June, is hampered by many lowhead dams that must be portaged.

The Souris River, which loops down from Canada and returns northward after traversing eighty miles of North Dakota, is a wildlife haven. Thousands of birds stop to feed and rest every year in its three national wildlife refuges, two of which contain guided canoe trails varying from three to 13 miles in length. But here, again, paddlers should watch out for lowhead dams.

Finally, the great Missouri itself is a favorite local playground for canoeists as well as power boaters, waterskiers and fishermen. It provides excellent canoeing from May to September. But state authorities say that because of its swift current it is best suited to experienced paddlers. Its many sandbars and gentle river bluffs make it an attractive float, good for picnicking and sunbathing.

For more detailed broadsheets describing each river's main characteristics, with maps and tables, contact the state's Parks and Recreation Department, 1835 E. Bismarck Expressway, Bismarck, ND 58504-6708, tel. (701) 328-5357.

NORTH DAKOTA

Cross Ranch State Park
North Dakota Parks & Recreation Dept.
HC2, Box 152
Sanger, ND 58567
(701) 794-3731
Missouri River
Max. rapids: None

Cross Ranch State Park rents canoes from May through September. Trips from 1 hour to 3 days are available to beginners or experienced canoeists, with camping available. Wildlife on the majestic Missouri includes Canada geese, other waterfowl, and beaver.

Fort Ransom State Park
North Dakota Parks & Recreation Dept.
5983 Walt Hjelle Parkway
Fort Ransom, ND 58033
(701) 973-4331
Sheyenne River

Fort Ransom State Park rents canoes from May 1 through September for easy, peaceful, novice-level trips in the wooded Sheyenne River valley. It is an unspoiled, uncrowded area where paddlers may spot deer, beavers, ducks, mink, turkeys, and songbirds. Trips last from 2 hours to 2 days and give fishermen a chance to catch roughfish, walleye, and northern pike.

250

Paddle America

Lake Metigoshe State Park

North Dakota Parks & Recreation Dept.
#2 Lake Metigoshe State Park
Bottineau, ND 58318-8044
(701)-263-4651
Lake Metigoshe
Max. rapids: None

Lake Metigoshe State Park is located in the scenic Turtle Mountains and provides canoe rentals from May through September. Visitors can spend the day paddling on Lake Metigoshe, noted for its northern pike, walleye, and perch. The more adventurous can explore School System Lake. Motorized boats are banned from this lake, which makes it an ideal area to view deer, moose, mink, and beaver in their natural habitat. It also contains native mallard, great blue heron and red-necked grebe.

North Dakota State University

Outing Center, Memorial Union
Fargo, ND 58105
(701) 237-8241
BWCA, Crow Wing River
Max. rapids: None

The Outing Center, a non-profit organization at NDSU, offers guided canoe trips and canoe rentals on the Crow Wing River and in Minnesota's Boundary Waters Canoe Area. Guided trips are chiefly for NDSU students, faculty, and staff, who receive preference in making reservations. However, the general public is encouraged to participate on a "space available" basis. Canoe rentals and rentals of full camping equipment are available at very reasonable rates.

Guided trips run from 1-7 days and canoe rentals are by the day or week. Canoeing on both the Crow Wing River and BWCA is easy, flatwater paddling in clear waters with good scenery and fishing for trout, walleye, northern pike, bass, and panfish. The Outing Center's canoe trips and rentals are available from May to October. In the winter, the Center rents cross-country skis and snowshoes.

Ohio

G ung-ho whitewater paddlers go elsewhere in search of thrills, but others find plenty of interesting canoe trails in Ohio. Actually some rivers, even in the flat northwest corner of the state, have rapids rated up to Class IV in springtime or after dam releases. But most Ohio streams offer different appeal, such as wetland canoeing through swampland alive with muskrats, raccoons, waterfowl, hawks and owls. It's a matter of taste.

Popular for family paddling is the Mohican River complex close to the center of the state. The Main Branch and the Black Fork can be paddled year-round, unlike the Clear Fork which is runnable only from December to June. Lake Fork is open ten months of the year, from December to September. Of these four, Clear Fork offers the most unspoiled scenery. This Class I stream runs through Clearfork Gorge, a slice cut out of pine-forested hill country that rates as a National Natural Landmark. Lake Fork is less remote but allows two miles of peaceful paddling before the stream runs into the Main Branch with its mass of canoeists from Black Fork.

The Black Fork, with its riverside campgrounds, restaurants and carryouts, is crowded in the summer season with family paddlers. But just because of its popularity this slow-moving Class I stream — often called the Muddy Fork — may not be everyone's choice. The Main Branch, too, tends to be crowded with Black Fork paddlers in its ten-mile section closest to Loudonville. But then it offers more secluded floating through a wide, forested valley.

South of Springfield is the Little Miami River, Ohio's first stream to be federally designated Wild and Scenic. Regarded by some as the state's prettiest river, the Little Miami attracts thousands of paddlers between April and October each year. During its 105-mile course to the Ohio River it flows mostly between cornfields and wooded hills.

Just north of Springfield is a stretch of the Mad River that ranks as another of Ohio's most popular canoeing streams. Sycamore and cottonwood trees form an overhead canopy as the paddler glides along a narrow channel some two to three feet deep. Despite its name, the Mad River is sane and friendly, a gentle stream of crystal-clear water with few riffles to disturb

OHIO

its surface. It is a fine trout stream, flowing through a wide plain of wheat and cornfields in its northern reaches before entering built-up areas south of Springfield.

The Sandusky and Maumee Rivers in the northwest offer Class III-IV rapids at highwater season. The Sandusky rates as a state scenic river from Upper Sandusky to Fremont. Paddlers enjoy its treelined seclusion and plentiful wildfowl. Where the broad Maumee flows down to Lake Erie at Toledo it offers great fishing, especially at spawning time in April-May. Canoeists more interested in scenery may prefer to stay further upstream, amid the sycamores and cottonwoods of the agricultural plain west of Napoleon. The Maumee is good for family floating and its banks and islands are well stocked with deer and birdlife.

In northeastern Ohio the Grand River provides fast-moving waters in an unspoiled natural setting from April through June.

Barefoot Canoes, Inc.
Bill Barefoot
3565 W. Frederick-Gingham Road
Tipp City, OH 45371
(513) 698-4351
Stillwater River, Great Miami River
Max. rapids: None

Barefoot Canoes, Inc., offers guided and unguided canoe trips of 1-3 days on the Stillwater River and Great Miami River. These scenic, flatwater trips are perfect for families and paddlers of all ages. The rivers wind along unspoiled, tree-lined banks and offer excellent fishing for bass, bluegill, northern pike and catfish. The quiet setting is also good for spotting turtles, ducks, cranes, raccoons, deer, squirrels, and other wildlife.

Barefoot Canoes, which also has liveries in Troy and West Milton, is open from April to October. During this time, the company also offers camping, bonfires, moonlight floats, and field games.

Camp Toodik Campground &
Canoe Livery
Britt & Nancy Young
7700 TR 462
Loudonville, OH 44842
(800) 322-2663
Lake Fork Branch of Mohican River,
Walhonding, Muskingum Rivers
Max. rapids: None
PPA, ARVC

Operating from two locations about 10 miles apart, this is the only canoe livery on the relatively uncrowded and scenic big branch of the Mohican River. The outfitter rents canoes from May 1 through October for trips of 2 hours to a week through farmland, woods, and wetlands with abundant fish and wildlife.

Downstream floats are suited to novices, families, and the physically challenged, while intermediate paddlers enjoy the upstream waters.

The owners' second location is Lake Fork Canoe Livery at 14765 SR3, Loudonville, OH 44842, (419) 994-5484.

Canal Fulton Canoe Livery
Michael G. Thomas
219 W. Cherry St., P.O. Box 458
Canal Fulton, OH 44614
(216) 854-0880
Tuscarawas River, Nimisila Reservoir
Max. rapids: None
PPA

Canal Fulton Canoe Livery rents canoes for scenic trips through heavily wooded areas with plentiful deer, beavers, turtles, and other wildlife. It offers paddling lessons and trips best suited for families, church groups, scouts, and nature lovers. Paddlers can also fish for smallmouth bass, rainbow trout, catfish, and carp.

The outfitter's season runs from May to November 1.

Dillon Lake Water Sports
Ernest & Liz Grimm
6275 Clay Littick Drive
Nashport, OH 43830
(614) 453-7964
Licking River, Dillon Lake
Max. rapids: I-II
PPA

Dillon Lake Water Sports rents canoes and kayaks for easy day trips of up to 6 hours. These are suitable for beginners, with some challenge on the Class I river. The river trips pass through the Black Hand Gorge interpretative nature preserve. Beavers, deer, fox, mink, and many kinds of birds may be observed. Fish include smallmouth and largemouth bass, saugeye, and muskie. The outfitter's season runs from April to October.

Hocking Valley Canoe Livery
Lewis Barbini
31251 Chieftain Dr.
Logan, OH 43138
(614) 385-8685, (800) 683-0386
Hocking River
Max. rapids: I-II
PPA

Hocking Valley Canoe Livery operates guided and unguided tours aboard canoes, kayaks, and rafts on the uncrowded waters of the Hocking River. Paddlers float through one of Ohio's most scenic regions, with abundant plant and wildlife. The run is of easy to moderate difficulty, and offers excellent fishing for smallmouth bass and catfish. The company's season lasts from April until October.

The Great Miami River is acclaimed as one of Ohio's prettiest rivers. Courtesy of Barefoot Canoes, Tipp City, Ohio.

Indian River Canoe Outfitters
Indiana Bob
215 Market St.
Canal Fulton, OH 44614
(800) 226-6349
Tuscarawas River
Max. rapids: None
PPA

Indian River rents canoes and kayaks from April-October for easy trips on the shallow Tuscarawas. The company provides service with a smile and emphasis on local Native American history. These outings, suitable for novice paddlers and families, take canoeists through scenic countryside, tree-shaded amid rolling hills. Freshwater clams, catfish, bluegill, and some bass may be caught and shore wildlife includes beaver, turtle, heron and duck.

Lake Fork Canoe Livery
Nancy Young
14765 SR3
Loudonville, OH 44842
(419) 994-5484, (800) 322-2663
Mohican, Wahonding, Muskingum Rivers
Max. rapids: I-II
PPA

This outfitter rents canoes and kayaks for paddlers to explore a unique former Indian water trail from Lake Erie to the Ohio River. They can also see old canals, active canal locks, and abandoned railroad bridges. Only experienced paddlers should come in the spring, but beginners and families are welcome at other times during the April-November season.

Bass, northern pike, and catfish may be found, and the fields and woods contain heron rookeries.

Mohican Canoe Livery and Fun Center
Doug Shannon
3045 State Rte. 3, Box 263
Loudonville, OH 44842
(419) 994-4097, (419) 994-4020,
(800) MO-CANOE
Mohican River, Black Fork River, Clear Fork River
Max. rapids: None
PPA, *Ohio Canoe Association*

Mohican Canoe Livery and Fun Center rents canoes, kayaks, rafts, and tubes for trips of 2 hours to 2 days on the Mohican, Black Fork, and Clear Fork Rivers. All floats are easy enough for beginners and offer attractive woodland scenery with views of large cliffs, birds, and other river wildlife.

During its April-to-November season, Mohican Canoe Livery and Fun Center also offers horseback riding, a waterslide, go-karts and adventure golf.

Mohican Reservation Campgrounds and Canoeing
Christopher J. Snively
23270 Wally Road
Loudonville, OH 44842
(800) 766-CAMP
Mohican River, Clear Fork River, Black Fork River, Tuscarawas River, Muskingum River
Max. rapids: I-II

Mohican Reservation Campground & Canoeing rents canoes, kayaks, rafts, and tubes for trips of 2 hours to 6 days on the Mohican, Clear Fork, Black Fork, Tuscarawas, and Muskingum Rivers. Paddling is easy on these rivers, allowing families, beginners, and advanced canoeists time to enjoy the area's wooded, hilly scenery and views of deer, raccoons, pheasants, squirrels, buzzards, turkeys, and rabbits. Paddlers can also fish for muskie, walleye, catfish, carp, bass, and sucker.

Tent and R.V. camping is available at riverfront and shaded sites. The campground's facilities include modern restrooms, hot showers, playing fields, a camp store, laundry, catering, and entertainment. Mohican Reservation

The Stillwater River, a scenic, unspoiled flatwater river with good fishing. Courtesy of Barefoot Canoes, Tipp City, Ohio.

Campground & Canoeing is open from April to November.

Mohican Valley Camp & Canoe
Al Bechtel
3069 St. Rte. 3
Loudonville, OH 44842
(800) 682-2663, (419) 994-5204
Blackfork, Mohican Rivers
Max. rapids: I
PPA

This company rents canoes and kayaks for a wide range of trips suitable for everyone from the novice to the seasoned paddler. Floaters explore attractive scenery with rolling hills and many species of birds and other wildlife. Overnight trips with camping are available, and fishing includes smallmouth bass, brown trout, rock bass and catfish.

Morgan's Mad River Outpost
Bob & June Morgan
5605 Lower Valley Pike
Springfield, OH 45502
(513) 882-6925
Mad River
Max. rapids: I-II
PPA

Morgan's offers guided canoe trips and rents canoes, kayaks, rafts, and tubes to paddlers on the clear and sparkling Mad River. Although the water runs fast, floats are suitable for novices. The Mad River ranks as Ohio's only natural trout stream. Its banks feature abundant birdlife. Morgan's season runs April-November.

New World Expeditions
William P. Cacciolfi
209 Xenia Avenue
Yellow Springs, OH 45387
(513) 767-7221
Rivers worldwide
Max. rapids: V+

New World Expeditions offers guided canoe, kayak, raft, and dory trips and rents kayaks. An adventure travel company, New World Expeditions runs trips world-wide for paddlers of all levels of ability. Paddle trips last 1-30 days and offer a range of activities, including fishing, camping, and lessons.

NTR Canoe Livery
Ann Swain
State Route 212
P.O. Box 203
Bolivar, OH 44612
(216) 874-2002
Tuscarawas River
Max. rapids: None

NTR Canoe Livery rents canoes, kayaks, and tubes on the Tuscarawas River for trips of 1-2 days. The trips are easy and scenic, passing through wooded wilderness that offers camping spots and views of deer, beavers, blue herons, and other native wildlife. Paddlers can also enjoy fishing for northern pike, bass, bluegill, and crappie.

Ohio Canoe Tours
Vincent Reis
2894 Daisybrook St.
N. Canton, OH 44720
No phone listed
Little Beaver Creek, E. Branch Mahoning River, Lake Milton, Walhonding River
Max. rapids: I-II
PPA

Ohio Canoe Tours runs 1-day guided trips for canoeists and kayakers through the Gateway to the Appalachians gorge, filled with hemlock and hardwoods. It prides itself on having top-quality equipment and an excellent guide service.

During its April-to-October season, it provides paddling lessons, bass fishing,

and a chance to spot deer, beavers, other mammals, and herons. Its outings are suitable for all swimmers age six or older.

Pleasant Hill Canoe Livery
Michael Dresch
914 State Route 39, Box 10
Perrysville, OH 44864
(419) 938-7777, (800) 442-2663
Mohican, Black Fork Rivers
Max. rapids: None
PPA

Pleasant Hill Canoe Livery rents canoes and kayaks for 1/2- hour to multiday trips on the Black Fork and Mohican Rivers. The rivers are forgiving, suitable for both beginners and experienced paddlers, and offer scenic views of rolling hills and wildlife. Pleasant Hill's most popular trips are on the less-populated Black Fork Branch of the Mohican River. The livery's season runs from April to November.

Raccoon Run Canoe Rental
Thomas Fellenstein
1129 State Road
Geneva, OH 44041
(216) 466-7414, (216) 466-8360
Grand River
Max. rapids: I-II

Raccoon Run Canoe Rental offers guided and unguided 1- and 2-day canoe trips on the scenic and exceptionally clear Grand River. The trips, which are fine for paddlers of all ages and abilities, have stretches that pass through deep, picturesque gorges. Paddlers also can spot deer, beavers, foxes, minks, and raccoons, and anglers can fish for northern pike, muskie, smallmouth bass, trout and crappie. Camping, swimming, and lessons are also available.

Raccoon Run's season is from April to November.

Rivers Edge Outfitters
Rhett and Andrea Rohrer
3928 State Route 42 S
Waynesville, OH 45068
(513) 862-4540, (800) 628-2319
Little Miami River
Max. rapids: I-II
PPA, Ohio Canoe Livery Association,
North American Paddlesport

Rivers Edge Outfitters rents canoes and kayaks for 1-5 day trips on the Little Miami River, a state and nationally designated scenic river. The Little Miami, a classic meandering midwestern river, is suitable for all skill levels and is set in a peaceful landscape of rolling wooded hills, cliffs, gorges, meadows, and fields. In addition to the scenery, paddlers can enjoy fishing for smallmouth bass, rock bass, sunfish, and bluegill, and spotting wildlife, including deer, beavers, muskrats, minks, raccoons, herons, ducks, geese, hawks, and owls.

The livery, which adjoins the 800-acre Spring Valley Wilderness Area, has a spacious riverfront campground with a modern bathhouse, paddle sports shop, and picnic area. Also available during the April-to-October season are hayrides and a "float and feast" trip that concludes with a barbecue or pig roast.

Riverside Landing
Hancock Park District
819 Park Street
Findlay, OH 45840
(419) 423-6952
Blanchard River
Max. rapids: None

Hancock Park District Riverside Landing rents canoes for 1-day trips on the Blanchard River. The river has no rapids but is not suitable for novices, as paddling skills are required to skirt occasional logjams. Trips pass through scenic, unspoiled parkland and surrounding woods, offering views of deer, raccoons, and squirrels, and fishing for white bass, carp, bluegill, and catfish.

The park also offers hiking and biking trails and primitive camping.

The park, open year-round, rents canoes between May and September.

Willow Grove Marina
Henry & Barb Cordray
14217 Painesville Warren Rd.
Painesville, OH 44077
(216) 254-4499, (216) 639-1265
Grand and Cuyahoga Rivers, Ladue Reservoir
Max. rapids: I-II

Willow Grove offers guided canoe trips and rents both canoes and kayaks to paddlers on the wild and scenic Grand River and in the wetlands of the Cuyahoga. These 1-day outings provide interesting scenery and glimpses of wildlife ranging from beavers and raccoons to ducks and woodchuck.

These trips also offer fishing for walleye, trout, bass, northern pike, catfish, and panfish. The outfitter's season runs from May through October.

Oklahoma

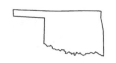

Two great river systems drain Oklahoma, the Red and the Arkansas. The Red River, which forms the state's boundary with Texas, draws water from southern Oklahoma. Most of the north and east of the state is drained by the Arkansas River and its long tributaries that reach into the Panhandle.

For canoeists, the best paddling is in eastern Oklahoma, notably on the Illinois River above and below the town of Tahlequah. The Illinois, running through the heart of the Oklahoma Ozarks with their clear, swift streams and steep-sided river valleys. Especially on the upper 70 miles designated scenic, floaters enjoy interesting and sometimes challenging waters amid oak-hickory forest rife with wildlife.

The Illinois has easy Class II rapids with waves up to three feet, and wide, clear channels. Although water levels vary, the Illinois is a river for all seasons. There are many developed campsites along the way, which are shown on maps of the river put out by the Oklahoma Scenic Rivers Commission, P.O. Box 292, Tahlequah, OK 74465, tel. (800) 299-3251. The commission's "floater's guide" leaflet says that 80,000 canoe trips are taken on the Illinois every year. Many of these paddlers are fishermen, for the river is said to be one of the few in Oklahoma that have the clean, clear conditions needed by smallmouth bass. All told, nearly 70 kinds of fish populate the Illinois.

Spring River canoe trail in the extreme northeast corner of the state runs through three separate state parks. These contain boat ramps, campgrounds and other facilities in an attractive Ozark foothills region close to a popular Oklahoma resort, the Grand Lake O' the Cherokees.

Grand Lake itself covers nearly 60,000 acres and boasts ten state parks, many marinas, campgrounds, accommodations and restaurants. Power boats, waterskiers and sailboats rule the waves, but canoeists can find sheltered coves to paddle in peace. Fish are plentiful: crappie, three species of bass, channel catfish, bluegill and hybrid striper. Grand Lake's chief attraction for the naturalist is that it is a favorite stopping-place for migrating white pelicans. The occasion is marked with a Pelican Festival in September.

Fort Gibson Lake, further south between Tulsa and Tahlequah, also attracts paddlers. Like Grand Lake, it has many tourist facilities: 26 parks and recreational areas, lakeside cabins, boat docks and restaurants. Fort Gibson Lake is well supplied with black bass, white bass and catfish for what is claimed to be some of the best fishing in the country. The Oklahoma Department of Wildlife Conservation manages a 4,500-acre waterfowl refuge and a 17,300-acre public hunting area full of deer, quail, dove, duck, geese and rabbit.

Arrowhead Camp
Bill and Mary Blackard
HD 61, Box 201
Tahlequah, OK 74464
(918) 456-1140, (800) 749-1140
Illinois River
Max. rapids: I-II

Arrowhead Camp offers canoe rentals for trips of 1-3 days on the Illinois River. These tours pass through a scenic region of bluffs, hills, and woods. The Illinois is clean and clear, with good fishing for catfish, bass, and crappie. Along its banks are deer, raccoons, rabbits, birds, and other wildlife. Paddling is easy on these trips, which have gentle Class I-II rapids.

During its May-September season, Arrowhead offers cabin rentals, bunkhouse lodging, and both tent and R.V. camping. A camp store with ice, groceries, tackle, and other supplies is also available.

Blue Hole Canoe Floats, Inc.
Chet and Susan Brewington
Route 1, Box 144
Quapaw, OK 74363
(918) 542-6344
Spring River
Max. rapids: None

Blue Heron Canoe Floats rents canoes for trips of 2 hours to 2 days along a 29-mile stretch of the Spring River. These trips are scenic, passing through a region of bluffs and pine forest inhabited by deer, cranes, and eagles. Also, the river boasts good fishing for crappie, bass, and catfish.

These Spring River trips, available from May to September, are on flat water and are fine for beginners, families and groups, as well as experienced paddlers.

Cedar Valley Camp
Richard King
Star Route 1, Box 101
Proctor, OK 74457
(918) 456-4094
Illinois River
Max. rapids: I-II

Cedar Valley Camp offers guided canoe trips and canoe rentals on the Illinois River. This small family-owned business with but 20 canoes specializes in low prices and personal service. Its trips, with mainly Class I rapids, are fine for families and beginners as well as more experienced paddlers. Trips last from 1-4 days and pass through a scenic, heavily wooded region around Sparrowhawk Mountain. Along the way, paddlers can view abundant wildlife, including deer, foxes, eagles, and great blue herons. Anglers can enjoy excellent fishing in the Illinois' clear spring-fed waters for a wide variety of fish, ranging from smallmouth bass to 50-lb. flathead catfish.

Cedar Valley Camp's season lasts from Memorial Day to Labor Day. However, trips in the early spring and late fall are available by reservation.

OKLAHOMA

Paddling on the Illinois River. Courtesy of Eagle Bluffs Resorts, Tahlequah, Oklahoma.

Diamond Head Resort
Tom Eastham
HC 61, Box 264
Tahlequah, OK 74464
(800) 722-2411
Illinois River
Max. rapids: I-II

Diamond Head Resort rents canoes and rafts for trips of 1-3 days on the Illinois River. These trips are easy outings suitable for families and novices, as well as experienced paddlers. Along the Illinois, paddlers can enjoy fishing, camping, swimming, and views of rocky bluffs and wildlife, including deer, raccoons, and birds. Diamond Head's season runs from April to October.

Eagle Bluff Resorts
Jeff and Vicki Bennett
H.C. 61, Box 230
Tahlequah, OK 74464
(800) 366-3031
Illinois River
Max. rapids: I-II

Eagle Bluff Resorts offers guided and unguided canoe and raft trips of 1-4 days on the Illinois River. These pass through a scenic region of rolling hills, bluffs, and hardwood forests. With only minor rapids, the Illinois is easy paddling for novices and families as well as experienced canoeists. While underway, paddlers can also enjoy fishing for brown bass and catfish, and glimpsing occasional deer, beavers, and other wildlife.

Eagle Bluff Resorts, open from April-October, provides riverside tent and R.V. camping, cabin rentals, a modern shower house, a guest lodge, snack shop, and catered riverside meals.

Hanging Rock Camp
Jim & Linda Wofford
HC61, Box 199-2
Tahlequah, OK 74464
(918) 456-3088, (800) 375-3088
Illinois River
Max. rapids: I-II

Easy family floats on a scenic river with clear water, wooded banks, and good fishing are offered by this company from April to October. As the river winds through hill country with occasional caves and cliffs, its rapids are very mild and therefore suitable for all ages.

Deer, eagle, water fowl, and wild turkey may be seen, and fishing is for catfish, bass, walleye, crappie, and drum.

Kamp Paddle Trails

Katherine and David Pickle
Route 1, Box 1320
Watts, OK 74964
(918) 723-3546
Illinois River, Lake Tenkiller
Max. rapids: I-II

Kamp Paddle Trails is a summer camp for boys and girls which also rents canoes to the general public. The camp, set on the Illinois River in the foothills of the Ozarks, specializes in teaching young people to canoe, camp, enjoy nature study and protect the environment. Camp sessions run from the start of school summer vacation through the first week in August. From then until November 1, Kamp Paddle rents its canoes to others, for trips of 1-4 days. Canoe rentals are also available to the public in the spring and early summer, provided spring rains do not make the river dangerously high.

Paddlers can run 146 gentle Class I-II rapids over a 75-mile stretch of the Illinois, enjoying free camping, and varied fishing amid profuse wildlife. Trips are not difficult but require previous river paddling experience.

Peyton's Place Canoes

Route HC-61, Box 231
Tahlequah, OK 74464
(918) 456-3847, (800) 359-0866
Illinois River
Max. rapids: I-II

Peyton's Place has both canoes and rafts for use on the scenic Illinois River with its rich wildlife and fishing. The oldest canoe camp on the river, Peyton's has a campground, airconditioned cottages, a convenience store and shuttle equipment.

Fine for family floats year-round, the clean river is good for swimming as well as bass, bream and channel cat fishing. Trips are through beautiful woodland

with deer, beavers, raccoons, herons, egrets, and eagles.

Tenkiller Valley Ranch

Larry and Paula Tharp
P.O. Box 231
Gore, OK 74435
(918) 489-5895, (800) 299-5895
Illinois River
Max. rapids: I-II

Tenkiller Valley Ranch rents canoes and rafts for 1- day trips on a 12-mile stretch of the Lower Illinois River below the Lake Tenkiller Dam. This stretch features sparkling clear waters, scenic bluffs and woods, gravel bars, and several swimming holes complete with rope swings. Fishing is especially good on this stretch, which is stocked with trout, and also contains abundant striped bass, walleye, pike, black bass, crappie, channel catfish, and sand bass. Sharp-eyed paddlers may also see deer, squirrels, red foxes, raccoons, beavers, muskrats, ferrets, cranes, herons, and kingfishers.

The outfitter's trips, offered from May-September, have only minor rapids and are easy enough for beginners and families.

Oregon

Rugged Oregon is surrounded on three sides by water — the Pacific to the west, the mighty Columbia River to the north and the Snake River along much of the Idaho state line to the east. Within these borders, this land of forests and mountains contains other rivers that invite exploration. Among them are the whitewater Rogue River in the southwest, the John Day, Oregon's longest river, the Deschutes in the northwest, and the Owyhee in the southeast. Paddlers can find daunting rapids with names like Bodacious Bounce and Widowmaker, as well as white sandy beaches, deep gorges, sparkling clear water, desert canyons, and endless pine forests. Oregon's abundant wildlife includes bighorn sheep, bear, deer, mink, otter, bald and golden eagles, osprey, and heron.

The Rogue River is a charter member of the National Wild and Scenic Rivers club founded by Congress in 1968. The floater who puts in near Grants Pass can spend several days paddling through a wilderness of forested canyons, rock slides, cascading side streams and ferny grottoes. Its numerous rapids are mostly Class III-IV, and thrilling for seasoned rafters as well as comparative novices. The 33-mile wild section of the Rogue is so popular that permits for individual boaters in the season from June 1 through September 15 are issued by lottery. Chances of a winning ticket are said to average one in ten, so it is easier to explore the river by booking with an outfitter. Fishing for steelhead begins in early September and lasts until mid November, while salmon are caught in spring and summer.

The Deschutes cuts through the arid desert of central Oregon on its way northward to join the Columbia. In this semi-wilderness the paddler floats past desert hills and rocky canyons. With rapids no fiercer than Class III+ the Deschutes is good for families and experienced floaters alike.

Only expert paddlers should run the Middle Owyhee with its Class IV-V rapids. Of these adventurers, only the most daring attempt the notorious Widowmaker rapids in the steepsided canyon. Below this obstacle the walls of the chasm widen and for the last seven miles of the trip down to Rome on US 95 the boater has to paddle on the flat, often against strong afternoon headwinds.

While the Middle Owyhee can only be run between March and May, the Lower Owyhee — from Rome to Owyhee Lake — is runnable from April through June. This downstream section is also less fearsome, with somewhat easier rapids rated Class III-IV. It is therefore accessible to thrill-seeking novices as well as experts. Its pristine desert canyon wilderness, with its multi-colored rock turrets, offers interesting geology as well as birdlife.

Another whitewater trip of similar excitement is the North Umpqua — the name derived from an Indian word meaning satisfaction. Designated recently as a state and federal scenic waterway, the Umpqua has become one of Oregon's favorite whitewater rivers. It is an ideal weekend outing since the trip down its back-to-back Class III-IV rapids lasts only 1-2 days. Runnable from April through July, the North Umpqua winds its way through a narrow, forested gorge. Its waters near Steamboat Creek have long been beloved by anglers including Zane Grey, who wrote books on game fishing as well as his popular novels of the American West.

Gentler floating through grand scenery is to be found on the 275-mile John Day River. The Upper John Day between Service Creek and Clarno in northcentral Oregon is normally floatable only in April and May. But it offers Class II-III rapids and superb views of cattle ranching country amid the Blue Mountains. The Lower John Day from Clarno down to Cottonwood Canyon Bridge is runnable until late July and has easy Class I-II rapids for the novice. It runs through semi-arid canyonland where the paddler feels the solitude of Oregon's great wide spaces.

OREGON

Adventure Whitewater
Gene Allred, M.D.
P.O. Box 321
Yreka, CA 96097
(800) 888-5632
Salmon River, Scott River, Klamath River, Trinity River
Max. rapids: V+
America Outdoors

Adventure Whitewater offers guided kayak and raft trips for gentle Class II to expert Class V runs. Trips feature great whitewater and spectacular mountain scenery of snow-capped peaks, deep granite gorges, and heavily forested slopes. Set in the Marble Mountains and Trinity Alps, the trips offer fishing for trout, steelhead, and salmon and chances to view bears, deer, coyotes, otters, eagles, ospreys, and herons. The company has personable, intelligent, highly-qualified guides.

All Rivers Adventures & Co.
Bruce Carlson
P.O. Box 12
Cashmere, WA 98815
(509) 782-2254, (800) 74 FLOAT
Deschutes, Wenatchee, Tieton, White Salmon Rivers
Max. rapids: III-IV

All Rivers Adventures offers guided raft trips on the Wenatchee, Tieton, White Salmon, and Deschutes Rivers.

These trips pass through the beautiful North Cascades, featuring scenic forest, canyons, wildflowers, and abundant wildlife, including deer, eagles, ospreys, minks, otters, ducks, herons, and geese. Anglers also can fish for salmon, steelhead, and rainbow trout.

Trips last 1-3 days, run between April and September, and range widely in difficulty, from scenic, flatwater trips to Class IV whitewater. All Rivers Adventures also offers parties, barbecue grills, campfires, day care, volleyball, moonlight floats, inflatable kayak trips, and scenic floats led by naturalist guides.

American River Touring Association
Steve Welch
24000 Casa Loma Rd.
Groveland, CA 95321
(800) 323-2782, (209) 962-7873
Rogue River, Illinois River, Umqua River, Green River, Yampa River, Colorado River, Middle Fork and Main Salmon Rivers, Selway River, Merced River, Tuolumne River, Klamath River
Max. rapids: V+
America Outdoors, Oregon Guides and Packers, Idaho Outfitters and Guides, Utah Guides and Outfitters

ARTA offers a total of 16 raft trips in five Western states. The trips, in California, Oregon, Utah, Idaho, and Arizona, are by oar rafts, paddle rafts, oar/paddle combination rafts, and inflatable canoes.

Most trips are of Class III difficulty and appropriate for novices and families, as well as those with more experience. Other trips of up to V+ difficulty challenge even the most advanced paddler. Depending on the location, the trips feature such added attractions as wildflowers, side streams, swimming holes, Indian ruins, warm water, abundant wildlife, good hiking and fishing, and hot springs.

ARTA, a non-profit company, also offers whitewater schools, professional guide training, and family discounts.

Davis Whitewater Expeditions
Lyle Davis
Box 86
Winnemucca, NV 89445
(800) 261-9451, (702) 623-2048
Snake, Owyhee, Lower Salmon Rivers
Max. rapids: V

Davis Whitewater Expeditions offers guided kayak and raft trips on the Owyhee River, on the Snake River through Hells Canyon, and through the Gorge of the Lower Salmon River. These tours pass through deep, narrow, high-desert canyons, offering pristine wilderness; excellent fishing for trout, bass, catfish, and sturgeon; swimming, and a chance to spot bears, otters, elk, goats, sheep, and raptors.

Trips are small and personal, provide good food and last 3-6 days. Davis floats, which run between April and October, vary greatly in difficulty from gentle, scenic excursions to very demanding Class V adventures. Both oar-powered and paddle trips are available.

ECHO: The Wilderness Company
Dick Linford and Joe Daly
6529 Telegraph Avenue
Oakland, CA 95609
(510) 652-1600, (800) 652-ECHO (3246)
Rogue, Main Salmon, Middle Fork Salmon, Tuolumne, American Rivers
Max. rapids: III-IV
Oregon Guides and Packers Association, America Outdoors

ECHO runs guided trips on the Rogue in Oregon; the Middle and Main Salmon in Idaho, and the Tuolumne and South Fork American in California. The company has 1-11 day trips available for paddlers at all skill levels. It offers a variety of boats, including paddle rafts, oar rafts, oar/paddle rafts, and inflatable kayaks.

ECHO also offers a large number of special trips, including White (and Red) Wine and Whitewater, Bluegrass on Whitewater, River Trips for Kids, the Rogue String Quartet, Yoga Workshop,

Rafters tackle Class IV "Blossom Bar Rapid" on the Rogue River. Courtesy of Wildwater Adventures, Eugene, Oregon.

and Aegean Odyssey on the Turkey Coast. ECHO's season runs from April to September.

Hells Canyon Adventures, Inc.
Bret Armacost
P.O. Box 159
Homestead Road
Oxbow, OR 97840
(800) 422-3568, (503) 785-3352
Snake River
Max. rapids: III-IV
America Outdoors, Idaho Outfitters & Guides

The company combines rafting with power boating to offer trips through some of the largest rapids in Hells Canyon. Guests can take a raft trip down some of the canyon's most famous rapids and return upstream aboard a jet boat, all within a day. Jet boat tours enable passengers of all ages to examine the remains of an Indian village, pictographs, an abandoned homesteaders' ranch, and other attractions in the deepest part of Hells Canyon.

Guests can fish for trout, bass, sturgeon, crappie, and catfish and swim in the warm water. Goats, sheep, elk and deer frequent the canyon shores.

James Henry River Journeys
James Katz
P.O. Box 807
Bolinas, CA 94924
(415) 868-1836, (800) 786-1830
Rogue River, Stanislaus River, Carson River,
Upper Klamath River, Colorado River,
Tatshenini-Alsek River
Max. rapids: III-IV
Idaho Outfitters and Guides

James Henry River Journeys runs guided canoe, kayak, and raft floats in California, Arizona, Idaho, Oregon, and Alaska. In Oregon, trips of 3, 4- and 5-days run on the Class III Rogue. Trips in Idaho, of 4, 5- or 6-days, run on the Class III-IV Main Salmon. In California, the outfitter offers trips on the Stanislaus, East Fork of the Carson, and the Lower Klamath. In Arizona, the company runs Grand Canyon trips, and in Alaska it offers a natural history expedition on the Tatshenshini-Alsek Rivers. (See separate state listings.)

Many special-interest trips are also available. These include Salmon River Bluegrass, Country, Folk and Cajun Music Trips; Whitewater Workshops; Organizational Development and Teambuilding; Wine Tasting and Gourmet

Kayaker David Gilmore jumps a 15-ft waterfall on Brice Creek in an inflatable kayak. Photo by Melinda Allan, courtesy of Wildwater Adventures, Eugene, Oregon.

Cuisine; Lodge Trips on the Rogue and Salmon; Rogue and Salmon Natural History Trips; Alaska Nature Photography; and Alaska Wilderness Literature.

All trips run through especially scenic wilderness areas and are carefully planned to move at a leisurely pace, allowing ample time for side hikes, fishing, photography, and general relaxation. Participation is open to anyone active and in good health. The company's season runs from May to September.

Jim's Oregon Whitewater, Inc.
Jim & Jane Berl
56324 McKenzie Highway
McKenzie Bridge, OR 97413
(541) 822-6003
McKenzie, Deschutes, North Umpqua Rivers
Max. rapids: III-IV

Jim's Oregon Whitewater offers exciting whitewater raft floats and fishing trips for trout, steelhead, or salmon on some of Oregon's most scenic rivers. The whole family, from novices to experts, can enjoy these floats, which range from 1/2-5 days and are led by experienced guides with safety as their top concern. The outfitter's camps are very comfortable, with hearty riverside meals. The company can handle large groups and customize to meet any need.

O.A.R.S.
George Wendt
P.O. Box 67
Angels Camp, CA 95222
(209) 736-4677, (800) 446-7238 (CA), (800) 346-6277 (U.S)
Rogue, San Juan, American,
Cal-Salmon, Merced, Stanislaus,
Tuolumne, Colorado, Snake, Salmon and
Middle Fork Salmon Rivers
Max. rapids: V+
America Outdoors

O.A.R.S. runs guided dory, raft and kayak trips in five Western states. It offers tours in California on the American, Cal-Salmon, Merced, Stanislaus and Tuolumne Rivers; in Oregon on the Rogue; in Arizona on the Colorado; in Wyoming on the Snake, and in Utah on the San Juan River. These outings last 1-13 days and, depending on the class of river, are fine for children, novices, families, intermediate, and expert rafters. O.A.R.S. trips run between April and October and provide fishing, swimming, camping, side hikes, wildlife viewing and other activities.

Oregon River Experiences
Craig Wright
2 Jefferson Pkwy #D7
Lake Oswego, OR 97035
(800) 827-1358, (503) 697-8133
Rogue, Salmon, Deschutes,
Grande Ronde, John Day, McKenzie,
Owyhee, Santiam Rivers
Max. rapids: III-IV
America Outdoors

Oregon River Experiences runs a wide variety of guided kayak, raft and dory trips on exciting Class III rivers with a few Class IV spring trips for thrill-seekers. Clear, cold, uncrowded rivers traverse a pristine wilderness with scenery ranging from coastal forest to desert.

The outfitter says its Class III floats are suitable for families. With camping available, trips last up to 6 days and allow paddlers to fish for trout, salmon, cutthroat and steelhead. Bear, otter, deer, eagles and other diverse wildlife may be seen.

Outdoor Adventures
Bob Volpert
P.O. Box 1149
Point Reyes, CA 94956
(415) 663-8300
Tuolumne River, Kern River, Salmon River,
Rogue River
Max. rapids: V+
America Outdoors, Idaho Outfitters and
Guides, Oregon Outfitters Association

Outdoor Adventures specializes in guided raft trips and raft rentals on federally designated wild and scenic rivers in Idaho, Oregon, and California. In Oregon, 3- and 4-day trips are available on the Rogue River, featuring lively rapids, wonderful hiking trails, and abundant wildlife. On these trips, the last night is spent at Half Moon Bar, a rustic lodge by the river where paddlers can enjoy hot showers, comfortable beds, and home-cooked meals.

The company's season is from April to September.

Ouzel Outfitters
Kent Wickham
Box 827
Bend, OR 97709
(503) 385-5497, (800) 788-RAFT
*Rogue River, Owyhee River, North Umpqua
River, Deschutes River, McKenzie River,
Salmon*
Max. rapids: III-IV
Oregon Guides and Packers

Ouzel Oufitters specializes in trips of
1-5 days on the "loveliest and liveliest"
rives in the Northwest. These rivers
include the Rogue, North Umpqua,
McKenzie, Lower and Middle Owyhee,
and Deschutes Rivers in Oregon, and
the Lower Salmon in Idaho. All trips
but the Middle Owyhee runs have class
III-IV rapids and are fine for families
and guests of all levels of experience to
paddle in rafts, inflatable kayaks, or
guide-accompanied, "row-your-own"
oar-rafts. The Middle Owyhee run, with
class IV-V rapids, is a challenging, expedition-like trip for adventurous, experienced rafters only.

Ouzel Outfitters' trips run between
May and September. Depending on the
river traveled, guests can view bears,
deer, eagles, and otters, and fish for bass
trout, steelhead, and salmon.

Rapid River Rafters
Martin Smith
Box 8231
Bend, OR 97708
(800) 962-3327, (503) 283-1514
Lower Deschutes, McKenzie Rivers
Max. rapids: III-IV
America Outdoors, Oregon Guides & Packer

Rapid River Rafters offers professionally guided whitewater tours for beginning to experienced rafters, using
self-bailing paddle boats with footcups
for improved stability, safety, and excitement. Operating from April 1-October
15, the company provides scenic runs
through high desert canyons with starlit
nights or old growth forests resplendent
with Douglas fir and hanging mosses.
Wildlife is plentiful and diverse and
geologic formations are impressive.
Paddling lessons, swimming, and fishing

Paddle rafting. Courtesy of Ouzel Outfitters, Bend, Oregon.

re available on 1-3 day trips suitable for
guests aged 8 to 80.

River Adventure Float Trips
Mel and Diane Norrick
P.O. Box 841
Grants Pass, OR 97526
(503) 476-6493, (800) 790-RAFT
Rogue River
Max. rapids: III-IV
America Outdoors, Oregon Guides and
Packers

River Adventure Float Trips runs
guided raft and dory trips on the Rogue
River in southern Oregon. These oar-
boat trips, of 1-4 days, are exciting but
not strenuous. However, for those who
want to paddle, the company brings inflatable kayaks for guests to use along
select stretches. While underway, guests
can enjoy wilderness scenery with views
of woods, canyons, eagles, ospreys,
herons, egrets, deer, and, occasionally,
bears, minks, and otters. Anglers also
relish the Rogue's excellent fishing for
steelhead, salmon, and sturgeon.

On multi-day trips, guests can camp
or stay in rustic, comfortable river
lodges. Fall steelhead fishing trips are
also available. River Adventure's season
runs from May to November.

River Outfitter, Inc.
Dave Helfrich
47555 McKenzie Hwy.
Vida, OR 97488
(541) 896-3786
McKenzie, Rogue, Owyhee, Middle Fork of
Salmon, Lower Main Salmon Rivers.
Max. rapids: III-IV
America Outdoors

Luxury guided fishing trips in comfortable McKenzie driftboats are the
specialty of River Outfitter, a company
operated by three generations of the
Helfrich family. It sends a supply boat
ahead on camping trips to set up camp,
and its professional guides serve three
delectable meals a day.

Aboard custom-designed rafts as well
as driftboats, guests float through desert
canyons, past forests and Indian petro-

Rafting on the Owyhee River in Oregon, a great wilderness trip in April or May. Courtesy of
Turtle River Rafting Company, Mt. Shasta, California.

Kayaker demonstrates a brace while "hole riding" on the McKenzie River. Photo by Melinda Allan, courtesy of Wildwater Adventures, Eugene, Oregon.

glyphs. Smallmouth bass and trout may be caught from July-September, steelhead from September-November. Trips last up to 1-6 days, and the season starts in May.

River Trips Unlimited, Inc.
Irv Urie
4140 Dry Creek Rd.
Medford, OR 97504-9253,
(800) 460-3865
Rogue, Chetco, Elk, Umpqua, Coquille Rivers
Max. rapids: III-IV
America Outdoors, Oregon Guides &
Packers, Rogue River Guides Assn.

River Trips Unlimited offers guided kayak, raft, and dory trips of 1/2-4 days, primarily on the wild and scenic section of the Rogue River. One of the original Wild and Scenic rivers, the Rogue is a great challenge to boaters in kayaks, rafts, and drift boats. It is also one of the West's top fishing rivers, containing four kinds of salmon and summer-run steelhead, rainbow, and cutthroat trout.

River Trips, celebating its 30-year anniversary and one of the largest river fishing outfitters in Oregon, claims 90-95 per cent repeat and referral business. Its outings, available year-round, are suitable for people age 6 to 90.

Rogue River Raft Trips, Inc.
B.A. & Elaine Hanten
8500 Galice Road
Merlin, OR 97532
(541) 476-3825, (800) 826-1963,
FAX (541) 476-4953
Rogue River
Max. rapids: III-IV
American Outdoor Assn., Oregon Outdoor Assn.

In business since 1967, Rogue River Raft Trips runs guided raft and dory floats amid the quiet solitude of a beautful pine forested canyon. The limited-access Rogue is a great family paddling river, unique in that it has lodges along the way with clean beds and showers daily.

...addle rafters at "Martin's Rapid" on the McKenzie River. Courtesy of Wildwater Adventures, ...ugene, Oregon.

The company's people-oriented ...uides set out to make everyone's river ...xperience enjoyable. Rafting may be ...njoyed on 3-4 day trips from May to ...eptember, and fishing for salmon and ...eelhead until November. Deer, bear, ...tter, mink, blue heron, osprey, golden ...d bald eagles may be seen.

...OW (River Odysseys West), Inc.
...eter Grubb
...O. Box 579-PA
...oeur d'Alene, ID 83814
...08) 765-0841, (800) 451-6034
...ake River
...ax. rapids: III-IV
...merica Outdoors, Idaho Outfitters and
...uides Association, Oregon Guides and
...ckers Association

ROW, one of the country's best-
...nown outfitters, offers a wide array of
...ips on Idaho and Oregon rivers to suit
...dventurers of all ages and levels of abil-
...y. Trips vary in length from 1-17 days
...d offer wilderness scenery ranging
...om desert to high alpine terrain.

In addition to its diverse offerings,
...OW also takes particular pride in the
...uality of its guides and its annual
..."amily Focus" trips, which are designed

with special activities for children. On
ROW's trips, which run between May
and October, paddlers may see bears,
moose, bighorn sheep, mountain goats,
river otters, deer, elk, and eagles. Fishing
is for cutthroat and rainbow trout, smallmouth bass, and sturgeon.

Wapiti River Guides
Gary Lane
Box 1125
Riggins, ID 83549
(208) 628-3523, (800) 488-9872
Grande Ronde River, Owyhee River,
Salmon River, rivers throughout Alaska
Max. rapids: V+
Oregon Guides and Packers Association,
Idaho Outfitters and Guides Association

Wapiti River Guides, with trips in
Idaho, Oregon, and Alaska, specializes
in small personalized trips of moderate
difficulty "for ages 3 to 103, families,
and nature lovers." The outfitter's trips
are distinctive, too, for their guides'
emphasis on natural history and Native
American culture, and for the fine
scenery, which includes caves, spires, pictographs, petroglyphs, and historic sites.

Trips, ranging in length from 1-12
days, also allow time for interesting side
hikes and viewing elk, deer, bald eagles,
bobcats, cougars, bears, bighorn sheep,
minks and other wildlife. Fishing is for
steelhead, trout, and bass.

Whitewater Voyages
William McGinnis
P.O. Box 20400
El Sobrante, CA 94820-0400
(509) 222-5994, (800) 488-RAFT
Rogue, Colorado, Kern, Merced,
Tuolumne, Cache Creek, American,
Yuba, Klamath, Stanislaus, Trinity, Middle
Fork and Salmon Rivers
Max. rapids: III-IV
America Outdoors, American River
Recreation Association

Whitewater Voyages offers an extensive array of trips, with guided oar- and
paddle-boat runs in California, Arizona,
Oregon, and Idaho. Trips by kayak and
raft range in length from 1-5 days and in
difficulty from Class II to Class V. With
runs on nine Wild and Scenic Rivers
and on more California rivers than any
other outfitter, Whitewater Voyages has
trips for paddlers of all levels of experience.

The outfitter also has specialty trips,

including whitewater schools, family
trips, low-cost river-cleanup trips,
"teambuilding" trips and excursions in
the former Soviet Union to paddle with
Russians as part of project R.A.F.T.

Wild Water Adventures
Al Law, Melinda Allan
P.O. Box 249
Creswell, OR 97426
(503) 895-4465, (800) 289-4534
Rogue, Owyhee, Deschutes, McKenzie, John
Day, Klickitat, North Umpqua, Grande
Ronde, Upper Klamath, and North Santiam
Rivers
Max. rapids: V+
Oregon Guides and Packers Associaiton

Wild Water Adventures specializes in
running guided and unguided inflatable
kayak trips on wilderness rivers. Trips in
rafts and inflatable kayaks range in
length from 1/2-9 days and run on rivers
ranging from mountain streams to desert
waterways and from scenic floats to
crashing whitewater. On these trips, in
addition to paddling, guests can fish,
view Indian pictographs and pioneer ruins, and spot deer, eagles, otters, hawks,
minks, beavers, and other wildlife.

During the season, which runs from
March to November, and year-round for
"wetsuiters," guests can also take inflatable kayak lessons, learning brace
strokes, ferrying, river rescue, and how
to "read" rivers. Kayaking students can
enjoy instruction by Melinda Allan,
coauthor of the *Inflatable Kayak Hand-*
book.

Wilderness Adventures
Dean Munroe
P.O. Box 938
Redding, CA 96099
(800) 323-7238
Upper Klamath River, Cal-Salmon River,
Scott River, Wooley Creek
Max. rapids: V+

Wilderness Adventures runs a
number of remarkable trips on rivers
along the California-Oregon border.
Among the unusual offerings is a raft

ip begun on the Class V Woodley
reek after a horseback ride into the
Marble Mountain Wilderness. Another
xciting trip, called "Hell and High
Water," combines all the Class V sec-
ons of the Salmon, Scott and Upper
lamath into a weekend trip.

Trips range in length from 1-4 days,
in between April and October, and are
or intermediate to advanced paddlers.
et in wilderness, trips offer fishing for
out and views of eagles, ospreys,
inks, otters, and beavers.

Wilderness River Outfitters
. Bruce Greene
567 Main St.
pringfield, OR 97477
503) 726-9471
McKenzie, Willamette, Umpqua & Rogue Riv-
rs (Oregon), Lower Main Salmon River
daho)
Max. rapids: V+

Wilderness River Outfitters, open
anuary-December, offers easy to diffi-
ult guided raft trips suitable for every-
ne. These trips, of 1-6 days, emphasize
afety and pampering guests with gour-
net meals. Knowledgeable guides escort
roups through canyons with old-growth
r trees and mountain views.

Deer, bears, beavers, eagles, and
erons may be seen, and trout, salmon,
eelhead, and bass lurk below the
ver's surface. Camping is available and
uests can enjoy clear, refreshing swim-
ing holes.

Wy-East Expeditions
Michael Gehrman
6700 Cooper Spur Rd.
Mt. Hood, OR 97041
(503) 352-6457
Deschutes, John Day, Rogue, Columbia &
Willamette Rivers. Also Puget Sound.
Max. rapids: III-IV
Deschutes Public Outfitters, Oregon Guides
& Packers

Wy-East Expeditions, named after a
legendary son of the Indian "Great
Spirit," offers guided canoe, raft, and
drift boat trips on a wide variety of
waters, from wild rivers to sea estuaries.
These excursions are said to be suited to
"anyone who can ride two hours in a car
or would like the thrill of mountain
climbing." Trips last up to 6 days, with
camping and swimming.

Fishing trips in search of smallmouth
bass, sturgeon, trout, and steelhead are
run on several rivers. The company also
specializes in authentic dugout canoes,
using a 51-foot replica of a Kwakiuti war
canoe, which carries 35 people, 24 of
them paddling. The season runs from
April to November.

Pennsylvania

The Keystone State is a wide land of mountains, plateaus and plains, w tered by big rivers as well as some of the most exciting whitewater strean in the East. Along its eastern border flows the majestic Delaware, rival by the mid-state Susquehanna and the Allegheny and Monongahela rive in the west. Pennsylvania's backbone is the massive range of Appalachi: ridges that divides the Allegheny Plateau in the northwest from the Atla tic coastal plain in the southeast. This topography defines a river system whi offers the rafter and canoeist everything from wilderness thrills to placid flo: ing on streams lined with campgrounds and restaurants.

For sheer popularity the Delaware River has few rivals. Surprisingly fr of dams for a river flowing through such a thirsty conurbation, the Del ware brings clean water down from the Catskills of New York. Its 76-mi stretch from Hancock to Port Jervis has long been a favorite canoe trip. takes three days and can be run in April-May and again in Septembe October. In the summer months paddlers depend upon adequate releas from Cannonsville and Pepacton reservoirs. The scenery is superb. But E ward Gertler, in his excellent book *Keystone Canoeing* (Seneca Press, 198& writes that the upper Delaware on a crowded summer weekend has "hu dreds of boaters, in all stages of ineptness, with no concept of river curren canoemanship, or even that a life vest is not just a funny-shaped seat cus ion. Many do not really care, their minds pickled by drugs or alcohol. Th drown and injure themselves on this simple river with amazing frequency Gertler adds that some "river pirates" even direct neophytes into roug sections of rapids in the hope that they will capsize, spilling valuables in the water which can be looted before the victims slog their way ashore. D spite all this, he says that most Delaware canoeists have a great time.

The West Branch of the Susquehanna drives through relatively emp unspoiled countryside in the heart of Pennsylvania. It is flanked by mile up mile of forest and the paddler can camp freely almost wherever he choose

Whitewater buffs head for the hills, and in Pennsylvania the best rapi lurk in the state's southwest corner adjoining Maryland and West Virgin The Youghiogheny — pronounced Yokagaynee or simply "Yok" for short a Mecca for paddlers from Pennsylvania, Ohio, Maryland, Virginia and Vest Virginia. The river's most exciting whitewater is on the Upper Yough cross the border (see Maryland). Within Pennsylvania the Middle Yough till offers plenty of scope for novice and family floating on gentle Class I-II aters. The Yough flows through the Laurel Mountains, with rhododendron nd mountain laurel adorning steep canyon walls. While other streams dry p in the summer, the dam-controlled Yough just keeps rolling along.

The Lower Yough ranks as an intermediate stream with Class III-IV apids, good for novices and veterans alike. And the scenery, largely pro-ected by the Ohiopyle State Park, is great. According to one recent count, 00,000 rafters enjoy the 7.5 miles of whitewater from Ohiopyle Falls through he park to Bruner Run every season.

Much beloved among Pennsylvania and New York paddlers is the Lehigh .iver in the Pocono Mountains. This popular stream is less than three hours rive from New York City and barely two hours from Philadelphia. Many oaters start at White Haven, right next to Interstate 80, and head 26 miles ownstream to the town of Jim Thorpe. But the whole river provides inter-sting canoeing. In the summer its rapids are tame, but until May and on ubseqent weekends when water is released from the Francis E. Walters Dam :heck with outfitters for dates) they are exciting. The trip through the .ehigh Gorge State Park combines grand scenery with plenty of thrills for he novice.

Pine Creek is another popular river, described by some as the crown jewel f Pennsylvania's scenic wilderness regions. Its chief attraction is the wooded orge claimed to be Pennsylvania's "Grand Canyon" but bearing little re-emblance to the original. Runnable usually from the "ice-out" in mid-March) mid-June and again from mid-September to mid-November, it has mostly entle rapids and good scenery.

PENNSYLVANIA

Adventure Sports
John Jacobi
P.O. Box 175
Marshalls Creek, PA 18335
(717) 223-0505, (800) 487-2628,
FAX (717) 223-1728
Delaware River
Max. rapids: I-II
PPA

A family business, Adventure Tours rents canoes and rafts as well as running guided canoe and raft tours on the Delaware River through the Delaware Water Gap National Recreation Area. Trips last from 1-7 days during a season that runs from April to October. Featuring rapids of Class I-II, the trips are suitable for beginners as well as more experienced paddlers.

On the river segments covered, the Delaware is above national purity standards, and it offers good swimming, camping and fall foliage. Pike, muskie, shad, bass and walleye are plentiful.

Blue Mountain Outfitters
Douglas Gibson
103 State Road, Rtes. 11 & 15
Marysville, PA 17053
(717) 957-2413
Susquehanna, Juniata Rivers, and tributaries
Max. rapids: I-II
PPA, NAPSA

Blue Mountain Outfitters rents canoes and kayaks for 1-3 day trips in which guests choose difficulty level, boat design, trip length, and camp sites. The scenery is a mixture of towns and countryside, including Rockville Bridge, the world's longest stone arch bridge.

Paddlers may also fish for smallmouth bass, catfish, muskie, and walleye, and view egrets, herons, ospreys, eagles, ducks, and geese.

Bucks County River Country
Tom McBrien
2 Walters Lane
Pt. Pleasant, PA 18950
(215) 297-5000, FAX (215) 297-5643
Delaware River
Max. rapids: I-II
PPA

This outfitter caters particularly to families looking for fun on the Delaware River through New York, New Jersey and Pennsylvania. Although the river is mostly calm, its bends and turns amid great mountain scenery make for continual excitement. The company has a record of over 30 years' service and rent top-notch equipment — canoes, kayaks rafts and tubes — from May-October.

The river contains no fewer than 36 species of fish, and the shore wildlife includes bear, deer, fox, beaver, and many birds. Clients may snorkel and swim as well as fish during camping trips lasting up to 10 days.

Chamberlain Canoes
Bob Sweeney
P.O. Box 155, River Road
Minisink Hills, PA 18341
(800) 422-6631
Delaware River
Max. rapids: I-II
PPA, ACA, U.S. Canoe Association

Chamberlain Canoes rents canoes, rafts and tubes for trips on the scenic Delaware River lasting from an hour or 2-5 days. Paddlers can explore the Delaware Water Gap recreation area, with it 38 miles of river. Open April-October, the company is geared to meet each customer's personal needs, with delivery and pickup according to his/her schedule. Overnight camping is free.

The Delaware, with Class I-II rapids, is suitable for novices and families. They may fish for bass, shad, walleye, muskie, trout and striper while looking out for bears, deer, fox, small game and birds including eagle and ospreys.

Cook Forest Canoe Livery
Carl Lipford
Box 14, Route 36
Cooksburg, PA 16217
(814) 744-8094
Clarion River
Max. rapids: I-II
PA

Cook Forest Canoe Livery, located on the Clarion River in the heart of Cook Forest State Park, specializes in family canoeing. The Clarion's clean, clear waters appeal to many as they course through a scenic wilderness. Rapids are nowhere more difficult than Class I-II. The 22-year-old livery rents canoes, kayaks and tubes for one to three days during an April-November season.

As they float through the woods, paddlers can glimpse deer, bears, and raccoons, and fish for trout and bass. Campgrounds, picnic areas and hiking trails abound.

Delaware River Canoe Adventures, Inc.
Thomas W. McBrien IV
R.D. #1, Box 154-B
Route 611
Easton, PA 18042
(215) 252-0877, (215) 982-5697
Delaware River
Max. rapids: I-II
PPA

A small, friendly family business, Delaware River Canoe Adventures provides canoe, kayak, raft and tube rentals for use on over 175 miles of the Delaware River. Open from mid-April to mid-November, this enthusiastic young company has no long lines. Its trips encounter only Class I-II rapids and are suitable for beginners and advanced paddlers.

Trips last from 1-10 days, ranging through a varied landscape. Two national parks and 50 islands are to be found on this long stretch of the Delaware, with its excellent campsites, abundant wildlife and numerous fish.

Rafting on the Lower Youghiogheny. Courtesy of Laurel Highlands River Tours, Ohiopyle, Pennsylvania.

Doe Hollow Boat Rentals
Donna Healey
1770 Riverton Rd., Dept. PA
Bangor, PA 18013
(610) 498-2193
Delaware River
Max. rapids: I-II

Doe Hollow rents canoes and 14-foot
fishing boats for great fishing on the
Delaware, the only undammed, navigable river in the East. Located on the
river, the company offers novice trips
lasting anywhere from 1 hour to 10 days,
with camping and swimming available.
Paddlers may view bear, deer, turkey,
and bird species ranging from ducks to
eagles. The outfitter's season runs April-
October.

Evergreen Outdoor Center
William Nesbit
RD #15, Union Deposit Road
Harrisburg, PA 17111-4708
(717) 657-9476
*Susquehanna River, Lehigh River, Delaware
River, most central PA streams*
Max. rapids: III
PPA

Evergreen Outdoor Center rents
canoes and runs guided canoe trips on
the Susquehanna, Lehigh and Delaware
rivers, along with most central Pennsylvania streams. It helps paddlers plan
their trips, choosing easy flat water or
Class II whitewater. Lessons are given
by certified instructors well versed in all
the streams traveled. Camping is available.

Trips run 1-10 days during a season
lasting from mid-April to mid-October.
They cover some excellent native trout
and bass streams unaffected by drought.
Paddlers see limestone springs along
with deer, hawks, eagles and other
wildlife.

Foxburg Livery & Outfitters
Dick Garrard
Main St., Box 352
Foxburg, PA 16036
(412) 659-3752
Allegheny, Clarion Rivers
Max. rapids: None
PPA

Foxburg rents canoes and kayaks for
easy trips of 3 to 52 miles in a federally
designated wild and scenic area. The
scenery is beautiful, with bare rock cliffs
steep hills covered in dense foliage, and
waterfalls tumbling into the river. Rates
are reasonable.

Many kinds of fish may be caught,
including walleye, bass, muskie, bluegill
and perch. Deer, snakes, bears, and
numerous bird species can be spotted.
Campsites are also available during the
April-to-October season.

Hazelbaker Recreation Service
Callen & Faith Hazelbaker
RD 2, Box 15G
Perryopolis, PA 15473
(412) 736-8155, (800) 42-RIVER
Youghiogheny River
Max. rapids: I-II
PPA

Hazelbaker rents canoes, kayaks, and
tubes for 1- and 2-day trips on six miles
of river in an area free of roads and
houses. With its gentle Class I water,
this float is suitable for people of all
ages and normal ability.

During its mid-April to mid-October
season, the company caters to large and
small groups. This area in the Laurel
Mountain foothills boasts some of Penn
sylvania's best bass fishing and is home
to deer, ducks, geese, and otters.

...anoeing the Delaware River. Courtesy of Kittatinny Canoes, Dingman's Ferry, Pennsylvania.

...m Thorpe River Adventures, Inc.

...avid and Robert Kuhn
...Adventure Lane
...m Thorpe, PA 18229
...17) 325-2570, (717) 325-4960,
...00) 424-RAFT FAX (717) 325-2688
...:high River
...ax. rapids: II-III
...merican Rivers, America Outdoors

Jim Thorpe River Adventures offers ...uided raft trips on the Lehigh River, ...ith its spectacular mountain scenery ...nd profusion of wildlife, from March ...hrough October. Whitewater is at its ...xciting best during March, April, May, ...nd June. These trips meet various skill ...vels. The company caters to beginners ...nd intermediate paddlers, with tough-...st rapids rated Class II and III.

During the hot summer months of ...uly and August it offers summer rafting ...ips. Excellent for beginners, these trips ...ffer easy rapids and deep quiet pools, ...ith lots of swimming and splashing at ...leisurely pace.

Anglers fish for bass, trout, pickerel, ...nd muskies in the Lehigh's waters. ...he company also offers kayak lessons, ...nd camping is available nearby.

Kittatinny Canoes

Ruth Jones
HC 67
Dingmans Ferry, PA 18328
(800) FLOAT KC
Delaware River
Max. rapids: I-II
PPA, America Outdoors

Family-owned for three generations, Kittatinny Canoes offers trips on over 100 miles of the Delaware River. Canoes, kayaks, rafts, tubes and campsites are all available, for periods of 1-7 days. Beginners can start on flat water and experienced paddlers can enjoy Class I-II whitewater. Lessons are available. The Delaware is crystal clear, with tall cliffs, forested mountains and wooded islands. Eagles, osprey and many other birds and animals may be seen, with bass, shad, muskies and pike awaiting the fisherman. Kittatinny's season runs from April to October.

Laurel Highlands River Tours
Mark and Linda McCarty
P.O. Box 107
Ohiopyle, PA 15470
(412) 329-8531, (800) 4 RAFTIN
*Middle Youghiogheny River, Lower
Youghiogheny River, Cheat River*
Max. rapids: III-IV
America Outdoors

Laurel Highlands River Tours, one of the oldest whitewater companies in the East, claims to have the largest fleet of equipment anywhere. It operates on the Cheat River as well as the Lower, Middle and Upper Youghiogheny from bases in Albright, W.Va., Ohiopyle, Pa. and Friendsville, Md. In a season running from March to October, it offers guided raft trips and rents both rafts and canoes for floats on both rivers. All are 1-day trips.

The "Yok" has the most popular whitewater in the East and the Cheat is famed for its spring thrills. Canoeing and kayaking instruction is available and acommodations range from camping to luxury motels.

Millers Canoe Rental
George & Ruth Miller
RD2 Box 13
Millerstown, PA 17062
(717) 589-3159
Juniata River
Max. rapids: I
PPA

Millers Canoe Rental offers canoes for trips of up to 6 days on an 80-mile stretch of the Juniata from Huntington to its confluence with the Susquehanna. These are easy floats, excellent for family outings. The river is peaceful, relatively remote, and exceptionally clean.

Millers prides itself on offering good equipment and prompt and flexible service during its April-November season. Wildlife to be seen includes deer, otters, mink, ospreys, bald eagles, herons, and egrets. The river contains smallmouth bass, muskie, walleye, channel catfish, and panfish.

Rafting on the Lower Youghiogheny. Courtesy of Laurel Highlands River Tours, Ohiopyle, Pennsylvania.

Mountain Streams and Trails
Michael S. McCarty
P.O. Box 106, Route 381
Ohiopyle, PA 15470-0106
(800) 245-4090
Lower, Middle, and Upper Youghiogheny
River, Cheat River, Gauley River,
Tygart River, Big Sandy Creek
Max. rapids: V+
America Outdoors

Mountain Streams and Trails operates on all three sections of the Youghiogheny as well as the Class III-IV Cheat, the challenging Tygart, isolated Big Sandy Creek and the Class III-VI Upper and Lower Gauley rivers. It runs guided raft and kayak trips in addition to renting canoes, kayaks and rafts, tailoring its trips to suit the needs of every paddler.

The company has skilled guides, trained in first aid and equipped with radios. They take guests through the spectacular panorama of maples, pines and rhododendrons that blanket the walls of the Middle and Lower Yough River canyon, habitat for deer, beavers, bears, ospreys, heron and an occasional wildcat. One- and two-day tours are offered during a March-October season.

Northbrook Canoe Company
Ezekiel Hubbard
1810 Beagle Road
West Chester, PA 19382
(215) 793-2279, (215) 793-1553
Brandywine Creek
Max. rapids: I-II
PPA

Based directly on the Brandywine River, Northbrook Canoe has canoes and tubes for rent to people who enjoy paddling gentle waters amid diverse scenery and wildlife. These leisurely trips last anywhere from 1-6 hours and are available from April to October. Ideal for beginners and families, they take paddlers through no riffles more difficult than Class I-II.

Observant floaters can admire herons, raccoons, foxes, otters, and turtles while fishing for bass, trout, and other fish.

Pack Shack Adventures, Inc.
John C. Greene and Family
88 Broad Street
P.O. Box 127
Delaware Water Gap, PA 18327
(717) 424-8533
Pine Creek, Delaware River, Broadheads
Creek
Max. rapids: III-IV
PPA

Pack Shack Adventures specializes in 5-day canoeing/camping trips for scouts, other youth groups and families. These and other guided tours are by raft and canoe on Pine Creek, the Delaware River and Broadheads Creek with its spring wildwater. In addition, Pack Shack rents canoes, rafts, kayaks and tubes with equipment and shuttle service.

The most difficult rapids on these waters are Class III-IV in springtime on Broadheads Creek. Otherwise they rank Class II-III. The Pine River is noted for its trout while bass fishing is great on the Delaware, with its plush green valley and distant mountains. Paddling lessons are available. Campsites are available in the Delaware Water Gap National Recreation Area.

The Pale Whale Canoe Fleet
Michael J. McMurray
P.O. Box 109
Cooksburg, PA 16217
(814) 744-8300
Clarion River
Max. rapids: I-II
PPA

Pale Whale rents canoes and tubes for trips of 1-3 days on the clean and undeveloped Clarion River. It is a nice, flowing stream, suitable for families, groups and others.

Pale Whale, with 175 canoes and 150 tubes, is the largest and oldest livery on the river. Camping and swimming are available, fishing is for brown trout and smallmouth bass, and the wildlife includes deer, bears, turkeys and waterfowl. The company's season runs from April to October.

Pine Creek Outfitters, Inc.

Chuck Dillon
RD #4, Box 130B
Wellsboro, PA 16901
(717) 724-3003
Pine Creek
Max. rapids: I-II
PPA

Pine Creek Outfitters offers guided
trips and rents rafts and canoes for trips
of 1-3 days through Pine Creek Gorge,
Pennsylvania's "Grand Canyon." Experienced and knowledgeable guides take
rafters nearly 20 miles through the gorge
from the March ice thaw until the water
gets too low to float — usually mid-June
— and again from mid-September to
mid-November.

Various overnight camping and inn-
to-inn tours are also provided. The
wilderness scenery, fishing and wildlife
are excellent.

Pocono Whitewater Adventure Center

Douglas Fogal
Route 903
Jim Thorpe, PA 18229
(717) 325-3656
Lehigh River
Max. rapids: III-IV
America Outdoors

Pocono Whitewater Adventure
Center runs guided raft trips and rents
rafts on the scenic Lehigh River with its
1,000-foot deep gorge. Rapids are rated
Class III-IV and trips last 1-2 days. The
company's season lasts from March to
November and its customers enjoy
swimming as well as paddling this popular stream.

The river is clean and undeveloped
despite its proximity to major population
centers. Rafters may catch a glimpse of
bears, deer and hawks, while anglers go
for trout and bass.

Riversport

Robert Ruppel
213 Yough Street
Confluence, PA 15424
(814) 395-5744
Youghiogheny River, Big Sandy River,
Cheat River, Casselman River
Max. rapids: III-IV
PPA

An excellent paddling school in the
Pennsylvania area, Riversport runs 1-day
canoe and kayak trips as well as renting
rafts, canoes and kayaks. It operates on
the challenging and beautiful Youghiogheny, Big Sandy, Cheat and Casselman
rivers from March to November.

Riversport's trips are suitable for
youngsters, adults and senior citizens in
good health. Its lessons teach the skills
beginners and intermediate paddlers
need to run the Class III-IV rapids of
nearby rivers, with their hemlocks, rhododendrons, mountain laurel and rich
wildlife.

Shawnee Canoe Trips

Shawnee Group
Box 93
Shawnee on Delaware, PA 18356
(717) 424-1139
Delaware River
Max. rapids: I-II
PPA

Shawnee Canoe Trips rents canoes,
kayaks and tubes for periods of 1 day to
2 weeks and serves the Delaware Water
Gap area. These are mostly flatwater
floats with a few rapids along the way,
suitable for novices and experienced
paddlers alike. Most of the trips go
through the national park with its beautiful mountainsides and wealth of wildlife. Bass, pickerel and muskie lurk in
the waters, plus shad in the spring.
Lessons are also available during
Shawnee's May-to-September season.

Valley Forge Canoe, Tube & Rafting
Tim Reeser
Rte. 724
Monocacy, PA 19542
(800) FLOAT-PA
Schuylkill River
Max. rapids: I-II
PPA, America Outdoors

Valley Forge Canoe, Tube & Rafting rents canoes, kayaks, rafts, and tubes at affordable rates. Guests of all ages and levels of experience can enjoy calm water trips and Class II beginner whitewater on a river with low usage and no motorboats. It is deep enough throughout the season, which runs from April 1 through October.

Trips last from 2 hours to 2 days and take paddlers through scenery varying from wooded hills to small old industrial towns. While fishing for smallmouth bass, carp, catfish, and muskie, customers can watch deer, fox, turtles, great blue herons, and ospreys. Camping and paddling lessons are available.

Whitewater Adventurers, Inc.
Robert and Shirley Marietta
P.O. Box 31
Ohiopyle, PA 15470
(412) 329-8850,
(800) WWA-RAFT (992-7238)
Upper, Middle, and Lower Youghiogheny River, Cheat River
Max. rapids: III-IV
America Outdoors, West Virginia Eastern Professional Outfitters

Whitewater Adventurers runs guided raft and kayak trips on the Lower, Middle and Upper Youghiogheny as well as renting canoes, kayaks and rafts from March to November. Paddlers can take their pick; the dam-controlled Yough is rated Class V on its upper section and Classes III and II on its lower and middle stretches respectively. Trips are suitable for "folks from 12-100 who are willing to paddle a bit and have a good time."

A highly professional staff and the best modern equipment are mainstays of the company, which offers lessons and provides a guide for every raft on the steep and technical Upper Yough. Trout, walleye and bass can be caught on the "Yok" as it winds through the Laurel Highland Mountains.

In West Virginia, Whitewater Adventurers of Cheat River Canyon runs "very thrilling" guided raft trips from March to July through Class IV-V rapids on the free-flowing Cheat River. The stream cuts through a very steep canyon in an historic part of West Virginia. It has beautiful wildflowers and mountain laurel, along with deer, wild turkeys, and grouse.

Whitewater Challengers, Inc.
Kenneth Powley
P.O. Box 8
White Haven, PA 18661
(717) 443-9532
Hudson, Moose, Lehigh Rivers, Black River Canyon
Max. rapids: V+
America Outdoors

Whitewater Challengers runs guided raft and kayak trips and rents rafts on the Lehigh, Hudson, Moose, and Black rivers, with their varying demands on paddlers' skills. The Lehigh is Class II/III and suitable for novices, the Hudson and Black are adventurous Class IV and the Moose is for Class V experts only.

Conveniently located near major interstate highways, the company has a excellent 20-year safety record. Its paddling waters are clean, scenic, and full of fish and wildlife ranging from trout to bears, hawk and blue heron. During its March-October season, the company also offers kayaking lessons.

Whitewater Rentals
Robert Marietta
P.O. Box 31
Ohiopyle, PA 15470
(412) 329-8850, (800) WWA-RAFT
Middle and Lower Youghiogheny River
Max. rapids: III-IV
America Outdoors

Whitewater Rentals has rafts, canoes and kayaks for 1-day use on the Middle and Lower Youghiogheny. Its professional staff is skilled at outfitting individual paddlers according to their particular needs. Trips range from mild water suitable for family floating to wild Class III-IV rapids.

The "Yough" is very clean and provides outstanding cold-water fishing for rainbow and brown trout, walleye and bass. Whitewater Rentals operates from March to November. Its clients enjoy the rugged mountain landscape with its hardwoods and mountain laurel.

Wilderness Voyageurs, Inc.
Eric Martin
P.O. Box 97, Dept. SP
Ohiopyle, PA 15470
(412) 329-5517, (412) 329-4752,
(800) 272-4141, FAX (412) 329-0809
Middle and Lower Youghiogheny, Cheat,
Big Sandy, Potomac Rivers
Max. rapids: III-IV
America Outdoors

Wilderness Voyageurs rents canoes, kayaks, rafts and duckies and provides guided trips in all these craft. With professional river guides dedicated to giving a quality wilderness experience, the company has an outstanding safety record. It claims to have been the first commercial outfitter east of the Mississippi when founded in 1964.

One-half and one-day trips start downstream of an impressive 20-foot waterfall and run seven miles through a wilderness gorge. The season runs from April 1 to October 15 and Wilderness Voyageurs can accommodate people of all ages on gentle floats or through Class III-IV whitewater.

Youghiogheny Outfitters, Inc.
James N. Falcon
Box 21
Ohiopyle, PA 15470
(412) 329-4549
Youghiogheny River
Max. rapids: III-IV

Challenging floats through spectacular mountain scenery are offered by this company from April through October. Suitable for athletic persons aged 12 and up, these trips take paddlers through the largest state park in Pennsylvania. Before boarding rental canoes and rafts, clients get a personal orientation and safety briefing.

Deer, bear, and turkey may be seen, and fishing is for trout. Camping is available, along with swimming in the clean water.

Rhode Island

Tiny Rhode Island has a surprising amount to offer the paddler who is content to relax, fish and birdwatch. Great Swamp, near Kingston in the south, is a state wildlife management area and home to sun turtles, water moccasins, herons, mallards, wild turkeys, deer, opossums, and redwing blackbirds. Seabirds such as herons, egrets, and sandpipers can be admired near the coast. Wood River in Exeter has good trout, bass and pike fishing.

Great Swamp, famous for the colonists' defeat of Narragansett Indians led by King Philip (Metacomet) in 1676, can be reached along the tiny Chipuxet River from a put-in at West Kingston. The trip starts under a heavy tree canopy and canoeists may have to duck under low branches. But then it opens up into a smooth ride through marshy wetlands, finally emerging on to Worden Pond. Here the paddling is heavy slogging when headwinds whip up whitecaps.

Narrow River, also known as the Pettaquamscutt, runs southward parallel to the Narragansett Bay shore until it flows into the sea at Narrow River Inlet. It is a tidal waterway, enabling the paddler who times it right to ride the ebb tide when he sets out from Gilbert Stuart's birthplace and the flood tide for the return trip. Small ocean fish known as "buckies" spawn in the upper reaches of the river every spring. A pastoral stretch upstream turns built-up and popular with summer powerboats further down, and only daring paddlers attempt the surf at Narrow River Inlet.

Wood River, in western Rhode Island, is a particularly appealing stream — not just for its fish and wildlife but also its wooded scenery as it flows through the Arcadia Management Area. Its most popular section runs for 13 miles to the village of Alton.

In the northwest corner of the state the Pascoag even offers the paddler a taste of fast water. Soon after the put-in at Harrisville, the river runs over two dams. One is easily runnable but the second can be a tricky three-foot drop when the river is in spate. Further downstream the scenic Pascoag provides a good marshy area for fishing and picnicking before it turns lively again and changes its name to the Branch River. At this point there is a dam by an old factory that must always be portaged, and finally a 100-yard dash of shallow rock rapids which can scratch and dent at low water.

Baer's River Workshop
Joseph Baer
222 South Water St.
Providence, RI 02903
(401) 453-1633
Wood, Charles, Pawcatuk, Providence, Woonosquatucket, Blackstone, Barrington, Palmer Rivers, Narragansett Bay, Great Swamp Management Area.
Max rapids: None
NAPSA

Baer's River Workshop offers guided and unguided canoeing, kayaking, and sea kayaking trips on a variety of southern New England waterways. Guests may enjoy bird and wildlife watching on hundreds of miles of sheltered coastline, pristine rivers and rich lakes. Or they may take an urban float down the historic Providence and Woonosquatucket Rivers, or an eco-tour with an experienced naturalist. Advanced kayak and canoe instruction is given by knowledgeable and friendly staff. Alternatively, paddlers may rent canoes and kayaks and make their own adventure.

Baer's River Workshop's season runs year-round.

Narragansett Kayak Co., Inc.
Ron Johnson & Patricia Thornton
1 Charlestown Beach Rd.
Charlestown, RI 02813
(401) 364-2000
Ninigret Pond, Narragansett Bay, Wood/Pawcatuck Watershed
Max. rapids: None
PPA

This company runs guided and unguided kayak trips in the 2,000-acre Ninigret Pond, which is mostly only a foot deep and great for clamming, crabbing and basking on miles of sandy beach. These are ideal outings for families and experts alike. Trout, flounder, and striped bass may be caught in these calm, serene coastal waters. Along with hundreds of bird species, paddlers may see deer, raccoon, fox and coyote.

Quaker Lane Bait and Tackle
Michael S. Betwick
4019 Quaker Lane
North Kingstown, RI 02852
(401) 294-9642
Wood River
Max. rapids: I-II
PPA

Quaker Lane Bait and Tackle rents canoes, kayaks and johnboats for trips of 1-3 days on the scenic Wood River. This river, with only gentle rapids, is fine for beginners as well as seasoned canoeists. Its clean waters offer great fishing for trout, bass, and pike, and its tranquil, wooded setting shelters deer, otters, birds, and other wildlife for paddlers to observe. Quaker Lane, open year-round, has helpful staff on hand seven days a week, from 4.30 a.m. to 8 p.m., to help paddlers plan trips and get underway.

South Carolina

Compared to its neighbors, South Carolina has only a tiny slice of the Appalachian Mountain system which stretches from Pennsylvania to northern Georgia. Only some 500 square miles of South Carolina terrain, in the extreme west, can be termed mountainous. As a result, most river paddling in the state is relatively serene.

But there is one great exception — the celebrated Chattooga River which marks the state line between South Carolina and Georgia. Familiar to moviegoers as the setting for the whitewater film *Deliverance*, the Chattooga has some of the most exciting rapids in the East. One of the nation's first Wild and Scenic Rivers, it attracts tens of thousands of rafters annually as it churns through the scenic Sumter and Chattahoochee national forests. Yet the river is less crowded than many other famous streams, since rafts are spread out over a 20-mile distance.

The Chattooga's hairiest section is the eight-mile stretch from the US 76 bridge to Lake Tugaloo. There the river roars through a remote and inaccessible canyon, dropping nearly 50 feet per mile. Rafters must negotiate Class IV-V rapids with names like Corkscrew and Sock-Em-Dog in quick succession. Their only chance to admire the scenery — lofty cliffs, handsome rock formations and waterfalls — is when the river slackens its headlong rush in the late summer and fall.

For a more laid-back experience, the Edisto River gives floaters a fine opportunity to view wildlife: alligators, otters, snakes, foxes, white-tailed deer, bobcats, wild turkeys and bird species from kingfishers to hummingbirds. The Edisto canoe and kayak trail offers 56 miles of pastoral paddling within easy reach of Charleston. The river is claimed to be the nation's longest free-flowing black water stream — the term black water denoting its dark tannin-rich color.

Canoes, kayaks and johnboats find their place under the moss-draped live oaks and black maples of the Edisto all summer long. The river can be run safely by novices and access is easy at many points. Fishing is first-rate for largemouth bass, bream, catfish, jackfish and crappie. Floaters can interrupt their gentle progress down this scenic river to picnic and camp on the sandbars and banks of its upper reaches, or at developed campgrounds further downstream.

Adventure Carolina, Inc.
Richard B. Mikell
1107 State St.
Cayce, SC 29033
(803) 796-4505
Congaree, Saluda, Edisto Rivers, Congaree Swamp, and others
Max. rapids: I-II
PPA

Operating year-round, Adventure Carolina runs guided and unguided raft, canoe, and kayak trips of 1- and 2-days. These trips are suitable for paddlers of all ages and skill levels. The Congaree combines wildlife with rapids and historic Columbia; the Saluda has cold water, lots of easy rapids and a Columbia trip; and the Edisto is famous for its foliage, sandy beaches, and tea-colored water. Congaree Swamp National Park displays the last significant stand of old-growth river bottom hardwood forest.

Fishing, camping, swimming and paddling lessons are available.

Black River Expeditions
William C. Unger III
21 Garden Ave.
Georgetown, SC 29440
(803) 546-4840
Black, Great Pee Dee & Waccamaw Rivers, Georgetown Harbor, Huntington Marsh
Max. rapids: None
PPA

Year-round floats on the slow, meandering waters of South Carolina's tidelands are this outfitter's specialty. Scenery varies from blackwater cypress swamps to saltwater marsh creeks and abandoned ricefield canals. People of all ages and skill levels can enjoy guided and unguided trips by canoe and kayak through thousands of acres of wildlife preserves.

These outings last up to 5 days, with camping and paddling lessons available. Bass, catfish, panfish, mullet, and shrimp may be caught, and alligators also roam the waters.

Blackwater Adventures
Louis J. Nexsen
Box 4639
Pinopolis, SC 29469
(800) 761-1850
Central coastal plain of S. Carolina
Max. rapids: None
PPA

Located 20 miles from Charleston, Blackwater Adventures runs year-round guided and unguided canoe and kayak floats on wilderness waters colored by the leaves of hardwood swamps. The paddling is very easy and suitable for all. Trips can be combined with clay, trap, and skeet shooting, horseback riding, catered meals, camping and lodge stays.

Catfish, bass, panfish, crappie, and redbreast may be caught, and birdlife is abundant. Paddling lessons are available.

Carolina Heritage Outfitters
Beau D. Kennedy, S. Scott Kennedy
Hwy. 15
Canadys, SC 29433
(803) 563-5051, (800) 563-5053
Edisto River
Max. rapids: None
PPA

Carolina Heritage Outfitters offers guided and unguided canoe, kayak, and raft trips on the Edisto River Canoe and Kayak Trail. The Edisto was chosen as the state's first canoe trail because it offers the best flatwater paddling opportunities. Its clean tea-colored water has a gentle flow suitable for paddlers of all ages. Trips run from one-half to 10 days, with primitive camping and eco-lodging available at a private wildlife refuge. On these floats, which run year-round, paddlers can also spot many types of birds, reptiles and small game. The company offers professional guides and experienced instructors to teach basic to advanced canoe and kayak skills.

Cassina Point Livery
Bruce & Tecla Earnshaw
North End Clark Rd., Box 535
Edisto Island, SC 29438
(803) 869-2535
Tidal creeks & inlets throughout Edisto Is.
Max. rapids: None
PPA

Located on a pristine barrier island, this livery is operated in conjunction with a bed and breakfast in an antebellum plantation home. Open year-round, it offers guided and unguided canoe and kayak trips on salt marshes little touched by man's presence.

Fishing is for spot tail, bass, trout, and flounder. Aside from paddling, birdwatching, and swimming, guests can ride the plantation's horses.

Chattooga Whitewater Shop
Bruce Hare
14239 Long Creek Hwy.
Long Creek, SC 29658
(803) 647-9083
Chattooga River
Max. rapids: III-IV

Chattooga Whitewater Shop offers experienced paddlers intermediate Class III-IV trips as well as easy Class I-II floats on the National Wild and Scenic Chattooga River.

Open all year, the company provides paddling lessons and service derived from nearly two decades' experience. All kinds of wildlife and various fish can be found. The outfitter offers guided canoe and kayak trips as well as renting canoes, kayaks, and rafts. Camping and paddling lessons are available.

Coastal Expeditions
Anne Goold
514-B Mill St.
Mt. Pleasant, SC 29464
(803) 884-7684
Edisto, Cumbahee, Ashepoo, Santee, Cooper, Wando Rivers, Wambaw & Rimini Swamps, Atlantic Ocean, salt marsh creeks
Max. rapids: None
PPA

Coastal Expeditions offers both fresh and salt water floats for people of all ages and experience levels. Certified instructors and naturalist guides lead custom kayak tours to bird rookeries and undeveloped barrier islands. The company also rents canoes and kayaks during its year-round season. Fishing is available for both fresh and salt water game, along with camping and paddling lessons.

Edisto River Canoe & Kayak Trail Commission.
P.O. Box 1763
Walterboro, SC 29488
(803) 549-9595, (803) 549-5591
Edisto River, Combahee River
Max. rapids: None

The Edisto River Canoe & Kayak Trail Commission offers guided canoe and kayak trips on the Edisto River, the world's longest blackwater river. Trips last a half day or full day, run year-round, and are easy enough for beginners. Along the way, paddlers can view river otters, deer, turkeys, ducks, alligators, snakes, and other wildlife. Anglers can also fish for red breast, catfish, and bass. Wildflowers bloom along the banks in spring and fall, amid giant live oaks, red swamp maple, black willows, cypress, tupelo, gum, and tall pines.

Along the Edisto River Canoe and Kayak Trail are two state parks, Colleton (803) 538-8206 and Givhan's Ferry (803) 873-0692. Both offer canoeing and picnicking.

Nantahala Outdoor Center
41 U.S. Highway 19 West
Bryson City, NC 28713
(704) 488-2175, (800) 232-RAFT
Chattooga River, Nantahala River, French
Broad River, Ocoee River, Nolichucky River
Max. rapids: V+
America Outdoors

Nantahala Outdoor Center (NOC)
runs guided and unguided trips of 1-21
days on five rivers in North Carolina,
South Carolina, and Tennessee. Trips
are by canoe, raft, or inflatable kayak.

Nantahala River trips, run near Great
Smoky Mountain National Park, offer
an excellent whitewater experience for
beginners and families. Runs on the
French Broad River, another ideal river
for family rafting, wind through a spectacular gorge in the Pisgah National
Forest. The Ocoee is a favorite of whitewater enthusiasts, with big waves and
constant action on its course through
Cherokee National Forest. The Nolichucky offers high-water excitement
in spring, gentler rafting and kayak trips
in late spring and early summer, and
stunning scenery at any time. The
Chattooga boasts some of the finest
whitewater in the Southeast as it tumbles through the Chattahoochee and
Sumter National Forests. NOC has
Chattooga trips to match any paddler's
skill, beginner to advanced.

NOC also offers lessons during its
March-to-November season.

Outside Hilton Head
Mike Overton
Plaza at Shelter Cove
Hilton Head, SC 29928
(800) 686-6996
Okatie, Colleton, New Rivers, Skull Creek,
Pinckney Is. National Wildlife Refuge
Max. rapids: None
PPA

This outfitter, which caters to all levels of paddlers, is a good bet for people
seeking a comprehensive introduction to
paddling. It runs guided kayak trips on
clean and pristine salt marshes rich in

birdlife. It also rents both kayaks and
canoes. Outside Hilton Head offers trips
every day of the year and also provides
paddling and windsurfing lessons. In addition to profuse saltmarsh life, clients
can admire numerous bottlenosed dolphins.

Rolling Thunder River Company
Ken and Dina Miller
P.O. Box 88
Almond, NC 28702
(704) 488-2030, (800) 344-5838
Chattooga River, Nantahala River, Ocoee
River, French Broad, Nolichucky River
Max. rapids: III-IV
America Outdoors

Rolling Thunder River Co. runs
guided canoe, kayak, and raft trips and
rents canoes, kayaks, rafts, and "funyaks" on five rivers in North Carolina,
Tennessee, and South Carolina. Trips
on the Nantahala have Class II-III rapids, are easy enough for beginners and
families, and pass through the beautiful
Nantahala Gorge. Full-day, wild-water
raft trips are available on the Ocoee.
These trips, with Class III and IV rapids,
are suitable for anyone age 12 and older.
Private canoe and kayak instruction on
the Ocoee is also available.

On the Chattooga, Rolling Thunder
offers an exciting overnight whitewater
canoe trip with Class II-IV rapids, spectacular scenery, and abundant wildlife.
No experience is necessary on this
guided trip. Finally, a combination
French Broad River-Nolichucky River
raft trip is available. This 2-day expedition includes a night of camping at one
of the company's base camps.

Rolling Thunder's season runs from
April to October.

Water Walk Touring Co.
Jea Chapman
The Kayak Farm
1289 Sea Island Parkway
St. Helena Is., SC 29920
(803) 838-2008
Cumbahee River, ACE Basin, St. Helena
Sound, Port Royal Sound
Max. rapids: None
PPA

Water Walk runs guided and un-guided sea kayaking trips into the heart of the ACE Basin and other unique coastal areas abounding in wildlife. Coastal South Carolina has thousands of acres of undeveloped wilderness, full of rivers, swamps, estuaries, and barrier islands.

With camping available, customers can take trips of up to 3 days and fish for sea trout, red fish, tarpon, sheep-head, and striped bass. The company also gives paddling lessons during its year-round season.

Wildwater Limited
Jim Greiner
P.O. Box 100
Longcreek, SC 29658
(800) 451-9972
Chattooga, Nantahala, Ocoee, Big Pigeon
Rivers
Max. rapids: V+
America Outdoors

Wildwater Limited operates in Geor-gia, North Carolina, South Carolina, and Tennessee, offering more than a dozen trip options for paddlers age 8 and over, ranging from novices to experts. The Chattooga is a National Wild and Scenic River, the Nantahala adjoins the Great Smoky Mountains National Park, and the Ocoee has been chosen for the 1996 Olympic whitewater events.

The company has served over 400,000 customers in 25 years of opera-tion, and prides itself on its staff, facili-ties, and safety record. It rents rafts and kayaks as well as running guided canoe, kayak and raft trips during a March-to-mid-November season.

Wind N Sea
Rick & Vicki Gardner
803 28th Ave. S.
North Myrtle Beach, SC 29582
(803) 272-4420
Waccamaw, Little Pee Dee Rivers, Coastal
salt marsh to Bird Is.
Max. rapids: None
PPA

Salt marsh tours with excellent bird-watching are the specialty of Wind N Sea, a family business which caters year-round to families. Although its kayak trips are not difficult, the company in-sists that customers must have paddling experience. Children under 10 are welcome to paddle with adults on 1/2-day tours. With camping, other guided and unguided trips can last up to a week.

Favorite destinations are undeveloped Bird Island and the Waccamaw wildlife preserve with its enormous cypress trees.

South Dakota

S outh Dakota is good canoeing country, with rivers flowing through interesting scenery into the mighty Missouri, which slashes through the middle of the state. Furthermore, the state government has made it easy for paddlers to plan trips. Write the Game, Fish and Parks Department at 445 East Capitol, Pierre, SD 57501, for their excellent leaflet, *Canoe South Dakota*, and separate brochures describing the James River and Big Sioux River canoe trails.

Streams in the eastern part of the state drive through rolling hardwood forests while western creeks cascade from the Black Hills and converge into prairie rivers. The landscape runs the gamut from glacial plain croplands through short-grass prairie hills to steep chalk bluffs and ponderosa pine-covered foothills.

Some South Dakota rivers can be paddled year-round, others only in spring and early summer, after snowmelt or rain. Some offer lazy floating while others have lively currents or require portages around dams and livestock fences. Campsites and parks flank a few rivers, while other streams wander through empty grasslands.

One of the state's favorite canoeing rivers is the Big Sioux, much of which can be floated all summer long. Its slow current takes it on a winding course through a thin belt of timber, with wildlife ranging from whitetail deer to painted turtles. The 52-mile stretch from Sioux Falls to Newton Hills — along the Iowa border — can be paddled comfortably in four days. Markers placed 300 feet upstream of lowhead dams warn of danger ahead, and portage signs indicate take-out points. For water levels, call the Newton Hills State Park weekdays at (605) 987-2263. Canoeists wanting to explore the upper segments of the Big Sioux can start at Brookings, but there is only enough water during the spring and early summer. In season, the entire 270-mile distance from Brookings to the river's confluence with the Missouri can be canoed.

The James River, a typical prairie stream which slices north-south through the state, has been called the longest unnavigable river in the world. But this does not apply to canoeists, who can float a 76-mile trail (from a put-in near Mitchell to Olivet) until early July, and sometimes through the summer. Normally this is a five-day trip but it can vary with current and winds. The slow-moving, curving river contains many species of wildlife including wood ducks. Six lowhead dams, three of them close to Mitchell, must be portaged but eight access points are available. Water levels can be obtained from the Mitchell Parks and Recreation Department at (605) 996-0708 weekdays.

Whitewater enthusiasts enjoy Split Rock Creek, which rises near the Pipestone National Monument in Minnesota and follows a picturesque course through Minnehaha County to join the Big Sioux near East Sioux Falls. In late spring and after heavy rain its rapids may be hazardous for the novice. The stream runs through Palisades State Park and parts of it run between sheer cliffs of red quartzite.

State officials recommend two segments of the Missouri for canoeing: the 40-mile stretch from Fort Randall Dam to Running Water, opposite the Nebraska town of Niobrara, and the 60-mile run from Gavins Point Dam to Ponca State Park, Nebraska. On both stretches the river is wide and clear, with sandbars and small islands. The lower section, which has several developed campsites and picnicking areas, has been designated a National Recreation River within the National Wild and Scenic River system.

In western South Dakota, the Belle Fourche River offers scenic floating through rolling plains dotted with buttes, peaks and pinnacles. A popular run, water level permitting, is on Spearfish Creek and the Red Water River to the Belle Fourche and thence to its confluence with the Cheyenne. The Cheyenne itself, flowing through remote grassland and rolling hills, has a good 55-mile run ending at the SD 63 bridge. Other recommended canoe trails in the west are on the White, Little White, Little Missouri, Moreau and Grand rivers.

Cottonwood Corral
Jerry and Deanna Mueller
Route 1, Box 241
Yankton, SD 57078
(605) 665-9589
Lewis and Clark Lake, Missouri River, James River, Yankton Lake
Max. rapids: None

Cottonwood Corral rents canoes from mid-April to mid-October for relaxed paddling, fishing, camping and swimming in Lewis and Clark Lake, Yankton Lake and adjoining rivers. The river paddling — on the Missouri above and below the lakes and on the James — is relatively easy. Anglers go for walleye and bass, among other fish. Wildlife in the area consists chiefly of birds.

Missouri River Outfitters
124 Court Street
Vermillion, SD 57069
(605) 624-4823
Missouri River
Max rapids: None

Missouri River Outfitters offers guided and unguided canoe trips of 1-4 days on the Missouri River and area lakes and ponds. The stretches paddled boast exceptionally clean water and attractive scenery of bluffs, trees, islands, and sandbars. These gentle, flatwater trips also offer fishing for catfish, walleye, carp, sturgeon, and sauger. Bird watchers can enjoy views of eagles, turkey buzzards, and blue herons. MRO's season runs from April to October.

Tennessee

Tennessee's star year-round attraction for thrill-seeking paddlers is the dam-controlled Ocoee River, venue of the 1996 Olympic whitewater events. Located less than an hour's drive east of Chattanooga, the Ocoee winds through a deep and beautiful gorge in the Cherokee National Forest. Over a five-mile stretch its level drops at an average rate of 50 feet a mile, making it a continuous Class III-IV whitewater experience. Its rapids have such colorful names as Hell's Hole, Broken Nose and Double Trouble. But local rafting outfitters say that with their experienced guides, the adventure is safe for everyone. Nearby is the comparatively gentle Hiwassee, a scenic river offering Class I-II rapids and a glimpse of deer, bear, raccoon, and numerous bird species.

Elsewhere in the Appalachians, too, Tennessee boasts some of the most challenging whitewater and spectacular scenery in the East. But the hazardous rapids on many mountain streams are runnable only in the winter and early spring. Take, for example, two awesome gorges in the state's northeast corner alongside Virginia and North Carolina. Paddlers on the Doe River thrill to the excitement of a narrow torrent confined between the 1000-foot bluffs of Cedar Mountain and Fork Mountain. The Doe's Class IV gorge on the seven-mile stretch above the town of Hampton is strictly for advanced canoeists prepared to scout the hazards cautiously. In the same area the celebrated Watauga River gorge cuts its way across the North Carolina state line. With rapids of up to Class V difficulty, gradients reaching 200 feet per mile, huge boulders and hazardous drops, it should be attempted only by experts. Even they should be accompanied by a person familiar with the river in all its moods. But both the Doe and the Watauga can only be run from December to April, or after heavy downpours.

Another of Tennessee's spectacular whitewater runs is the Big South Fork Gorge —a trip to be undertaken in the spring runoff weeks between late March and early May. This Class III-IV run on the Big South Fork of the Cumberland River is within the Big South Fork National River and Recreation Area. The nearby Obed River is the state's only National Wild and Scenic River, a pristine wilderness stream. Another springtime run through a handsome gorge, the trip from Obed Junction to Emory River provides many Class III-IV rapids with such names as Rockgarden and Oh My God!

For the family canoeist, the Elk River in south central Tennessee is a good bet, with its gentle current and profusion of trout, bass, blue herons, and basking turtles. Also in the middle of the state is the Harpeth State Scenic River, with many historic sites, mills and Indian mounds. Here, too, floaters find easy paddling and good catches of smallmouth bass, brim, crappie, and catfish. The Sequatchie River canoe area near Dunlap northwest of Chattanooga offers clean water, fishing and wildlife including fox, mink, muskrat, blue heron, wood duck, and Canada geese.

Dubbed a "paddler's dream" are the wildlife-rich headwaters of the Wolf River in the southwest corner of the state. The 16-mile stretch from La Grange to Moscow runs through a swamp considered impassable until a trail was blazed in 1990. Canoeists are warned: miss a single blue marker on the trees and you may get lost.

Around Gatlinburg, back in the Smokies, families can enjoy rafting on the Nantahala, Big Pigeon and French Broad Rivers in waters providing varying degrees of excitement. And the Buffalo River, which parallels the Tennessee River for part of its length, is great for fishing.

Adventures Unlimited, Inc.
Carlo J. Smith
648 Harpeth Bend Drive
Nashville, TN 37221
(800) 662-0667
Ocoee River
Max. rapids: III-IV
PPA

Adventures Unlimited conducts guided rafting trips down the Ocoee River. With a continuous run of Class III and IV rapids, Adventures Unlimited offers a great adventure for novice and experienced paddlers alike. In their new self-bailing boats, everybody can enjoy the Ocoee on a four-and-a-half mile stretch through Cherokee National Forest. Trips are available from March through November, as are camping, caving, and climbing.

The Buffalo River Canoe Rental Co.
Alf M. and Patricia Ashton
Route 4, Box 510
Flatwoods, TN 37096
(615) 589-2755
Buffalo River
Max. rapids: I-II
PPA

Buffalo River Canoe Rental Co. offers canoe, kayak, and flat-bottom boat trips and canoe, kayak, and raft rentals on the Buffalo River. The river, with Class I-II rapids, is challenging but fine for beginners. Its clear, cool, spring-fed waters also offer excellent fishing for smallmouth bass, largemouth bass, rock bass, crappie, pike, trout, catfish, and perch. The river is scenic, with views of rock bluffs, deer, turkeys, ducks, geese, and beavers. Trips run from 1-7 days.

During the mid-March to mid-October season, Buffalo River Canoe Rental also operates an attractive, primitive campground at the river's edge.

TENNESSEE

Canoe the Sequatchie

Scott and Ernestine Pilkington
U.S. Highway 127 South & River
Dunlap, TN 37327-0211
(423) 949-4400, FAX (423) 949-2745,
Chattanooga 855-4961,
Knoxville 694-3188
Sequatchie River
Max. rapids: I-II
Tennessee Association of Canoe Liveries and Outfitters

Canoe the Sequatchie rents canoes for trips of 1-7 days on the Sequatchie River. The river, fine for beginners and experienced paddlers, has exceptionally clean water and good fishing for smallmouth bass, rock bass, bream and sunfish. On its course through a unique rift valley, the Sequatchie offers many scenic spots to picnic, swim, and watch for deer, beavers, foxes, minks, muskrats, wood ducks, and wild geese.

Canoe the Sequatchie's season runs from April to October.

Cherokee Adventures, Inc.

Dennis Nedelman
Route 1, Box 605
Erwin, TN 37650
(423) 743-7733, (800) 445-7238
Nolichucky, Russell Fork, Pigeon Rivers
Max. rapids: IV+
America Outdoors

Cherokee Adventures, Inc., runs guided raft and funyak trips on the Nolichucky River 7 days a week from March through October. The river is located in a national forest in a 3,000 foot canyon. It has Class III-IV rapids and is for paddlers 12 and older. No previous experience is required. The Lower Nolichucky has Class II-III rapids and the minimum age is 5. The Russell Fork Canyon trips, with Class IV+ whitewater, are in funyaks only at appropriate low dam releases, for experienced paddlers 18 and older. Trips on the Pigeon River, close to the Smokies with continuous Class III and IV rapids, are fully guided. No prior experience is required, but paddlers must be at least 10 years old.

Rafting on the Ocoee River. Courtesy of Adventures Unlimited.

There is also fishing for trout, muskie, bass, and catfish. Riverfront camping is available for rafters on the Nolichucky, and packages include primitive lodging and meals.

Elk River Canoe Rental
Don and Lou Ann Townsend
Route 1, Box 20
Kelso, TN 37348
(615) 937-6886
Elk River
Max. rapids: None
PPA

Elk River Canoe Rental rents canoes for trips of 1/2 day to several days on the Elk River. This scenic, flatwater river has clean, clear water, a gravel bottom, and steady flow throughout the season. Paddling is easy, allowing time to enjoy the Tennessee hill country of rocky bluffs, woodlands, and wildflowers. Along the way, paddlers can also enjoy fishing for trout, smallmouth and large-mouth bass, and many types of panfish. On the banks, herons, wild turkeys, minks, beavers, muskrats, and deer are often seen. Elk River Canoe Rental's season runs from April to the end of October.

Flatwoods Canoe Base
Richard and Julia Rotgers
Route 4, Box 612 B
Highway 13
Flatwoods, TN 37096
(615) 589-5661
Buffalo River
Max. rapids: I-II

Flatwoods Canoe Base rents canoes for trips of 1-7 days on the Buffalo River from Natchez Trace to Blue Hole Bridge. With Class I-II rapids, the river is safe for beginners yet challenging for experienced canoeists. The clear, spring-fed waters offer good fishing for black perch, bream, smallmouth bass, and catfish. Paddlers also can enjoy beautiful views of limestone bluffs, waterfalls, wild flowers, fall foliage, and wildlife, including turtles, beavers, raccoons, and deer

Flatwoods' season runs from May to October.

Hiwassee Outfitters
David A. Smith
Box 62
Reliance, TN 37369
(800) 338-8133, (423) 338-8115
Hiwassee, Lower Ocoee Rivers
Max. rapids: III-IV
PPA, AO

Hiwassee Outfitters runs guided raft and dory trips as well as renting rafts, inflatable kayaks and tubes for 1/2-day trips on scenic waters suitable for the whole family. As a licensed fishing guide service, the company helps anglers hook rainbow and brown trout. It also maintains a complete fishing center and a riverbank campground.

Open from March to November, the outfitter offers a wide range of accommodations in a beautiful location among mountains rich in wildlife.

Nantahala Outdoor Center
41 U.S. Highway 19 West
Bryson City, NC 28713
(704) 488-2175, (800) 232-RAFT
Ocoee River, Nolichucky River, Chatooga River, Nantahala River, French Broad River
Max. rapids: V+
America Outdoors

Nantahala Outdoor Center (NOC) runs guided and unguided trips of 1-21 days on five rivers in North Carolina, South Carolina, and Tennessee. Trips are by canoe, raft, or inflatable kayak.

Nantahala River trips, run near Great Smoky Mountain National Park, offer an excellent whitewater experience for beginners and families. Runs on the French Broad River, another ideal river for family rafting, wind through a spectacular gorge in the Pisgah National Forest. The Ocoee is a favorite of white-water enthusiasts, with big waves and constant action on its course through Cherokee National Forest. The Nolichucky offers high-water excitement in spring, gentler rafting and kayak trips in late spring and early summer, and stunning scenery at any time. The Chattooga boasts some of the finest whitewater in the Southeast as it tumbles through the Chattahoochee and Sumter National Forests. NOC has Chattooga trips to match any paddler's skill, beginner to advanced.

NOC also offers lessons during its March-to-November season.

Ocoee Inn Rafting, Inc.
Jerr Hamby
Route 1, Box 347
Benton, TN 37307
(615) 338-2064, (800) 272-7238
Ocoee River
Max. rapids: III-IV
America Outdoors

Ocoee Inn Rafting runs guided raft trips on the Ocoee, through five miles of exciting Class III-IV whitewater. These trips, fine for anyone over 12, are all in light, self-bailing rafts, a point of pride for the company. Paddlers pass through the beautiful Ocoee River Gorge, known for its mountain wilderness scenery. Trips run from April to November.

In addition to rafting, the Ocoee Inn offers rustic motel rooms, cabin rentals, family-style meals, and a boat dock on Lake Ocoee, where guests can rent canoes, pontoon boats, and fishing boats inside Cherokee National Forest.

Ocoee Outdoors
J.T. Lemons
P.O. Box 72
Ocoee, TN 37361
(800) 533-PROS, (615) 338-2438
Ocoee, Hiwassee Rivers
Max. rapids: III-IV
America Outdoors, Ocoee River Outfitters Association

Ocoee Outdoors runs guided raft trips and rents both rafts and kayaks for 1/2-day outings from March to November. Its friendly, professional guides have led 35,000 river trips and logged 175,000 safe miles on the Ocoee alone.

Paddlers who rent craft on the Hiwassee, a state scenic river, may catch trout and glimpse deer, bears and boar. The minimum age for Ocoee rafting is 12 years; 6 is the minimum for the Hiwassee.

Ocoee Rafting, Inc.
John and Diana Holloran
P.O. Box 461
Ducktown, TN 37326
(615) 496-3388, (800) 251-4800
Ocoee River
Max. rapids: III-IV
America Outdoors

Ocoee Rafting Inc. runs guided 1-day trips on the Ocoee River, site of the 1996 Olympic whitewater events. The trips feature continuous Class III-IV rapids but are fine for beginners and anyone over 12. The Ocoee, running through the Cherokee National Forest, also offers beautiful wilderness scenery, trout and bass fishing, and plentiful wildlife, including deer, beavers, and, occasionally, bears.

Ocoee Rafting's season runs from March to November. During this time, guests on river trips can camp for free at the company's campground, equipped with hot showers and attractive sites.

Outdoor Adventures of Tennessee
Doug and Connie Simmons
P.O. Box 109
Welcome Valley Road
Ocoee, TN 37361
(615) 338-8634, (800) OARSMEN
Ocoee River
Max. rapids: III-IV
America Outdoors

Outdoor Adventures of Tennessee offers guided raft trips and tube rentals for 1/2-day trips on the Ocoee. With Class III-IV rapids, the Ocoee is suitable for beginners and exciting for experienced paddlers as well. Set in the Cherokee National Forest, the Ocoee trips feature wilderness scenery and views of soaring birds and other wildlife.

During its March-to-November

eason, the outfitter also offers a picnic area and camping on wooded sites.

Outland Expeditions
Lamar Davis
5501 Waterlevel Highway S.E.
Highway 64
Cleveland, TN 37323
(615) 478-1442, (615) 478-3553,
(800) 827-1442
Hiwasseee River, Lower Ocoee River
Max. rapids: III-IV

Outland Expeditions offers guided raft trips and canoe, kayak, raft, and tube rentals on the Ocoee and Hiwassee Rivers. The Ocoee trips cover five-and-a-half miles of continuous Class III-IV whitewater, a challenging and exciting run for beginners and experts alike. Hiwassee trips are leisurely, scenic, and particularly good for beginners, families, and trout fishermen. On both rivers, paddlers may be able to spot black bears, woodchucks, deer, and other wildlife.

Outland's season runs from March to November. During this time, the company offers free camping on wooded sites at its headquarters.

Quest Expeditions
Keith Jenkins
P.O. Box 499
Benton, TN 37307
(615) 338-2979, (800) 277-4537
Ocoee River
Max. rapids: III-IV
America Outdoors

Quest Expeditions specializes in guided raft trips for small groups on the Ocoee River. These trips last a 1/2-day and are challenging, fun whitewater runs with Class III-IV rapids, and are suitable for almost anyone. Ocoee trips, which run between April and October, also offer beautiful mountain scenery. In addition to its Ocoee runs, Quest offers fall and winter river trips on Class IV rapids through North America's last remaining tropical rain forest on the Rio Usumacinta in southern Mexico.

Rafting In The Smokies/Pigeon River Outdoors, Inc.
Andrew R. MacKinnon
P.O. Box 592, Highway 321 N.
Gatlinburg, TN 37738
(615) 436-5008, (800) 776-RAFT (7238)
French Broad River, Nantahala River, Big Pigeon River
Max. rapids: III-IV
America Outdoors

Rafting in the Smokies runs guided paddle-raft trips on the French Broad, Nantahala, and Big Pigeon Rivers. The Nantahala trips, for beginners and intermediate paddlers, feature the dramatic wilderness scenery of Nantahala Gorge, good trout fishing, and crystal-clear water. The Big Pigeon River offers a challenging, roaring five-mile run through the Great Smoky Mountains National Park and Pisgah National Forest. This trip is for intermediate to advanced paddlers. Finally, the French Broad River offers a quiet, scenic float on the placid waters for everyone aged 3 and up. The French Broad River has bass fishing; the Nantahala has trout fishing.

Rafting in the Smokies/Pigeon River Outdoors runs trips between March and October.

River Sports Outfitters
Ed McAlister
2918 Sutherland Avenue
Knoxville, TN 37919
(615) 523-0066
French Broad River, Nolichucky River, Little River
Max. rapids: V+
ACA

River Sports Outfitters offers guided canoe, kayak, and raft trips and rents canoes and kayaks for trips on the French Broad, Nolichucky, and Little Rivers. These trips, of 1-18 days, run year-round through unspoiled wilderness, offering fine scenery, trout fishing, swimming, and camping. River Sport Outfitters has trips for paddlers of all abilities, and also offers river adventures in Costa Rica and the Grand Canyon.

Rolling Thunder River Company
Ken and Dina Miller
P.O. Box 88
Almond, NC 28702
(704) 488-2030, (800) 344-5838
*Ocoee River, Chattooga River, Nantahala
River, French Broad, Nolichucky River*
Max. rapids: III-IV
America Outdoors

Rolling Thunder River Co. runs
guided canoe, kayak, and raft trips and
rents canoes, kayaks, rafts, and funyaks
on five rivers in North Carolina, Tennessee, and South Carolina. Trips on the
Nantahala have Class II-III rapids, are
easy enough for beginners and families,
and pass through the beautiful Nantahala Gorge. Full-day, wild-water raft
trips are available on the Ocoee. These
trips, with Class III and IV rapids, are
suitable for anyone age 12 and older.
Private canoe and kayak instruction on
the Ocoee is also available.

On the Chattooga, Rolling Thunder
offers an exciting overnight whitewater
canoe trip with Class II-IV rapids,
spectacular scenery, and abundant
wildlife. No experience is necessary on
this guided trip. Finally, a combination
French Broad River-Nolichucky River
raft trip is available. This 2-day expedition includes a night of camping at one
of the company's base camps.

Rolling Thunder's season runs from
April to October.

Sunburst Adventures, Inc.
P.O. Box 329
Welcome Valley Rd.
Benton, TN 37307
(800) 247-8388, (423) 338-8388
Ocoee River
Max. rapids: III-IV
America Outdoors, American Rivers

Sunburst Adventures offers guided
raft trips with highly experienced guides
for anyone age 12 and up. During its
March-to-November season, the company operates from a 35-acre facility
and specializes in camp, church, and
scout groups.

Rafters can enjoy five miles of continuous Class III-IV whitewater in
Cherokee National Forest's Ocoee
Gorge. Guests also can fish for trout,
bass, and panfish, learn about local
history, and enjoy the scenery. Wildlife
includes bears, wild turkeys, wild hogs,
and many raptors.

Tip-A-Canoe Stores, Inc.
D.J. Spear
1279 Highway 70
Kingston Springs, TN 37082
(615) 254-0836, (615) 646-7124
Harpeth River
Max. rapids: I-II
*Tennessee Association of Canoe Liveries and
Outfitters*

Tip-A-Canoe Stores, Inc., rents
canoes on the Harpeth River for trips of
1-4 days. With Class I-II rapids, the river
is easy enough for beginners, and offers
fishing for smallmouth bass, brim, crappie, and catfish. Paddlers can enjoy the
river's natural beauty, with its bluffs,
tree-lined banks, and beavers, otters,
deer, ducks, birds, and other wildlife.
Designated a state scenic river, the
Harpeth also has historic significance,
named for two bandit brothers, "Big"
and "Little" Harp, who terrorized the
region during the late 18th century.
Various Indian artifacts remain to be
seen. These include mounds, mills,
tunnels, carvings, and paintings.

During its March-to-November season, Tip-A-Canoe offers primitive camp
sites, picnic supplies, canoe accessories,
and custom trips.

USA RAFT
Mary Kay Heffernan
P.O. Box 277
Rowlesburg, WV 26425
(800) USA RAFT
North Fork Potomac River, Gauley River,
Cheat River, Tygart River, New River, Upper
Youghiogheny River, Nolichucky River, Ocoee
River, Nantahala River, French Broad River
Max. rapids: II-III
America Outdoors

USA Raft offers outings on ten of the best whitewater rivers in the East — the Russell Fork in Kentucky; the Upper Youghiogeny in Maryland; the Nolichucky, French Broad, and Nantahala in North Carolina; the Nolichucky and Ocoee in Tennessee; and the New, Gauley, Cheat, and Tygart in West Virginia. With this selection of trips, rivers, and outfitters, USA Raft offers affordable outings to suit paddlers of all skill levels at locations convenient to residents throughout the Middle Atlantic and Southeast.

Webb Bros. Float Service, Inc.
Harold Webb
Hiwassee River/Box 61
Reliance, TN 37369
(423) 338-2373
Hiwassee River
Max. rapids: I-II
PA

Webb Bros. rents rafts, tubes, and duckies for 5-mile trips through the Cherokee National Forest on the Hiwassee River. The oldest outfitter on the river, Webb Bros. is open year-round. Its run begins at the Appalachia powerhouse and ends at the company's own landing in the heart of the Reliance Historic District.

Wildwater Limited
Jim Greiner
P.O. Box 507
Ducktown, TN 37326
(800) 451-9972
Chattooga, Nantahala, Ocoee Rivers,
Big Pigeon
Max. rapids: V+
America Outdoors

Wildwater Limited operates in Georgia, North Carolina, South Carolina, and Tennessee, offering more than a dozen trip options for paddlers age 8 and over, ranging from novices to experts. The Chattooga is a National Wild and Scenic River, the Nantahala adjoins the Great Smoky Mountains National Park, and the Ocoee has been chosen for the 1996 Olympic whitewater events.

The company has served over 400,000 customers in 25 years of operation, and prides itself on its staff, facilities, and safety record. It rents rafts and kayaks as well as running guided canoe, kayak and raft trips during a March-to-mid-November season.

Texas

Clear and cold, the spring-fed streams of the Hill Country attract more canoeists than any other rivers of Texas. This area stretches from the central section of the Texas-Mexico border to the Colorado River in the east. Many of its streams are seasonal and susceptible to flash flooding due to high runoff after heavy rains. But the San Marcos, for instance, runs year-round and its clean water appeals to novice and expert paddlers alike. Located between Austin and San Antonio, it is mostly flat water and only one of its rapids is classified. Naturalists can find several species of plants and wildlife that are said to be unique in the world. While paddlers fish for bass, perch, catfish, and bluegill, they can observe hawks, owls, kingfishers, and herons overhead.

Hill Country streams typically contain whitewater rapids, small waterfalls and boulder gardens. River banks are lined with tall bald cypress, sycamore, pecan, and live oak trees, and cliffs are crowned with mesquite, cedar, and yucca. The Guadalupe River, flanked by rolling hills and rocky bluffs, has rapids for both novice and expert as well as good fishing.

Further west lies the Mountain Region, with the Rio Grande offering some of the most exciting scenery and canoe water in the state. At the heart of this country is the Big Bend National Park, a truly spectacular wilderness of desert canyons. With sheer walls rising 1800 feet or more, the Big Bend ravines rank behind only the Grand Canyon and Hell's Canyon on Idaho's Snake River.

Big Bend's deserts abound with cacti, while river cane, mesquite, salt cedar and cottonwood line the Rio Grande's banks. Canoeing and rafting can be enjoyed all year, but many paddlers say the best period is from Thanksgiving to Easter. In summer the river is at its lowest and in its rocky bed temperatures often rise above 110 degrees. The Rio is highly susceptible to flash flooding, especially during spring and fall. Some Texans insist that when the river is brown, this color denotes mud, not pollution. But one recent analysis found that the Rio "suffers from just every type of pollution imaginable." A popular trip in the Big Bend is Santa Elena Canyon, a 17-mile float between 1500-foot canyon walls. It is enlivened by the tricky "Rock slide" rapid, side canyons, fern-covered waterfalls, and cool swimming holes

Wildlife along this stretch includes eagles, rare peregrine falcons, bank beavers, wild burros, and javelina.

Elsewhere in Texas the scenery may be less awesome but the rivers are still appealing to many paddlers. The forested region of East Texas has a wealth of slow-moving, coffee-colored streams which owe their hue to tannic acid. And in the coastal area many vacationers enjoy paddling the bayous, rivers, and streams.

Abbott's River Outfitters
Jane Abbott
HCR 3 Box 871
New Braunfels, TX 78132
(210) 625-4928
Guadalupe River
Max. rapids: I-II

Abbott's rents canoes, kayaks, rafts, and tubes for 1/2- and 1-day trips on the scenic Guadalupe River in the heart of the Texas Hill Country. Customers can choose between three convenient locations along the river.

These floats are suitable for everyone, with good equipment and a wide variety of trips. The valley is beautiful, with cypress and pecan trees, and the dam-controlled river contains bass, perch, trout, and catfish. The company's season runs from April-October.

Big Bend River Tours
Beth Garcia
P.O. Box 337
Terlingua, TX 79852
(915) 424-3219, (800) 545-4240
Rio Grande
Max. rapids: III-IV
America Outdoors

Big Bend River Tours runs year-round guided raft tours through the dramatic wilderness of canyons and whitewater that comprises the Big Bend National Park. Trips last anywhere from 1/2 a day to 3 weeks. Most are suitable for rafters of all ages and skill levels. Within this mysterious and alluring desert-mountain country may be found deer, javelina, fox, beavers, and more bird species, including eagles, peregrine falcons and hawks,

than in any other National Park.

BBRT's friendly guides enjoy describing the flora and fauna, geology, folklore, and history as they steer the rafts through the canyons with rapids of up to Class III-IV difficulty. Floaters can enjoy fishing, camping, swimming and paddling lessons.

Bighorn Expeditions
P.O. Box 508
Junction, TX 76849
(915) 475-2118
Rio Grande, Pecos, Devils, and Gila Rivers
Max. rapids: III-IV
America Outdoors, Utah Guides and Outfitters

Bighorn Expeditions offers 2-8 day guided oar-boat trips on the Devils, Pecos, and Rio Grande Rivers in Texas and the Gila River in New Mexico. Unlike most outfitters offering oar-boat trips, Bighorn encourages guests to do the rowing. The company provides 11-foot, one-person rafts that are lively and riverworthy but small enough for easy handling. Trips include thorough lessons and begin on calm stretches, so they are fine for those with no rowing experience. Those wishing to row, however, should be in good physical condition. If you are unsure of your conditioning or prefer to concentrate on photography or bird-watching, you can elect to ride on one of the company's larger, guide-operated rafts.

Bighorn's trips run from March to November through scenic canyon terrain and offer good instruction in whitewater boating and wilderness ethics.

Canoes of Big Bend
Huck Geschke
Box 181
Terlingua, TX 79852
(915) 371-2613
Lower Rio Grande through Big Bend Nat.
Park
Max. rapids: II-III

Floats through spectacular canyon
and desert scenery are offered by Canoes
of Big Bend on 300 miles of river. The
company rents canoes to beginners and
experts alike for trips of varied difficulty.
Winter conditions are excellent, with
lows of 45 and highs of 75 degrees.

Five canyons, some with walls rising
1,600 feet, and the Chihuahua Desert
make for superb scenery along the way,
with wildlife ranging from peregrine
falcons to mule deer. The season runs
Sept.-May.

An oar-raft trip on the Rio Grande. Photo by
Jim Hudson, Rio Grande River Tours,
Lajitas, Texas.

Far Flung Adventures, Inc.
Steve Harris/Mike Davidson
P.O. Box 377
Terlingua, TX 79852
(915) 371-2489, (800) 359-4138
Lower Rio Grande
Max. rapids: III
Big Bend Assn., Texas River Runners

Far Flung Adventures specializes in
taking rafters on camping trips through
the ruggedly beautiful Big Bend region
of Texas as well as in other states in the
U.S. and Mexico. Its tours last from 1-7
days and run year-round. It caters to
everyone from novices to whitewater
experts seeking Class V+ challenges.
Floats specializing in such themes as
music, birding, and archeology are also
available.

The remoteness of the Rio Grande's
Big Bend National Park, its spectacular
canyons and wildlife, combine with good
fishing to make these trips unforgettable.
Far Flung Adventures offers paddling
lessons as well as camping and swimming.

Forest Cove Marina
Patti Carothers
1078 Marina Dr.
Kingwood, TX 77339-4068
(713) 359-FISH (3474)
Colorado, Brazos, San Jacinto, Guadalupe,
San Marcos Rivers, Houston, Conroe,
Livingston, Amistad Lakes, Christmas, West,
Matagorda Bays
Max. rapids: III-IV
PPA

Forest Cove Marina offers guided
canoe and kayak tours as well as renting
canoes, kayaks, rafts, and tubes for family-oriented trips of varying difficulty.
Most of the waters are flat and the fishing is good for bass, crappie, catfish,
flounder, and speckled trout.

The flat countryside is enlivened by
such species as roseate spoonbills and
alligators.

High Trails Co.
Bob Narramore
610 Marquis Drive
Garland, TX 75042
(214) 272-3353
All rivers in Texas, Arkansas, and Oklahoma
Max. rapids: I-II

High Trails, located at Garland, close to Dallas, rents canoes, kayaks and rafts for easy family paddling on rivers in Texas, Oklahoma, and Arkansas. Although not on a river, the company is within driving distance of many good paddling waters in all directions. Open year-round, it loads rivercraft on customers' cars or aboard its own trailers for large groups.

Some of the rivers its clients paddle, like the Guadalupe, are challenging. Mostly they are clear streams offering great fishing and camping, along with glimpses of wildlife including many kinds of birds. Trips last from 1-7 days.

Kimbo's
Rocky Shepler
HCR 4, Box 73
Canyon Lake, TX 78133
(512) 964-3113
Guadalupe River, Canyon Lake
Max. rapids: None

Kimbo's rents rafts and tubes from March-October for day-trip paddlers on the attractive Guadalupe River and Canyon Lake. The waters involved are clean and cold, with what is claimed to be the best rainbow trout fishing in Texas. Anglers can also catch catfish, perch, striper and walleye. Floats are easy, safe and suitable for families and large groups.

Set in the Texas hill country, the Guadalupe gives paddlers a view of cliffs and large trees. Deer, turkeys, armadillo, buffalo, Texas longhorn cattle and birds also enliven the scenery.

Mountain Breeze
Paul W. Rich
HC 3 Box 796, River Road
New Braunfels, TX 78132
(210) 964-2484
Guadalupe River
Max. rapids: I-II
PPA

Mountain Breeze offers fun and refreshing family trips on the cold, clear waters of the Guadalupe River in the scenic Texas hill country. It rents canoes, rafts, and tubes for trips of 1-10 hours. At normal water flow the river's rapids are rated Class I.

Deer, raccoons, and wild turkeys may be spotted as anglers fish for bass, trout, perch, and catfish. Camping and swimming are also available.

Northwest Passage
Rick Sweitzer
1130 Greenleaf Avenue
Wilmette, IL 60091
(847) 256-4409, (800) RECREATE
Current River, Rio Grande, Chicago River,
BWCA, Lake Michigan, Lake Superior
Max. rapids: III-IV

Northwest Passage offers guided raft trips on the New and Gauley Rivers in West Virginia; canoe trips on the Current River in Missouri, the Rio Grande in Texas, the Chicago River, and the Boundary Waters Canoe Area in Minnesota; and sea kayak trips on Lake Michigan in Illinois, in Door County, Wisconsin, and Lake Superior in Michigan. Most of these trips, which last 1-7 days, are designed for beginners; some require prior experience. Depending on the location, these trips offer excitement, challenge, remoteness and beauty.

An adventure travel company, Northwest Passage also offers skiing, hiking, cycling, backpacking, dogsledding, and rock climbing. Outings run year-round in the U.S., Canada, the Arctic, Greenland, Switzerland, New Zealand, Costa Rica, Belize, Crete, Tanzania, southern Africa, and Antarctica.

Paddlers enjoy a fresh-cooked meat on the Rio Grande. Photo by Jim Hudson, Rio Grande River Tours, Lajitas, Texas.

Piney Woods Canoe Co.
Nick & Leni Rodes
P.O. Box 1994
Kountze, TX 77625
(409) 274-5892
Village Creek, Neches & Trinity Rivers, Pine Is. Bayou
Max. rapids: None
PPA

The Piney Woods Canoe Co. is an experienced firm that prides itself on giving friendly, on-time service with good equipment and accurate river information. Open year-round, the outfitter rents canoes and runs guided canoe trips on a beautiful, meandering river through closed canopy forest. It is a unique area for wildflowers, cypresses, and southern birds, with pristine sandbars for picnics and swimming.

Camping is available during trips that last up to a week. Guests can also fish for largemouth bass, catfish, and bluegills.

Red River Canoe Co.
Bruce Keeler
497 N. Main St.
Moab, UT 84532
(801) 259-7722
Colorado, Green, and San Juan Rivers
Max. rapids: I-II
PPA, ACA

Red River rents canoes for use on mostly calm water in desert terrain. Deer, bighorn sheep, beavers, and an array of birds frequent the scenic landscape with its red sandstone canyons. Trips range from 1 day to a week and are suitable for all ability levels. Some Class II and III sections are available for seasoned whitewater canoeists.

The company offers personalized, custom trips from April to November.

Rio Grande Outfitters
Bill C. Ivey
Box 211
Terlingua, TX 79852
(915) 371-2424, (800) 226-2046
Rio Grande
Max. rapids: III-IV

Rio Grande Outfitters rents rafts for floats of up to Class III-IV difficulty through the spectacular canyons of the Rio Grande. The scenery is rugged, with chasms 1,500 feet deep amid the desert landscape. During the year-round season, the company arranges one-half to 10-day trips suitable for people of all ages and levels of experience.

Camping is available, swimming is good and fishermen angle for catfish.

Rio Raft Co.
John F. Guenzel
P.O. Box 2036
Canyon Lake, TX 78130
(210) 964-3613
Guadalupe River
Max. rapids: I-II
PA

Rio Raft Company rents canoes, rafts, and tubes for 1-day trips on the Guadalupe River above and below Canyon Dam. The Guadalupe passes through a region of sheer bluffs, limestone cliffs, rolling green hills, and tall cypress and pecan trees. In this area, attentive floaters can also spot turkeys, deer, hawks, squirrels, cranes, and turtles. The river has deep pools and small rapids, making for easy trips for novices and intermediate paddlers. Also, the river's cold, clear waters offer fishing for bass, perch, and rainbow and brown trout. Rio Raft's rentals are available year-round.

Rockin' R River Rides
Dick & Zero Rivers
1405 Gruene Rd.
New Braunfels, TX 78130-3334
(210) 629-9999, (800) 55 FLOAT,
(506) 556-1575 (Costa Rica)
Guadalupe, Comal, Rio Grande Rivers, also operates in Costa Rica
Max. rapids: I-II in US, II-IV in Costa Rica
PA, W. Virginia Rivers Coalition

Rockin' R rents canoes, rafts, and tubes and offers guided raft trips in the Texas Hill Country, with its towering rocky cliffs, boulders, and beautiful vegetation. The waters are cool and clean, and rapids are short and fun to run. Trips are safe for novices and families with children. Camping and fishing, for trout, smallmouth bass, catfish, carp and stripers, are available. The company's season runs from March to November.

Rockin' R operates in Costa Rica as "Dos Rios Whitewater Rafting," conducting guided raft trips year-round through the rain forest.

Roy's Rentals
Roy L. Vordenbaum
HCR 3, Box 869
New Braunfels, TX 78132
(512) 964-3721
Guadalupe River
Max. rapids: I-II
PPA

Roy's Rentals, located between Austin and San Antonio, rents canoes, tubes and rafts for paddling down the Guadalupe River from Canyon Lake to New Braunfels. From March to September, its courteous staff helps novices and experienced paddlers arrange 1-2 day trips of varying difficulty. At high water the river with its Class I-II rapids gains added excitement.

Unlike large parts of Texas, the countryside along this stretch of the Guadalupe has rolling hills and riverside cliffs. Deer and ducks are plentiful, and the fish include catfish, rainbow trout, perch and bass.

Rafting on the Rio Grande. Photo by Jim Hudson, Rio Grande River Tours, Lajitas, Texas.

SouthWest Paddlesports
Patti Carothers & James Graham
1101 Hamblen Rd.
Kingwood, TX 77339
(713) 359-3474, (713) 359-7468,
FAX (713) 358-3167
San Jacinto, Brazos, Colorado, Guadalupe,
San Marcos Rivers, Houston, Conroe,
Livingston, Amistad Lakes, Christmas, West,
Matagorda Bays
Max. rapids: III-IV
PPA

Southwest Paddlesports runs guided
canoe and kayak trips year-round on
mostly flat waters, suitable for beginners
and families. It also rents canoes,
kayaks, rafts, and tubes. Only the
Guadalupe and San Marcos Rivers have
whitewater here and there. With camping, trips last up to 3 days. Fishing is
usually good for bass, crappie, gar,
drum, catfish, flounder, and speckled
trout.

The company, which prides itself on
its friendly, personal service, also gives
paddling lessons.

**Spencer Canoes/Shady Grove
Campground**
Pat Spencer
9515 FM 1979
Martindale, TX 78655
(512) 357-6113
San Marcos River
Max. rapids: I-II
PPA

Spencer Canoes/Shady Grove Campground, conveniently based on the San
Marcos River between Austin and San
Antonio, rents, sells and builds canoes.
Offering a full-service retail operation,
private shuttles and rental trips on a
clean, spring-fed river, the Spencer
family prides itself on the personal service it gives clients. This includes a video
orientation of the San Marcos River and

asic paddling tips for novices. They will
elp guests choose a river section of the
esired length and level of difficulty.

The San Marcos is a beautiful, rela-
ively undeveloped river with stretches
anging from flat to Class II or III. It has
everal unique plant and wildlife species
nd water temperature of 72 degrees
ear-round.

'G Canoe Livery

)uane and Evelyn TeGrotenhuis
O. Box 177
Iartindale, TX 78655
512) 353-3946
an Marcos River, Blanco River
Iax. rapids: I-II
'PA

TG Canoe Livery calls itself a person-
ble Mom and Pop business which sets
ut to ensure that individuals and
roups alike have safe and enjoyable
anoeing and kayaking. Operating
ear-round, it rents canoes and kayaks,
roviding guided day-trip paddling on
he San Marcos and Blanco Rivers.

The 72-degree spring-fed San Marcos
said to be the cleanest river in Texas
nd it combines lush vegetation with
mall, interesting rapids. In addition to
s rich birdlife, the river contains bass,
erch, catfish, bluegill and gar.

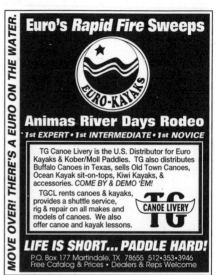

Utah

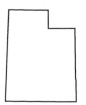

U tah boasts 400 miles of raftable rivers ranging from the Green ar Colorado to their lesser-known tributaries such as the Yampa, the San R; fael and the San Juan. Spectacular red-rock canyons, exotic wildlife, son of the most exciting whitewater in the West, easy rapids, calm floating – Utah has all of the above.

You can sign up with Utah outfitters for Grand Canyon rafting exped tions (see Arizona), which typically start at Lee's Ferry, just south of the Utai Arizona state line. If you want still more, you can go on package tours th; combine horseback or mountain bike riding with river running, or he; expert guides discuss history, folklore, geology, wildlife, and other topics local interest.

If Utah cannot match the majesty of Arizona's unique Grand Canyon, comes close. Utah's Green River gorge is as deep as the Grand Canyon ar the rapids in the Colorado's Cataract Canyon rival any in the world-famo chasm for power and difficulty.

From Sand Wash on the Green River, floaters can take an 84-mile fiv day trip over some 60 rapids — exciting but not technically difficult — a ternating with swift, calm water. They pass through Desolation Canyon, tortuous chasm with sculpted cliffs, crags and towering peaks on either sid It was Major John Wesley Powell who gave Desolation Canyon its nan during his epic 1869 descent of the Green and Colorado Rivers. But althoug its colorful rock strata remain unchanged, it is not so desolate — or deser ed — today. Rafters gaze upward at pine-covered desert mesas or relax : the cool, clear waters of pools and side streams.

Elsewhere on the Green River floaters may enjoy Labyrinth and Stil water Canyons, great places for canoeing, or the one-day run through Gr; Canyon near Interstate 70. Fishermen take special delight in the stretch the Green River just below Flaming Gorge Dam in the far northeast corn of the state. It is said to provide some of the best fishing water in the worl with the largest trout population of any river in the lower 48 states.

Upstream on the Colorado is Westwater Canyon, with its narrow Blac Granite Gorge and its feisty rapids: Funnel Falls, The Steps, Last Chan

nd Skull Rapid. On the upper canyon's calmer stretches, rafters may float
n silent contemplation of a wilderness in which beaver, muskrat, raccoon,
nd great blue heron make their home, along with the occasional golden
agle. Westwater permits for individual paddlers are scarce: call 801-259-
421 for information on how to apply.

In Cataract Canyon, within Canyonlands National Park, the Colorado
after encounters 26 rapids bearing such names as Brown Betty, Mile Long
nd the Button, followed by the Big Drops. This whitewater is described as
truly awesome" in the spring runoff season from late May through most of
une. The scenery is fantastic, with the gorge deepening to 2,000 feet and
s colorful walls crowned with buttes and castellations. Rafters can hike to
ndian ruins and view the confluence of the Green and Colorado rivers.

Adrift Adventures
Mike Hughes
O. Box 577
78 N. Main Street
Moab, UT 84532
(01) 259-8594, (800) 874-4483
olorado River, Green River
Max. rapids: V+
tah Guides and Outfitters, America
utdoors

Adrift Adventures runs guided raft
ips of 1-7 days on the Colorado and
Green Rivers, passing through the stun-
ing red-rock canyons of Canyonlands
National Park. The trips vary greatly in
ifficulty, depending on the river, time of
ear, and whether guests elect to ride in
n oar boat or paddle themselves. On all
ips, beginners and experts alike can en-
y the spectacular rock formations and
oundant Indian ruins, pictographs, and
etroglyphs. Guests also can view wild-
fe, including bighorn sheep, deer, ot-
rs, beavers, and cougars.

Adrift Adventures' season is from
March to November. During that time
he company also offers jeep trips, jet-
oat tours, and mountain bike trips.

Adventure River
Skip Bell
Box 2133
Salt Lake City, UT 84110
(801) 363-1222
Green, Colorado Rivers
Max. rapids: III-IV

Guided raft trips through the Canyonlands National Park, with its sheer
desert canyon walls and spires, are Adventure River's specialty. Partly owned
by its guides, the company takes clients
to Cataract and Westwater Canyons,
which can be challenging with Class III-
IV rapids and are for persons aged over
10. Desolation Canyon on the Green
River is good for all ages with its Class
III rapids. Both Desolation and Cataract
have numerous Indian ruins and rock
art. Camping trips of up to 6 days are
available during the April-October
season.

UTAH

American River Touring Association
Steve Welch
24000 Casa Loma Rd.
Groveland, CA 95321
(800) 323-2782, (209) 962-7873
Green River, Yampa River, Colorado River,
Middle Fork and Main Salmon Rivers,
Selway River, Merced River, Tuolumne River,
Klamath River, Rogue River, Illinois River,
Umpqua River
Max. rapids: III
America Outdoors, Oregon Guides and
Packers, Idaho Outfitters and Guides, Utah
Guides and Outfitters

ARTA offers a total of 16 raft trips in
five Western states. The trips, in California, Oregon, Utah, Idaho, and Arizona,
are by oar rafts, paddle rafts, oar/paddle
combination rafts, and inflatable canoes.

Most trips are of Class III difficulty
and appropriate for novices and families,
as well as those with more experience.
Other trips of up to Class V+ difficulty
challenge even the most advanced
paddler. Depending on the location,
the trips also feature wildflowers, side
streams, swimming holes, Indian ruins,
warm water, abundant wildlife, good
hiking and fishing, and hot springs.

ARTA, a non-profit company, also
offers whitewater schools, professional
guide training, and family discounts.

Bighorn Expeditions
Pitchfork Enterprises
P.O. Box 365
Bellvue, CO 80512
(303) 221-8110
Green River, Dolores River, Rio Grande
Max. rapids: III-IV
America Outdoors, Utah Guides and
Outfitters

Bighorn Expeditions offers 2-8 day
guided oar-boat trips on the Rio Grande
River in Texas, the Dolores River in
Colorado, and the Green River in Utah.
Unlike most outfitters offering oar-boat
trips, Bighorn encourages guests to do
the rowing. The company provides 11-
foot, one-person rafts that are lively
and riverworthy but small enough for

easy handling. Trips include thorough
lessons and begin on calm stretches, so
they are fine for those with no rowing
experience. Those wishing to row,
however, should be in good physical
condition. If you are unsure of your con
ditioning or prefer to concentrate on
photography or bird-watching, you can
elect to ride on one of the company's
larger, guide-operated rafts.

Bighorn's trips run from March to
November through scenic canyon terrain and offer good instruction in white
water boating and wilderness ethics.

Bill Dvorak's Kayak and Rafting
Expeditions
Bill and Jaci Dvorak
17921 US Highway 285
Nathrop, CO 81236
(719) 539-6851, (800) 824-3795
Arkansas, Colorado, Green, Gunnison,
North Platte, Dolores, Middle Fork Salmon
and Main Salmon, Rio Grande, and Salt River
Max. rapids: V+
America Outdoors, Colorado River Outfitte
Association, Utah Guides and Outfitters, an
New Mexico River Outfitters Association

Dvorak's runs a wide array of guided
and unguided trips through 29 canyons
on a total of 10 rivers in Colorado,
Utah, and New Mexico. Scenery ranges
from Alpine to desert, and whitewater
ranges from Class I to Class V. Guests
also have a choice of touring by canoe,
kayak, or raft. With this selection of
locations and trips, Dvorak's has offerings to suit any individual or group.

Trips run for one to 13 days between
March and October and permit time
for trout fishing and viewing deer, elk,
bears, eagles, beavers, and coyotes.

Canyon Voyages
Don & Denise Oblak
Box 416
Moab, UT 84532
(800) 733-6007, (801) 259-6007
Colorado, Dolores, Green Rivers
Max. rapids: III-IV
America Outdoors

Canyon Voyages, unlike some outfitters, caters to couples, families and small groups rather than heavy volume business. Its raft and kayak guided trips through the breathtaking scenery of the Canyonlands and the Colorado Plateau operate in relative seclusion. The company also rents canoes, kayaks, and rafts during its March-November season.

Camping and paddling are available, wildlife is plentiful. Trips last up to 3 days and suit novices as well as people seeking whitewater excitement.

Colorado River and Trail Expeditions
Vicki and David Mackay
5058 S. 300 West
Salt Lake City, UT 84107
(801) 261-1789
Green River, Colorado River
Max. rapids: III-IV

Colorado River & Trail Expeditions runs guided raft trips of 5-12 days on the Colorado River in Utah and Arizona, the Green River in Utah, and Glacier Bay and the Arctic National Wildlife Refuge in Alaska. These trips offer excellent whitewater and magnificent scenery in remote locations. Their difficulty varies with the river and season. Generally, all trips are fine for people in good health and good physical condition.

During its May-September season, Colorado River & Trails also offers educational trips, which study photography, history, natural history or ecology.

Dinosaur Expeditions
Tim Mertens
PO. Box 3387
Park City, UT 84060
250 E. Main Vernal, UT 84078
(801) 649-8092, (801) 781-0717
Yampa, Green Rivers
Max. rapids: III-IV
America Outdoors, Utah Outfitters & Guides

Dinosaur Expeditions is a small, dedicated company that has been in business since 1979 and takes fewer than 400 people down the Yampa and Green rivers each year. This is intentional, since the company wants to pay utmost attention to each passenger. The Yampa joins the Green River in Dinosaur National Monument, and the area is rich in fascinating geology, wildlife, Indian lore and shades of Major John Wesley Powell's epic 1869 exploration.

The company runs its guided raft and dory trips, lasting 1-5 days, from April to September.

Don Hatch River Expeditions, Inc.
Meg Hatch
Box 1150
Vernal, UT 84078
(800) 342-8243, (801) 789-4316
Middle Fork of the Salmon (Idaho), Cataract of the Colorado, Yampa, Green Rivers
Max. rapids: V+
America Outdoors

With over 60 years' experience, this outfitter has expert staff to handle its varied guided raft expeditions over waters ranging from "mild to wild." The spectacular scenery includes Alpine forests in the Idaho trips and deep desert-terrain canyons in the more southerly tours of Utah and Colorado.

With new, state-of-the-art equipment, the emphasis is on safety and service. Paddlers can spot deer, bighorn sheep, and beaver in the wilderness while fishing for trout and catfish. Camping trips last up to 6 days, and the company's season runs May-September.

Eagle Outdoor Sports, Inc.
Rex Mumford
1507 S. Haight Creek
Kaysville, UT 84037
(801) 451-7238, (800) 369-6635
Green River, Yampa River
Max. rapids: III-IV
Utah Guides and Outfitters

Eagle Outdoor Sports, Inc. runs guided fishing trips and guided scenic raft trips on the Green River from Flaming Gorge Dam to the Colorado state line. They also run whitewater trips on the Green and Yampa Rivers within Dinosaur National Monument. Trips are from 2-5 days in length. All trips offer spectacular canyon scenery, private campsites, excellent meals, knowledgeable guides, and the opportunity to see deer, elk, bighorn sheep, and smaller wildlife. Trips are by oar or paddle raft and are ideal for families. The minimum age is six for scenic trips and 11 for whitewater trips. Eagle Outdoor's season runs from April through October.

Flaming Gorge Lodge
Craig W. Colletti
Greendale U.S. 191
Dutch John, UT 84023
(801) 889-3773
Green River
Max. rapids: I-II

Flaming Gorge Lodge offers guided raft and dory trips and raft rentals of 1-3 days on the Green River. Guided trips are by oar boat and geared for those who want to sample the Green River's excellent fishing for cutthroat, rainbow, brook, and brown trout. Raft rentals for self-guided float trips run on the river just below Flaming Gorge Dam. These trips feature gentle rapids and scenic canyons, and are fun for families and paddlers of all ages.

Open year-round, Flaming Gorge Lodge also offers motel rooms, condominium units, a general store, and shuttle service. Nearby campgrounds are also available.

Four Corners School
P.O. Box 1029
Monticello, UT 84535
(801) 587-2156, (800) 525-4456
San Juan River
Max. rapids: II-III

Four Corners School offers guided raft trips on the San Juan River. These trips last 5-8 days and pass through a region of spectacular geological formations, Anasazi ruins and abundant wildlife, including raptors, deer, coyotes, and

lizards. With Class II-III rapids and the choice of either paddle or oar boats, floating the river is not strenuous. However, guests should be fit enough to participate in 3-6 mile day hikes to archaeological sites and rock formations. Four Corners' trips run from April to October.

Hawk, I'm Your Sister
Beverley Antaeus
Box 9109
Santa Fe, NM 87504
(505) 984-2268
Green River
Max. rapids: I-II
Worldwide Outfitter & Guide Assn.

Hawk, I'm Your Sister of Sante Fe specializes in women's wilderness canoe and raft trips. Its year-round program is geared to "women of all ages, shapes, sizes and skill levels" with guided trips in five states and three foreign locations. Its aim is to "teach you the language of the forests, canyons, deserts and waterways" in a safe and non-competitive environment. It takes paddlers on Heron Lake in New Mexico and the Missouri River in Montana, with other excursions to Mexico, Peru, and Russia.

Holiday River and Bike Expeditions
544 East 3900 Street
Salt Lake City, UT 84107
(801) 266-2087, (800) 624-6323
Colorado River, Green River, San Juan River, Yampa River,
Max. rapids: V+
Utah Guides and Outfitters

Holiday River and Bike Expeditions rents canoes and rafts as well as running guided canoe, kayak, and raft trips on the Colorado, Green, San Juan, and Yampa Rivers in Utah and the Snake, Main Salmon, Lower Salmon, and Lochsa Rivers in Idaho. These trips last 1-12 days, offer oar and paddle options, and range in difficulty from beginners' runs to expert-level whitewater adventures. Floaters pass through pristine areas with spectacular scenery ranging from arid desert canyons to alpine forests. Along the way, guests can camp, swim, fish for trout, and catfish, and spot deer, bighorn sheep, raptors, otters, and beavers.

Holiday's season runs from April to October.

Hondoo Rivers and Trails
Gary George
Box 750098
95 E. Main
Torrey, UT 84775
(801) 425-3519, (800) 33 CANYONS
Green River
Max. rapids: I-II
Utah Guides and Outfitters, Worldwide Guides and Outfitters

Hondoo Rivers and Trails runs guided kayak and raft trips on the Green River. Trips last up to 6 days and are designed for beginning and intermediate paddlers who want to learn whitewater skills and become comfortable with progressively larger rapids. Oar-boat trips are also available for families with young children and anyone preferring a less challenging ride. On Hondoo's trips, which run between May and October, guests can enjoy canyon scenery, swimming, sandy beaches, warm water, and fishing for catfish. In this wilderness area, one can often spot deer, geese, eagles, and an occasional bear or bighorn sheep.

Lake Powell Tours, Inc.
P.O. Box 40
St. George, UT 84771-0040
(801) 673-1733
San Juan River, Lake Powell
Max. rapids: I-II

Lake Powell Tours offers small guided kayak and raft trips and rents kayaks for trips of 2-5 days on the San Juan River and Lake Powell. River trips are good for beginners but also offer enough eddies and rapids to interest intermediate and advanced kayakers. On all tours, paddlers can enjoy the soothing desert landscape, unusual geology, and views of beavers, birds, deer, snakes, and bighorn

sheep. One can also fish in Lake Powell for bass and trout and on the San Juan for catfish. Lake Powell Tours' season is from April-October.

Laughing Heart Adventures
Dezh Pagen
Trinity Outdoor Center
P.O. Box 669
Willow Creek, CA 95573
(916) 629-3516, (800) 541-1256
Green River
Max. rapids: I
PPA, America Outdoors, ACA, NORS

Laughing Heart Adventures offers canoe outings on the Green River in the Canyonlands of Utah. Trips last 5 days and cover 75 miles of moving flatwater where the canyon walls rise dramatically 1,000 feet above the river. The Green River meanders through an incredibly scenic wilderness canyon containuing Anasazi ruins, clear water tributaries, bighorn sheep, caves, and a geological fantasyland of exposed color and shape. LHA suggests combining this river trip with a visit to Canyonlands or Arches National Park.

Moab Rafting Company
Pierce Nelson
Box 801
Moab, UT 84532
(801) 259-RAFT, (800) RIO MOAB
Colorado, San Juan Rivers
Max. rapids: III-IV

Moab Rafting runs guided raft and kayak trips through 1,000-foot deep red canyons, passing interesting geology and ancient Indian ruins. The rapids are moderate and safe for people of all ages. The company emphasizes smallness and quality in its camping tours, which last up to 6 days.

Catfish may be caught and the shore wildlife includes bighorn sheep, deer, eagle and much more. The season runs March-October.

Moki Mac River Expeditions, Inc.
Richard, Clair and Robert Quist
P.O. Box 21242
Salt Lake City, UT 84121
(801) 268-6667, (800) 284-7280
Colorado River, Green River
Max. rapids: V+
Utah Guides and Outfitters, PPA

Moki Mac River Expeditions runs guided canoe, raft and "funyak" trips of 1-14 days on the Colorado and Green Rivers. Runs on the Colorado go through the Westwater, Cataract, and Grand Canyons, and on the Green River through the Desolation, Labyrinth, and Stillwater Canyons. Oar boats are available on all runs, motorized boats are available in Cataract Canyon and the Grand Canyon, and oar-boat/funyak trips run through Desolation Canyon. The Grand Canyon has the largest, most frequent rapids, Desolation Canyon is milder and Cataract Canyon offers great excitement during the high-water run-off season.

Moki Mac also rents canoes for trips through the Labyrinth and Stillwater Canyons. All trips, set on the Colorado Plateau, offer chances to spot eagles, cranes, Canada geese, bighorn sheep, and the occasional bear. Guests can also fish for catfish and trout. Moki Mac's season is from April to October.

NAVTEC Expeditions
John and Chris Williams
321 North Main
Box 1267
Moab, UT 84532
(801) 259-7983
Colorado River
Max. rapids: III-IV

NAVTEC Expeditions offers guided kayak and raft trips of 1/2-4 days on the Colorado through Westwater, Fisher Towers, and Cataract Canyons. These trips feature spectacular canyon scenery, red-rock cliffs and white-sand beaches, with abundant great blue herons, mule deer, beavers, bighorn sheep, and other wildlife. Guests can elect either paddle-

boat or motor-raft trips to suit their adventurousness. NAVTEC's trips on the Colorado run between April and October. From December to March the company offers whale-watching trips on the Sea of Cortez in Baja, Mexico.

Nichols Expeditions
Chuck and Judy Nichols
497 North Main
Moab, UT 84532
(801) 259-3999, (800) 648-8488
Copper River, Green River, Koyakuk River,
Main Salmon River, Sea of Cortez,
Magdalena Bay
Max. rapids: II-IV
Utah Guides and Outfitters, Idaho Guides
and Outfitters

Nichols offers a 6-day "Green River Wilderness Quest" in Utah's Labyrinth Canyon. The trip's "movement and and sensory awareness exercises help tune in the wilderness within ourselves."

Nichols Expeditions also offers sea kayaking in Baja, Mexico, featuring sandy beaches, clear water, sea lions, whales, and warm winter days. Beginners are welcome. Operating year-round, Nichols Expeditions also offers mountain biking trips.

O.A.R.S.
George Wendt
P.O. Box 67
Angels Camp, CA 95222
(209) 736-4677, (800) 446-7238 (CA),
(800) 346-6277 (U.S.)
San Juan River, American River, Cal-Salmon
River, Merced River, Stanislaus River,
Tuolumne River, Rogue River, Colorado River
Snake, Salmon and Little Fork Salmon Rivers
Max. rapids: III-IV
America Outdoors

O.A.R.S. runs guided dory, raft and kayak trips in six Western states. It offers tours in California on the American, Cal-Salmon, Merced, Stanislaus, and Tuolumne Rivers; in Oregon on the Rogue; in Arizona on the Colorado; in Wyoming on the Snake, and in Utah on the San Juan River. These outings last

1-13 days and, depending on the class of river, are fine for children, novices, families, intermediate, and expert rafters. O.A.R.S. trips provide fishing, swimming, camping, side hikes, wildlife viewing and other activities. Tours run from April to October.

The National Outdoor Leadership School
Nancy Siegel, River Manager
Box AA
Lander, WY 82520
(307) 332-6973
Green River, Prince William Sound, other Alaskan waters
Max. rapids: III-IV
America Outdoors, Colorado River Outfitters Association, Utah Guides and Outfitters Organization

The National Outdoor Leadership School specializes in teaching a wide array of backcountry skills including kayaking, rafting, mountaineering, rock climbing, glacier travel, backpacking and cross-country skiing. Its rafting trips

run through Desolation Canyon on the Green River in Utah and Lodore Canyon on the Green River at the Colorado-Utah border. NOLS also offers sea kayaking in Alaska and Baja, Mexico. These instructional trips range in length from 14-31 days, with some trips geared for teenagers 16 and older and some for paddlers 25 and older. All runs are physically challenging.

These trips, which run between June and late October, feature beautiful scenery and sufficient challenge to ensure that all participants can test and improve their paddling skills.

Red River Canoe Co.
Bruce Keeler, Lisa Katz
497 North Main
Moab, UT 84532
(801) 259-7722
Green, Colorado, Dolores, San Juan Rivers, Lake Powell
Max. rapids: III
America Outdoors

Red River Canoe offers both guided

Kayak clinics on the Green River taught by Cully Erdman of Slickrock Adventures. Photo: Lucy K. Wallingford/Slickrock Adventures.

An oar-boat trip on the Green River. Photo by Norm Shrewsbury, courtesy of Sheri Griffith Expeditions.

and unguided canoe trips suitable for novices as well as advanced paddlers. Moderate physical condition is required for flatwater trips, good physical shape for whitewater. The small family-owned business provides gourmet cooking and certified instructor/guides.

Red rock canyons, rock arches, high deserts, and vast panoramas abounding in deer, bighorn sheep, beaver, heron, and eagles provide the setting for these trips. Camping trips of up to 5 days are available during the March-October season.

River Runner Sports
Don & Denise Oblak
401 N. Main St.
Moab, UT 84532
(801) 259-4121
*Colorado, Dolores, Green, San Juan Rivers,
Lake Powell*
Max. rapids: V+

Trips of 1-10 days through superb scenery are on offer by River Runner Sports. The company rents canoes, kayaks, and rafts to beginners as well as seasoned paddlers. Some multi-day camping trips are on flatwater while others involve exciting rapids. Many trips require advance official permits, which restrict numbers of boaters.

The company provides top-line equipment, certified instruction and complete information on area rivers. Its season runs March-November.

Sheri Griffith Expeditions, Inc.
Sheri Griffith
P.O. Box 1324
2231 S. Highway 191
Moab, UT 84532
(801) 259-8229, (800) 332-2439,
FAX (801) 259-2226
Colorado, Green, Dolores Rivers
Max. rapids: III-V
*America Outdoors, Utah Guides and
Outfitters, Colorado River Outfitters Assn.*

Sheri Griffith Expeditions runs guided raft and kayak trips of 1-6 days through Westwater and Cataract Canyons on the Colorado River, Desolation Canyon on the Green River, and along the Dolores River. All trips are through protected lands — national parks and landmarks, wild and scenic rivers — where permits limit the number of boats and ensure a true wilderness experience. On all trips, guests can enjoy exciting rapids, spectacular canyons, excellent food and a chance to view bighorn sheep, golden eagles, and other wildlife.

Guests can choose between oar boats, paddle boats, inflatable kayaks and motorized J-rig rafts. Trips are of moderate to advanced difficulty, depending on iver, dates, and choice of boat. During ts May-Sept. season, Sheri Griffith also offers special family trips, camping trips, uxury trips, women-only floats, combination mountain bike/raft trips, and norseback/raft trips.

Slickrock Adventures
Cully Erdman
P.O. Box 1400
Moab, UT 84532
(800) 390-5715, FAX (801) 259-6996
Green River
Max. rapids: II

Slickrock Adventures combines two sports on its tour of the Canyonlands area near Moab. Beginning with 3 days of sea kayaking, guests journey 44 miles downstream through the flatwater stretch of Labyrinth Canyon. The steady current and sleek hull design of the sea kayaks allow easy travel. On Day 4 the paddlers meet mountain bike guides and continue by bike on the famous White Rim Trail. The ride is rated easy to moderate and is vehicle supported. On both halves of the trip clients enjoy numerous side hikes and camp on sandy beaches or atop huge sandstone cliffs. Customers have the option of joining either the bike trip or the kayak portion separately. Open all year, Slickrock also offers paddling trips in Belize and Mexico.

Tag-A-Long Expeditions
Bob Jones
452 N. Main St.
Moab, UT 84532
(800) 453-3292, (801) 259-8946,
FAX (801) 259-8990
Colorado, Green Rivers
Max. rapids: V+

Tag-A-Long runs guided canoe and raft trips as well as renting canoes for trips through the Westwater and Cataract Canyons on the Colorado River and the Desolation, Stillwater and Labyrinth Canyons on the Green River.

Lasting up to 6 days, these outings involve Class I to Class V rapids, with something for everyone. Guides are licensed and very experienced. The deep red rock canyons contain bighorn sheep, deer, and many raptors. The season runs April-October.

Western River Expeditions
Larry Lake
7258 Racquet Club Drive
Salt Lake City, UT 84121
(801) 942-6669, (800) 453-7450 (outside UT)
Colorado River, Green River, Main Salmon River
Max. rapids: III-IV
America Outdoors, Professional River Outfitters

Western River Expeditions runs guided raft trips and rents rafts and inflatable kayaks on the Colorado River in Colorado, Utah and Arizona; the Green River in Utah and the Main Salmon in Idaho. Green River trips, by oar or paddle raft, provide thrilling whitewater and views of towering red rock cliffs and arches, deep gorges, frontier cabins, and Indian petroglyphs.

Colorado River tours offer spectacular scenery in Cataract Canyon, Westwater Canyon or the Upper and Lower Grand Canyon. Rapids are moderate to large, and paddlers can swim, take side hikes and view historic Indian and Old West sites. Finally, trips on the Main Salmon involve scenic blue-green waters, pine-covered mountains, stops at hot springs and abandoned mining camps, and camping on white sand beaches.

All trips are suitable for anyone of good health above the minimum age set for each trip, depending on its difficulty. During Western River's March-September season, some trips can be combined with a ranch stay.

Vermont

Exploring Vermont by canoe puts its delightful scenery, so familiar to the traveling motorist, in a new perspective. The Green Mountain State is graced with many rivers to take the paddler through its pastures, woods and rocky gorges amid the forested hills. Vermont streams are made for tranquil floating, not for crashing down thunderous rapids. Such whitewater as exists is modest by West Virginia or western standards. Vermont's charms are different: relaxed paddling under covered bridges, past red barns and through wooded valleys spiced with inviting country inns. And of course the ideal time to go is in the fall when the foliage can be admired in all its glory.

Of the three big rivers that cut through the Green Mountain Range, the Winooski is the most scenic. It flows westward from its source in the cheese-making area of Cabot to empty into Lake Champlain at Burlington. The Winooski is dammed at intervals and must be portaged, but runnable all summer long. It has deep gorges and views of Mount Mansfield to starboard and the Camel's Hump to port.

Spaced further north, flowing parallel to the Winooski, are the Lamoille and Missisquoi Rivers, both of which also help feed Lake Champlain. One Lamoille run combines gentle floating past woods and meadows with the occasional easy rapid. The Missisquoi takes a loop across the Canadian border before returning to Vermont. Both are appealing rivers.

The White River is one of the most beloved canoe trails in New England. It provides easy rapids — Class I-II — as well as water so pure that it was chosen as a spawning-ground by the Atlantic Salmon Restoration Project. On its way down to join the Connecticut River, the White flows through a scenic valley that was once a main Indian route between lower New England and Montreal.

The Black River in northcentral Vermont offers a slow, meandering float downstream from Albany, providing the paddler with pretty scenery and deep forests as it follows a curving valley. The Clyde River which flows northwest from Island Pond provides a Class II run when the water level is right. Its lower stretch is secluded and has been called one of Vermont's best canoe ing trails. Like the Black, the Clyde flows into Lake Memphremagog astride the Canadian border.

Near the pleasant little town of Waitsfield at the foot of the Green Mountains, the Mad River flows northward to its confluence with the Winooski below Middlesex. It offers easy Class I-II rapids amid forested scenery.

New Englanders seeking Vermont's best whitewater head for the West River on the first weekends of May and October (or maybe the last weekend of September). This stream in southern Vermont has lively Class II-IV rapids, scene of whitewater kayaking championships, in a gorgeous Green Mountain setting. It can only be run when the Ball Mountain Dam releases water — currently just those two weekends. Pick the autumn date if you want to combine paddling with fall foliage.

Another appealing destination in southern Vermont is Somerset Reservoir, a wilderness lake between Mount Snow and Stratton Mountain which can be reached only by dirt road. Campers can view nesting loons, hawks, bears, and an occasional moose.

The Connecticut is a river on a different scale. More than 400 miles long, it divides Vermont from New Hampshire as it rolls majestically down toward Long Island Sound. Since the state line is drawn at the low-water mark on the Vermont side, the upper Connecticut actually belongs to New Hampshire.

Balloon Inn Vermont Vacations
Scott Wright
RR 1, Box 8
Fairlee, VT 05045
(802) 333-4326, (800) 666-1946
Connecticut River
Max. rapids: I-II

Balloon Inn Vermont rents canoes from May-October for self-guided trips on the Connecticut River between Woodsville, N.H. and Orford, N.H. These trips, of 1-3 days, include lodging at historic inns along the river. With only Class I-II rapids to contend with, paddling is only moderately difficult, even for beginners. Along the way, floaters can enjoy the natural beauty of the river valley, and fishing for trout, pike, bass, and walleye. The company also offers bicycling, hiking and balloon trips.

BattenKill Canoe
Jim Walker
Vermont Canoe Trippers
Box 65, Historic Route 7A
Arlington, VT 05250
(802) 362-2800, (800) 421-5268
Winooski River, Lamoille River, Missiquoi River, Clyde River, White River, Black River, Connecticut River, Maine Coast
Max. rapids: III-IV

BattenKill Canoe offers guided and unguided canoe trips of 2-10 days on the Winooski, Lamoille, Missisquoi, Clyde, Black, Connecticut, and White Rivers. These outings are exceptionally well organized and widely varied to suit all skill levels and tastes. Participants can choose either whitewater or scenic trips, with lodgings either at country inns or at secluded riverside camp sites. Also available throughout the March-November season are instructional trips for all skill levels; river sampler trips that

VERMONT

A covered bridge along the Battenkill River. Courtesy of Karen Krough/BattenKill Canoe, Arlington, Vermont.

offer paddling on a different river each day; historic tours retracing explorers' routes, and fall foliage trips. Finally, BattenKill also offers a 5-day trip along the mid-coast of Maine with 2 days paddling among islands.

With this array of offerings, Batten-Kill gives paddlers a chance to view scenic regions throughout the state, from mountain to lush flatlands.

Clearwater Sports
Barry Bender
Route 100
Waitsfield, VT 05673
(802) 496-2708
Mad River, Winooski River, White River, Waterbury Reservoir
Max. rapids: III-IV

Clearwater Sports offers guided canoe, kayak, and raft trips and rents canoes, kayaks, rafts, and tubes for trips on the Mad, Winooski and White Rivers as well as Waterbury Reservoir. Guided 1-day canoe trips are available, along with escorted full-moon outings

which include dinner as well as adventurous paddling. For kayakers, Clearwater offers 2-day courses for beginners through advanced paddlers. Sea kayaking lessons are also available.

Canoeists and kayakers can run rapids that challenge novices, intermediate paddlers, and — at high water — advanced paddlers, too. The scenery, fishing, and wildlife are great. Clearwater also offers windsurfing, hiking, and mountain biking during its April-October season.

Connecticut River Safari
451 Putney Rd. (Rte. 5)
Brattleboro, VT 05301
(802) 257-5008, (802) 254-3908
Connecticut, West Rivers, Harriman, Somerset Reservoirs
Max. rapids: None
PPA

Floats through mountains, rolling hills, farmland and typical New England villages are offered by this company from May 1-October 20. Paddlers may take guided canoe and kayak tours or rent canoes, kayaks, and rowboats. Camping and swimming are available, along with fishing for bass, northern pike, walleyed pike, and brown trout.

The wide and meandering Connecticut River lends itself to peaceful canoeing, and nearly all species of northeastern wildlife are found.

Pine Ridge Adventure Center
Skip Dewhirst
1079 Williston Rd.
Williston, VT 05495
(802) 434-5294
Lamoille, Winooski, Missisquoi, Connecticut Rivers in VT; Oswegatchie, Raquette, Saranac Rivers in NY; Temagami River in Ontario, Allagash, Moose Rivers in Maine
Max. rapids: I-II

Pine Ridge Adventure Center has guided canoe trips for all ages from May to October, but its summer trips focus on 9-18 year olds. Its professional staff gives personal instruction and it runs camping trips lasting up to 14 days.

Wildlife includes moose, otter, mink, loon, eagle and other birds, while the fishing is for trout, bass, walleye, and northern pike.

Smugglers Notch Canoe Touring
Bette and Kelley Mann
Route 108S
RR 2, Box 4319
Jeffersonville, VT 05464
(802) 644-8321, (800) 937-MANN
Lamoille River, Greer River Reservoir
Max. rapids: I-II

Smugglers Notch Canoe Touring offers guided and self-guided canoe trips of 1-2 days on the Lamoille River as well as the Greer River Reservoir. The scenery on these trips is picturesque, with views of the Green Mountains, pristine countryside, and pine and maple forests. There is also abundant wildlife, including hawks, loons, deer, beavers, and sometimes bears and moose. Paddlers can also enjoy fishing for trout, perch, and bass. These trips, on placid waters,

are fine for all canoeists. Lodging packages at the outfitter's Mannsview Inn are available and include canoeing, lodging and meals.

Stowe Action Outfitters
Dan Susslin
Box 2160
Stowe, VT 05672
(802) 253-7975
Winooski River, Lamoille River, Waterbury Reservoir
Max. rapids: I-II

Stowe Action Outfitters provides guided canoe trips and canoe and tube rentals on the Winooski and Lamoille Rivers and Waterbury Reservoir. These trips run on scenic, flatwater waterways that are well-suited for family trips and beginners. Guided canoe trips last 1/2 a day, with longer outings available by special arrangement. Rentals are for 1- and 2-day trips. On all outings, paddlers can enjoy fishing for rainbow, brown and brook trout, and watching for deer, moose, otters, eagles, falcons, and other wildlife. Stowe's season runs from March to November.

Umiak Outfitters
Steve Brownlee, Heidi Krantz
849 S. Main St. East.
Stowe, VT 05672
(802) 253-2317
Lamoille, White, Mad & West Rivers, Waterbury Reservoir
Max. rapids: III
PPA

Umiak rents canoes and kayaks and provides guided canoe and kayak trips for floats of 1- and 2-days through beautiful Vermont farmland. Its certified instructors introduce paddling to people of all ages.

During the April-October season, clients can enjoy clean waters, great fishing for trout, bass and pickerel, abundant wildlife, and scenery adorned with covered bridges and the Green Mountains.

Vermont Waterways, Inc.
Mark & Hope McAndrew
RR1, Box 322
East Hardwick, VT 05836
(802) 472-8271, (800) 492-8271
Connecticut, White, Lamoille, Winooski
Rivers, Green River Reservoir, Waterbury
Reservoir, Lake Champlain
Max. rapids: I-II
ACA

Vermont Waterways offers guided
canoe trips, walk-and-paddle, and sea
kayak floats geared mostly for novices
and others happy to paddle at a relaxed
pace. But the company also caters to
those who want to learn new maneuvers
or travel longer distances. Groups are
limited to 10 or less and itineraries are
flexible. The outfitter promises great
food and comfortable lodging in lovely
country inns.

A wide variety of aquatic life, including otters, beavers, and great blue herons frequent the riverbanks against a
backdrop of the Green and White
Mountains. The season runs from June
25-Oct. 10.

The Village Sport Shop
John G. Hibsman
P.O. Box 173, 74 Broad Street
Route 5
Lyndonville, VT 05851
(802) 626-8448
Connecticut River, Passumpsic River, Black
River, Willoughby Lake
Max. rapids: I-II

The Village Sport Shop rents canoes
for trips of 1-5 days on the Connecticut,
Passumpsic and Black Rivers and on
Lake Willoughby. The rivers, with Class
I-II rapids, require whitewater paddling
experience in the spring. However, by
June 1 water levels have dropped
enough to make all trips suitable for beginners as well. The trips pass through
some of the loveliest country in Vermont, complete with covered bridges,
red barns, sugar houses and lush forests.
The region also contains moose, deer,
foxes and bears, along with good trout,
perch, bass, and pickerel fishing. The
Village Sports Shop's season is April to
October.

Paddling on the Winooski River. Courtesy of Karen Krough/BattenKill Canoe, Arlington,
Vermont.

Virginia

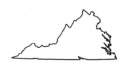

Canoeing in Virginia naturally centers on the mountain streams in the west. The Old Dominion, like its neighbors to the north and south, stretches from mountains to the sea. Down in the Tidewater area adjoining Chesapeake Bay the land is divided into peninsulas by the broad Potomac, Rappahannock, York and James Rivers. But the action, in terms of whitewater and recreational canoeing, is chiefly in the Shenandoah Valley between the Blue Ridge and the Allegheny Mountains.

Shenandoah, an Indian name, is said to mean "daughter of the stars." As a canoeing waterway, the South Fork of the Shenandoah is a favorite playground for paddlers from the Washington-Baltimore metropolitan area. It can be run year-round and it has enough Class I-III rapids to lend spice to the trip without endangering the novice. Outfitters run trips of various lengths along the meandering stretch of river between Luray and Front Royal. Here the hill scenery is mostly unspoiled as the South Fork winds its way alongside the George Washington National Forest. Game species include bear, raccoon, deer and wild turkey, along with quail and grouse. Bald eagles and hawks circle overhead. Anglers go for small and largemouth bass, perch, catfish, carp and bluegill. A canoeing trip can be combined with visiting one of the many caves in the area or hiking a woodland trail.

Further southwest along the valley lies another good canoeing area, the James River Basin around Lexington. Here flow the headwaters of the James and many smaller streams including the Maury. It is a region of beautiful scenery, mostly easy rapids, clean water, good fishing, and relaxation for those seeking solitude.

But not all the rapids in the James River Basin are easy. Whitewater buffs flock to the Maury in its upstream Goshen Pass area. Outfitters say this is probably the most popular whitewater run in Virginia. Depending on water levels, the rapids rate Class II-III and possibly Class IV for the first three miles. Then follow nine miles of Class II-III whitewater before the river turns tame in its lower reaches. The Maury joins the James at Glasgow, ten miles south of Buena Vista.

The James is mostly easy Class I-II paddling in this headwater region.

325

VIRGINIA

The only exception is its Balcony Falls stretch, which rates Class II+. Canoeists exploring the lower reaches of this river find that the most interesting stretch along the 185-mile section from Lynchburg to Richmond is a 13-mile trip just downstream from Scottsville. The area is fairly wild, with only a nearby railroad as a sign of civilization. There are over 300 islands along this stretch as the river splits up into a skein of narrow channels. At low water there are various rapids, none tougher than Class II.

Far down at the James River estuary the Tidewater area offers countryside steeped in history. Paddlers roam rivers and creeks that the Jamestown settlers explored when they set foot in the New World in 1607. A leisurely tour of the new indoor museum at Jamestown, with its expert guides, is thoroughly worthwhile. The waters of the James estuary, the Pagan and Blackwater Rivers and neighboring creeks yield bass, catfish, and sea trout. The wildlife includes beaver, otter, muskrat, and birds of prey.

Atlantic Canoe & Kayak Co.
Judy Lathrop
9015 Captain's Row
Alexandria, VA 22308
(703) 780-0066, FAX (703) 780-6765
Chesapeake Bay, including tidal tributaries,
Atlantic Ocean
Max. rapids: None

Kayaking down the Potomac past Mount Vernon and other historic plantations is one of the attractions offered by this outfitter. Operating from March to November, the company runs sea kayak trips with knowledgeable guides through salt, brackish and fresh waters alive with flora and fauna. Most trips are for novices, but intermediate and advanced paddlers can also build their skills.

Paddling lessons, camping and fishing for bass and crabs are also available.

Downriver Canoe Co.
John Gibson
Box 10
Bentonville, VA 22610
(540) 635-5526
South Fork Shenandoah River
Max. rapids: I-II
PPA

Downriver Canoe Company rents canoes on a remote section of the South Fork of the Shenandoah River, which

flows north between Shenandoah National Park and George Washington National Forest. The river is especially scenic, flanked by the Appalachian Mountains and offering views of beavers, otters, bald eagles, turtles, and other wildlife. Anglers also will enjoy the South Fork's profusion of smallmouth bass, as well as good fishing for bluegill, perch, catfish, and largemouth bass.

Trips last 1-5 days and are ideal for novices as well as experienced canoeists. The river's Class I-II rapids are fun and exciting but not dangerous. Downriver's season is from April to October.

Front Royal Canoe Co.
Don Roberts
P.O. Box 473
Front Royal, VA 22630
(540) 635-5440
South Fork Shenandoah River
Max. rapids: I-II
PPA, America Outdoors

Front Royal Canoe Co. offers canoe, kayak, raft and tube trips on the South Fork of the Shenandoah. These trips offer views of the Blue Ridge Mountains and abundant wildlife, including deer, squirrels, beavers, and occasional bears and bobcats. Anglers also can enjoy fine fishing on this clean mountain river for smallmouth bass, catfish, panfish, muskie, and largemouth bass.

Canoe trips last from 1-7 days, are fine for paddlers aged six and older, and available from March to November. On overnight trips free camping is available on government land. Tube trips cover three miles and last 3-4 hours. FRCC also has a store offering bait, tackle, and other paddling supplies.

Harpers Ferry River Riders, Inc.
Mark Grimes
P.O. Box 267
Knoxville, MD 21758
(301) 834-8051, (800) 326-7238
Shenandoah River, Potomac River, Tygart River
Max. rapids: I-III

Harpers Ferry River Riders offers 1-day guided raft and tube trips, and canoe and kayak rentals on the Shenandoah, Potomac, and Tygart Rivers. Trips on the Potomac and Shenandoah, with Class I-III rapids, are fine for beginners and offer scenic views of historic Harpers Ferry, wooded mountains, and abundant wildlife, including great blue herons, egrets, nesting bald eagles, turtles, geese, deer, and ducks. The two rivers also feature good fishing for smallmouth and largemouth bass, catfish, panfish, and carp.

The Tygart River, also scenic, has more challenging whitewater with up to Class V rapids, requiring previous paddling experience. The outfitter's season is from April to October and it also offers a professional river gear shop.

James River Basin Canoe Livery, Ltd.
RFD #6, Box 125
Lexington, VA 24450
(540) 261-7334
James, Maury, Jackson, Cowpasture, Calfpasture, Tye, Maury, South, Piney Rivers and Catawba, Craig, Buffalo, Kerrs, and Irish Creeks
Max. rapids: III
American Rivers

James River Basin Canoe Livery rents canoes on the James and Maury Rivers. Trips are also available by special arrangement on the Maury, Jackson, Cowpasture, Calfpasture, Tye, and Piney Rivers and the Catawba, Craig, Buffalo, Kerrs, and Irish Creeks. With this array of trips, the livery has canoeing with fast water, flat water, game fish, camping, beautiful scenery, and other attractions.

Some trips feature high cliffs, others are pastoral, and all have views of the Blue Ridge Mountains. Along the way, paddlers can spot deer, herons, otters, beavers, turtles, turkeys, and ospreys, and fish for rock bass, smallmouth bass, perch, and bluegill. Floaters can select Class I, II or III runs, which last from 1-7 days. The livery's season runs from March-November.

James River Runners, Inc.
Rte. 4, Box 106
Scottsville, VA 24590
(804) 286-2338
James, Rockfish Rivers
Max. rapids: I-II
PPA, ACA, VAPPA

Located 25 miles south of Charlottesville, James River Runners offers easy, novice whitewater trips suitable for families, church groups, scouts, and others. In business for 17 years, the company has served thousands of clients with an emphasis on safety and reliability.

Canoes, rafts, and tubes can be rented for camping trips of up to 4 days. The James River is famed for its rich history and smallmouth bass fishing. Its water is clear and the scenery idyllic. The company's season runs from March to October. Trips on Rockfish River run only in the spring.

Massanutten Canoe & Kayak Voyages

P.O. Box 6
McGaheysville, VA 22840
(703) 289-WILD
South Fork Shenandoah River
Max. rapids: I-II
PPA

Massanutten Canoe offers half-day Shenandoah excursions departing from Massanutten Resort. Trips run April through October, weather permitting. Class I rapids are fine for beginners and experts alike.

Rappahannock Outdoors

Bill & Denise Micks
3219 Fall Hill Ave.
Fredericksburg, VA 22401
(703) 371-5085, (703) 373-5830
Rappahannock, Rapidan, Shenandoah, Potomac
Max. rapids: I-II

A family-run business, Rappahannock Outdoors rents canoes, rafts, and tubes and provides guided canoe and raft trips for guests of all ages. Many outings cater to those interested in wildflowers, birds, and history. Families, youth groups, canoe campers, and fishermen are welcome. The company says that with 4,800 acres of camping available, paddlers need not worry about camping on private land.

Unspoiled woodland on the riverbanks contains deer, geese, turkeys, beavers, eagles, hawks, and reptiles. Fish include smallmouth bass, brim, and sun perch.

Rappahannock River Campground

Steve and Sheila Stephens
33017 River Mill Rd.
Richardsville, VA 22736
(540) 399-1839, (800) 78-4-PADL
(reservations only)
Rapidan and Rappahannock Rivers
Max. rapids: II-III
PPA

Rappahannock River Campground rents canoes and tubes at its attractive, wooded 50-acre site for trips of 1-4 days.

It can handle large groups and offers varied fare: an 8-mile trip for beginners, a 17-mile tour for enthusiasts, and several outings for intermediates.

Bass fishing is great in the clean river with its good rapids, undeveloped banks, and abundant wildlife. The company's season runs from April through October or beyond.

Richmond Raft Co.

M.S. Bateman & John Alley
4400 East Main St.
Richmond, VA 23231-1103
(804) 222-7238, FAX (804) 222-7655
James River
Max. rapids: III-IV
America Outdoors

Floating the "Falls of the James," a seven-mile stretch of whitewater on the James River at Richmond, is the specialty of this rafting company. It offers 1-day guided trips from March-November on this moderately difficult float, suitable for families, church groups and business outings. Since the trip is within city limits, paddlers see the skyline of modern downtown Richmond as well as historic buildings from Colonial and Civil War days. They can also fish for bass, bluegill, shad and herring.

River Rental Outfitters

Trace Noel & Edith Appleton
Rtes. 613 & 629, P.O. Box 145
Bentonville, VA 22610
(703) 635-5050
South Fork Shenandoah River
Max. rapids: I-II
PPA

River Rental runs guided and unguided canoe, kayak, raft, and tube trips for runs of 2 hours to 3 days. These are beginners' outings — "we have folks who don't know the difference between a school bus and a canoe and have a good day." The outfitter prides itself on personal service, top-quality equipment, river lore, and knowledge of German and Spanish.

The Shenandoah's South Fork

presents great scenery between the Blue Ridge and Massanutten mountain chains. Wildlife is abundant, with fishing for bass, muskie, and catfish. The season runs from March 15 to October 31.

Shenandoah River Outfitters
Route 3, Box 144
Luray, VA 22835
(540) 743-4159
South Fork Shenandoah River
Max. rapids: I-II

Shenandoah River Outfitters rents canoes and tubes on the South Fork of the Shenandoah for trips of 1-7 days. These trips are scenic, passing between two mountain ranges, and offering views of cliffs, caves, farmland, and abundant wildlife, including deer, ducks, and turkeys. Also, fishing in the Shenandoah is especially good, particularly for smallmouth bass, sunfish, perch, largemouth bass, catfish, crappie, and muskie. These trips are not difficult, offering only Class I-II whitewater, which is ideal for beginning whitewater paddlers.

Shenandoah River Outfitters, open from April to November, also offers a steak dinner and lunch for groups of 20 or more.

Smithfield Paddler, Inc.
Gary Parsons
15017 Mill Swamp Road
Smithfield, VA 23430
(804) 357-4165
Pagan River, Cypress Creek, Jones Creek, Blackwater River, James River
Max. rapids: None
PPA

Smithfield Paddler offers guided and unguided canoe and kayak rentals on the Pagan, Blackwater, and James Rivers, and on Cypress and Jones Creeks. These trips provide easy paddling for families, groups, and nature lovers on flatwater rivers. On these 1-day outings, paddlers can view historic ruins and other remains dating back to the 1600s. The area also displays wilderness scenery

and opportunities to view beavers, otters, hawks, eagles, egrets, and muskrats. Anglers also can enjoy excellent fishing for largemouth and smallmouth bass, catfish, and sea trout. Smithfield's season runs from April to November.

Tidewater River Adventures, Inc.
Sally Mills
P.O. Box 157
Walkerton, VA 23177
(804) 769-1602
James, York, Rappahannock, Chickahominy, Mattaponi, Pamunkey, and Dragon Run Rivers
Max. rapids: None
PPA, ASA

Tidewater River Adventures operates on Virginia's tidal rivers. It rents canoes and kayaks for easy guided and unguided trips by paddlers seeking retreat and quiet. Paddling lessons, swimming, camping, and fishing — for bass, catfish, and yellow perch — are available.

The company also offers conservation education for individuals and groups, who can observe rare and endangered plant species in the wetlands and bald eagles and osprey nesting in the trees. The season runs from March 15 to Dec. 15.

West View Livery & Outfitters, Inc.
Nancy H. Waldrop
1151 West View Rd., Box 258
Goochland, VA 23063
(804) 457-2744
James River
Max. rapids: None
PPA

This company rents canoes and tubes for 1- and 2-day floats on smoothflowing waters with a few riffles, suitable for everyone. The scenery is attractive on this historic river, and fishing is excellent for large- and smallmouth bass, perch, and catfish. Wildlife includes deer, muskrat, herons, ducks, and geese. The season runs May through October.

Washington

Breathtaking is the word for Washington's scenery: majestic mountain evergreen forests, semidesert flatlands and snow-fed rivers slicing throug to the Pacific. This is the land of the Cascades, of Mount Rainier, Moun Baker and the Olympic National Park. With such a majestic backdrop, pac dlers can take in the spectacle by simply floating on a lake amid snowcap ped peaks reflected in the water.

For those with zest for more excitement, the Evergreen State has an abur dance of fast-flowing wilderness rivers. They vary greatly in difficulty wit the flow of water. In the spring — April through June — they are typicall in spate from melting snow. From July until the end of the season in Sep tember they are fed by dam releases or melting glaciers. In any event th water is always cold, whether one is paddling in the mountains or the de sert. So wet suits are recommended for whitewater runs, and floaters shoul check water levels before setting out.

The most popular river in the state is the Wenatchee, which runs off th east flank of the Cascades — the warmer and sunnier side. Its rapids rate a Class III-IV and some previous paddling experience is recommended dur ing peak run-off. With a highway beside the river for much of the run, civ lization is never far away and there tends to be junk on the riverbank.

Superb scenery is to be found along the Sauk River, which flows throug dense forest between snowy mountains on the west side of the Cascade The Upper Sauk run, starting some 16 miles from Darrington, is eight mile long and has tough rapids at the beginning and the end which demand ex pert paddling. The Middle Sauk trip down to Darrington from the Whit Chuck River confluence is still more challenging, with its Class III-IV rap ids rising to Class V and hazardous at peak river levels. The Sauk is note for its rapid fluctuations in water flow, which may double from one day t the next. Parts of it are very difficult to scout because of the terrain and th whole river is subject to logjams.

One of the tougher rivers in the state is the Skykomish, with an eigh mile run rated Class III-V. The put-in is near Index, just off US 2 and onl an hour's drive northeast of Seattle. Its most famous rapid is the Class V

Boulder Drop which many paddlers prefer to portage. But it is a very clean river with magnificent views of 5,000-foot mountains, and its banks are forested with evergreen and deciduous growth.

Only 30 miles from Seattle is the Green River Gorge, a boulder-choked chasm with Class III-IV rapids dropping into deep green pools. Although it is one of the state's most beautiful river canyons, its waters are dam-controlled and unpredictable far in advance. So outfitters cannot schedule trips through this lush rain forest gorge except at short notice, and then only in the spring.

A great float for families all summer long is the Skagit within North Cascades National Park. Although several dams control its flow, the Skagit is still relatively unspoiled and scenic, with salmon spawning in the fall and bald eagles circling overhead during the winter. The put-in for the nine-mile Class II-III run is near Newhalem and paddlers enjoy views of high Cascades peaks.

Washington State is not only blessed with magnificent mountains and rivers; it also has the superb San Juan Islands between the mainland and Canada's Vancouver Island. Here sea kayakers may watch whales and other prolific wildlife including dolphins, seals, sea turtles, water birds, and bald eagles. The strait also boasts unspoiled wooded islands, historic sites, and sheltered waters rich in salmon, cod, and rockfish.

All Rivers Adventures Wenatchee Whitewater & Co.
Bruce Carlson
Box 12
Cashmere, WA 98815
(509) 782-2254, (800) 74 FLOAT
Wenatchee, Methow, Tieton, White Salmon, Klickitat, Yakama, Skagit Rivers
Max. rapids: III-IV

All Rivers Adventures Wenatchee Whitewater & Co. offers guided raft trips on the Wenatchee, Tieton, White Salmon, and Deschutes Rivers. These boats pass through the beautiful North Cascades and Columbia Gorge area, featuring scenic forest, canyons, wildflowers, and abundant wildlife including deer, eagles, ospreys, minks, otters, ducks, herons, and geese. Anglers can fish for salmon, steelhead, and rainbow trout.

Trips last 1-3 days, run between April and September and range widely in difficulty from scenic flatwater trips to Class IV whitewater. The company also offers parties, barbecue grills, campfires, daycare, volleyball, moonlight floats, inflatable kayak trips, and scenic floats led by naturalist guides.

Downstream River Runners, Inc.
Casey Garland
12112 NE 195th
Bothell, WA 98011
(206) 483-0335
Suiattle River, Nooksack River, Wenatchee River, Methow River, Tieton River, Skykomish River, Sauk River, Green River, Grande Ronde
Max. rapids: V+
America Outdoors, Professional River Outfitters of Washington
Downstream River Runners conducts

"mild to wild" guided trips on the Eagle, Upper Skagit, Suiattle, Nooksack, Wenatchee, Methow, Tieton, Skykomish, Sauk, Green, Cascade and Klickitat rivers, as well as streams in Oregon. Some of these are recommended for beginners, others have rapids of Class V+ difficulty.

Downstream prides itself on quality and safety, with all its river guides certified as Swiftwater Rescue Technicians. Open from March to September, it provides instruction and runs trips of 1-5 days' duration. It offers 25 different wetsuit sizes to protect against hypothermia on the cold mountain streams.

MacKaye Harbor Inn

Brooks & Sharon Broberg
Route 1, Box 1940
Lopez Island, WA 98261
(360) 468-2253
Puget Sound
Max. rapids: None

Mackaye Harbor Inn, a beachfront bed and breakfast on Lopez Island, rents kayaks and conducts guided kayak trips among the San Juans between April and October. The tours, for beginners as well as intermediate paddlers, take guests along a beautiful shoreline in one of the world's loveliest island regions. They can view many marine birds as well as seals, otters and deer, while eagles soar above. Salmon and cod are among the local fish.

North Cascades River Expeditions

Gerald and Lori Michalec
P.O. Box 116
Arlington, WA 98223
(206) 435-9548, (800) 634-8433
Methow, Skagit, Wenatchee, Green, Klickitat, Noosuck, Skykomish, Tieton, Deschutes Rivers
Max. rapids: III-IV
Professional River Outfitters of Washington

North Cascades River Expeditions provides guided raft trips on many rivers: the Methow, Skagit, Suiattle, Wenatchee, Green, Klickitat, Nooksack, Skykomish, Tieton, White Salmon and

Deschutes. It offers beginners' and advanced trips, mostly through rugged mountains, with the advanced paddlers running Class III-IV rapids. The season runs from March 1 through September.

Paddlers can fish for salmon and steelhead trout, and view bears, otters, ospreys, eagles, and other wildlife.

Northwest Outdoor Center

Bill Stewart, John Meyer, Herb Meyer
2100 Westlake Avenue North
Seattle, WA 98109
(206) 281-9694
Skykomish River, Wenatchee River, Saltwater inlets and bays
Max. rapids: III-IV
TASK

Northwest Outdoor Center was founded in 1980 to provide safe, high quality boating instruction in the Pacific Northwest. It has since expanded into providing guided sea and river kayaking trips and renting both kayaks and canoes. Most of its floats are in sheltered flat water, suitable for beginners. Sea kayaking tours run through Puget Sound and the scenic San Juan Islands, while river paddling is on five rivers in the beautiful Cascades and the Rogue in Oregon. NWOC operates trips varying from 3 hours to 5 days and its season runs year-round.

Wildife includes whales, seals, bald eagles, waterbirds, and shorebirds.

Orion River Expeditions, Inc.

James Moore
2366 Eastlake Ave. E. #305
Seattle, WA 98072
(206) 322-9130, (800) 553-7466
Methow, Skykomish, Sauk, White Salmon, Tieton, Skagit, Deschutes, Siuattle, Wenatchee Rivers
Max. rapids: III-IV
Washington Outfitters and Guides, America Outdoors

Orion Expeditions offers whitewater and calm water guided trips by raft and kayak on many of Washington's most ex citing rivers — the Methow, Skykomish, auk, White Salmon, Tieton, Skagit, Deschutes, Siuattle, and Wenatchee Rivers. Most trips are suitable for beginners; some are for experienced paddlers only. The landscape varies from alpine to high desert canyon scenery. Orion's season runs from April to September and from December to February. Trips last 1-6 days. Guests can see elk, bighorn sheep, black bears, eagles, and ospreys, and fish for several species of trout.

Outland Adventures
Daniel Clarke
Box 16343
Seattle, WA 98116
(209) 932-7012
Straits of Juan de Fuca, Frederick Sound in AK
Max. rapids: None

Outland Adventures runs guided sea kayaking trips lasting from 3-10 days for novice and intermediate paddlers in a variety of waters amid stark natural beauty. It has expert guides, top equipment, and offers great food and campsites.

Open all year, the company offers tours at many points from Alaska to Honduras. Whales and porpoises may be seen, along with many species of birds.

Pacific Water Sports, Inc.
Lee Moyer
16055 Pacific Highway South
Seattle, WA 98188
(206) 246-9385
Puget Sound
Max. rapids: None
PA, NAPSA, TASK

Pacific Water Sports has been serving paddlers for over 20 years, renting canoes and kayaks, giving paddling instruction and running guided trips. It teaches sea kayaking on Puget Sound and whitewater kayaking on inland rivers, using classrooms, pools and lakes for instruction.

Guided sea kayak trips run from 1-5 days and PWS is open year-round. Tours include such destinations as Hammerslay Inlet, Deception Pass, and Jetty Island, and offer impressive scenery, birdwatching, and fishng.

Sea Quest Expeditions
Zoetic Research
P.O. Box 2424M
Friday Harbor, WA 98250
(206) 378-5767
Puget Sound/San Juan Islands; Sea of Cortez/ Baja California; Prince William Sound/ Alaska
Max. rapids: None
TASK

Sea Quest Expeditions is different from most outfitters in that it sets out to give sea kayakers a learning experience as well as an outdoor adventure. Owned by a non-profit research and education organization, it has skilled biologists as guides to describe the natural history of the San Juan Islands, the Alaskan rainforest and the Baja region. They lead sea kayak expeditions to the best whale-watching areas in North America. No previous kayaking experience is needed, trips last from 1-7 days, and paddlers camp on islands accessible only by boat.

In addition to humpback, minke and orca whales, the marine life includes porpoises, seals, sea turtles, eagles and sea birds. Salmon and bottomfish may be caught. A highlight in Alaska is visiting tidewater glaciers as they calve icebergs into the sea, while in the Baja area guests enjoy nocturnal snorkeling forays.

Wenatchee Water Sports, Inc.
Morey S. Zimmerman
15735 River Road
Leavenworth, WA 98826
(509) 763-3307
Wenatchee River
Max. rapids: III-IV
PPA

Wenatchee Water Sports is a rafting, kayaking and canoe livery with experienced river guides, located on scenic land with unspoiled views of the Wenatchee River and Big Jim Mountain. Open May-September, the company caters to people of all ages with both rentals and guided trips varying from 1-7 days. Tubes are also rented.

Wildlife to be seen in this alpine setting includes mountain lions, bears, deer, coyote, beavers and many bird species such as osprey and bald eagle. Salmon and trout tempt fishermen.

West Virginia

Mountainous West Virginia calls itself the undisputed Whitewater Capital of the East, with nearly 30,000 miles of streams coursing through the Appalachians. More than 60 rivers in the state may be rafted, kayaked or canoed, and some of them, notably the Cheat, the Gauley and the Tygart, are highly challenging. They have rapids rated up to Class V+ which demand great skill, especially during the spring runoff. Less adventurous paddlers enjoy the Shenandoah with its pastoral scenery as it meanders through the eastern panhandle of West Virginia to join the Potomac at historic Harpers Ferry. (See Virginia.) But even the Shenandoah has Class III rapids on its Staircase segment to enliven the journey.

The Cheat River in the north of the state is a wild stream that winds through an impressive canyon with massive boulders, overhanging rock walls and waterfalls. It has 38 rapids in eleven miles, including Big Nasty and Even Nastier. They are rated Class II-IV except in high water when some reach Class V. When the flow slackens in midsummer the Cheat allows paddlers to relish the scenery. Unfortunately, the Cheat is plagued by acid pollution from coalmines which has killed all life in its turbulent waters. After a heavy spring runoff in 1994, the river's boulders turned bright orange and its waters stank of sulfur.

Efforts are currently underway to secure permanent protection for the Cheat and a dozen other "crown jewel" rivers within the Monongahela National Forest. The West Virginia Rivers Coalition is battling formidable opposition to have them designated National Wild and Scenic streams.

The Gauley River, variously listed as number seven or eight in the world, features more than 100 rapids on a 26-mile stretch that drops 670 feet. The toughest part is the upper Gauley, with its steep chutes and rocky routes which test the most experienced paddler's skill. The Lower Gauley still ranks as Class III-V but demands less technical expertise, so inexperienced rafters can safely enjoy its huge waves. But since the river is controlled by Summersville Dam the whitewater season is short — only 22 days in the fall when the sluicegates are opened. With space so limited, many of the rafters who flock to the Gauley from all the United States and Canada make reservations a year ahead. So early booking is essential. But in the summer, when water levels are lower, the river still offers enjoyable family rafting.

The uncrowded Tygart in northcentral West Virginia contains Wells Falls which rates as the most powerful runnable drop in the whole Monongahela River basin. Another Tygart thrill is Valley Falls, described as a short but incredibly intense 25-foot water slide. The most demanding of the Tygart's raftable stretches is the Gorge. It consists of Class II-III whitewater with intervening technical Class IV-V rapids. Placid Tygart Lake, which curves for 13 miles through wooded valleys, is a popular boating center with its camp site, cabins, lodge and restaurant. But the Tygart, too, has been hurt by acid mine drainage (AMD), for which no effective remedy has been found.

Despite its name, the New River is said to be the world's second oldest river after the Nile. Its celebrated gorge, dubbed the Grand Canyon of the East, has walls 700 to 1,300 feet high. Named in this section the New River Gorge National River, the stream drops 240 feet in 14 miles, creating the biggest whitewater in the east. The Upper New is comparatively gentle, suitable for leisurely floating and fishing. The middle section offers moderate Class II-III rapids. Only in its lower, and most popular, section does the New unleash its full fury. The New River season runs from mid-March through November, with the greatest rafting challenge in April and May.

The Greenbrier, a major tributary of the New River, and the South Branch of the Potomac, in the eastern mountains, rank among the best canoeing waters in West Virginia. The 150-mile Greenbrier flows through superb Allegheny scenery containing old logging communities, farmlands and state forests. The South Branch altered course in 1985 when floods permanently changed its streambed. Paddlers able to move at short notice can float the more remote Bluestone and Meadow with their Class III-V rapids and great mountain scenery. But these rivers, in the south and central sections of the state, are only raftable when swollen by spring rains.

ACE Whitewater Ltd.
Jerry Cook
Box 1168
Oak Hill, WV 25901
(800) 223-2641
New River, Gauley River, Russell Fork River
Max. rapids: V+
America Outdoors

ACE Whitewater offers guided canoe, kayak, and raft trips on the New and Gauley Rivers in West Virginia and the Russell Fork River in Virginia and Kentucky. On the New River, paddlers can enjoy all 52 miles of the 1,000 foot-deep New River Gorge, with rapids of up to Class V. The Gauley offers 26 miles of clean water in the wilderness of the Gauley River Recreational Area. Depending on the river and season, these trips range from mild to wild, from family fun to world-class whitewater. Trips last 1-5 days.

Pillow Rock Rapids on the Upper Gauley River. Courtesy of USA Raft, Rowlesburg, West Virginia.

During its April-November season, ACE also offers horseback riding, camping, hot showers, use of its recreation lodge, and base camp hiking trails and fishing lakes.

Blackwater Outdoor Center
Jim Browning
Rte. 1, Box 239
St. George, WV 26290
(800) 328-4798
Cheat River
Max. rapids: V+

Blackwater Outdoor Center provides guided and unguided canoe, kayak, and raft trips during a March-November season. It specializes in catering to small groups, providing "quality on a first-name basis."

The outfitter serves the entire 275-mile Cheat River with trips that last from 1-14 days. Many undisturbed tributaries provide good campsites. Bears and eagles are among the wildlife, while fishing is for bass, redeye, smallmouth and other species of trout.

Cheat River Outfitters
Eric & Peggy Neilson
River Road, Rte. 26
Box 134
Albright, WV 26519
(304) 329-2024, (410) 489-2837
Cheat River
Max. rapids: V
America Outdoors

Cheat River Outfitters, a 20-year-old family business, provides exciting 1-day guided trips for all skill levels. For families and youth groups it offers the 8-mile Cheat Narrows run with Class II-III rapids, while advanced paddlers tackle the Cheat Canyon, 13 miles of whitewater with Class III-V adventure.

The Cheat River is widely seen as the toughest whitewater in the East. It has clean, clear water containing smallmouth bass and trout. Deer, black bears and wild turkeys frequent the banks.

Class VI River Runners
David Arnold
Ames Heights Road
P.O. Box 78
Lansing, WV 25862-0078
(800) 252-7784 or (800) CLASS VI
*New River Gorge, Gauley River National
Recreation Area*
Max Rapids: V+
*West Virginia Professional River Outfitters,
America Outdoors.*

Class VI River Runners offers people
seeking whitewater adventure a variety
of guided raft and kayak trips on waters
ranging from Class I to V+. Tours last
1-4 days, with the whitewater said to be
"the best in the East."

Camping, swimming, and fishing for
smallmouth bass are also available during a March-to-November season. The
Gauley River has 100 major rapids in a
24-mile stretch and a 400-foot-deep
canyon, while the New River boasts a
forested, 1,000-foot-deep canyon.

Drift-a-Bit, Inc.
Box 885
Fayetteville, WV 25840
(800) 633-RAFT (7238)
New, Gauley Rivers
Max. rapids: V+

This company operates guided raft
trips to suit customers aged six and up
on wild and scenic rivers, including the
New River Gorge. It emphasizes laid-
back personal attention. With camping,
overnight trips are available.

Customers may fish for smallmouth
bass and catfish and look out for deer,
beaver, mink, and many bird species.

Eastern River Expeditions
John Connelly
Box 1173
Greenville, ME 04441
(207) 695-2411, (800) 634-7238
*Gauley River, Kennebec River, Penobscot
River, Dead River, Moose River*
Max. rapids: V+
*Maine Professional River Outfitters
Association, America Outdoors*

Eastern River Expeditions offers
canoe rentals and guided raft and inflatable-kayak trips on five rivers in Maine,
New York, and West Virginia. In Maine,
paddlers can choose among whitewater
trips on the Kennebec, Penobscot, and
Dead Rivers. Most Maine trips are fine
for novice paddlers, combining excellent
wilderness scenery with Class II-IV
whitewater. Trips on the Dead and
Penobscot Rip Gorge, however, require
excellent conditioning. Penobscot Rip
Gorge also requires intermediate or advanced paddling skills. Advanced rafting
experience is a prerequisite for trips on
New York's Moose River and West Virginia's Gauley River, which have Class
IV-V rapids.

All trips, of 1-2 days, pass through
wilderness, offering camping spots, clear
water, fishing, and chances to spot deer,
coyotes, loons, ducks, beavers, foxes,
great blue herons, and other wildlife.

Greenbrier River Campground
Virgil Hanshaw
P.O. Box 265
Ronceverte, WV 24970
(800) 775-2203
Greenbrier River
Max. rapids: I-II
PPA, ACA, USCA

Greenbrier offers guided canoe trips
and rents canoes and tubes for outings
of up to 5 days on the clean Greenbrier,
with its deep gorges and wilderness scenery. Paddling instruction, an eight-acre,
four-star rated campground, swimming,
mountain bike rentals and bass fishing
are available.

The company claims to be the oldest,
most experienced, and most complete
canoeing outfitter on the Greenbrier. Its
season runs from April through October.

Harpers Ferry River Riders, Inc.
Mark Grimes
P.O. Box 267
Knoxville, MD 21758
(304) 535-2663, (800) 326-7238
Tygart River, Shenandoah River, Potomac River
Max. rapids: V+

Harpers Ferry River Riders offers 1-day guided raft and tube trips and canoe and kayak rentals on the Shenandoah, Potomac, and Tygart Rivers. Trips on the Potomac and Shenandoah, with Class I-III rapids, are fine for beginners and offer scenic views of historic Harpers Ferry, wooded mountains, and abundant wildlife, including great blue herons, egrets, nesting bald eagles, turtles, geese, deer, and ducks. The two rivers also feature good fishing for smallmouth and largemouth bass, catfish, panfish, and carp.

The Tygart River, also scenic, has more challenging whitewater with up to Class V rapids, requiring previous paddling experience. The outfitter's season is from April to October and it has a professional river gear shop.

Laurel Highlands River Tours
Mark and Linda McCarty
P.O. Box 107
Ohiopyle, PA 15470
(412) 329-8531, (800) 4 RAFTIN
Middle Youghiogheny River, Lower Youghiogheny River, Cheat River
Max. rapids: III-IV
America Outdoors

Laurel Highlands River Tours, one of the oldest whitewater companies in the East, claims to have the largest fleet of equipment anywhere. It operates on the Cheat River as well as the Lower, Middle and Upper Youghiogheny from bases in Albright, W.Va., Ohiopyle, Pa., and Friendsville, Md. In a season running from March to October, it offers guided raft trips and rents both rafts and canoes for floats on both rivers. All are 1-day trips.

The Yough has the most popular whitewater in the East and the Cheat is famed for its spring thrills. Canoeing and kayaking instruction is available and accommodations range from camping to luxury motels.

Wild whitewater on the Lower New River. Courtesy of Whitewater Information, Glen Jean, West Virginia.

Mountain River Tours, Inc.
Box 88 Sunday Road
Hico, WV 25854
(800) 822-1386
New, Gauley Rivers
Max. rapids: V+
America Outdoors

Mountain River Tours runs guided raft trips on the New and Gauley Rivers. Trips pass through lush green forests with 1,000-foot rocky cliffs, and range widely in difficulty, from gentle runs through scenic wilderness to awesome Class V adventures. With this array of offerings, the company has trips for everyone.

Taking pride in being flexible, Mountain River Tours will adapt trip times, meals, and river trips as desired. The company offers tours of 2 hours to 2 days and a choice of duckies or rafts. The season runs from March to November. Adventure packages include mountain biking, rock climbing, and horseback riding with meals and lodging.

Mountain Streams and Trails
Michael S. McCarty
P.O. Box 106, Route 381
Ohiopyle, PA 15470-0106
(800) 245-4090
Cheat River, Gauley River, Tygart River, Big Sandy Creek, Youghiogheny River
Max. rapids: V+
America Outdoors

Mountain Streams and Trails operates on all three sections of the Youghiogheny as well as the Class III-IV Cheat, the challenging Tygart, isolated Big Sandy Creek and the Class III-VI Upper and Lower Gauley rivers. It runs guided raft and kayak trips in addition to renting canoes, kayaks and rafts, tailoring its trips to suit the needs of every paddler.

The company has skilled guides, trained in first aid and equipped with radios. They take guests through the spectacular panorama of maples, pines and rhododendrons that blanket the walls of the Middle and Lower Yough River canyon, habitat for deer, beavers, bears,

Riding a rapid on the Cheat River. Courtesy of Laurel Highlands River Tours, Ohiopyle, Pennsylvania.

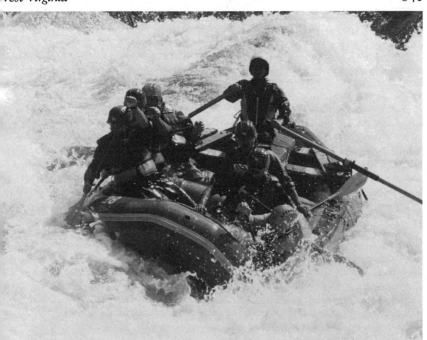

A paddle/oar boat trip on the Gauley River. Courtesy of New River Scenic Whitewater Tours, Hinton, West Virginia.

ospreys, heron and an occasional wild-cat. One- and two-day tours are offered during a March-October season.

New River Scenic Whitewater Tours, Inc.
P.O. Box 637
Hinton Bypass
Hinton, WV 25951
(304) 466-2288, (800) 292-0880
New River, Gauley River, Bluestone River, Greenbrier River
Max. rapids: V+
America Outdoors
New River Scenic Whitewater Tours offers guided canoe and raft trips as well as canoe and "funyak" rentals on the New, Gauley, Bluestone, and Greenbrier Rivers. All trips offer beautiful mountain scenery, exciting rapids, good fishing for smallmouth bass, catfish, and redeye,

and abundant wildlife such as beavers, deer, muskrats, rare turtle species, falcons, herons, and migratory birds.

Rapids on these trips range from mild to wild, to suit everyone from young children and seniors to the most adventurous, skilled paddlers. Trips last from 1/2-3 days; special fishing trips are also available.

New River Scenic Whitewater Tours also offers oar-powered raft trips during its March-October season.

North American River Runners
Frank Lakacs
Box 81
Hico, WV 25854
(800) 950-2585
New, Cheat, Gauley, Upper Yough Rivers
Max. rapids: V
America Outdoors

This company offers guided raft and kayak trips from March through October for paddlers of all skill levels. It is committed to providing "a consistent high quality river service" with tours well-organized from start to finish. Its excursions run through the New River Gorge National River and the Gauley River National Recreation Area.

Paddlers float past lush green banks, beautiful cliffs, and abandoned mining towns. Peregrine falcons, whitetail deer, and mink may be spotted ashore. These rivers also feature good smallmouth bass fishing.

Northwest Passage
Rick Sweitzer
1130 Greenleaf Avenue
Wilmette, IL 60091
(847) 256-4409, (800) RECREATE, FAX (847)-256-4476
New, Gauley, Current, Rio Grande, Chicago Rivers, BWCA, Lake Michigan, Lake Superior
Max. rapids: III-IV

Northwest Passage offers guided raft trips on the New and Gauley Rivers in West Virginia; canoe trips on the Current River in Missouri, the Rio Grande in Texas, the Chicago River and the Boundary Waters Canoe Area in Minnesota; and sea kayak trips on Lake Michigan in Illinois, in Door County, Wisconsin, and on Lake Superior in Michigan. Most of these trips, which last 1-7 days, are designed for beginners; some require prior experience.

An adventure travel company, Northwest Passage also offers skiing, hiking, cycling, backpacking, dogsledding, and rock climbing. Outings run year-round in the U.S., Canada, the Arctic, Greenland, New Zealand, Costa Rica, Belize, Crete, southern Africa, and Antarctica.

Passages to Adventure
Benjy Simpson
P.O. Box 71
Fayetteville, WV 25840
(304) 574-1037, (800) 634-3785
Cheat River, New River, Gauley River, Uppe Youghiogheny River
Max. rapids: V+
America Outdoors

Passages to Adventure provides guided canoe, inflatable kayak, and raft trips as well as renting canoes and inflat able kayaks on the Cheat, New, and Gauley Rivers in West Virginia and the Upper Youghiogheny in Maryland. It runs instructional courses in kayaking, commercial guiding, river rescue, and wilderness medicine.

With this variety, the company caters to all paddlers, from beginners to experts. The wild Cheat River has challenging, technical rapids that come in quick succession down a majestic canyon. The Lower New River offers huge rolling waves, giving a "rollercoaster" ride that is the company's most popular trip. The Upper New is wide, scenic and has Class II rapids — ideal for families and first-time rafters. The Upper Gauley has superb whitewater that requires previous paddling experience. The Lower Gauley has huge waves but doesn't require prior experience. Finally, the Upper Yough is famous for its technical Class IV-V+ rapids.

River Riders, Inc.
Mark Grimes
Route 3, Box 1260
Harpers Ferry, WV 24525
(304) 535-2663
Shenandoah River, Potomac River, Tygart River
Max. rapids: V+

River Riders offers guided raft and tube trips as well as canoe rentals on the Shenandoah, Potomac, and Tygart Rivers. All three rivers feature mountain scenery, clean water, and good fishing for smallmouth and largemouth bass, catfish, carp, and panfish. The Shenandoah

nd Potomac, with Class I-III rapids, are
ine for beginners. They also offer good
iews of historic Harper's Ferry.

Tygart trips, with Class V rapids, are
or experienced paddlers only, and offer
xceptional challenge. River Riders'
rips last either a 1/2 or a full day and
un from April to October.

The Rivermen
Brian Campbell
P.O. Box 360
Fayetteville, WV 25840
(800) 545-7238
New and Gauley Rivers
Max. rapids: V
WVPRO, America Outdoors

The Rivermen offers a wide range of
raft trips on some of the best whitewater
in the East, with expert guides and first-
rate equipment. People of all ages take
-day or multi-day tours through "mild
to wild" rapids, with camping and meals
provided. Each trip is carefully rated for
difficulty, with minimum age and skill
levels set accordingly. The "Gauley Riv-
r Gauntlet" trip, for instance, covers 26

miles in a day and is "not recommended
for those who have a heart condition,
(are) overweight, underweight, or just a
plain wimp," the brochure says.

The Rivermen's season runs from
April to October.

RIVERS
Karen Calvert
P.O. Drawer 39
Lansing, WV 25862
(304) 574-3834, (800) 879-7483
Upper and Lower New River, Upper and
Lower Gauley River, Cheat River
Max. rapids: V+
America Outdoors

Rivers runs guided raft and kayak
trips on the New, Gauley, and Cheat Rivers. The New River offers breathtaking scenery and fun, moderate rapids.
The Cheat features thrills for early-sea-
son rafters, and the Gauley offers the
ultimate whitewater experience for paddlers who crave non-stop action. All
trips run through wild, unspoiled gorges
in a historic region of coal-mining and
lumber towns. Varying with the river

*A family oar-boat trip on the Upper New River. Courtesy of Whitewater Information, Glen Jean,
West Virginia.*

and season, difficulty ranges from Class I-III for families with young children, Class IV- V for adults and children over 12 and Class V for experienced rafters.

Open March-October, Rivers also offers camping, cabins, multi-day trips, ducky outings, kayak clinics, float-fishing trips, motel packages, an outfitter shop, hiking, and horseback riding.

Riversport
Robert Ruppel
213 Yough Street
Confluence, PA 15424
(814) 395-5744
Big Sandy River, Cheat River, Casselman River, Youghiogheny River
Max. rapids: III-IV
PPA

A well-known Pennsylvania paddling school near the borders of West Virginia and Maryland, Riversport runs 1-day canoe and kayak trips as well as renting rafts, canoes and kayaks. It operates on the challenging and beautiful Youghiogheny, Big Sandy, Cheat and Casselman rivers from March to November.

Riversport's trips are suitable for youngsters, adults and senior citizens in good health. Its lessons teach the skills beginners and intermediate paddlers need to run the Class III-IV rapids of nearby rivers, with their hemlocks, rhododendrons, mountain laurel, and rich wildlife.

Songer Whitewater, Inc.
Len and Susie Hanger
P.O. Box 300
Fayetteville, WV 25840
(304) 658-9926, (800) 356-RAFT
New River, Gauley River, Greenbrier River, Bluestone River, Meadow River
Max. rapids: V+
America Outdoors

Songer Whitewater runs guided raft trips of 1-4 days on the New, Gauley, Greenbrier, Bluestone, and Meadow Rivers. All trips are through scenic mountains and gorges, with the most popular excursions running through large, nationally protected areas with big rapids and especially clean air and water. These areas also boast good fishing for bass,

Paddling an inflatable kayak through Surprise Rapids on the Lower New River. Courtesy of USA Raft, Rowlesburg, West Virginia.

Lower New River. Courtesy of Whitewater Information, Glen Jean, West Virginia.

catfish, and muskie, and opportunities to spot deer, turkeys, and other wildlife.

Songer, whose season runs from March to November, has trips to suit all skill levels — novice to expert.

USA RAFT
Mary Kay Heffernan
P.O. Box 277
Rowlesburg, WV 26425
(800) USA RAFT
North Fork Potomac River, Gauley River, Cheat River, Tygart River, New River, Upper Youghiogheny River, Nolichucky River, Ocoee River, Nantahala River, French Broad River
Max. rapids: II-III
America Outdoors

USA Raft offers outings on ten of the best whitewater rivers in the East — the Russell Fork in Kentucky; the Upper Youghiogeny in Maryland; the Nolichucky, French Broad, and Nantahala in North Carolina; the Nolichucky and Ocoee in Tennessee; and the New, Gauley, Cheat, and Tygart in West Virginia.

With this selection of trips, rivers, and outfitters, USA Raft offers afford-able outings to suit paddlers of all skill levels at locations convenient to residents throughout the Middle Atlantic and Southeast.

Whitewater Adventurers of Cheat River Canyon
Robert and Shirley Marietta
P.O. Box 31
Ohiopyle, PA 15470
(412) 329-8850, (800) WWA-RAFT
Cheat River, Upper, Middle and Lower Youghiogheny River
Max. rapids: III-IV
America Outdoors, West Virginia Eastern Professional Outfitters

Whitewater Adventures runs guided raft and kayak trips on the Lower, Middle and Upper Youghiogheny as well as renting canoes, kayaks and rafts from March to November. Paddlers can take their pick; the dam-controlled Yough is rated Class V on its upper section and Classes III and II on its lower and middle stretches respectively. Trips are suitable for "folks from 12-100 who are willing to paddle a bit and have a good time."

A highly professional staff and the best modern equipment are mainstays of the company, which offers lessons and provides a guide for every raft on the steep and technical Upper Yough. Trout, walleye and bass can be caught on the Yough.

In West Virginia, Whitewater Adventurers of Cheat River Canyon runs "very thrilling" guided raft trips from March to July through Class IV-V rapids on the free-flowing Cheat River. The stream cuts through a very steep canyon in an historic part of West Virginia. It has beautiful wildflowers and mountain laurel, along with deer, wild turkeys, and grouse.

Whitewater Information
P.O. Box 243
Glen Jean, WV 25846
(304) 465-0855, (800) 782-RAFT
New River, Gauley River, Bluestone River, Greenbrier River
Max. rapids: V+

Whitewater Information offers guided canoe, raft, and dory trips as well as canoe, raft and tube rentals on the New, Gauley, Bluestone, and Greenbrier Rivers. Trips on the Lower New River cover some of the best whitewater rafting in the East, and can be run all season from April through October. The Upper New is great for scenic family floats and overnight excursions. And the Gauley offers wild excitement on one of the country's most challenging whitewater rivers. All rivers provide terrific mountain scenery, good fishing, and abundant wildlife.

Trips last 1 or 2 days and can be tailored to almost anyone's wishes. During its April-November season, the company also offers guided fishing trips on the New and Gauley Rivers. Acclaimed in outdoors magazines, these tours offer great fishing for many species from bass and walleye to yellow perch.

Whitewater World
Douglas Fogal
Route 903
Jim Thorpe, PA 18229
(717) 325-3656
Cheat River
Max. rapids: V+
America Outdoors

Whitewater World has guided raft trips on the Cheat River with its thrilling Class V+ rapids. Only for the experienced, these spring floats from May to June last 1- and 2-days. The company keeps the size of its groups small, uses up-to-date equipment and serves steak dinners.

Part of the appeal of Whitewater World trips is the amount of time actually spent rafting the rapids. Deer may be spotted on the riverbanks and bass caught in the fast-moving water.

Wildwater Expeditions Unlimited
Box 155
Lansing, WV 25862
(800) WVA-RAFT, (304) 658-4007
New, Gauley Rivers
Max. rapids: V+

Guided raft trips on some of America's best whitewater are offered by this outfitter from April to October. It caters to everyone over six years of age, providing scenic floats and high adventure. The staff is experienced and professional, as well as full of fun. Fishing for bass and catfish is available, along with camping and paddling lessons. Trips last up to 3 days and provide views of deer and numerous bird varieties.

Wisconsin

From the lake country of the north to the rolling Mississippi in the west and vast Lake Michigan in the east, Wisconsin has a wide variety of floats for every taste. All told, the state has 144 canoe trails covering nearly 3,500 miles on rivers of all shapes and sizes. One of the best is the Flambeau, with its tranquil upstream waters and turbulent Class III-IV whitewater in its southern reaches. Still more challenging is the Peshtigo, whose upper waters flow through the beautiful Nicolet National Forest and contain some of the most difficult whitewater in the Midwest. And state officials warn that parts of the Menominee River separating Wisconsin from Michigan are so dangerous that they should be run only by experts in decked boats.

Canoeists in search of kinder and gentler trips are drawn to the Wisconsin River. On its lower reaches, where the 430-mile-long river bends westward to join the Mississippi, the Wisconsin provides lovely scenery and many islands. Canoes may be rented at many locations from Wisconsin Dells to Muscoda. Far upstream, on the quiet stretch between McNaughton and Rhinelander, ospreys, eagles, and blue herons delight floating birdwatchers.

Wisconsin's Parks and Recreation Department (P.O. Box 7921, Madison, WI 53707, phone 608-266-2181) puts out a visitors' guide listing canoeing rivers. These include the delightfully-named Kickapoo River in the southwest, known as "the crookedest river in the world."

The Yellow River in the northwest may be choked by aquatic growth in the summer, but the nearby Apple River, which runs into the Mississippi near Minneapolis, is recommended for family floating in tubes. Another popular canoeing region in the northwest is the St. Croix National Scenic Riverway, with its many National Park Service primitive campsites. Both the St. Croix and its tributary, the Namekagon, may be enjoyed, especially in May and June when the spring runoff creates Class II and III rapids. World-famous for trout fishing is the Bois Brule River in the state's far northwest close to Lake Superior.

Another well-known fishing stream is the Lower Wolf River in the east, where anglers pursue walleye and white bass. Canoeing is possible on the sloughs and backwaters of the Mississippi, but not on the river itself because of its heavy commercial traffic and currents. Some outfitters offer sea kayaking on Lake Michigan.

9 Mile Resort & Tavern
Herb and Carm Echeler
W-10590 Hwy 70
Park Falls, WI 54552
(715) 762-3174
North Fork Flambeau River
Max. rapids: III-IV

9 Mile Resort & Tavern rents canoes for trips of 1-4 days on the Flambeau River. These trips vary in difficulty, to suit novices and advanced paddlers. The first 30 miles below 9 Mile Resort is tranquil and good for beginners. The next 15 miles has Class III-IV rapids to challenge experienced canoeists.

Along the way, paddlers can enjoy the scenic northwoods country of the Flambeau State Forest, which offers free camping; good fishing for bass, walleye, muskie and sturgeon; and abundant wildlife, including ospreys, deer, bears, otters, ducks, and bald eagles. 9 Mile Resort's season runs from May to October.

Bender's Bluffview Canoe Rentals
Ruth Huerth Bender
614 Spruce Street
Sauk City, WI 53583
(608) 643-8247
Wisconsin River
Max. rapids: None

Benders Bluffview Canoe Rentals rents canoes on the Wisconsin River, the "river of a thousand islands." This wide, gentle river offers good fishing, camping on beautiful sand islands and scenic surroundings of high bluffs and woodlands. Trips on the river last 1-5 days and are fine for paddlers of all ages. Along the way, canoeists can fish for walleye, bass, and catfish. They can also admire bald eagles, ospreys, wild turkeys, turkey vultures, and deer.

Benders Bluffview Canoe Rentals' season runs from May to October.

Blue Heron Tours, Inc.
Marc & Gayl Zuelsdorf
Blue Heron Landing
Hwy. 33 at the Bridge, P.O. Box 6
Horicon, WI 53032-0006
(414) 485-4663
Horicon Marsh, Rock River
Max. rapids: None

Blue Heron Tours rents canoes and runs guided trips through Horicon Marsh, a wetland of international importance. It contains Wisconsin's largest heron and egret rookery and 260 other species of birds. Shuttles are available.

Brule River Canoe Rental, Inc.
Brian Carlson
P.O. Box 145
Brule, WI 54820
(715) 372-4983
Bois Brule River
Max.rapids: III-IV
PPA

Brule River Canoe Rental rents canoes and kayaks for 1-3 day outings suitable for novices to experienced paddlers. The company has 30 years' experience of outfitting on the spring-fed river, which flows northward through the Brule River State Forest into Lake Superior. The area, with its cedar swamps and white pine, is famous for its fishing and beauty.

Fishermen can angle for brook, rainbow and brown trout, and paddlers may spot black bears, wolves, and eagles. The season runs from May 1 to October 15.

Cardarelli's Resort & Canoe Rental
Dorothy Cardarelli
Rte. 2, Box 2019
Trego, WI 54888
(715) 635-2959
Namekagon River
Max. rapids: I

Cardarelli's rents canoes, kayaks, and rafts and runs guided canoe trips on the clean and relaxing Namekagon for periods of a full day or more. Camping, cabins, and fishing for walleye and smallmouth bass are available. Deer, beavers, and numerous birds can be seen. The season runs from May 1 to October 15.

Flambeau River Lodge
Robert B. Felske
N7870 Flambeau Road
Ladysmith, WI 54848
(715) 532-5392
North and South Fork Flambeau River
Max. rapids: I-II

Flambeau River Lodge rents canoes on Class I-II sections of the North and South Forks of the Flambeau River for trips of 1-5 days. These trips, fine for paddlers of all ages, run through unspoiled old-growth forest, offering views of bald eagles, ospreys, blue herons, deer, and other wildlife. Along the North Fork, paddlers can also camp at free sites maintained by the Department of Natural Resources. There's no camping on the South Fork.

Flambeau River Lodge, open year-round, also has its own private tent and R.V. campground, a dining room and bar.

Homestead Canoe Rental
Donald & Arlene Kuba
Rte. 1, Box 446
Gordon, WI 54838
(715) 376-4491
Upper St. Croix, Eau Claire Rivers.
Max. rapids: III-IV

Homestead Canoe Rental rents canoes for trips ranging of 1 hour to 2 days in a wilderness setting where deer, eagles, bears, and otters may be seen. Waters are suitable for people of all ages, with rapids up to Class III, and offer fishing for bass, walleye, and panfish. The company's season runs from April 1 to October 1.

Kayaking Adventure of Door County
Tim Pflieger
4497 Ploor Rd.
Sturgeon Bay, WI 54235
(414) 746-9999
Lake Michigan, Mink River
Max. rapids: None

This company rents sea kayaks and runs sea kayaking trips for tours on Lake Michigan from Baileys Harbor to Washington Island. The paddling is suitable for novices, but the outfitter also runs advanced skill workshops. Fishing is good for several kinds of trout, bass, and salmon.

Camping is available during excursions which can last up to 4 days during the May-October season.

Kosir's Rapid Rafts
Dan Kosir
H.C.R. Box 161
Athelstane, WI 54104
(715) 757-3431
Peshtigo River, Menominee River
Max. rapids: III-IV

Kosir's Rapid Rafts runs guided raft trips and rents kayaks and rafts on the Peshtigo and Menominee Rivers. These rivers offer continuous stretches of Class III-IV whitewater but are fine for beginners as well as experienced paddlers. Both rivers are also extremely clean, offering good fishing for bass, northern pike, walleye, and trout. The Menominee features 200-foot high cliffs, and both the Menominee and Peshtigo offer opportunities to spot deer, bald eagles, and occasional otters.

During Kosir's season, which runs from April to October, the outfitter also offers camping, cabin rentals, and a restaurant and bar.

Life Tools Adventure Outfitters
John Hermonson & Craig Charles
1035 Main St.
Green Bay, WI 54301
(414) 432-7399, FAX (414) 432-4509
*Green Bay, Lakes Michigan & Superior,
inland rivers*
Max. rapids: None

This outfitter runs guided sea kayaking tours suitable for all ages and also rents canoes. Some athletic ability is needed for 3-4 day camping trips. Friendly and outgoing staff equip clients with high quality gear and trips are scenic and relaxed.

Customers enjoy scenic bluffs, miles of sandy beaches, rare forest ecologies, and evening sunset tours open to everybody. Wildlife is plentiful and fishing is for trout, salmon, perch, and bass. The season runs May-September.

Northern Waters
Wayne Overberg
P.O. Box 2087
6009 Highway 70 W.
Eagle River, WI 54521
(715) 479-3884, (715) 479-2966
Rivers of northern Wisconsin, Lake Superior
Max. rapids: I-II
PPA

Northern Waters offers guided canoe and sea-kayak trips and rents canoes, sea kayaks, and tubes for trips of 1-3 days. The canoe trips, on several Northern Wisconsin rivers, have Class I- II rapids and are fine for both novices and experienced canoeists. Sea kayaking trips, also easy enough for beginners, are on Lake Superior. On guided trips, guests wanting lessons can learn paddling skills from the outfitter's ACA-certified instructors. On all trips, paddlers can also enjoy pristine wilderness, clean waters, good camping, fishing for bass, walleye, muskie, and northern pike as well as views of eagles, ospreys, bears, deer, beavers, otters, and other wildlife.

Northern Waters' season runs from May to October.

Northwest Passage
Rick Sweitzer
1130 Greenleaf Avenue
Wilmette, IL 60091
(847) 256-4409, (800) RECREATE,
FAX (847) 256-4476
*Current River, Rio Grande, Chicago River,
BWCA, Lake Michigan, Lake Superior*
Max. rapids: III-IV

Northwest Passage offers guided sea kayak trips on Lake Michigan in Door County, Wisconsin, and on Lake Superior in Michigan. It also has raft trips on the New and Gauley Rivers in West Virginia; canoe trips on the Current River in Missouri, the Rio Grande in Texas, and the Boundary Waters Canoe Area in Minnesota. Most of these trips, which last 2-7 days, are designed for beginners; some require prior experience. Depending on the location, these floats offer excitement, challenge, remoteness and beauty.

An adventure travel company, Northwest Passage also offers skiing, hiking, cycling, backpacking, dogsledding, and rock climbing. Outings run year-round in the U.S., Canada, the Arctic, Greenland, Switzerland, New Zealand, Costa Rica, Belize, Crete, Tanzania, southern Africa, and Antarctica.

Old Homestead
Don and Arlene Kuba
Route 1, Box 446
Gordon, WI 54838
(715) 376-4491
Eau Claire River, St. Croix River
Max. rapids: III-IV

Old Homestead rents canoes on the Eau Claire and St. Croix Rivers, two clean, secluded streams with trips fit for all paddlers from beginners to experts. Trips last from 2 hours to 5 days and offer camping, good fishing for walleye, northern pike, bass, and panfish, and a chance to spot deer, bears, eagles, hawks, and other wildlife. Old Homestead's season runs from April to October.

Quest Recreation
John Wright
Highway 8 and 35
St. Croix Falls, WI 54024
(800) 992-2692
St. Croix River
Max. rapids: None

Quest Recreation rents canoes for trips of 1-6 days on the St. Croix, one of the eight original Wild and Scenic rivers. A gentle river, the St. Croix is fine for paddlers of all ages. It offers unspoiled wilderness, good fishing, and abundant deer, raccoons, eagles, and other wildlife. Quest's season is from May to September.

River Forest Rafts
Jim Stecher
N 2755 Sunny Waters Lane
White Lake, WI 54491
(715) 882-3351
Wolf River
Max. rapids: III-IV

River Forest Rafts offers guided and unguided trips by raft, canoe and kayak on clean waters through a wilderness full of wildlife. During the spring runoff, rapids become Class III-IV and require paddling experience. But in the summer the river is gentler and suitable for families and youth groups. Each paddler gets experienced instruction before setting out.

Camping is available, along with trout and smallmouth bass fishing.

Riverview Hills
Albert J. Bremmen
Route 1, Box 307
Muscoda, WI 53573
(608) 739-3472
Wisconsin River, Pine River
Max. rapids: None

Riverview Hills rents canoes for trips of 1-7 days on the Wisconsin and Pine Rivers. On the Wisconsin River alone the outfitter offers access to 100 miles of river along which to paddle, swim, fish, and camp. The rivers feature scenic bluffs, canyons, woods, clean water and good fishing for walleye, crappie, bass,

catfish, sturgeon, bluegill, and sunfish. Paddlers on these gentle flatwater trips can also enjoy viewing deer, beavers, squirrels, turkeys, ducks, seagulls, foxes, and other wildlife. Riverview Hills' season runs from May to September.

Rutabaga, Inc.
Gordy Sussman
220 W. Broadway
Madison, WI 53716
(608) 223-9300, (800) I-PADDLE
(472-3353)
Lake Superior, BWCA
Max. rapids: None
NAPSA, America Outdoors

Rutabaga rents canoes and kayaks from its location in Madison. Customers generally rent touring kayaks for trips on Lake Michigan and canoes for touring the Boundary Waters. The outfitter's staff also offers solo canoes and advice on where to paddle.

St. John Mine Canoe Rental
Harry D. Henderson
129 Main Street
Potosi, WI 53820
(608) 763-2121
Grant River, Platte River, Mississippi River
Max. rapids: I-II

St. John Mine Canoe Rental offers guided and unguided canoe rentals for trips on the Grant, Platte, and Mississippi Rivers. These rivers, with Class I-II rapids, are especially well suited for beginners and families. The trips pass through the scenic, unglaciated "Hidden Valley" area of southwest Wisconsin, offering views of rocky ledges, steep bluffs, and woodlands. The wildlife includes deer, muskrats, otters, blue herons, eagles, several species of duck, and many smaller birds.

Paddlers on these 1-3 day trips can also enjoy primitive camping, excursions to nearby historic lead mines and unusual ethnic sites, and fishing for smallmouth bass, northern pike, catfish, suckers, and bluegill. St. John Mine's season is from May through October.

Sea Isles Boat Livery
Ronald C. Schams
107 First Avenue South
Onalaska, WI 54650
(608) 783-5623
Black River, Mississippi River, Lake Onalaska
Max. rapids: None

Sea Isles Boat Livery rents canoes for flatwater trips on the Black River, Mississippi, and Lake Onalaska. These waters offer excellent fishing for bluegill, crappie, bass, catfish, walleye, and northern pike. The livery also operates a camp store and a 30-site campground with electric hook-ups, shaded riverside sites, and a modern bathhouse.

Shotgun Eddy, Inc.
6074 Sherrie Lane
Gillett, WI 54124
(414) 855-2355
Wolf River
Max. rapids: III-IV

Shotgun Eddy, Inc., rents rafts for half-day and full-day trips on the Wolf River. The river has Class III-IV rapids, but is easy enough for beginners age 16 or older. In fact, 90 percent of the outfitter's customers are first-time rafters. In addition to the rapids, paddlers also can enjoy the river's exceptionally clear, spring-fed waters and its wilderness scenery of canyons, waterfalls, and abundant birds, fish, raccoons, and other wildlife. The banks are also free of litter, as no bottles or cans are allowed on the river.

During the May-to-October season, Shotgun Eddy also operates a rustic campground.

Trek & Trail
Greg Swevak, Ken Pobloske
Granary-Wagon Trail Resort
Highway ZZ
Ellison Bay, WI 54210
(414) 854-9616
Lake Michigan, Lake Superior, Lake Huron, Green Bay
Max. rapids: None

Trek & Trail Inc. offers guided sea-kayak trips and sea-kayak rentals for 1-14 day trips on Lake Superior and Lake Michigan. From the company's base on the Apostle Islands National Lake Shore, paddlers can quickly reach colorful sea caves, shipwrecks, lighthouses, and an abandoned fishing village. En route one can also fish for lake trout and salmon and view wildlife, including eagles, ospreys, deer, otters, loons, cormorants, and possibly bears. On guided trips, paddlers can also receive basic or advanced instruction, learn about the region's geology and natural history, and enjoy combination sailing/kayaking trips, which enable kayakers to reach some of Lake Superior's most remote and spectacular areas.

Some extended trips and ones including long crossings of open water require previous sea-kayaking experience. However, no experience is necessary for most trips. In fact, 95 percent of Trek & Trail's guests have never kayaked before. The company, whose season runs from May to October, also runs a paddle sport retail and mail-order shop.

Twin Lakes Canoe Shop
John Kropp
1968 E. Lake Shore Dr.
Twin Lakes, WI 53181
(414) 877-3329
Nippersink Creek, Fox River
Max. rapids: None

This outfitter rents canoes for day trips on the beautiful Nippersink canoe trail in northern Illinois and the pastoral Fox River canoe trail in Wisconsin.

These are easy trips suitable for all, and the outfitter promises personal service with top equipment.

Paddlers can watch deer, turtles, ducks, beavers, muskrat, and blue heron, and fish for bass, catfish, bluegills, and walleye. The season lasts from May to October. Swimming and paddling lessons are available.

University of Iowa Rec. Services
Wayne Fett
Touch the Earth
E216 Field House
Iowa City, IA 52242
(319) 335-9293, (310) 335-5256
Wolf River, Red River, Wisconsin River, Upper Iowa River, BWCA, Upper Iowa River, Ocoee River, Chattooga River, Nantahala River, St. Francis River, Poudre River
Max. rapids: III-IV

University of Iowa Recreation Services offers guided canoe, kayak, and raft trips and rents canoes for trips in Iowa on the upper Iowa River; in Minnesota in the Boundary Waters Canoe Area; in Wisconsin on the Wolf, Red, and Wisconsin Rivers; and in the southeast on the Ocoee, Chattooga, Nantahala, St. Francis, and Poudre Rivers. These trips, open to students and the general public, feature a low student-to-instructor ratio and are geared for beginning to intermediate paddlers. All trips run through scenic, remote, and wild areas. Trips last 1-4 days.

The department of recreation services, open year-round, also offers rock climbing, cross-country skiing, backpacking, and bicycle touring.

Whitewater Specialty
Bill Kallner
N3894 Hwy. 55
White Lake, WI 54491
(715) 882-5400
Wolf, Red, Peshtigo, and Menominee Rivers
Max. rapids: III-IV

Whitewater Specialty offers guided, instructional canoe and kayak trips on the Wolf, Red, Peshtigo, and Menominee Rivers in northern Wisconsin. On these 1-day trips, professional instructors teach participants how to paddle skillfully, safely, and confidently and how to break complex rapids down into manageable parts. These trips, geared for paddlers of all experience levels, feature challenging, clean whitewater, outstanding scenery, and many opportunities to view bald eagles, ospreys, herons, ducks, otters, deer, mink, and other wildlife. Paddlers also can fish for trout. Whitewater Specialty is open from May to September.

Wild River Outfitters
Marilyn Chesnik and Jerry Dorff
15177 Highway 70
Grantsburg, WI 54840
(715) 463-2254
Upper St. Croix River, Namekagon River
Max. rapids: I-II

Wild River Outfitters provides canoe rental and shuttle service on over 150 miles of the Upper St. Croix and Namekagon Rivers. Both streams are designated Wild and Scenic Rivers managed by the National Park Service. Trips last 1-6 days, have Class I-II rapids and are suitable for beginning to advanced paddlers. These clean and clear rivers provide good fishing for smallmouth bass, walleye, northern pike, muskie, catfish, and sturgeon. Along the riverway are many scenic, secluded campsites provided at no charge to canoeists. Opportunities abound to see native wildlife, including deer, bears, raccoons, otters, foxes, bald eagles, blue herons, ducks, and geese.

During its April-to-November season, Wild River Outfitters also operates a campground with hot showers and a store selling bait, tackle, camping supplies and other convenience items.

Wolf River Trips, Inc.
Clair Flease
Route 3, Box 122
New London, WI 54961
(414) 982-2458
Little Wolf River
Max. rapids: I-II

Wolf River Trips rents canoes and tubes for 1-day trips on the Wolf River. The river, with gentle Class I-II rapids, is fine for beginners and offers clean water good for swimming and fishing for black bass. For all trips, a shuttle bus takes paddlers to upstream put-ins for floats back to the campground. The campground, open from May to October, offers tent and R.V. sites, swimming, tennis, hiking and volleyball.

Wyoming

Where the Great Plains meet the Rocky Mountains, the classic western state of Wyoming bestrides the Continental Divide. Wyoming's cold, clear waters therefore flow both ways: eastward toward the Gulf and the Atlantic, westward to the Pacific. Mountains, desert, grasslands and wild rivers make for some of the best recreational country in the world, not least for rafting, kayaking and canoeing. River names like the Snake, the North Platte and the Big Horn stir the imagination. Parts of three great river systems — the Missouri, the Colorado and the Columbia — have their headwaters in the Wyoming mountains.

Outfitters run several popular trips on the Snake River, which rises in Yellowstone National Park and flows southward through the Grand Teton National Park before crossing into Idaho through a magnificent canyon. This Grand Canyon of the Snake offers whitewater rafting amid great scenery. Some of the rapids are rated Class III-IV but the trip is billed as a very safe float for families with children. Overnight trippers camp in wooded meadows with a chance of seeing eagles and ospreys overhead. The canyon walls display intriguing geological formations.

Further upstream, people can float on the Snake's headwaters or take a very gentle ten-mile paddle from Dead Man's Bar to Moose Village. Since the latter trip is entirely within the Grand Teton National Park it runs beneath the beautiful alpine backdrop of the Grand Tetons and is rich in wildlife. Floaters may spot moose, elk, beaver, deer, heron and osprey, especially in the early morning and at dusk. In addition to running rivers, visitors to the national parks can paddle on Yellowstone and Jackson Lakes.

The Clarks Fork of the Yellowstone River is one of the wildest rivers outside Alaska and the only federally-designated wild and scenic river in Wyoming. Yet it is on American Rivers' list of most-endangered rivers because of Canadian mining company's plan to open a gold mine in headwaters just outside Yellowstone National Park.

In the southeast corner of Wyoming near the Colorado state line, the North Platte comes roaring northward through North Gate Canyon. This is wild country where rafters battle rugged whitewater — mostly Class III-

WYOMING

IV but up to Class V+ at high water — as the river thunders through canyons and past meadows, wildflowers and forests. Bighorn sheep, black bear,
elk deer, beaver, golden eagles, bald eagles, herons and Canada geese may
be glimpsed from the river. The 64-mile stretch of the North Platte between
the Colorado border and the Wyoming town of Saratoga has been nationally designated a blue ribbon trout fishery. It is claimed to be Wyoming's
best trout stream with 3,200 catchable trout (rainbow, brown and cutthroat)
per mile.

As a rule, Wyoming's rivers are best run in June and July. The choice is
wide: every paddler to his (or her) taste. The upper reaches of the Green
River, the source and fount of the Colorado, provide a 16-mile Class II day
trip near the town of Pinedale. Greys River is a real high-country stream in
the 3,440,000-acre Bridger-Teton National Forest bordering Grand Teton and
Yellowstone National Parks. The 43-mile section starting at the Corral Creek
Campground is only Class II, but other stretches are virtually unrunnable.

In the Shoshone National Forest, the first National Forest in the United
States (created by President Benjamin Harrison in 1891), the North Fork
of the Shoshone River offers a 9-mile day trip from Wapiti to Buffalo Bill
Reservoir. Its rapids rate Class II and it has the advantage that it can be run
until early August. The broad Big Horn River, running vertically through
the north-central area of the state, provides good scenery and great fishing
all summer long. There are no rapids in the Thermopolis area and the waters are uncrowded.

Barker-Ewing Scenic Float Trips
Dick and Barbara Barker
Box 100
Moose, WY 83012
(307) 733-1800, (800) 365-1800
Snake River
Max. rapids: None
America Outdoors

Barker-Ewing Scenic Float Trips offers
half-day scenic trips on the Snake River
in Grand Teton National Park. These
cover 10 miles and offer spectacular
views of the Teton Mountains and plentiful wildlife, including moose, elk, deer,
bald eagles, ospreys, beavers, otters, and
occasional bison and bears. These flatwater outings, suitable for all ages, are
led by experienced guides who interpret
the park's wildlife and natural history.
During Barker-Ewing's season, which

runs from May to September, the company also offers cookout tours that provide either breakfast or dinner.

Flagg Ranch Village
P.O. Box 187
Moran, WY 83013
(307) 733-8761
Snake River
Max. rapids: III-IV

Flagg Ranch Village offers guided oar-
boat trips and canoe rentals for trips of
1-4 hours on the Snake River. These
family-oriented trips offer spectacular
views of the Teton Mountains and wilderness in Grand Teton National Park.
Guests also can view abundant wildlife
and fish for trout. Flagg Ranch's season
runs from June 1 to July 30.

Great Rocky Mountain Outfitters, Inc.
Thomas H. Wiersema,
Robert G. Smith
Box 1636, 216 E. Walnut Ave.
Saratoga, WY 82331
(307) 326-8750
Upper North Platte, Encampment Rivers
Max. rapids: III-IV

Great Rocky Mountain Outfitters, Inc. offers guided wade and drift boat fishing and scenic trips on Wyoming's Upper North Platte and Encampment Rivers. These floats offer a spectacular array of scenery ranging from steep mountain canyons to hay meadows and desert terrain with large limestone bluffs. Guests may encounter a wide variety of wildlife, including bighorn sheep, elk, deer, antelope, beaver, coyote, fox, bald and golden eagles, ospreys, and herons. Anglers find a nationally known blue ribbon stream with large numbers of brown, rainbow and cutthroat trout.

Trips are offered from April through October and may run from one-half to 5 days. Shuttle service, and canoe and raft rentals are also available.

Green River Outfitters
Bill Webb
Pinedale, WY 82941
(307) 367-2416
Green, New Fork, Gros Ventre
Max. rapids: None
Wyoming Outfitters Association

Green River Outfitters offers guided raft trips from May to September for 1-3 days amid the beauty and isolation of the Green River headwaters. The company caters to fly fishermen and others who "just want to get away from it all." In business for 15 years, it has experienced guides who help fishermen land five species of trout.

The outfitter runs wilderness camping outings and float trips. The abundant wildlife in this Bridger-Teton National Forest area includes moose, elk, deer, coyotes, ospreys, and bald eagles.

Gregg & Goodyear Rendezvous River Sports
Aaron Pruzan
Box 9201, 1035 W. Broadway
Jackson, WY 83001
(800) 733-2471, FAX (307) 733-7171
Yellowstone, Lewis, Shoshone Lakes, Snake, Hoback, Greys Rivers
Max. rapids: III-IV

Rendezvous River Sports offers guided kayak and rental kayak and canoe trips amid superb scenery in the Yellowstone-Grand Teton area. Floats vary from beginner flatwater to expert whitewater and last 1-5 days. While trout fishing, paddlers view a wide range of wildlife including bear, moose, and bald eagles.

Camping and paddling lessons are available during the April-October season.

Heart 6 Ranch
The Garnick Family
P.O. Box 70
Moran, WY 83013
(307) 543-2477
Snake River, Buffalo River, Yellowstone lakes, Jackson lakes
Max. rapids: None

Heart 6 Ranch provides guided raft and dory trips and canoe rentals on the Snake and Buffalo Rivers and Jackson and Yellowstone Lakes. These trips run at the base of the Tetons, offering spectacular mountain scenery and abundant wildlife, including elk, moose, deer, bears, eagles, coyotes, and marmots. Paddling is on flat water, which makes it easy for people of all ages. Anglers also enjoy excellent trout fishing.

Heart 6 Ranch's season runs from June 1 to September 15.

O.A.R.S.
George Wendt
P.O. Box 67
Angels Camp, CA 95222
(209) 736-4677, (800) 446-7238 (CA),
(800) 346-6277
*Snake, San Juan, American, Salmon, Middle
Fork Salmon, Cal-Salmon, Merced, Stanis-
laus, Tuolumne, Rogue, Colorado Rivers*
Max. rapids: III-IV
America Outdoors

O.A.R.S. runs guided dory, raft, and
kayak trips in six Western states. It offers
tours in California on the American,
Cal-Salmon, Merced, Stanislaus and
Tuolumne Rivers; in Oregon on the
Rogue; in Arizona on the Colorado; in
Wyoming on the Snake, and in Utah on
the San Juan River. These outings last
1-13 days and, depending on the class
of river, are fine for children, novices,
families, intermediate, and expert rafters. O.A.R.S. trips provide fishing,
swimming, camping, side hikes, wildlife
viewing and other activities.

O.A.R.S. tours run from April to
October.

Ottertail Outings
Jefferson M. Brown
Box 1312
Pinedale, WY 82941
(307) 367-4363
Wyoming rivers and lakes
Max. rapids: None

Ottertail Outings offers a unique
service: custom trips in a replica of the
birch-bark trade canoes known as North
canoes. They were 20-30 feet long and
used by French-Canadian employees of
the fur companies for hundreds of years
over much of North America. The replica is made of both modern and traditional materials.

The outfitter takes 4 to 6 paddlers
on flatwater rivers and lakes within the
state of Wyoming. Reservations should
be made at least a week in advance during the June 15-Sept. 15 season.

Platte River Drifters
Bill White
383 Glendo Park Rd.
Glendo, WY 82213
(307) 735-4216
North Platte River, Glendo Reservoir
Max. rapids: I-II

Platte River Drifters run 1/2- and 1-
day trips in dories and drift boats for
people of all ages who enjoy uncrowded,
scenic waters and superb fishing. It rents
drift boats and runs guided trips in dories.
The outfitter, which has friendly, knowledgeable guides and new equipment, is
open from April through October.

Several minor rapids enliven the
North Platte, which has large trees in
part of the canyon. Generally the waters
are very quiet and the weather is sunny.

Richard Brothers, Inc.
James Richard
2215 Rangeview Lane
Laramie, WY 82070
(307) 742-7529
North Platte River
Max. rapids: V+
America Outdoors

Richard Brothers offer guided raft trips
and raft rentals on the North Platte River through North Gate Canyon. These
trips run through magnificent canyon
country of pine, spruce, fir, and aspen forests. These harbor abundant wildlife ranging from elk, deer, black bears, and bighorn sheep to eagles, herons, and Canada
geese. The wild and free-flowing North
Platte has technical Class III-IV rapids,
which the company runs in oar boats for
guests of all ages. Paddle raft trips are
more demanding, requiring experience.

Whitewater trips of 1 and 2 days are
scheduled each weekend from mid-May
through July 4. Custom trips of 1-7 days
are also available, along with 3-5 day
trips contracted through the National
Audubon Society and American Wilderness Alliance. During Richard Brothers
May-to-July season, the company also
offers drift boat trout fishing trips for
serious fly fishermen.

Sands Wild Water River Trips
Charles Sands
P.O. Box 696
Wilson, WY 83014
(307) 733-4410, (800) 223-4059
Snake River
Max. rapids: III-IV

Sands Wild Water River Trips offers guided oar- and paddle-raft trips on the Snake River. These outings, which last from 1/2-2 days, pass through a spectacular river canyon in the Tetons that offers exciting Class III-IV rapids, interesting geology, and spectacular views of surrounding mountains. Participants can also enjoy viewing abundant bald eagles, ospreys, ducks, geese, beavers, otters, and other wildlife.

Oar-boat trips are fine for guests of all ages. Paddle-boat trips are best suited for active adults and teens. During Sands' season, which runs from May to September, guests can also camp at the company's "Pine Bar" campsite, set in a forest with beautiful mountain meadows.

Snake River Kayak and Canoe School
Donald S. Perkins
P.O. Box 3482
345 West Gill
Jackson, WY 83001
(307) 733-3127, (800) 529-2501
Hoback River, Snake River, Gros Ventre River
Max. rapids: III-IV
America Outdoors, ACA

Snake River Kayak & Canoe School offers guided and unguided canoe, kayak, sea kayak, and raft trips for paddlers of all levels of ability. These trips, which last from 3 hours to 3 days, run in Yellowstone Lake and the Hoback, Snake, and Gros Ventre Rivers through the spectacular mountain country in and around Grand Teton National Park, Yellowstone National Park and the Jackson Hole Valley. Both oar-boat and paddle-boat trips are available, making Class III-IV whitewater runs accessible to guests of all ages. Day trips run in morning, afternoon, and evening, include a hearty homemade meal, and last

for either three or six hours. Special scenic trips and combination "pedal & paddle" trips are also available. Finally, the company also offers a complete array of kayak, raft, and canoe lessons.

On all of Snake River Kayak & Canoe School's trips, guests have an excellent chance of spotting wildlife, including ospreys, eagles, deer, moose, and bears. The company's season runs from May to September.

Triangle X Ranch
Moose, WY 83012
(307) 733-5500
Snake River
Max. rapids: I-II
NTA

Operating in Grand Teton National Park, Triangle X Ranch provides guided raft trips lasting 1-3 hours amid some of the world's finest scenery. These floats are suitable for families, groups, and seniors, who may fish for trout and watch for moose, elk, deer, buffalo, bald eagles, and ospreys. The company's season runs from May 1 through September.

Wind River Canyon Outfitters
Daniel E. Miller
P.O. Box 269
Thermopolis, WY 82443
(307) 864-3617
Big Horn River, Wind River, North Platte River, Shoshone River
Max. rapids: None

Wind River Canyon Outfitters runs guided drift-boat fly- and spin-fishing trips on the Bighorn, Wind, North Platte, and Shoshone Rivers. These 1/2-day and full-day trips offer exceptional fishing for rainbow, brown, and cutthroat trout and beautiful scenery in this region bounded by the Big Horn and Absaroka Mountains. On these trips, which run from April to October, guests can also see abundant deer, waterfowl, birds of prey and other wildlife.

In addition to fishing, the outfitter also offers or can arrange hunting, horsepacking, sightseeing, and photography.

Resources

America Outdoors, David Brown, exec. dir., P.O. Box 1348, Knoxville, TN 37901, tel. (423) 524-4814, FAX (423) 525-4765.

American Canoe Association (ACA), Jeffrey Yeager, exec. dir., 7432 Alban Station Blvd., Suite B-226, Springfield, VA 22150, tel. (703) 451-0141, FAX (703) 451-2205.

American Rivers. Rebecca Wodder, president, 1025 Vermont Avenue, N.W., Suite 720, Washington, D.C. 20005. Tel. (202) 547-6900.

American Whitewater Affiliation, Phyllis Horowitz, exec. dir., P.O. Box 85, Phoenicia, NY 12464, tel. (914) 688-5569.

North American Paddlesports Association (NAPSA), Neil Wiesner-Hanks, exec. dir., 12455 N. Wauwatosa Road, Mequon, WI 53092, tel. (414) 242-1539, FAX (414) 242-5228.

Professional Paddlesports Association (PPA), Jim Thaxton, exec. dir., R.R. 2, Box 248, Butler, KY 41006, tel. (606) 472-2205, FAX (606) 472-2030.

Trade Association of Sea Kayaking (TASK), Neil Wiesner-Hanks, 12455 N. Wauwatosa Road, Mequon, WI 53092, tel. 414-242-5228, FAX 414-242-4428.

U.S. Canoe Association (USCA), Jim Mack, exec. dir., 606 Ross Street, Middletown OH 45044, tel./FAX (513) 422-3739.

U.S. National Park Service, (202) 208-4747.

Note: Your nearest canoe club probably belongs to either the ACA or the USCA. Contact these groups for information on local clubs.

Bibliography

Following is a selection of some of the best guidebooks on canoeing and rafting in he United States.

A *Canoeing and Kayaking Guide to the Streams of Florida*, by Elizabeth F. Carter and John L. Pearce, 1985-87, Menasha Ridge Press, Hillsborough, N.C.

A *Canoeing and Kayaking Guide to the Streams of Kentucky*, by Bob Sehlinger, 1978, Thomas Press, Ann Arbor, Mich.

A *Canoeing and Kayaking Guide to the Streams of Ohio*, by Richard Combs, 1983, Menasha Ridge Press, Hillsborough, N.C.

Adirondack Canoe Waters, North Flow, by Paul Jamieson, 1986, Adirondack Mountain Club, Glen Falls, N.Y.

Adirondack Canoe Waters, South and West Flow, by Alec C. Proskine, 1985, Adirondack Mountain Club, Glen Falls, N.Y.

The Alaska River Guide, by Karen Jettmar, 1993, Alaska Northwest Books, Anchorage, Alaska.

AMC River Guide, Massachusetts, Connecticut, and Rhode Island, ed. by Steve Tuckerman, 1990, Appalachian Mountain Club Books, Boston, Mass.

AMC River Guide. Maine, Ed. Katharine Yates and Carey Phillips, 1991. Appalachian Mountain Club, New York, N.Y.

An Illustrated Canoe Log of the Shenandoah River and its South Fork, by Louis J. Matacia and Owen S. Cecil III, 1974, Matacia, Oakton, Va.

Back to Nature in Canoes: A Guide to American Waters, by Rainer Esslen, 1976, Columbia Publishing Co., Frenchtown, N.J.

The Big Drops: Ten Legendary Rapids, by Robert O. Collins and Roderick Nash, 1978, Sierra Club Books, San Francisco, Calif.

Boundary Waters Canoe Area, by Robert Beymer, 1994, Wilderness Press, Berkeley, Calif.

Boundary Waters: Canoe Camping with Style, by Cliff Jacobson, 1995, ICS Books, Merrillville, Ind.

Brown's Guide to the Georgia Outdoors, ed. by John W. English, 1986, Cherokee Publishing Co., Atlanta, Ga.

California Whitewater: A Guide to the Rivers, by Jim Cassady and Fryar Calhoun, 1990, North Fork Press, Berkeley, Calif.

Canoe Camping, Vermont and New Hampshire Rivers, by Roioli Schweiker, 1985, Backcountry Publications, Woodstock, Vt.

Canoe Guide, by Indiana Dept. of Natural Resources, 1975, Dept. of Nat. Resources, Indianapolis, Ind.

Canoe Trails of the Deep South, by Chuck Estes et al., 1991, Menasha Ridge Press, Birmingham, Ala.

Canoeing and Kayaking Ohio's Streams, 1994, Backcountry Publications, Woodstock, Vt

Canoeing the Jersey Pine Barrens, by Robert Parne, 1994, Globe Pequot Press, Old Saybrook, Conn.

Canoeing and Rafting: The Complete Where-to-go Guide to America's Best Tame and Wild Waters, by Sara Pyle, 1979, Morrow, New York, N.Y.

Canoeing Guide: Western Pennsylvania and Northern West Virginia, by American Youth Hostels, Inc., 1975, AYA Pittsburgh Council, Penn.

Canoeing Maine #1, by Eben Thomas, 1979, Thorndike Press, Thorndike, Maine.

Canoeing Maine #2, by Eben Thomas, 1979, Thorndike Press, Thorndike, Maine.

Canoeing Mass., Rhode Island and Conn., by Ken Weber, 1980, New Hampshire Pub. Co., Somersworth, N.H.

Canoeing Michigan Rivers, by Jerry Dennis, 1986, Friede Publications, Davison, Mich.

Canoeing the Jersey Pine Barrens, by Robert Parnes, 1990, Globe Pequot Press, Chester, Conn.

Canoeing Waters of California, by Ann Dwyer, 1973, GBH Press, Kentfield, Calif.

Canoeing Western Waterways, the Mountain States, by Ann Schafer, 1978, Harper & Row, New York, N.Y.

Canoeing White Water: River Guide, Virginia, Eastern West Virginia, North Carolina, Grea Smoky Mountain Area, by Randy Carter, 1974, Appalachian Books, Oakton, Va.

Canoeing Wild Rivers, by Cliff Jacobson, 1989, ICS Books, Merrillville, Ind.

Canoeing: Trips in Connecticut, by Pamela Detels and Janet Harris, 1977, Birch Run Press, Madison, Conn.

The Complete Guide to Whitewater Rafting Tours, by Rena K. Margulis, 1986, Aquatic Adventure Publns., Palo Alto, Calif.

The Concord, Sudbury and Assabet Rivers, by Ron McAdow, 1990, Bliss Publishing Co., Marlborough, Mass.

Carolina Whitewater, by Bob Benner, 1981, Menasha Ridge Press, Hillsborough, N.C.

Cataract Canyon via the Green or Colorado Rivers, by Donald L. Baars, 1987, Canon Publishers, Evergreen, Colo.

Down the Wild Rivers: A Guide to the Streams of California, by Thomas Harris, 1972, Chronicle Books, San Francisco, Calif.

Downstream, A Rafting and Tubing Guide to Florida's Rivers and Streams, by Robert Tabor, 1978, SSAM Publishing Company, Ft. Pierce, Fla.

Exciting River Running in the U.S., by Elizabeth Medes, 1979, Contemporary Books, Chicago, Ill.

The Floater's Guide to Colorado, by Doug Wheat, 1983, Falcon Press Publishing Company, Helena, Mont.

The Floater's Guide to Missouri, by Andy Cline, 1992, Falcon Press, Helene, Mont.

The Floater's Guide to Montana, by Hank Fischer, 1986, Falcon Press Publishing Company, Helena, Mont.

Garden State Canoeing, by Edward Gertler, 1992, Seneca Press, Silver Spring, Md.

Guide to Floating Whitewater Rivers, by R.W. Miskimins, 1987, F. Amato Publications, Portland, Ore.

Florida by Paddle and Pack, by Mike Toner, 1979, Banyan Books, Miami, Fla.

Idaho Whitewater: The Complete River Guide, by Greg Moore and Don McClaran, 198⁹ Class VI Whitewater, McCall, Id.

inois Country Canoe Trails, by Philip E. Vierling, 1979, Illinois Country Canoe Guides, Chicago, Ill.

troduction to Water Trails in America, by Robert Colwell, 1973, Stackpole Books, Harrisburg, Penn.

eystone Canoeing, by Edward Gertler, 1988, Seneca Press, Silver Spring, Md.

he Lower Canyons of the Rio Grande, by Louis F. Aulbach and Joe Butler, 1988, Wilderness Area Map Service, Houston, Texas.

Maryland and Delaware Canoe Trails, by Edward Gertler, 1992, Seneca Press, Silver Spring, Md.

Midwest Canoe Trails, by John W. Malo, 1978, Contemporary Books, Chicago, Ill.

Mississippi Solo, by Eddy L. Harris, 1988, N. Lyons Books, New York, N.Y.

ew Mexico Whitewater, by New Mexico State Park Division, Natural Resources Dept., 1983, Santa Fe, N.M.

iobrara River Canoeing Guide, by Duane Gudgel, 1990, Plains Trading Co. Archives, Valentine, Neb.

o Two Rivers Alike: 50 Canoeable Rivers in New York and Pennsylvania, by Alec C. Proskine, 1995, Purple Mountain Press, Fleishmanns, N.Y.

orthern Georgia Canoeing, by Bob Sehlinger and Don Otey, 1980, Menasha Ridge Press, Hillsborough, N.C.

ne and Two Day River Cruises: Maryland, Virginia, West Virginia, by H. Roger Corbett, Jr., and Louis J. Matacia, 1973, Blue Ridge Voyageurs, Oakton, Va.

regon River Tours, by John Garren, 1991, Garren Publishing, Portland, Ore.

ddle Routes of Western Washington, by Verne Huser, 1990, Mountaineers, Seattle, Wash.

ddle Washington, by Dave LeRoux and Martha Rudersdorf, 1984, Neah Bay Books, Seattle, Wash.

ddler's Atlas of U.S. Rivers West, by Ken Hulick, 1993, Stackpole Books, Harrisburg, Penn.

ver Runners Guide to Utah and Adjacent Areas, by Gary Nichols, 1986, Univ. of Utah Press, Salt Lake City, Utah.

vers of the Southwest, by Fletcher Anderson and Ann Hopkinson, 1987, Pruett Publishing Co., Boulder, Colo.

inning the Rivers of North America, by Peter Wood, 1978, Barre Publishing, Barre, Mass.

erra Whitewater, by Charles Martin, 1974, Fiddleneck Press, Sunnyvale, Calif.

ggy Sneakers: A Guide to Oregon Rivers, by Willamette Kayak and Canoe Club, 1994, Corvallis, Ore.

uthern Georgia Canoeing, by Bob Sehlinger and Don Otey, 1980, Menasha Ridge Press, Hillsborough, N.C.

ill Waters, White Waters: Exploring America's Rivers and Lakes, by Ron M. Fisher, 1977, Nat. Geographic Soc., Washington D.C.

rde River Recreation Guide, by Jim Slingluff, 1990, Golden West Publishers, Phoenix, Ariz.

ashington Whitewater I: A Guide to 17 of Washington's Most Popular Whitewater Tours, by Douglass A. North, 1988, Mountaineers, Seattle, Wash.

ashington Whitewater II: A Guide to 17 of Washington's Lesser Known Whitewater Trips, by Douglass A. North, 1987, Mountaineers, Seattle, Wash.

Washington Whitewater, by Douglass A. North and Lynn Conant, 1984, North
    Publishing, Seattle, Wash.

West Branch of the Penobscot and the Kennebec Gorge, by Ron Rathnow, 1989, Menasha
    Ridge Press, Birmingham, Ala.

Whitewater Adventure, Running the Great Wild Rivers of America, by Richard Bangs,
    1989, Thunder Bay Press, San Diego, Calif.

Whitewater Rafting in Eastern North America, by Lloyd D. Armstead, 1989, Globe
    Pequot Press, Chester, Conn.

Whitewater Rafting in Western North America, by Lloyd D. Armstead, 1990, Globe
    Pequot Press, Chester, Conn.

The Whitewater Source Book, by Richard Penny, 1989, Menasha Ridge Press,
    Birmingham, Ala.

*Whitewater, Quietwater: A Guide to the Wild Rivers of Wisconsin, Upper Michigan and
    Northeast Minnesota*, by Bob and Jody Palzer, 1983, Evergreen Paddleways, Two
    Rivers, Wis.

Wild Rivers of North America, by Michael Jenkinson, 1981, E.P. Dutton, New York, N.Y.

Wildwater: Exploring Wilderness Waterways, by Buddy Mays, 1977, Chronicle Books,
    San Francisco, Calif.

Wildwater: the Sierra Club Guide to Kayaking and Whitewater Boating, by Lito Tejada-
    Flores, 1978, Sierra Club Books, San Francisco, Calif.